THE GUINNESS
DICTIONARY OF
Poisonous
QUOTES

—— COMPILED BY COLIN JARMAN ——

GUINNESS PUBLISHING

Editor: Honor Head
Assistant Editor: Paola Simoneschi

Design and Layout: Cathy Shilling

First published in 1991 by Guinness Publishing Ltd,
Publication copyright © Guinness Publishing Ltd 1991
Published in Great Britain by Guinness Publishing Ltd,
33 London Road, Enfield, Middlesex

Typeset in Plantin Light by
Ace Filmsetting Ltd, Frome, Somerset
Printed and bound in Great Britain by
BPCC Hazell Books, Aylesbury, Buckinghamshire

'Guinness' is a registered trade mark of Guinness Publishing Ltd

A catalogue record for this book is available from the British Library.

ISBN 0-85112-958-7

CONTENTS

HOW TO USE THIS BOOK

All quotes are alphabetically listed within their individual sections.

The contents page lists the sub-sections within the major groups.

The Guinnness Dictionary of Poisonous Quotes has been compiled to be used as either Reading or Reference material.

1. Reading

Reading sections as a whole will give an insight into each subject, in both an entertaining and educational way.

2. Reference

By using the extensive index certain subjects or reviewers can be traced through the book.

There are 2 indexes – the first lists all the names of those quoted or quoted about, while the second is a general reference index.

For example, the following quote found in 'Actors':

Cliff Osmond
After he had auditioned for a singing role – He has Van Gogh's ear for music.   *Billy Wilder*

is indexed under:

Cliff OSMOND, Singers, Vincent VAN GOGH and Billy WILDER.

EDITORIAL NOTES

Biographical details include date of birth and death, where known. This information is given to place the quotes in a 'time' context rather than in the interests of providing a definitive biographical reference.

Sections containing reviews are alphabetically listed in two fashions – either by reviewer or by subject as indicated on the Contents page.

INTRODUCTION

Criticism is venom from contented rattlesnakes – *Percy Hammond*

The Guinness Book of Poisonous Quotes originally started life as a cauldron of critical consciousness – a tribute to critics and their stock-in-trade – criticism, or, as I have come to call it, the trade of 'potshots and pans'.

This critical tribute soon resembled a tributary joining a raging river in flood – full of mud, full of slime, full of sticks and stones, scraped from the depths, and flung at any upstanding object in its path. At the end, this river's mouth spewed out an anthology on the art of acetic analysis. No stone was left unturned and no turn left unstoned (thanks, G. B. Shaw) in the search for the ultimate insult.

Since 'insult' comes from the Latin *insultus* meaning 'a leaping upon', this book can still be regarded as a tribute – a tribute to those who do not 'look before they leap'.

But what kind of people are these no-look abusers? From all ages, all walks of life – even the most reserved people have been caught with their tongue in the cookie jar. Normally genteel ladies like Queen Victoria, Grace Kelly, Doris Day and Julie Andrews have all felt the need to let slip a scathing shot about someone or something.

If you find it shocking that these paragons of virtue appear more like 'Ladies of the slight' – wait until you encounter the odious outpourings from cyanogenic cynics like Samuel Johnson and George Bernard Shaw, or feel the 'hot-lead' from bitchy trigger-fingers like Dorothy Parker and Joan Rivers. We all have it inside of us; but some let it flow more freely.

Many of the criticisms, put-downs and reviews included are not just vituperative and damning, some are gems of stunning brilliance that radiate through the mire. There is a very thin line between being hailed as a shining wit or merely interpreted as Dr Spooner's muck-ridden alternative.

Throughout the pages of this book, you will discover a select band of people who convey a combination of wit and wilful damage across a wide range of targets. Apart from Johnson, Shaw, Parker and Rivers, other members of the verbal battery include Oscar Wilde, Mark Twain and William F. Buckley Jr. Each armed with an arsenal of hate-seeking missiles, they raze their many targets with razor-sharp accuracy.

'Princess Malice', 'The Butcher of Broadway' and 'Old Vitriol and Violets' are nicknames of three more needle-sharp critics who can be found weaving their tormenting threads into the equivalent of an 'Axe Monster' carpet.

The finale, 'Self-criticism', echoes nature, where many deadly poisons have an antidote – a soothing balm for the effects of thousands of poison-tipped darts. Of course, 'Praise' would be a more effective balm to soothe raw wounds – but that's another story!

COLIN M. JARMAN (1991)

CRITICS & CRITICISM

A critic is one who is quick-on-the-flaw. *Anon*

A critic is a man who pans for gold. *Anon*

A critic is a man who writes about things he doesn't like. *Anon*

A critic is a wet blanket that soaks everything it touches. *Anon*

The only two jobs that are paid to run people down are – critics and elevator operators. *Anon*

Before you criticise a person for letting the grass grow under his feet, you ought to find out if his lawn-mower is out of order. *Anon*

When you hear the voice of the Knocker,
As you listen to his hammer fall,
Remember the fact that the knocking act
    Requires no brain at all.
Anon – 'The Quarrelsome Trio'

Never criticise a man until you walk in his moccasins. *American Indian proverb*

Critics always want to put you into pigeon-holes, which can be very uncomfortable unless you happen to be a pigeon. *Max Adrian*

Critics are like eunuchs in a harem. They're there every night, they see it done every night, they see how it should be done every night, but they can't do it themselves. *Brendan Behan*

Artistic enthusiasm is alien to the critic. In his hand the art-work is the shining sword in the battle of minds.
Walter Benjamin – 'One-Way Street' (1925)

A critic is a person who boasts himself hard to please because nobody tries to please him. *Ambrose Bierce*

In the finest critics one hears the full cry of the human. They tell one why it matters to read. *Harold Bloom – 'Newsweek' (1986)*

The critics have given me lots of flowers. A few weeds will keep my soil moist. *Shirley Booth*

A cricket captain must always make his decision before he knows what will happen. A critic usually bases his statements on what has happened and thus takes no chances. *Sir Donald Bradman (1950)*

Critics, what good are they? They can't make music by rubbing their hind legs together. *Mel Brooks – 'New York Times' (1975)*

They're very noisy at night. You can't sleep because of them. *Mel Brooks – ibid.*

Praise not the critic, lest he think
    You crave the shelter of his ink.
Alice Brown – 'The Critic'

That gang of spiteful rascals that are always baiting us as if we had committed murder. *Annibale Carraci (1580)*

In judging others, folks will work overtime for no pay. *Charles Carruthers*

Great critics, of whom there are piteously few, build a home for the truth. *Raymond Chandler (1948)*

A great deal of contemporary criticism reads to me like a man saying, 'Of course, I do not like green cheese: I am very fond of brown sherry.' *G. K. Chesterton – 'All I Survey'*

Though by whim, envy, or resentment led,
They damn those authors whom they never read. *Charles Churchill*

Criticism may not be agreeable, but it is necessary. It fulfils the same function as pain in the body. It calls attention to an unhealthy state of things. *Sir Winston Churchill*

I do not resent criticism, even when, for the sake of emphasis, it parts for the time with reality. *Sir Winston Churchill (1941)*

I don't care what they say about me, as long as they say something about me, and as long as they spell my name right.   *George M. Cohan*

F*** the critics. They're like eunuchs. They can tell you how to do it, but they can't do it themselves.   *Harry Cohn*

One does not value even a dog if he wags his tail for everybody and it is the same with a critic.   *Frank Colby*

Criticism is like champagne, nothing more execrable if bad, nothing more excellent if good; if meagre, muddy, vapid and sour, both are fit only to engender colic and wind; but if rich, generous and sparkling, they communicate a genial flow to the spirits, improve the taste, and expand the heart.   *Charles Colton*

A critic may write for an institution, but he shouldn't be one.   *Richard Eder*

Criticism should not be querulous and wasting, all knife and root-puller, but guiding, instructive, inspiring, a south wind, not an east wind.   *Ralph W. Emerson – 'Journals'*

Taking to pieces is the trade of those who cannot construct.   *Ralph W. Emerson*

You'd scarce expect one of my age
    To speak in public on the stage;
And if I chance to fall below
    Demosthenes or Cicero,
Don't view me with a critic's eye,
    But pass my imperfections by
Large streams from little fountains flow,
    Tall oaks from little acorns grow.
          David Everett –
'Lines Written for a School Declamation' (1791)

A man is a critic when he cannot be an artist, just as a man becomes a stool-pigeon when he cannot be a soldier.   *Gustave Flaubert*

Criticising, like charity, should begin at home.
          B. C. Forbes

The good critic is he who relates the adventures of his soul amongst his masterpieces.
          Anatole France

The works that everybody admires are those that nobody examines.   *Anatole France*

Don't pay any attention to the critics – don't even ignore them.   *Samuel Goldwyn*

Criticism is not just a question of taste, but of whose taste.   *James Grand (1980)*

In some cases taking up the trade of critic is only an embittered form of renunciation.
          Albert Guinon (1900)

The Stones that Critics hurl with Harsh Intent
A Man may use to build his monument.
          Albert Guiterman – 'Poet's Proverb'

Now as through this world I ramble, I see lots
    of funny men,
    Some rob you with a six-gun, some with a
    fountain pen.   *Woody Guthrie*

A critic should be a pair of snuffers. He is oftener an extinguisher and not seldom a thief.
          J. C. & A. W. Hare

Extremely foolish criticism is likely to be uttered by those who are looking at the labouring vessel from the land.   *Thomas Helps*

A critic is a haunter of unquiet graves; he tries to evoke the presence of a living art, but usually succeeds only in disturbing the peace of the dead.   *M. J. Hodgcart – 'The Ballads'*

A good review from the critics is just another stay of execution.   *Dustin Hoffman*

What a blessed thing it is that Nature, when she invented, manufactured, and patented her authors, contrived to make critics out of the chips that were left!
          Oliver Wendell Holmes Jr –
'Professor at the Breakfast-table'

For critics, I care the five-hundred-thousandth part of the tythe of a half-farthing.
          Charles Lamb (1830)

The eyes of critics, whether in commending or carping, are both on one side, like a turbot's.
          Walter S. Landor

A critic is one who goes along for deride.
L. L. Levinson

He has a right to criticise, who has a heart to help.
Abraham Lincoln

Some critics are like chimney-sweepers; they put out the fire below, and frighten the swallows from their nests above; they scrape a long time in the chimney, cover themselves with soot, and bring nothing away but a bag of cinders, and then sing from the top of the house as if they had built it.
Henry Longfellow

The strength of criticism lies only in the weakness of the thing criticised.
Henry Longfellow

A wise scepticism is the first attribute of a good critic.
James Lowell – 'Among My Books'

Nature fits all her children with something to do,
He who would write and can't write, can surely review,
Can set up a small booth as a critic, and sell us his
Petty conceit and his pettier jealousies.
James Lowell – 'A Fable for Critics'

A critic is a gong at a railroad crossing clanging loudly and vainly as the train goes by.
Christopher Morley

If the critics were always right we should be in deep trouble.
Robert Morley

It is the heart that makes the critic, not the nose.
Max Muller

A bad review is even less important than whether it is raining in Patagonia.
Iris Murdoch

Insects sting, not from malice, but because they want to live. It is the same with critics – they desire our blood, not pain.
Friedrich Nietzsche – 'Miscellaneous Maxims and Opinions' (1879)

Critics are beasts, highly disturbed people, basically frustrated, totally insecure, and brutalised by the profession they're in. The

public should be warned – critics may be harmful to your health.
Lore Notto

So who's perfect? Washington had false teeth. Franklin was nearsighted. Mussolini had syphilis. Unpleasant things have been said about Walt Whitman and Oscar Wilde. Tchaikovsky had his problems, too. And Lincoln was constipated.
John O'Hara – 'Carte Blanche' (1965)

Reviewers are little old ladies of both sexes. Why do I let them bother me?
John O'Hara

Critics? – I love every bone in their heads.
Eugene O'Neill

Critics are a dissembling, dishonest, contemptible race of men. Asking a working writer what he feels about critics is like asking a lamp-post what he feels about dogs.
John Osborne

The trouble with most of us is that we would rather be ruined by praise than saved by criticism.
Norman V. Peale

A critic is someone who's at his best when you're at your worst.
Tony Pettito

Boredom, after all, is a form of criticism.
William Philips (1967)

A critic –
A eunuch judging a man's lovemaking.
A skydreaming eagle without wings.
Pygmies with poison darts who live in
The valley of the sleeping giants.
Dagobert Runes

To knock a thing down, especially if it is cocked at an arrogant angle, is a deep delight of the blood.
George Santayana

Critics are like mayors of New York; nobody really wants to like them.
Dore Scharry

O ye critics, will nothing melt ye!
Sir Walter Scott

Contemporary criticism only represents the amount of ignorance genius has to contend with.
Percy B. Shelley

Critics must excuse me if I compare them to certain animals called asses, who have by gnawing vines originally taught the great advantage of pruning them.   *William Shenstone*

The function of criticism should be to show how it is what it is, even that it is what it is, rather than to show what it means.
Susan Sontag

The critic's symbol should be the tumble-bug; he deposits his egg in somebody else's dung, otherwise he could not hatch it.   *Mark Twain*

The public is the only critic whose opinion is worth anything at all.   *Mark Twain – ibid.*

One mustn't criticise other people on grounds where he can't stand perpendicular himself.
Mark Twain – 'A Connecticut Yankee at the Court of King Arthur'

Critics are like pigs at the pastry cart.
John Updike

They search for ages for the wrong word, which, to give them credit, they eventually find.
Peter Ustinov (1952)

Critics are like those of whom Demetrius declared that he took no more account of the wind that came from their mouths than that which they expelled from their lower parts.
Leonardo da Vinci

Really to stop criticism they say one must die.
Voltaire – 'Les Trois Empereurs en Sorbonne'

Impressions are two a penny, but opinions are definitely precious, to be prized like jewels and defended; taken out of hiding from time to time, then polished and put back.
Auberon Waugh – 'Esquire' (1968)

When critics disagree the artist is in accordance with himself.
Oscar Wilde – 'The Picture of Dorian Gray'

A critic is a man who can translate into another manner or a new material his impression of beautiful things.   *Oscar Wilde – ibid.*

Critics are like brushers of noblemen's clothes.
Henry Wooton

CRITICS ON CRITICISM

There should be a dash of the amateur in criticism, for the amateur is a man of enthusiasm who has not settled down and is not habit-bound.
Brooks Atkinson – 'Once Around the Sun' (1952)

It is unfortunate that more and more we confuse the function of criticism with being a sort of racing tip-sheet. If you work for the mass media you're going to be used as a market report, a Good Housekeeping Seal of Approval.
Clive Barnes

Criticism, I take it, is the formal disease of the amateur.
R. P. Blackmur – 'Language as a Gesture' (1952)

A critic is a man who prefers the indolence of opinion to the trials of action.
John Mason Brown – 'Town & Country' (1966)

Reviewing is no easy matter. To begin with, you must be sure that writing is your vocation, next you must be convinced that reviewing is not writing, hence the conclusion that your vocation is not reviewing. Well, once you feel that, you can start.   *Cyril Connolly*

To be a critic, you have to have maybe three per cent education, five per cent intelligence, two per cent style and ninety per cent gall and egomania in equal parts.   *Judith Crist*

The whole absurdity of trying to write for the information of my friends about something that was plainly designed for the entertainment of their cooks.   *Woolcot Gibbs*

Critics are probably more prone to clichés than fiction writers who pluck things out of the air.
Penelope Gilliatt

It is through criticism that the race has managed to come out of the woods and lead a civilised life. The first man who objected to the general nakedness and advised his fellows to put on clothes was the first critic.
Edwin L. Godwin – 'Problems of Modern Democracy'

A critic is a man who expects miracles.
James Huneker

There is something fatally wrong about critics; what is good is good without our saying so.
Randall Jarrell

Criticism is a study by which men grow important and formidable at very small expense.
Samuel Johnson

In the arts, the critic is the only independent source of information. The rest is advertising.
Pauline Kael – 'Newsweek' (1973)

The best critic is one who illuminates whole provinces of an art that you could not see before, who helps the general public's taste (which is never good enough – they haven't the time) and who serves as a sounding board for serious artists.
Stanley Kauffman – 'A Life in Reviews' (1958)

No critic who is any good sets out deliberately to enlighten someone else; he writes to put his own ideas in order.
Alfred Kazan

A critic is a creature without a spiritual home, and it is his point of honour never to seek one.
Desmond McCarthy

When a modern critic hears the word 'beauty' he releases the catch on his fountain pen.
Dwight MacDonald

Criticism is prejudice made plausible.
Henry L. Mencken

A critic is a man who boasts he is hard to please, when nobody tries to please him.
Henry L. Mencken

Show me a critic without prejudices, and I'll show you an arrested cretin. *George J. Nathan*

The better and more honest a critic you are, the fewer friends will eventually send flowers up the funeral parlour. *George J. Nathan*

Don't be afraid of being labelled a destructive critic. You will be in good company. Where would you rather be: in Hell with Swift, Voltaire and Nietzsche or in the American Academy of Arts and Letters with Richard Burton, Clayton Hamilton and Hermann Hagedorn? *George J. Nathan*

The only way for a critic to get on with the world is to roast the living tar out of everything that calls for such roasting and never stop for a minute and to praise the living roses back into everything that calls for such praise and likewise never stop for a minute.
George J. Nathan

Criticism is the art wherewith the critic tries to guess himself into a share of the artist's fame.
George J. Nathan – 'The House of Satan'

Impersonal criticism is like am impersonal fist fight or an impersonal marriage, and as successful. *George J. Nathan – 'The Impersonal World of . . .' (1952)*

Criticism is the window and chandelier of art.
George J. Nathan – 'The Critic and the Drama' (1922)

Not only is there but one way of doing things rightly, but there is only one way of seeing them, and that is, seeing the whole of them.
John Ruskin – 'The Two Paths' (1859)

A critic is a man whose watch is five minutes ahead of other people's watches.
Charles Sainte-Beuve

The critic is not only the secretary of the public, but a secretary who does not wait to take dictation, and who divines, who decides, who expresses every morning what everybody is thinking. *Charles Sainte-Beuve*

Critics, like other people, see what they look for, not what is actually before them.
G. B. Shaw

Like dentists, critics spend a good deal of time in hurting sensitive people in sensitive places; and as they have to do it in an entertaining manner, which no doubt gives them an air of enjoying it, they produce an impression of sadism. *G. B. Shaw*

A critic is a man who knows the way but can't drive the car. *Kenneth Tynan*

When you are in the brick-throwing racket, you must expect to get hit with one occasionally.

My greatest thrill has been surviving my
imitators.   *Walter Winchell*

Critics are ink-stained wretches.
                            Alexander Woollcott

CRITICS AT LARGE

Joseph Addison - *(1672-1719)*
Damn with faint praise, assent with civil leer,
    And without sneering teach the rest to sneer;
Willing to wound, and yet afraid to strike,
    Just a hint a fault, and hesitate dislike;
    Alike reserv'd to blame or to commend,
A tim'rous foe, and a suspicious friend.
                            Alexander Pope

James Agate - *(1877-1947)*
On 'Here's Richness' - If provocation in a writer
is a sign of talent, then Mr James Agate is as
gifted as he gives the impression of thinking
himself to be, for I know of no modern essayist,
critic, and journalist who is capable of affording
so much annoyance to so many by the
expression of so few really significant thoughts.
                    'Shell Magazine' (1942)

James Agee - *(1909-55)*
James Agee was the most intriguing star-gazer
in the Middle-brow era of Hollywood films, a
virtuoso who capped a strange company of stars
on people's lips and set up a hailstorm of ideas
for other critics to use.
                    *Manny Farber - 'Star-gazing for
                    Middle-brows' (1958)*

Kelcey Allen - *(1875-1951)*
On spying his fellow critic asleep during a show - I
see that Kelcey's writing his review early.
                            Walter Winchell

Walter Bagehot - *(1826-77)*
More than any of his contemporaries he
excelled in the art of informal criticism - of
what it would be tempting to call talkative
criticism, if that didn't suggest the maundering
well-jacketed causerie of a later date.
                            John Gross

Walter Bagehot defies classification. He was
not a literary critic in the academic sense, nor a
political economist, nor a historian. He was all
of these and none of them. He was in fact an
amateur of genius with that breadth of mind
and wide range of interests which to us looking
back seems one of the most valuable and
agreeable characteristics of the Victorian age.
                        Norman St John Stevas

Pierre Bayle - *(1647-1706)*
He wreathed the rod of criticism with roses.
                            Isaac D'Israeli

Max Beerbohm - *(1872-1956)*
It always makes me cross when Max is called
'The Incomparable Max'. He is not
incomparable at all. He is a shallow, affected,
self-conscious fribble.
                    Victoria Sackville-West (1959)

He has the most remarkable and seductive
genius - and, I should say, about the smallest in
the world.   *Lytton Strachey*

The gods have bestowed on Max the gift of
perpetual old age.   *Oscar Wilde*

Robert Benchley - *(1889-1945)*
Robert Benchley has a style that is weak and
lies down frequently to rest.
            Max Eastman - 'Enjoyment of Laughter'

Arnold Bennett - *(1867-1931)*
He has described how, when as a young drama
critic, he went to a Lyceum first night, he
would saunter into the stalls and 'glancing at
the front row of the pit with cold and aloof
disdain' would think 'don't you wish you were
me?'   *Robert Lynd - 'Obituary' -
                    News Chronicle' (1931)*

Randolph Bourne - *(1886-1918)*
In his early death America lost a writer of great
promise, a critic at home in philosophy,
education, politics and literature, but homeless
in his contemporary world.   *Ernest Bates*

John Mason Brown - *(1900-69)*
Minister of fine arts to the people at large.
                            Brooks Atkinson

John would rather be caught in a loincloth in
Times Square, than with a sloppy phrase.
                            Norman Cousins

He treads the most extraordinary delicate line between principle and popularity, and he never seems to injure either. He doesn't respond to vulgar drives, whether ambition, sex or money.
Marya Manners

The confederate Aristotle.
Charles Poore – 'New York Times'

Henry Brougham – *(1778-1868)*
Article in 'Edinburgh Review' – It is long yet vigorous, like the penis of a jackass.
Sydney Smith

Edward Bulwer-Lytton – *(1803-73)*
What profits now to understand
  The merits of a spotless shirt –
  A dapper boot – a little hand –
If half the little soul is dirt.
Alfred, Lord Tennyson

J. Churton Collins – *(1848-1908)*
A louse in the locks of literature.
Alfred, Lord Tennyson

Cyril Connolly – *(1903-75)*
His virtue as a critic has always been the directness that comes from treating all writing as the personal expression of a particular human being in particular circumstances. *Anon*

William Cowper – *(1731-1800)*
The fairest critic, and the sweetest bard.
James Hurdis – 'Address to Criticism'

Alan Dent *(b 1905)*
I am the only critic who is too small for his boots.

John Dryden – *(1631-1700)*
The father of English criticism. *Samuel Johnson*

T. S. Earp
I heard a little chicken chirp:
My name is Thomas, Thomas Earp,
And I can neither paint nor write,
I can only put other people right.
All people that can write and paint,
  Do tremble under my complaint.
    For I am a chicken, and I chirp
  And my name is Thomas, Thomas Earp!
D. H. Lawrence

Roger Fry – *(1866-1934)*
Dear Roger Fry, whom I love as a man but detest as a movement. *Edward Marsh*

Sarah Fuller [Marchioness Ossoli] – *(1810-50)*
She was a great humbug; of course with much talent, and much moral ideality, or else she could not have been so great a humbug.
Nathaniel Hawthorne

She wrote so gracelessly and effusively, and sometimes with such lack of simple clarity, that reading her was anything but a pleasure even to her friends and neighbours. *Bernard Smith*

To whom Venus gave everything except beauty, and Pallas everything except wisdom.
Oscar Wilde

Percy Hammond – *(1873-1936)*
A newspaperman, whose sweetheart ran away with an actor. *Walter Winchell*

His editor had thought of sending Hammond to cover the war in Europe – For Christ's sake, you can't do that! Suppose he doesn't like it?
Ring Lardner

Eduard Hanslick – *(1825-1904)*
With him one cannot fight. One can only approach him with petitions. *Anton Bruckner*

Hanslick's writing represents one of the unlovelier forms of parasitism; that which, having the wealth to collect objets d'art and the birth and education to talk amusingly, does not itself attempt a stroke of artistic work, does not dream of revising a first impression, experiences the fine art entirely as the pleasures of a gentleman, and then pronounces judgement as if the expression of its opinion were a benefit and a duty to society.
Donald Tovey – 'Essays in Musical Analysis' (1935)

Jean François de la Harpe – *(1739-1803)*
M. de la Harpe is a man who uses his faults to hide his vices. *Nicholas de Chamfort*

William Hazlitt – *(1778-1830)*
If Hazlitt was a godsend to Edmund Kean, Kean was scarcely less of a godsend to Hazlitt.

The critic made the actor's reputation, but the actor made the critic's immortality as a theatrical critic. If Hazlitt had not had Kean to write about, he would certainly have written much less with far inferior life and gusto, and would probably never have collected his articles.

William Archer – 'Hazlitt on Theatre' (1895)

His manners are 99 in a 100 singularly repulsive. *Samuel T. Coleridge (1803)*

Hazlitt possesses considerable talent; but it is diseased by a morbid hatred of the Beautiful, and killed by the absence of the Imagination, & alas! by a wicked Heart of embruted Appetites. Poor wretch! he is a melancholy instance of the awful truth. *Samuel T. Coleridge (1816)*

He had the most uninteresting mind of all our distinguished critics.

T. S. Eliot – 'Essays: John Dryden'

There is nothing in the world which he seems to like, unless we except 'washerwomen'.

William Gifford (1817)

He is your only good damner, and if I am ever damned I should like to be damned by him.

John Keats

The Pit-trumpet of Mr Kean at Drury Lane.

'Philadelphia National Gazette'

A mere ulcer; a sore from head to foot; a poor devil so completely flayed that there is not a square inch of healthy flesh on his carcass; an overgrown pimple, sore to the touch.

'Quarterly Review'

He is not a proper person to be admitted into respectable society, being the most perverse and malevolent creature that ill-luck has thrown my way. *William Wordsworth (1817)*

Clive James – *(b 1939)*
Not satire, but name-dropping. He writes like a man who wishes he was invited to more parties.
Paul Theroux – 'Sunday Times' (1981)

Randall Jarrell – *(1914–65)*
He was bearded, formidable, bristling, with a high-pitched nervous voice and the wariness of a porcupine. *Stanley Kurnitz*

If God were a writer and wrote a book that Randall did not think was good, Randall would not have hesitated to give it a bad review. And if God complained, Randall would then set about showing God what was wrong with his sentences. *Robert Watson*

Francis Jeffrey – *(1773–1850)*
No one minds what Jeffrey says . . . it's not more than a week ago that I heard him speak disrespectfully of the Equator. *Sydney Smith*

Samuel Johnson – *(1709–84)*
The pompous preacher of melancholy moralities. *Jeremy Bentham*

The Caliban of literature. *Gilbert Cowper*

A dangerous person to disagree with. *T. S. Eliot*

There is no arguing with Johnson; for when his pistol misses fire, he knocks you down with the butt end of it. *Oliver Goldsmith*

Dr Johnson was a man without originality, compared with the ordinary run of men's mind, but he was not a man of original thought or genius, in the sense in which Montaigne or Lord Bacon was. He opened no new vein of precious ore, nor did he light upon any single pebbles of uncommon size and unrivalled lustre. We seldom meet with anything to 'give us pause'; he does not set us thinking for the first time. *William Hazlitt*

Here lies poor Johnson! have a care,
Tread lightly, lest you rouse a sleeping bear.
Religious, moral, gen'rous and humane,
He was, but self-conceited, rude, and vain:
Ill-bred, and overbearing in dispute,
A scholar and a Christian, yet a brute.
Would you know all his wisdom and his folly,
His actions, sayings, mirth, and melancholy,
Boswell and Thrale, retailers of wit,
Will tell you how he wrote, and talk'd, and spit.
Soame Jenyns – 'Epitaph for Samuel Johnson'

I have a notion that it is pleasanter to read Boswell's record of the conversations than it ever was to listen to Dr Johnson.

W. Somerset Maugham

Dr Johnson's sayings would not appear so
extraordinary, were it not for his bow-wow
way.   *Lord Pembroke*

That great Cham of literature.
                              Tobias Smollett (1959)

Johnson's aesthetic judgements are almost
invariably subtle, or solid, or bold; they have
always some good quality to recommend them
– except one: they are never right.
                              Lytton Strachey

Johnson made the most brutal speeches to
living persons; for though he was a good-
natured man at bottom, he was ill-natured at
top. He loved to dispute to show his
superiority. If his opponents were weak, he told
them they were fools; if they vanquished him,
he was scurrilous.   *Horace Walpole*

With a pig's eyes that never look up, with a
pig's snout that loves muck, with a pig's brain
that knows only the sty, and a pig's squeal that
cries only when he is hurt, he sometimes opens
his pig's mouth, tusked and ugly, and lets out
the voice of God, railing at the whitewash that
covers the manure about his habitat.
                              William A. White (1928)

Edvard Munch – *(1863–1944)*
After all his literary efforts had come to nought
and he had to wear dark glasses, he became an
art critic.   *Caricature in 'The Critic' (1911)*

George Jean Nathan – *(1882–1958)*
Nathan is a good game, but you've got to know
the rules.   *James Mason Brown*

'Art of the Night' – It acted upon me like so
much black coffee, and this in spite of the fact
that any book with 'Art' in its title usually
renders me unconscious as soon as I've cracked
it. Beating the head against a granite wall . . .
'Art of the Night' is the most valuable of his
works on the theater . . . He can, in short,
write. And so he makes almost all of the other
dramatic commentators (I can think, in fact, of
but three exceptions, and I'm not sure of two of
those) look as if they spelled out their reviews
with alphabet blocks.
                    Dorothy Parker – 'New Yorker' (1928)

Dorothy Parker – *(1893–1967)*
The belle dame sans merci has the ruthlessness
of the great tragic lyricists whose work was
allegorised in the fable of the nightingale
singing with her breast against a thorn. It is
disillusion recollected in tranquillity where the
imagination has at last controlled the emotions.
It comes out clear, and with the authentic
sparkle of a great vintage.
                              Henry Seidel Canby
[*This is popularly misquoted as a direct reference to
Miss Parker* – A nightingale singing with her
breast against a thorn.

[*Also note lines of a Dorothy Parker poem* –
His little trills and chirpings were his best,
No music like the nightingale's was born
Within his throat; but he, too, laid his breast
Upon a thorn.   *'Minor Poet'*]

She was an elfin woman who had two kinds of
magic about her. Her first magical quality was
that no one could ever consider her
dispassionately, and the other was that no one
could precisely define her.
                    John Keats – 'You Might As Well Live'

Petite, pretty, and deadly as an asp.
                              Howard Teichmann

Her acidic bon mots were the olives of the
martini age.   *'Vanity Fair' (1986)*

She has put into what she has written a voice, a
state of mind, an era, a few moments of human
experience that nobody else has conveyed.
                              Edmund Wilson

Her work is so potent a distillation of nectar
and wormwood, of ambrosia and deadly
nightshade, as might suggest to the rest of us
that we write far too much.   *Alexander Woollcott*

A combination of Little Nell and Lady
Macbeth.
          Alexander Woollcott – 'While Rome Burns'

Walter Pater – *(1839–94)*
Mr Walter Pater's style is, to me, like the face
of some old woman who has been to Madame
Rachel and had herself enamelled. The bloom is
nothing but powder and paint and the odour is
cherry-blossom.   *Samuel Butler – 'Notebooks'*

Faint, pale, embarrassed, exquisite Pater! He reminds me, in the disturbed midnight of our actual literature, of one of those lucent match boxes which you place, on going to bed, near the candle, to show you, in the darkness, where you can strike a light: he shines in the uneasy gloom – vaguely, and has a phosphorescence, not a flame.   *Henry James (1894)*

Alma Pater.   *Osbert Lancaster*

Jean Poueigh – *(1876–1958)*
Dear sir and friend, not only are you an arse, you're an unmusical arse. *Erik Satie - 'Postcard'*

Sir Arthur Quiller-Couch – *(1863–1944)*
Judged by subsequent Cambridge standards, he often seems impossibly florid, and on the whole his critical methods are what can only be described as under-ingenious. But in 1912 the world was younger, and professors could still talk about criticism in terms of adventure.
                                          John Gross

Rex Reed – *(b 1939)*
Rex Reed is either at your feet or at your throat.   *Ava Gardner*

All that bullshit with the New York critics is just cocktail party talk. I've become a multi-millionaire with things that Rex Reed hated.
                                     Jerry Weintraub (1975)

Frank Rich – *'The Butcher of Broadway'*
Some days I want to kill Frank Rich. He represents this Great Deaf Ear I must somehow get through to in order to reach a theatre-going public . . . the years have gone on and he's gotten harder and harder and harder.
                                    Christopher Durang

Frank Rich is a terrible critic. He's an unfortunate blot on the American theatre . . . He's a boy, he's an untutored boy, who doesn't realise there's anything higher than his own perceptions. As Tolstoy said, 'Mediocre men must of necessity have a mediocre idea of what constitutes greatness' and he was speaking of Mr Rich when he wrote it.   *David Mamet (1988)*

Frank Rich and John Simon are the syphilis and gonorrhea of the theatre.   *David Mamet*

This is a man who knows nothing about love.
                                   Andrew Lloyd Webber

John Ruskin – *(1819–1900)*
I takes and paints,
Hears no complaints,
And sells before I'm dry;
    Till savage Ruskin
He sticks his tusk in,
    Then nobody will buy.
                          Shirley Brooks – 'Punch' (1856)

A bottle of beautiful soda-water.
                                  Thomas Carlyle (1855)

He is a chartered libertine – he is possessed himself by prescription of the function of a general scold.   *Henry James – 'Nation' (1878)*

Ruskin is one of the most turbid and fallacious minds of the century. To the service of the most widely eccentric thoughts he brings the acerbity of a bigot. His mental temperament is that of the first Spanish Grand Inquisitor. He is a Torquemada of aesthetics. He would burn the critic who disagrees with him.
                                  Max Simon Nordau

A certain girlish petulance of style that distinguishes Ruskin was not altogether a defect. It served to irritate and fix attention where a more evenly judicial writer might have remained unread.   *W. R. Sickert - 'New Age'*

I doubt that art needed Ruskin any more than a moving train needs one of its passengers to shove it.   *Tom Stoppard – 'Times Literary Supplement' (1977)*

A life passed among pictures does not make a painter – else the policeman in the National Gallery might assert himself. As well as allege that he who lives in a library must needs die a poet. Let not Mr Ruskin flatter himself that more education makes the difference between himself and the policeman when both stand gazing in the Gallery.
    There they might remain till the end of time; the one decently silent, the other saying, in good English, many high-sounding empty things, like the crackling of thorns under a poet – undismayed by the presence of the Masters with whose names he is sacrilegiously familiar;

whose intentions he interprets, whose vices he discovers with the facility of the incapable, and whose virtues he descants upon with a verbosity and flow of language that would, could we hear it, give Titian the same shock of surprise that was Balaam's when the first great critic proffered his opinion.

James M. Whistler – 'Gentle Art of Making Enemies'

What greater sarcasm can Mr Ruskin pass upon than that he preaches to young men what he cannot perform! Why, unsatisfied with his own conscious power, should he choose to become the type of incompetence by talking for forty years of what he has never done!

James M. Whistler – 'Whistler v Ruskin: Art & Art Critics'

George Bernard Shaw – *(1856-1950)*
A freakish homunculus germinated outside lawful procreation.   *Henry A. Jones*

The noisiest of all cocks.   *Percy W. Lewis*

Shaw is like an old château, not even haunted by a spirit.   *Maurice Maeterlinck*

It is his life work to announce the obvious in terms of the scandalous.   *H. L. Mencken*

Mr Shaw is one of the cyclonic kind of talents that charge through their time as an express train tears through country stations, and if your mind be only a piece of straw or an empty paper bag, or is not pulled in any special direction by something else, it leaves all and follows the express until the express drops it a little farther on.   *C. E. Montague (1911)*

Intellectually he is beneath contempt. Artistically he appeals only to pseudo-philosophers. Are we not all a little tired of this blatant self-puffery?   *Alfred Noyes*

A desiccated bourgeois, a fossilised chauvinist.   *'Pravda'*

He went through the fiery furnace, but never a hair was missed
From the heels of our most Colossal Arch-Super Egotist.   *'Punch' (1917)*

I think Shaw, on the whole, is more bounder than genius; and though of course I admit him to be forcible, I don't admit him to be moral.   *Bertrand Russell (1904)*

As an iconoclast he was admirable, as an icon somewhat less so.   *Bertrand Russell*

George Too Shaw To Be Good.   *Dylan Thomas*

He was the Bradman of all letters: he scored all round the wicket off all kinds of ideological bowling; he hit centuries off all causes and men that were idle or unrealistic; but though he took great pains to command respect, he took none at all to inspire affection.

Kenneth Tynan – 'Observer' (1956)

The more I think you over the more it comes home to me what an unmitigated Middle Victorian ass you are.   *H. G. Wells*

As yet, Bernard Shaw hasn't become prominent enough to have any enemies; but none of his friends like him.   *Oscar Wilde*

At 83 Shaw's mind was perhaps not quite as good as it used to be. It was still better than anyone else's.

Alexander Woollcott – 'While Rome Burns' (1934)

Walter Winchell – *(1897-1972)*
I don't see why Walter Winchell is allowed to live.   *Ethel Barrymore*

He is more like some freak of climate – a tornado, say, or an electric storm that is heard whistling and roaring far away, against which everybody braces himself; and then it strikes and does its whirling damage.

Alistair Cooke – 'Listener' (1947)

The three of us are all in the same business – libel – but Winchell seems to know when to stop.   *H. L. Mencken to George J. Nathan*

Poor Walter. He's afraid he'll wake up some day and discover he's not Walter Winchell.

Dorothy Parker

Walter Winchell suffers from a chronic state of wild excitement, venom and perpetual motion of the jaw.   *Eleanor Patterson*

A Gents' Room Journalist. *Westbrook Pegler*

This is a dangerously ill-informed man who, in his tremendous egotism, who, with this great power, unaccompanied by greatness or nobility of thinking, is uttering sage opinions on what we should do. *Ed Sullivan*

Mr W. was an emotionalist who rarely succumbed to the chill demands of logic. Woollcott was less a critic than an amusing hysteric. *Tallulah Bankhead*

A Seidlitz powder in Times Square.
Heywood Broun

The smartest of Alecs. *Heywood Broun*

His life was what the marquees describe as a 'continuous performance'. *James Mason Brown*

He turned several books into bestsellers, single-handed. Woollcott's enthusiasms could make a book a bestseller more surely than anything else in the world. *Bennett Cerf*

Alexander Woollcott in a rage has all the tenderness and restraint of a newly-caged cobra; and, when striking, much the same admirable precision. There was always a sly, rococo twist to Woollcott; he was indubitably a character; in its highest sense he was what the French call an 'original'. *Noel Coward*

A New Jersey Nero who mistook a pinafore for a toga. *Edna Furber*
[*Edna Furber also described Woollcott as* 'A Colossal Fool', *which highly delighted the critic.*]

He wasn't exactly hostile to facts, but he was apathetic about them. *Wolcott Gibbs*

A pernickety fellow with more fizz than brain.
Ben Hecht

He was a serious young man, a very active one,

and a perfectly normal one until the end of his college years when he suffered a severe attack of the mumps and the complications that sometimes affect the male. After the attack the change in Aleck was apparent. He became, in effect, a eunuch, and he began to acquire eunuchoid characteristics. He grew pudgy and his hips broadened. He grew mincing in his ways . . . He became Buddha-like fat . . . The studied insult, the insulting term of endearment, even the dirty word at the dinner table – all these became Woollcottian hallmarks.
Edwin P. Hoyt – 'The Man Who Came to Dinner'

Trivia was Aleck's declared business.
Edwin P. Hoyt – ibid.

He looked like something that had gotten loose from Macy's Thanksgiving Day Parade.
Harpo Marx

He is just a big dreamer, with a good sense of double-entry bookkeeping. *Harpo Marx*

Woollcott's reviews resemble either a gravy bomb, a bursting gladiolus, a palpitating 'orissa cantata', an attack of psychic phobia, or a Roman denunciation.
George J. Nathan – 'Smart Set' (1921)

Woollcott's criticisms may be 'simply pathological in origin' or owing to Pa's high blood pressure perhaps, in an unfortunate chronic costiveness. Woollcott's approach is 'lump in the throat reviewing'.

George J. Nathan

Old Vitriol and Violets. *James Thurber*

A little fat boy, impish, disagreeable, even obnoxious at times, but one who creates amusement and wins friends. *Danton Walker*

He always praises the first production of each season, being reluctant to stone the first cast.
Walter Winchell

THE CREATIVE ARTS

There are certain things in which mediocrity is insupportable – poetry, music, painting, public speaking.   *Jean de la Bruyere*

A taste of sculpture and painting is in my mind as becoming as a taste of fiddling and piping is unbecoming to a man of fashion. The former is connected with history and poetry, the latter, with nothing that I know of but bad company.
Lord Chesterfield (1749)

Art never seems to make me peaceful or pure.
Willem de Kooning

In art the same elevator goes either to the basement or the penthouse.   *Piet Mondrian*

The art of our era is not art, but technology. Today Rembrandt is painting automobiles; Shakespeare is writing research reports; Michelangelo is designing more efficient bank lobbies.   *Howard Sparks – 'The Petrified Truth'*

The artist is a lucky dog. In any community of a thousand souls there will be nine hundred doing the work, ninety doing well, nine doing good, and one lucky dog painting or writing about the other nine hundred and ninety-nine.
Tom Stoppard (1972)

ANTIQUES

An antique is a work of art that isn't all it's cracked up to be.   *Anon*

An antique is something that's been useless so long it's still in pretty good condition.
Franklin P. Jones

ARCHITECTURE

Any work of architecture that does not express serenity is a mistake.
Luis Barragan - 'Time' (1980)

Owing to such things as town planning hurdles it is perhaps not surprising that buildings tend not to be designed to give delight, but to

achieve least displeasure.   *Prince Charles (1985)*

You have to give this much to the Luftwaffe – when it knocked down our buildings it did not replace them with anything more offensive than rubble. We did that.   *Prince Charles (1987)*

On how many newspaper staffs shall we find, besides the dramatic, literary and musical critics, an architecture critic? With how many casual dinner-party neighbours should we dare to substitute the latest London building for the latest London play as a feeder topic?
Clough W. Ellis – 'The Pleasure of Architecture' (1924)

No one, it would seem, has fairly estimated the indebtedness of architecture to lunatics. Most palaces and several towns owe their present form to the dementia of royal persons.
Philip Guedalla

Architecture isn't just about producing buildings that are photogenic. We must get away from the idea that an architect is like a concert pianist, a genius surrounded by Philistines.
Rod Hackney – President of RIBA (1987)

Too much of the urban scene is made up of buildings which toe the property line and shout their assertions of methods and structure to their neighbours across the street. The cacophony becomes a bedlam and we, the architect, little more than a huckster. Someone ought to 'whisper' a building.
James M. Hunter – 'Arizona Architect'

Architecture is the art of how to waste space.
Philip Johnson

Architecture is very much like the oldest profession in the world: it has only one aim, and that is to please for a fee.
Philip Johnson (1984)

Architecture is too important to be left to architects alone. Like crime, it is a problem for society as a whole.   *Berthold Lubetkin (1985)*

No architecture can be truly noble which is not imperfect.   *John Ruskin*

What we need is a race of discriminating two-inch-high pygmies who can be rented out to architectural offices to wander through their three-dimensional models and tell us how things look from down there. They may observe: 'Master, it may be breathtaking from up where you stand, but down here it's dull and tedious.'   *Fred Smith*

Suburbia is where the developer bulldozes out the trees, then names the streets after them.
                              Bill Vaughan

ARCHITECTS

An architect is two per cent gentleman and ninety-eight per cent renegade car salesman.
                              Anon

A large number of us have developed a feeling that architects tend to design houses for the approval of fellow architects and critics – not for the tenants.   *Prince Charles*

The brevity of human life gives a melancholy to the profession of the architect.
          Ralph W. Emerson – 'Journals' (1842)

Architects are pretty much high-class whores. We can turn down projects the way they can turn down clients, but we've both got to say yes to someone if we want to stay in business.
          Philip Johnson – 'Esquire' (1980)

Architects never felt the urge to establish ethical precepts for the performance of their profession, as did the medical fraternity. No equivalent of the Hippocratic Oath exists for them. Criticism within the profession – the only conceivable way to spread a sense of responsibility among its members – is tabooed by their own codified standards of practice. To bolster their own ego, architects hold their own beauty contests, award each other prizes, decorate each other with gold medals, and make light of the damning fact that they do not amount to any moral force in this country.
          Bernard Rudofsky – 'Streets for People' (1969)

No person who is not a great sculptor or painter can be an architect. If he is not a sculptor or painter, he can only be a builder.
          John Ruskin – 'Lectures on Architecture and Painting' (1853)

The relationship between architects and the media is based on trust and understanding. The architects don't trust the media, and the media don't understand the architects.
          Scorpio – 'Building Design' (1986)

Architects vary like doctors and lawyers, some are good – some bad. Unfortunately, in architecture, failure shows.
          Peter Shepherd – President of RIBA

A doctor can bury his mistakes, but an architect can only advise his client to plant vines.   *Frank Lloyd Wright*

Robert Adam – *(1782–92)*
Adam, our most admired architect, is all gingerbread, filigraine, and fan-painting.
          Horace Walpole (1775)

William Kent – *(1686–1748)*
William Kent was one of those generally accomplished persons who can do everything well up to a certain point, and nothing well.
          Sir Reginald Bloomfield

He was not a thinker; he was only a second-rate artist with a well-developed sense of decoration.
          J. Summerson

Mr Kent's passion, clumps – that is, sticking a dozen trees here and there till a lawn looks like a ten of spades.   *Horace Walpole (1743)*

Le Corbusier [Charles Jeanneret]
(1887–1965)
On his style – If I were building a house tomorrow – it would certainly not follow the lines of a dynamo or a steam shovel.
          Henry L. Mencken

Sir Joseph Paxton – *(1810–65)*
His life was simple, his ingenuity unfailing, his energy unbounded, his health robust, his taste dubious.   *R. Furneaux-Jordan*

Karl F. Schinkel - *(1781-1841)*
He paints like an architect and builds like a
painter.   *Anon*

Sir George Gilbert Scott - *(1811-78)*
We may be now too near the Victorian age to
be able to judge its heroes impartially; but will
anyone ever admire the works of Scott? It is
hard to believe that they will, for there is
nothing particular in them to admire.
                                    Basil Clarke

Gilbert Scott was the supreme model of a
Samuel Smiles self-made man - with all the
vigour and all the lack of subtlety that one
would expect.   *R. Furneaux-Jordan*

His enormous output of bad and indifferent
architecture reflects that Victorian philistinism
that sprang from the moralisation of art.
                                    R. Turnor

Sir John Soame - *(1753-1837)*
Soame affected an originality of form and
decoration, which, not being based on any well-
understood constructive principle, or any
recognised form of beauty, has led to no result,
and to us now appears little less than
ridiculous.   *J. Fergusson*

He never possessed any real strength, moral or
intellectual.   *George Wightwick - 'Recollections'*

James Wyatt - *(1746-1813)*
James Wyatt, of execrable memory.
                    A. W. N. Pugin - 'Contrasts'

BUILDINGS

MODERN ARCHITECTURE

Most buildings now are glorified wallpaper.
                                Alan Bird (1986)

I'm not sure modern office buildings are even
architecture. They're really mathematical
calculation, just three-dimensional investments.
                                Gordon Bunshaft

A Short Guide to Modern Architecture -
The planner is my shepherd.
He maketh me to walk; through dark tunnels
and underpasses he forceth me to go.

He maketh concrete canyons tower above me.
By the rivers of traffic he maketh me walk.
He knocketh down all that is good, he maketh
straight the curves.
He maketh of the city a wasteland and a car
park.   *Mike Harding*

Modern architecture is a flop. There is no
question that our cities are uglier today than
they were fifty years ago.   *Philip Johnson (1968)*

Post-war architecture is the accountant's
revenge on the pre-war businessman's dreams.
        Rem Koolhaas - 'Delirious New York' (1978)

What has happened to Architecture since the
Second World War that the only passers-by
who can contemplate it without pain are those
equipped with a white stick and a dog?
            Bernard Levin - 'The Times' (1983)

Modern buildings are not architecture, but
packaging glued together with epoxy or
neoprene. It is all a technological fun-fair of the
shift age of make-believe, high-turnover, low-
profile, covert operations and massage parlours.
Indeed, as could be expected, our art reflects
vividly a demented society that has had its day.
        Berthold Lubetkin - 'Lecture' (1985)

Perhaps the blank faceless abstract quality of
our modern architecture is a reflection of the
anxiety we feel before the void, a kind of visual
static which emanates from the psyche of us all,
as if we do not know which way to go.
    Norman Mailer - 'Cannibals and Christians'

The fundamental failure of modern
architecture was that in the shift from an
agrarian society to an industrialised society,
from handicrafts to the machine, from single
production to mass production, in trying to
produce in abundance for all the people, the
people themselves got left out.
                            John Portman (1984)

People get bored with too many modern
buildings, stripped and stark and functional.
They stay home when they might be window
shopping, and tourists go elsewhere, and the
city could be worse off than before. Experience
has shown in city after city that the big
standardised complexes that developers dream

up because they represent advanced design, and demonstrate functionalism, and have a cost-to-cubic-content ratio to delight an investment banker, fail to have any particular magnetism for people.   *Fred Smith*

In my experience, if you have to keep the lavatory door shut by extending your left leg, it's modern architecture.
       Nancy Banks-Smith – 'The Guardian' (1969)

Ninety-nine per cent of modern architecture is boring, banal, and barren, and usually disruptive and unharmonious when placed in older cities.   *James Stirling (1974)*

HIGH-RISE

Aside from all the aesthetic considerations, the continued erection of the so-called 'skyscraper', the excessively tall building, constitutes a menace to public health and safety and an offence which must be stopped.
                               David K. Boyd (1908)

Describing the office developments around St Paul's Cathedral, London – A jostling scrum of office buildings so mediocre that the only way you ever remember them is by the frustration they induce – like a basketball team standing shoulder to shoulder between you and the Mona Lisa.   *Prince Charles (1987)*

A high-rise building is like a 747 jet. I can't think of any advantages.
                               C. Allan Cornell (1972)

I don't know what London's coming to – the higher the buildings, the lower the morals.
                               Noël Coward (1922)

Skyscrapers are mountains for people to climb.
                               Bruce Graham (1984)

Skyscrapers are a hubristic tower of babel.
                               Reinhold Niebuhr (1974)

The skyscraper, which was such a prominent feature of American architecture from the 1920s onwards, was the precocious, and occasional delinquent, child of four grandparents: steel-framed construction, the invention of the electric elevator, high city land

values and competitive advertising. The last must be included because some of the most ambitious skyscrapers have hardly been economic as buildings, but have become so because of the commercial value of a company headquarters that visibly outreaches its neighbours.
          John Julius Norwich – 'Great Architecture of the World' (1975)

On Glasgow – When you think of some of the high flats around us, it can hardly be an accident that they are as near as one can get to an architectural filing cabinet.
                               Jimmy Reid (1972)

BUILDINGS (BY NAME)

Albert Hall and Albert Memorial, London
A Twelfth Night cake, from which some giant has removed the ornament on top and placed it on the other side of the road.   *Anon*

Biltmore Hotel, Los Angeles
Patterned after an Italian Renaissance palace, it is 88 times as large and one millionth as valuable to the continuation of man – the Pentagon of travelling salesmen.
          Norman Mailer – 'Esquire' (1960)

Blenheim Palace, Oxfordshire
A quarry of stone that looked at a distance like a great house.   Horace Walpole (1736)

The Brighton Pavilion, Sussex
The Pavilion at Brighton is like a collection of stone pumpkins and pepper-boxes. It seems as if the genius of Architecture had at once the dropsy and the megrims. The King's stud (if they were horses of taste) would petition against so irrational a lodging.
          William Hazlitt – 'Journey Through France & Italy' (1826)

Buckingham Palace, London
Uglier structures of the kind there may be many; yet scarcely any one that is more deficient in grandeur and nobleness of aspect.
          W. Leeds – 'Illustrations of Public Buildings in London' (1838)

Candlestick Park Stadium, San Francisco
Candlestick was built on the water. It should

have been built under it.   *Roger Maris*

Criminal Court Extension, London
The walls of the Old Bailey extension are built, not clad. Perhaps he wants it to look like a penitentiary – he has certainly succeeded.
George Whitby – 'Architects' Journal'

Crystal Palace, London
[*Architect: Sir Joseph Paxton*]
A dreadful sight . . . there was confusion enough in the universe, without building a crystal palace to represent it.   *Thomas Carlyle*

This block of glass is as monstrous as it is unsightly.   *Hector Horeau*

The quantity of thought it expresses is, I suppose, a single and very admirable thought of Sir Joseph Paxton's, probably not a bit brighter than thousands of thoughts which pass through his active and intelligent brain every hour – that it might be possible to build a greenhouse larger than ever a greenhouse was built before. This thought, and some very ordinary algebra, are as much as all that glass can represent of human intellect.   *John Ruskin*

Eiffel Tower, Paris
The Eiffel Tower is the Empire State Building after taxes.   *Anon*

A gigantic carrot that goes by the name of the Eiffel Tower.   *Elena Blavatsky*

The Escorial, Spain
This grandest and gloomiest failure of modern times.   *Anon*

Fox Theater, Atlanta
A popcorn palace of gargantuan gaudiness.
B. Drummond Ayres Jr – 'New York Times' (1978)

Gare d'Orsay, Paris
An obsolete pachyderm of tawny limestone.
Robert Hughes – 'Time' (1986)

Guggenheim Museum, New York
[*Architect: Frank Lloyd Wright*]
A war between architecture and painting in which both come out badly maimed.
John Canady – 'New York Times' (1959)

Wright's inverted oatmeal dish and silo with their awkward cantilevering, their jaundiced skin and the ingenious spiral ramp leading down past the abstractions which mirror the tortured maladjustments of our time.
Robert Moses (1959)

Heathrow Airport, London
I did not fully understand the dread term 'terminal illness' until I saw Heathrow Airport for myself.   *Dennis Potter*

House Office Building, Washington D.C.
The House Office Building is costing more than the combined cost of the Great Pyramids at Giza, the Colossus of Rhodes and the Hanging Gardens of Babylon. Three of the Seven Wonders of the World combined cost less than an office building for 200 congressmen.
David Brinkley – 'New York Herald/Tribune' (1964)

Hubert H. Humphrey Metrodome, Minneapolis
I don't like that Hubert H. Humphrey Metrodome. It's a shame a great guy like Humphrey had to be named after it.
Billy Martin

If this is a ball park, I'm a Chinese aviator.
Billy Martin

John F. Kennedy Center for the Performing Arts, Washington D.C.
The building is a national tragedy. A cross between a concrete candy box and a marble sarcophagus in which the art of architecture lies buried.   *Ada Louise Huxtable (1971)*

The Kingdome, Seattle
Everybody agrees on two things about the Kingdome:
1) It is the most efficient of the domes;
2) It is surpassingly ugly.   *Glenn Dickey*

Los Angeles
I have a theory about LA architecture. I think all the houses came to a costume party and they all came as other countries. *Michael O'Donoghue*

Manhattan Marriott Marquis Hotel, New York
A suburban mall turned vertical.
Paul Goldberger (1985)

Thank God this isn't a play. Critics can kill a play. But not a hotel.
John Portman – 'New York Times' (1985)

Mansion House, London
[*Architect: Mies van der Rohe*]
On the proposed Mansion House Square scheme – A giant glass stump better suited to downtown Chicago than to the City of London.
Prince Charles (1984)

Even the Germans did not succeed in doing the damage you propose to do.
Edward Finlayson (1985)

Milan Cathedral, Italy
The Cathedral is an awful failure. Outside the design is monstrous and inartistic. The over-elaborated details stuck high up where no one can see them; everything is vile in it.
Oscar Wilde (1875)

Moscow University
I have never seen a building so lacking in humanity. It suggested an enormous termitary of cement.
James Kirkup – 'One Man's Russia' (1968)

Mosque of Sophia, Istanbul
It is the rustiest old barn in heathendom.
Mark Twain – 'The Innocents Abroad' (1869)

National Gallery, London
The best view of London is from the National Theatre, because from there you can't see the National Theatre.
Anon

Windows without glass, a cupola without size, a portico without height, pepper-boxes without pepper, and the finest site in Europe without anything to show upon it.
'All the Year Round'

On the proposed extension – A kind of vast municipal fire station . . . what is proposed is like a monstrous carbuncle on the face of a much-loved, elegant friend.
Prince Charles (1984)
[*Two years later, the Prince repeated his view* – a carbuncle on the face of an old and valued friend.]

On Richard Rodgers' proposed design for the extension – The architecture of a man who says,

'Sod you! This is the way it's going to be!'
Owen Luder – President of RIBA

New London Theatre, Drury Lane, London
Upstairs the décor is airport lounge circa 1960 and although there's an attractive circular bar, the feeling that one's flight is about to be called at any moment is inescapable.
Sheridan Morley – 'Punch' (1973)

Old Executive Office Building, Washington DC
A mass of Victorian tiles and granite that resembles a battleship in the rain and a wedding cake in the sun.
Francis X. Clines – 'New York Times' (1985)

I think it's the greatest monstrosity in America.
Harry S. Truman (1958)

The Olivier Theatre, London
A space which might seem over-large for a full-scale revival of Ben Hur on ice.
Sheridan Morley

Post Office Tower, London
Stacked like a pile of green cotton reels.
A. J. Marshall

The Pyramids
As for the pyramids, there is nothing to wonder at in them so much as the fact that so many men could be found degraded enough to spend their lives constructing a tomb for some ambitious booby, whom it would have been wiser and manlier to have drowned in the Nile, and then given his body to the dogs.
Henry D. Thoreau (1854)

Queens High School, New York, USA
Designed by architects with honourable intentions but hands of palsy.
Jimmy Breslin – 'Table Money' (1986)

Ronan Point, East London
A modern 21-storey block of flats, Ronan Point was ripped open by a gas explosion in 1968, killing five people – The best thing that ever happened in British architecture was the collapse of Ronan Point.
Theo Crosby – 'How to Play the Environment Game' (1973)

Royal Festival Hall, South Bank, London
The chief architectural inspiration for the pile
of concrete blocks on the South Bank appears
to have been a cross between Speer's Atlantic
Wall and the Führerbank.
Christopher Booker – 'Dreams that
Crack like Concrete' (1976)

St Pancras Station, London
There is no relief or quiet in any part of the
work. The eye is constantly troubled and
tormented, and the mechanical patterns follow
one another with such rapidity and
perseverance, that the mind becomes irritated
where it ought to be gratified and goaded to
criticism where it should be led calmly to
approve. There is here a complete travesty of
noble associations, and not the slightest care to
save these from sordid contact. An elaboration
that might be suitable for a chapter-house, or a
Cathedral choir, is used as an 'advertising
medium' for bagmen's bedrooms and the costly
discomforts of a terminus hotel, and the
architect is thus a mere expensive rival of the
Company's head cook in catering for the low
enjoyments of the great travelling crowd . . .
Here the public taste has been exactly suited,
and every kind of architectural decoration has
been made thoroughly common and unclean.
J. M. Emmett

St Peter's Basilica, Rome
As a hole St Peter's is fit for nothing but a
ballroom, and it is a little too gaudy even for
that.   *John Ruskin (1840)*

Shakespeare Memorial Theatre,
Stratford-upon-Avon
A courageous and partly successful attempt to
disguise a gasworks as a racquets court.
Peter Fleming – 'The Times' (1951)

Sistine Chapel, Vatican
It has always been difficult to get very close to
the spirit of the Sistine Chapel; now that it has
been cleaned, it is like trying to get close to a
trumpet. *Nigel McGilchrist – 'The Times' (1986)*

Smithsonian Institution Extension,
Washington D.C.
A disaster where marble has been substituted
for imagination.
Ada Louise Huxtable – 'Saturday
Evening Post' (1964)

Statue of Liberty, New York
You have set up in New York harbour a
monstrous idol which you call Liberty. The
only thing that remains to complete the
monument is to put on its pedestal the
inscription written by Dante on the gate of
Hell: 'All hope abandon, ye who enter here.'
G. B. Shaw (1933)

Sydney Opera House
Like nuns in a rugby scrum.   *Anon*

It looks like a typewriter full of oyster shells;
like a broken Pyrex casserole dish in a brown
cardboard box.
Clive James – 'The Observer' (1983)

As if something had crawled up out of the sea
and was up to no good. It reminds me of one of
those films where giant ants and things take
over.
Beverly Nichols – 'Sydney Sun News' (1968)

The greatest public relations building since the
pyramids.   *Billy Wentworth*

Tower Bridge, London
The whole thing as far as architectural
expression is concerned is the most colossal
architectural gimcrack that has ever been seen.
H. H. Statham – 'The Builder' (1895)

Vancouver City Hall
I declare this thing open, whatever it is . . . ?
Prince Philip

The Vatican
One of the best warehouses I ever saw.
Arnold Wesker – 'Chips with Everything' (1962)

Washington D.C.
Washington is an endless series of mock palaces
clearly built for clerks.   *Ada Louise Huxtable*

Washington Monument, Washington D.C.
Saw Washington Monument. Phallic.
Appalling. A national catastrophe.
Arnold Bennett – 'Journal' (1911)

Windsor Castle
A stately pile from the outside, but in the
interior one sees that the state apartments are
decidedly shabby, like a second-class boarding
house. *Lilian Leland – 'Travelling Alone' (1890)*

CARTOON & COMIC STRIP

Comic strip is an eight-column diagram of an old, old joke.   *Anon*

Comic books are illiterature.   *Anon*

Anyone can be a cartoonist! It's so simple even a child can do it!   *Robert Crumb*

Comic strip artists do not make good husbands.
                                        Bud Fisher

Bud Fisher says comic strip artists do not make good husbands. And God knows they do not make good comic strips.   *Don Herold*

ENGRAVING

Engraving is the art of scratch.   John Ruskin

ENGRAVERS

Thomas Bewick – *wood engraver (1753–1828)*
He could draw a pig, but not an Aphrodite.
                                        John Ruskin

INTERIOR DECORATION

An interior decorator is simply an inferior desecrator of the work of an artist.
                                Frank Lloyd Wright (1959)

Mario Buatta – *interior decorator*
The Prince of Chintz – wears well and resists stains.   *Georgia Dullea (1986)*

Tina Turner
After seeing inside her house – You mean you can actually spend $70 000 at Woolworth's?
                                        Bob Krasnow

PAINTING

Everyone wants an artist on the wall or on the shelf, but nobody wants him in the house.
                                        James Baldwin

The emperor loves art in the same way a butcher loves a fat ox.
                        Napoleon Bonaparte – 'Bourrienne'

A Master of Art
Is not worth a fart.   *Andrew Boorde (1690)*

Good painters imitate art, bad ones spew it up.
                                Miguel de Cervantes

Art consists of limitation. The most beautiful part of every picture is the frame.
                                        G. K. Chesterton

Artistic temperament is a disease that afflicts amateurs.   *G. K. Chesterton – 'Heretics'*

Appreciation of art is a moral erection, otherwise it is mere dilettantism.   *Jean Cocteau*

An artist cannot speak about his art any more than a plant can discuss horticulture.
                                        Jean Cocteau (1955)

Art is the community's medicine for the worst disease of the mind, the corruption of consciousness.   *R. G. Collingwood*

An uninspired painter can be described as a blandscape artist.   *Vera Colyer*

'ART' is just a racket! A HOAX perpetrated on the public by so-called 'artists' who set themselves up on a pedestal, and promoted by pantywaist ivory-tower intellectuals and sob-sister 'critics' who think the world owes them a living.   *Robert Crumb (1970)*

Art is a jealous mistress.
                        Ralph W. Emerson – 'Conduct of Life'

What's an artist, but the dregs of his work – the human shambles that follows it around?
                                        William Gaddis

Art is either plagiarism or revolution.
                                        Paul Gauguin

A work of art is an exaggeration.   *André Gide*

All profoundly original art looks ugly at first.
                                        Clement Greenberg

The moment you cheat for the sake of beauty, you know you are an artist.
                        Max Jacob – 'Art Poetique' (1922)

If debased art is kitsch, perhaps kitsch redeemed by honest vulgarity may become art.
Pauline Kael

The more minimal the art the more maximum the explanation. *Hilton Kramer*

If people only knew as much about painting as I do, they would not buy my pictures.
Sir Edwin Landseer

I certainly do hate the act of painting: and although day after day, I go steadily on, it is like grinding my nose off. *Edward Lear*

Art for art's sake makes no more sense than gin for gin's sake. *W. Somerset Maugham*

The great artists of the world are never Puritans, and seldom even ordinarily respectable. *Henry L. Mencken*

The artist and the censor differ in this wise: that the first is a decent mind in an indecent body and that the second is an indecent mind in a decent body. *George J. Nathan*

Finding a businessman interested in the arts is like finding chicken shit in the chicken salad.
Alice Neel

Aesthetics is for me as ornithology must be for the birds.
Barnet Newman – 'Painters Painting' (1972)

Everyone wants to understand painting. Why don't they try to understand the singing of the birds? People love the night, a flower, everything which surrounds them without trying to understand them. But painting – that they 'must' understand. *Pablo Picasso*

The connoisseur of painting gives only bad advice to the painter. For that reason I have given up trying to judge myself. *Pablo Picasso*

Art is long, but a lot of artists are short.
'Philadelphia Inquirer'

A work of art that contains theories is like an object on which the price tag has been left.
Marcel Proust

Art is a kind of illness. *Giacomo Puccini*

Art disease is caused by a hardening of the categories. *Adina Reinhardt*

A mere copier of nature can never produce anything great. *Sir Joshua Reynolds (1770)*

We now live in the Age of Incompetence; we have painters who can't paint, poets who can't rhyme and composers who whistle dissonance.
Dagobert Runes

An artist should be fit for the best society and keep out of it. *John Ruskin*

The fact that many people prefer bad art to good art is not a matter for criminal prosecution but an ingredient in the human comedy, one by which other people will always know how to profit. *John Russell*

A portrait is a painting with something wrong with the mouth. *John Singer Sargent*

If more than ten per cent of the population likes a painting it should be burned, for it must be bad. *G. B. Shaw*

The true artist will let his wife starve, his children go barefoot, his mother drudge for his living at seventy, sooner than work at anything but his art. *G. B. Shaw*

An artist has been defined as a neurotic who continually cures himself with his art.
Lee Simonson

The artist, like the idiot, or clown, sits on the edge of the world, and a push may send him over it. *Osbert Sitwell*

What sight is sadder than the sight of a lady we admire admiring a nauseating picture?
Logan P. Smith

To be an artist at all is like living in Switzerland during a world war.
Tom Stoppard – 'Travesties' (1975)

The immature artist imitates. Mature artists steal. *Lionel Trilling*

I'm glad the old masters are all dead, and I only wish they had died sooner.   *Mark Twain*

An artist is someone who produces things that people don't need to have, but that he – for some good reason – thinks it would be a good idea to give them.   *Andy Warhol*

There are three kinds of people in the world: those who can't stand Picasso, those who can't stand Raphael and those who've never heard of either of them.   *John White*

A work of art is useless. So is a flower.
                    Oscar Wilde

Bad artists always admire each other's work.
                    Oscar Wilde

Pictures deface walls oftener than they decorate them.   *Frank Lloyd Wright – 'Saturday Evening Post' (1961)*

CRITICISM

Writing about art is like dancing about architecture.   *Anon*

Reply to female critic – You will never learn art criticism until you have had relations with the ice man.   *Albert C. Barnes*

To be continually pointing out those parts, the sum, or rather the combination, of which unite to produce significant form, is the function of criticism.   *Clive Bell – 'Art' (1923)*

Painting is the art of protecting flat surfaces from the weather and exposing them to the critics.   *Ambrose Bierce*

Every man ought to be a judge of pictures, and every man is so who has not been connoisseured out of his senses.
                    William Blake (1806)

Painting . . . I detest it . . . I spit upon and abhor all the saints and subjects of one half the impostures I see in the churches and palaces . . . of all the arts, it is the most artificial and unnatural – and that by which the nonsense of mankind is the most imposed upon.
                    Lord Byron (1817)

In matters of art it is more blessed to respond than to judge.   *Lord David Cecil*

Do not be an art critic; paint instead. That way salvation lies.   *Paul Cézanne (1904)*

Criticism is powerless to reach art. Art proceeds itself in a region quite beyond the reach of other expressions save itself.
                    John Jay Chapman – 'Memories and Milestones' (1915)

The ultimate criticism of art is the integration and application of conventional aesthetic definitions towards a silk screen of a car crash in green.   *Sue Coe – 'The Image' (1973)*

Surely when a man is painting a picture he ought not to refuse to hear any man's opinion, for we know very well that though a man may not be a painter he may have a true conception of the form of another man.
                    Leonardo da Vinci – 'Notebooks'

Criticism is easy, and art is difficult.
                    Phillipe Destouches – 'Le Glorieux'

How would any signpost dauber know
    The worth of Titian or of Angelo?
                    John Dryden (1677)

Do not arrogantly disdain to learn the opinion of every man concerning your work. All men are blind as to their own productions, and no man is capable of judging in his own cause.
                    Charles A. Dufresnoy – 'The Art of Painting' (1665)

Let none presume to measure the irregularities of Michelangelo or Socrates by village scales.
                    Ralph Waldo Emerson – 'Representatives Men – Plato'

Works of art exist to be seen, not talked about, except, perhaps, in their presence. I am thoroughly ashamed of all the babbling about art in which I used to join.
                    Johann Goethe – 'Italian Journey' (1788)

Genuine works of art carry their own aesthetic theory implicit within them and suggest the standards according to which they are to be judged.   *Johann Goethe (1808)*

I have generally found that persons who had studied painting least were the best judges of it.
William Hogarth (1761)

If you could say it in words there would be no reason to paint.
Edward Hopper

Criticism talks a good deal of nonsense, but even its nonsense is a useful force. It keeps the question of art before the world, insists upon its importance, and makes it always in order.
Henry James - 'On Some Pictures Lately Exhibited' (1875)

The ideal art critic would not be one who would seek to discover the 'mistake', 'ignorance', 'plagiarisms', and so forth, but the one who would seek to feel how this or that form has an inner effect, and would then impart expressively his whole experience to the public.
Wassily Kandinsky - 'Der Blaue Reiter' (1912)

Two and two continue to make four, in spite of the whine of the amateur for three, or the cry of the art critic for five.
James M. Whistler

The first duty of an art critic is to hold his tongue at all times and on all occasions.
Oscar Wilde - 'The English Renaissance of Art' (1882)

STYLES

Abstract, Surreal and Modern Art
Modern art is like trying to follow the plot in alphabet soup.
Anon

Modern art is when you buy a picture to cover a hole in the wall, and then decide the hole looks much better.
Anon

A modern artist is one who throws paint on a canvas, wipes it off with a cloth and sells the cloth.
Anon

It's easy to recognise modern art. It's the one you can't recognise.
Anon

It's easy to understand modern art. If it hangs on the wall it's a painting. If you can walk around it, it's a sculpture.
Anon

One reassuring thing about modern art is that things can't possibly be as bad as they are painted.
Anon

Pop art is the indelible raised to the unspeakable.
Leonard Baskin (1965)

Abstract art is a product of the untalented, sold by the unprincipled to the utterly bewildered.
Al Capp - 'National Observer' (1963)

What is there to bite on in the abstract? You might as well eat triangles.
Joyce Cary

The Impressionists provoke laughter and yet they are lamentable. They display the profoundest ignorance of drawing, of composition and colour. When children amuse themselves with a box of colour and a piece of paper, they do better.
'Le Chronique des Arts' (1877)

Modern art is what happens when painters stop looking at girls and persuade themselves that they have had a better idea.
John Ciardi - 'Saturday Review'

One sees a square lady with three breasts and a guitar up her crotch.
Noël Coward

Skill without imagination is craftsmanship and gives us many useful objects such as wickerwork picnic baskets. Imagination without skill gives us modern art.
Tom Stoppard (1972)

If that's art, I'm a Hottentot!
Harry S. Truman

I am of the opinion that so-called modern art is merely the vapouring of half-baked lazy people. There is no art at all in connection with the modernists.
Harry S. Truman

Another unsettling element in modern art is that common symptom of immaturity, the dread of doing what has been done before.
Edith Wharton - 'The Writing of Fiction' (1925)

American Art
One of the big problems of American painting is that it is American.
Emile de Antonio

The arts in America are a gigantic racket run by unscrupulous men for unhealthy women.
Sir Thomas Beecham

The only works of art produced by America are its plumbing and its bridges.
Marcel Duchamp (1917)

The smallest ham sandwich ever wrapped at the world's biggest and noisiest banquet.
Edwin Avery Park

The art of covering one thing with another thing to imitate a third thing, which, if genuine, would not be desirable.
Montgomery Schulyer – 'The Point of View' (1891)

An American artist is the unwanted cockroach in the kitchen of a frontier society.   *John Sloan*

A fog-horn chorus of blah.   *Forbes Watson*

British Art
His work was that curious mixture of bad painting and good intentions that always entitles a man to be called a representative British artist.   *Oscar Wilde*

French Art
French Art, if not sanguinary, is usually obscene.   *Herbert Spencer – 'Home Life with Herbert Spencer' (1906)*

Post-Impressionism
The drawing is on the level of that of an untaught child of seven or eight years old, the sense of colour that of a tea-tray painter, the method that of a schoolboy who wiped his fingers on a slate after spitting on them.
W. S. Blunt – 'My Diaries' (1920)

PAINTERS

Anon
They couldn't find the artist, so they hung the picture.   *Anon*

I found myself standing before an oil of a horse that I figured was probably a self-portrait, judging from the general execution.
Peter de Vries – 'Let Me Count the Ways' (1965)

What's it meant to be? A 'Study'? It doesn't say what of. Well, that's an easy way out for a painter.   *Ruth Draper*

I can truthfully say that the painter has observed the Ten Commandments. Because he hath not made to himself the likeness of anything in heaven above, or that which is on earth beneath, or that which is in the water under the earth.   *Abraham Lincoln*

He does watercolours like a girl of fourteen – when she was twelve.   *Ben Nicholson*

This is either a forgery or a damn clever original.   *Frank Sullivan*

Sir Lawrence Alma-Tadema – *(1836–1912)*
'*Anon*' – The general effect was exactly like a microscopic view of a small detachment of black beetles, in search of a dead rat.
John Ruskin

Aubrey V. Beardsley – *(1872–98)*
Duabaway Weirdsley.   *'Punch' (1895)*

A face like a silver hatchet, with grass green hair.   *Oscar Wilde*

Sandro Botticelli – *(1445–1510)*
If Botticelli were alive today, he'd be working for Vogue.   *Peter Ustinov*

Georges Braque – *(1882–1963)*
He constructs deformed metallic men of a terrible simplification. He is contemptuous of form, reduces everything, sites and figures and house, to schemes, to cubes.
Louis Vauxcelles – 'Gil Blas' (1908)
[*This quote is attributed as the first reference to 'Cubism'.*]

Ford Madox Brown – *(1821–93)*
Do you not see that his name never occurs in my books – do you think that would be so if I could praise him, seeing that he is an entirely worthy fellow? But pictures are pictures, and things that aren't aren't.   *John Ruskin (1862)*

Paul Cézanne – *(1839–1906)*
M. Cézanne must be some kind of a lunatic, afflicted with delirium tremens while he is

painting. In fact, it is one of the weird shapes, thrown off by hashish, borrowed from a swarm of ridiculous dreams. *Anon French art critic*

I like the work of old masters, because I can see how they've done it – and I can also see what they've done. But with Cézanne, I can see how he's done it, but I can't make out for the life of me just what he's done. *John Singer Sargent*

To me, apples are fruit – to Cézanne they were mountains! *David Smith*

John Sell Cotman – *(1782–1842)*
I think Cotman's a very overrated reputation; he was the slave of his watercolour technique, instead of its master. *Roger Fry*

Jean Baptiste Corot – *(1796–1875)*
Corot painted over three thousand pictures; at least ten thousand of them are in America.
Anon

Antoine Corregio – *(1489–1534)*
The properties of his figures are sometimes such as might be corrected by a common sign-painter. *William Hogarth – 'The Analysis of Beauty' (1753)*

Salvador Dali – *(1904–82)*
Señor Dali, born delirious,
Considers it folly to be serious.
Phyllis McGinley (1960)

Edgar Degas – *(1834–1917)*
He is nothing but a peeping Tom, behind the coulisses, and among the dressing rooms of ballet dancers, noting only travesties on fallen womanhood, most disgusting and offensive.
'The Churchman' (1886)

Degas is repulsive. *'New York Times' (1886)*

Tell him that in art there are certain qualities called drawing, colour, execution and control and he will laugh in your face.
Albert Wolff – 'Le Figaro' (1876)

Caspar D. Friedrich – *(1774–1840)*
'Monk by the Sea' – Because of its monotony and boundlessness, with nothing but the frame as foreground, one feels as if one's eyelids had been cut away. *Heinrich van Kleist*

William Frith – *(1819–1909)*
'Derby Day' – Is it really all done by hand?
Anon

Roger Fry – *(1866–1934)*
When he began to paint, he was Mr Facing Both-Ways; a thousand theories assailed him, paralysing every stroke of the brush. *M. Lilly*

Paul Gauguin – *(1848–1903)*
Don't talk to me of Gauguin. I'd like to wring the fellow's neck. *Paul Cézanne*

A decorator tainted with insanity.
Kenyon Cox – 'Harper's Weekly' (1913)

Vincent van Gogh – *(1853–90)*
Vincent van Gogh's mother painted all of his best things. The famous mailed decapitated ear was a figment of the public relations firm engaged by van Gogh's dealer. *Roy Blount Jr*

Benjamin Haydon – *(1786–1846)*
Haydon hardly ever contemplated a teaspoon without a desire to shout and hurl himself at it.
Edmund Blunden

Haydon believed himself Phidias in the morning, and retired as Michelangelo at night.
John Ruskin

William Hogarth – *(1697–1764)*
Is any one so foolish as to succeed?
On Envy's altar he is doomed to bleed!
Hogarth, a guilty pleasure in your eyes,
The place of executioner supplies.
Charles Churchill

William H. Hunt – *(1827–1910)*
'The Scapegoat' – A mere goat, with no more interest for us than the sheep which furnished yesterday's dinner. *Anon (1856)*

Peter Hurd – *(b 1904)*
On his portrait – The ugliest thing I ever saw.
Lyndon B. Johnson

Augustus John – *(1878–1961)*
That standard celebrity. *Percy W. Lewis*

He exaggerates every little hill and hollow of the face till one looks like a gypsy, grown old in wickedness and hardship. If one looked like any of his pictures the country women would take the clean clothes off the hedges when one passed, as they do at the sight of a tinker.

William Yeats (1907)

Paul Klee – *(1879–1940)*
His pictures seem to resemble, not pictures, but a sample book of patterns of linoleum.

Cyril Asquith

Percy Wyndham Lewis – *(1884–1957)*
A buffalo in wolf's clothing. *Robert Rose*

Mr Lewis's pictures appeared, as a very great painter said to me, to have been painted by a mailed fist in a cotton glove.

Edith Sitwell – 'Taken Care Of'

Claude Lorrain – *(1600–82)*
We know hundreds of painters who do counterfeit good paintings, but here's one (and almost the only one) who painted counterfeit bad pictures. *Roger Fry (1925)*

Edouard Manet – *(1832–83)*
You are the first in the decadence of your art.

Charles Baudelaire

'Venus et le Chat' – You scarcely know if you were looking at a parcel of nude flesh or a bundle of laundry.

Jules Clarette – 'Le Figaro' (1863)

'Le Dejeuner sur l'Herbe' – This is a young man's practical joke, a shameful open sore not worth exhibiting in this way. *Louis Etienne (1863)*

Henri Matisse – *(1869–1954)*
'The Red Studio' – This is not amusing, it is dismaying and disheartening. The other day, someone attributed to me the statement that 'the human race was nearing insanity'. I never said that but if anyone is trying to convince me that this is 'modern art', and that it is representative of our time, I would be obliged to think that statement is true.

Kenyon Cox – 'Harper's Weekly' (1913)

Matisse is an unmitigated bore. Surely the vogue of those twisted and contorted human figures must be as short as it is artificial.

Harriet Monroe – 'Chicago Tribune' (1913)

Michelangelo – *(1475–1564)*
An inventor of filthiness. *Anon*

If Michelangelo had been a heterosexual, the Sistine Chapel would have been painted basic white and with a roller. *Rita Mae Brown (1988)*

'Pieta' – The figure of Christ is as much emaciated as if He had died of consumption: besides, there is something indelicate, not to say indecent, in the attitude of a man's body, stark naked, lying upon the knees of a woman.

Tobias Smollett (1766)

Sir John Millais – *(1829–96)*
This strangely unequal painter – a painter whose imperfectly great powers always suggest to me the legend of the spiteful fairy at the christening feast. The name of Mr Millais's spiteful fairy is vulgarity.

Henry James – 'Nation' (1878)

Samuel Morse – *(1791–1872)*
He cannot design. There is no poetry about his paintings, and his prose consists of straight lines, which look as if they have been stretched to their utmost tension to form clothes-lines.

Philip Hone – 'Diary' (1833)

On a painting of Christ riding an ass into Jerusalem – Morse, your donkey is the saviour of your picture. *Abraham Lincoln*

Sir Alfred Munnings – *(1878–1959)*
His first job was designing chocolate box wrappers – a talent he clearly never lost.

Waldemar Januszcak – 'The Guardian' (1986)

Pablo Picasso – *(1881–1973)*
A Catalan wizard who fools with shapes.

Bernard Berenson

'Des Mesmoiselles d'Avignon' – It's as if you wanted to feed us scraps and give us gasoline to drink to make us spit. *Georges Braque*

A highbrow is the kind of person who looks at a sausage and thinks of Picasso. *A. P. Herbert*

A scream is always just that – a noise and not music. *Carl Jung*

Many painters and writers have made beautiful

works out of repulsive subjects; Picasso enjoys making repulsive works out of beautiful objects.
Raymond Mortimer – 'Picasso in Private'

'Desmesmoiselles d'Avignon' – It's the work of a madman. *Ambrose Vollard (1907)*

Camille Pissarro – *(1831–1903)*
No intelligence can accept such aberrations.
Albert Wolff (1876)

Jackson Pollock – *(1912–56)*
Pollock does not seem to be especially talented, there being too much of an air of baked macaroni about some of his patterns, as though they were scrambled baroque designs.
Parker Tyler – 'View' (1945)

Jean Puy – *(1876–1934)*
'Stroll under the Pines' – A pot of paint has been thrown in the public's face.
Camille Mauclair – 'Le Figaro'

Pierre Auguste Renoir – *(1841–1919)*
On the work of M. Auguste Renoir it is hard to speak with gravity. A glance at some of the canvases which bear his name will explain more fully than any words of mine the difficulty one might experience in taking such work seriously.
Philip Burne-Jones (1905)

Just explain to M. Renoir that the torso of a woman is not a mass of decomposing flesh, its green and violet spots indicating the state of complete putrefaction of a corpse. *Albert Wolff*

Sir Joshua Reynolds – *(1723–92)*
I consider Reynolds's 'Discourses to the Royal Academy' as the Simulations of the Hypocrite who smiles particularly where he means to Betray. *William Blake*

O reader, behold the philosopher's grave! He was born quite a fool but he died quite a knave. *William Blake*

Roebuck
Roebuck believes in the fine arts with all the earnestness of a man who does not understand them. *G. B. Shaw*

Salvator Rosa – *(1615–73)*
The quack doctor of painting.
William Blake (1808)

Dante Rossetti – *(1828–82)*
'The Rossetti Exhibition' – I have been to it and am pleased to find it more odious than I even dared to hope. *Samuel Butler*

I should say that Rossetti was a man without any principles at all, who earnestly desired to find some means of salvation along the lines of least resistance.
Ford Madox Ford – 'Ancient Lights'

Rossetti, dear Rossetti, I love your work,
  But you were really a bit of a jerk.
George MacBeth

Rossetti is not a painter, Rossetti is a ladies' maid. *James M. Whistler*

Henri Rousseau – *(1844–1910)*
He had enthusiasm, faith in his art of painting and also the instinctive qualities that are lacking in so many conquering heroes of the Salon. Unfortunately, taste, measure, everything that constitutes talent, are missing.
'Le Mercure de France' (1910)

John Singer Sargent – *(1856–1925)*
It is positively dangerous to sit next to Sargent. It is taking your face in your hands. *Anon*

John is very stiff, a sort of completely accentless mongrel . . . rather French, fauborg sort of manners. Ugly. *Vernon Lee*

A sepulchre of dullness and propriety.
James M. Whistler

Walter Sickert – *(1860–1942)*
I give you this cigar because I so much admire your writings. If I liked your paintings, I'd give you a bigger one. *Percy W. Lewis*

Graham Sutherland – *(1903–80)*
Portrait of Sir Winston Churchill – It makes me look as if I was straining a stool.
Sir Winston Churchill

Tintoretto – *(1518–94)*
He will never be anything but a dauber. *Titian*

Titian – *(1477–1576)*
If I hear the name Titian, I have to lie down.
Helen Bell

Why should Titians and the Venetitians be named in a discourse on art? Such idiots are not artists.　　　　　　*William Blake (1807)*

'Venus' – There, against the wall, without obstructing rag or leaf, you may look your fill upon the foulest, the vilest, the obscenest picture the world possesses. Without any question it was painted for a bagnio and it was probably refused because it was a trifle too strong.　　*Mark Twain – 'A Tramp Abroad (1880)*

Henri de Toulouse-Lautrec – *(1864–1901)*
A tiny blacksmith with little eye-glasses.
　　　　　　　　　　　　　　Jules Renard

A baron who has taken root in a brothel.
　　　　　　　　　　　　　　André Suare

Joseph M. W. Turner – *(1775–1851)*
His pictures appear to me to be like the works of an old man who had ideas but had lost his powers of execution.　　*Sir George Beaumont*

'Boats Carrying out Anchors & Cable to Dutch Men-of-War in 1665' – It seems to have been painted with a birch-broom and whitening.
　　　　　　　　　　　　　'The Sun' (1804)

'The Slave Ship' – It resembles a tortoise-shell cat having a fit in a plate of tomatoes.
　　　　　　　　　　　　　　Mark Twain

Leonardo da Vinci – *(1452–1519)*
He bores me. He ought to have stuck to his flying machines.　　　　　　*Auguste Renoir*

Andy Warhol – *(1930–80)*
The most famous living artist in America is Andy Warhol, unfortunately.
　　　　　　John Heilpern – 'Observer' (1979)

Warhol's art belongs less to the history of painting than the history of publicity.
　　　　　　　　　　　　　Hilton Kramer

The only genius with an IQ of 60.　　*Gore Vidal*

Benjamin West – *(1738–1820)*
That tame and wooden painter, West.
　　　　　　A. W. N. Pugin – 'Contrasts'

James M. Whistler – *(1834–1903)*
'Nocturne in Black and Gold' – For Mr Whistler's sake, no less than for the protection of the purchaser, Sir Coutts Lindsay ought not to have admitted works into the gallery, in which the ill-educated conceit of the artist so nearly approached the aspect of wilful imposture. I have seen, and heard, much of Cockney impudence before now; but never expected to hear a coxcomb ask two hundred guineas for flinging a pot of paint in the public's face.
　　　　John Ruskin – 'Fors Clavigera' (1877)
[*This critique led to two famous responses –*
a) a celebrated libel action – settled by the award of one farthing to Turner;
b) Whistler answered Ruskin's counsel's question –
'For two days' labour, you ask two hundred guineas?'
'No, I ask it for the knowledge of a lifetime!']

'Symphony in Grey and Green' – I never saw anything so impudent on the walls of any exhibition, in any country, as last year in London. It was a daub professing to be a 'harmony in pink and white' (or some such nonsense): absolute rubbish, and which had taken about a quarter of an hour to scrawl or daub – it had no pretence to be called a painting.　　　　　　　　　*John Ruskin*

With our James vulgarity begins at home, and should be allowed to stay there.　*Oscar Wilde*

He opened the eyes of the blind and has given great encouragement to the short-sighted.
　　　　　　　　　　　　　　Oscar Wilde

Wols – *(1913–51)*
Violent splashes of next-to-nothingness.
　　　　William Feaver – 'Observer' (1985)

GALLERIES

L'Ouvre, Paris
The finest collection of frames that I ever saw.
　　　　　　　　　　　Sir Humphrey Davy

PERFORMANCE ART

Performance art is created by thin young men and usually consists of dancerly women taking their clothes off, putting on masks, and

THE CREATIVE ARTS

dumping blood on each other while a sound-track screeches out machinery noises.

Ian Shoales

PHOTOGRAPHY

A bad photographer is a person who takes a dim view of things. *Anon*

Not everybody trusts paintings, but people believe photographs. *Ansel Adams*

A painting teaches us to know a man; a photograph can but recall him to our minds.
Comtesse Diane

Trick photography is merely focus-pocus.
Doris Dolphin

The best photographs have a terrible defect which excludes them from the domain of art: they have not been thought. *Octave Feuillet*

All camera work is a form of voyeurism.
Joseph Frick (1963)

The more gadgets you use, the worse the picture. *Felix Man (1971)*

Inside every photographer is a painter trying to get out. *Pablo Picasso*

A still photographer is a mechanic. He's not an artist, despite all you read.
Lord Snowdon (1968)

No photographer is as good as the simplest camera. *Edward Steichen*

No word-person writing on photography has ever said anything that helped me do better on Thursday what I'd done less well on Wednesday. *Ralph Steiner*

For half a century photography has been the 'art-form' of the untalented.
Gore Vidal – 'New Statesman' (1978)

My idea of a good picture is one that is in focus.
Andy Warhol (1979)

The difference between good and bad art lies in

the minds that created, rather than in the skill of hands. *Ed Weston*

To consult rules of composition before making a picture is a little like consulting the law of gravitation before going for a walk. *Ed Weston*

PHOTOGRAPHERS

Anon
To a press photographer – You are a pest, by the very nature of that camera in your hands.
Princess Anne

Photographers are the most loathsome inconvenience. They're imbeciles. They're the pits. *Paul Newman*

A photographer without a magazine behind him is like a farmer without fields.
Norman Parkinson – 'New Yorker' (1984)

Margaret Bourke-White
One thing I learned above all else from Margaret Bourke-White is the kind of woman I didn't want to be. *Peggy Sargent*

POTTERY

Even the most generous and benign souls might find it hard to enthuse about pottery.
Robin Dutt – 'Independent'

SCULPTURE

Sculptures are mud-pies which endure.
Cyril Connolly

SCULPTORS

Jacob Epstein – *(1880–1959)*
There is a famous family named Stein –
There's Gert, and there's Ep, and there's Ein;
  Gert's poems are bunk,
  Ep's statues are junk,
And nobody understands Ein. *Anon*

I've seen the Epstein. I confess it makes me physically a little sick. The wretched woman has two sets of breasts and hip joints like a merrythought! No, really! *John Galsworthy*

If people dug up the remains of this civilisation a thousand years hence, and found Epstein's statues and that man Ellis, they would think we were just savages.   *Doris Lessing*

Epstein is a great sculptor, but I wish he would wash.   *Ezra Pound*

John Flaxman – *(1755–1826)*
   I mock thee not, tho' I by thee am Mocked. Thou call's me Madman, But I call thee Blockhead.   *William Blake*

In these designs of Flaxman, you have gentlemanly feeling, and fair knowledge of anatomy, and firm setting down of lines, all applied, in the foolishest and worst possible way; you cannot have a more finished example of learned error, amiable want of meaning, and bad drawing with a steady hand.   *John Ruskin*

Horatio Greenhough – *(1805–52)*
His tongue was far cunninger in talk than his chisel was to carve.   *R. W. Emerson*

Henry Moore – *(1898–1986)*
It is a mistake for a sculptor or a painter to speak or write very often about his job. It releases tension needed for his work.
                    'Henry Moore on Sculpture' (1967)

'Less is more' and Moore is a bore.   *Anon*
[*Such a comment begs* 'Moore is less!'
                    Colin M. Jarman]

His statues are hideous beyond words, they seem to be a sort of primitive caveman production, and unworthy of a good place on any public building in London.
                    'Morning Post' (1929)

Hiram Powers – *(1805–73)*
He is a man of great mechanical talent and natural strength of perception, but with no poetry in his composition, and I think no creative power.   *William W. Story*

LITERARY

The best part of the fiction in many novels is the notice that the characters are purely imaginary.   *Franklin P. Adams*

Most writers, you know, are awful sticks to talk with.   *Sherwood Anderson*

All writing is pigshit. People who come out of nowhere to try to put into words any part of what goes on in their head are pigs.
Antonin Artaud – 'Selected Works' (1980)

A professional writer is an amateur who didn't quit.   *Richard Bach (1974)*

Some books are to be tasted, others to be swallowed, and some few to be chewed and digested.   *Francis Bacon*

Literature is the question minus the answer.
Roland Barthes (1978)

The llama is a woolly sort of fleecy hair goat
With an indolent expression and an undulating
    throat –
Like an unsuccessful literary man.
Hillaire Belloc

No wonder the really powerful men in our society, whether politicians or scientists, hold writers and poets in contempt. They do it because they get no evidence from modern literature that anybody is thinking about any significant question.   *Saul Bellow*

Every writer, without exception, is a masochist, a sadist, a peeping Tom, an exhibitionist, a narcissist, an unjustice collector and a depressed person constantly haunted by fears of unproductivity.   *Edward Bergler*

About the most originality that any writer can hope to achieve honestly is to steal with good judgement.   *Josh Billings*

A novel is never anything but a philosophy put into images.   *Albert Camus*

The majority of books of our time give one the impression of having been manufactured in a day out of the books read the day before.
Nicholas de Chamfort

The author who invents a title well
Will always find his covered dullness sell.
Thomas Chatterton

If writers were good businessmen, they'd have too much sense to be writers.   *Irvin S. Cobb*

The greatest masterpiece in literature is only a dictionary out of order.   *Jean Cocteau*

A man may as well expect to grow stronger by always eating as wiser by always reading.
Jeremy Collier

It may be observed of good writing, as of good blood, that it is much easier to say what it is composed of than to compose it.   *Charles Colton*

Many books require no thought from those who read them, and for a very simple reason. They made no such demand upon those who write them.   *Charles Colton*

The old Penny Dreadful which became the dime novel is now the Buck Ninety Awful!
Bill Copeland

The best photographs have a terrible defect which excludes them from the domain of art: they have not been thought. Literature also has its photographers; they are called realists. These are writers who reduce themselves to being only object-glasses in action, instead of being souls which feel and intelligences which interpret.   *Octave Feuillet*

To read a group of novels these days is a depressing experience. After the fourth or fifth, I find myself thinking about 'The Novel' and I feel a desperate desire to sneak out to a movie.
Leslie Fielding

Actors yearn for the perfect director, athletes for the perfect coach, priests for the perfect pope, presidents for the perfect historian. Writers hunger for the perfect reviewer. But this is an imperfect world, as actors, athletes, priests and presidents soon discover. Writers have known this from the day they read their first reviews.

Thomas Fleming – 'New York Times' (1985)

It is a mistake to think that books have come to stay. The human race did without them for thousands of years and may decide to do without them again. *E. M. Forster*

One always tends to overpraise a long book because one has got through it. *E. M. Forster*

The difference between an author and a horse is that the horse doesn't understand the horse-dealer's language. *Max Frisch*

Unprovided with original learning, unformed in the habits of thinking, unskilled in the arts of composition, I resolved to write a book.
Edward Gibbon

Contemporary literature can be classified under three headings: the neurotic, the erotic and the tommy-rotic. *W. Giese*

The public which reads, in any sense of the word worth considering, is very small, very small; the public which would feel no lack if all book-printing ceased tomorrow is enormous.
George Gissing

A detective digs around in the garbage of people's lives. A novelist invents people and then digs around in their garbage. *Joe Gore*

The novelist, afraid his ideas may be foolish, slyly puts them in the mouth of some other fool and reserves the right to disavow them.
Diane Johnson – 'New York Times Book Review' (1979)

I never desire to converse with a man who has written more than he has read. *Samuel Johnson*

When an author is yet living, we estimate his powers by his worst performance; and when he is dead, we rate them by his best.
Samuel Johnson

A transition from an author's book to his conversation is too often like an entrance into a large city after a distant prospect. Remotely, we see nothing but spires of temples and turrets of palaces, and imagine it is the residence of splendour, grandeur, and magnificence; but when we have passed the gates, we find it perplexed with narrow passages, disgraced with despicable cottages, embarrassed with obstructions, and clouded with smoke.
Samuel Johnson – 'The Rambler'

Authors are easy enough to get on with – if you are fond of children.
Michael Joseph – 'Observer' (1949)

How many young people have a good ear for literature but sing out of tune!
Joseph Joubert – 'Pensees'

Young writers give their minds plenty of exercise and very little nourishment.
Joseph Joubert

One man is as good as another until he has written a book. *Benjamin Jowett*

A woman who writes a book commits two sins; she increases the number of books, and decreases the number of women. *Alphonse Karr*

There are two literary maladies – writer's cramp and swelled head. *Coulson Kernahan*

Books are a load of crap.
Philip Larkin – 'A Study of Reading Habits'

Having been unpopular in high school is not just cause for book publication. *Fran Lebowitz*

It's a crazy business, anyway, writing; locking yourself in a room and inventing conversations, no way for a grown-up to behave. Then, your book is published, the sun comes up, as usual, and the sun goes down, as usual, and the world is in no way altered, and it must be someone's fault. *John Leonard – 'Esquire' (1975)*

Literature is mostly about having sex, and not much about having babies; life is the other way round. *David Lodge*

A writer is somebody for whom writing is more

difficult than it is for other people.
Thomas Mann

The idea of attending a writers' congress in
Moscow is rather like attending a human rights
conference in Nazi Germany.   *David Markstein*

If you have one strong idea, you can't help
repeating it and embroidering it. Sometimes I
think that authors should write one book and
then be put in a gas chamber.
John P. Marquand

If you want to get rich from writing, write the
sort of thing that's read by persons who move
their lips when they're reading to themselves.
Don Marquis

Only a mediocre writer is always at his best.
W. Somerset Maugham

I have never met an author who admitted that
people did not buy his book because it was dull.
W. Somerset Maugham

There are no dull subjects. There are only dull
writers.   *H. L. Mencken*

The chief knowledge that a man gets from
reading books is the knowledge that very few of
them are worth reading.   *H. L. Mencken*

A person who publishes a book wilfully appears
before the populace with his pants down. If it is
a good book nothing will hurt him. If it is a bad
book, nothing can help him.
Edna St Vincent Millay

A man with a belly full of classics is an enemy
of the human race.
Henry Miller – 'Tropic of Cancer' (1930)

An optimist is one who believes everything he
reads on the jacket of a new book.
'Milwaukee Journal'

First you're an unknown, then you write a book
and you move up to obscurity.   *Martin Myers*

It is a mean thief, or a successful author, that
plunders the dead.   *Austin O'Malley*

Only ambitious nonentities and hearty

mediocrities exhibit their rough drafts. It is like
passing around samples of one's sputum.
Vladimir Nabokov

Everywhere I go I'm asked if I think the
university stifles writers. My opinion is that
they don't stifle enough of them. There's many
a best seller that could have been prevented by
a good teacher.   *Flannery O'Connor*

So many people are writing books that 'tell all'
– soon we'll be having Book of the Mouth Club.
Robert Orben

When one says that a writer is fashionable one
practically always means that he is admired by
people under thirty.   *George Orwell*

All writers are vain, selfish and lazy, and at the
very bottom of their motives there lies a
mystery. Writing a book is a horrible,
exhausting struggle, like a long bout of some
painful illness. One would never undertake
such a thing if one were not driven on by some
demon whom one can neither resist nor
understand. For all one knows that demon is
simply the same instinct that makes a baby
squall for attention.
George Orwell – 'Why I Write' (1947)

On female writers – As artists they're rot, but as
providers they're oil wells – they gush.
Dorothy Parker

A pin has as much as some authors, and a good
deal more point.   *G. D. Prentice*

A work in which there are theories is like an
object which still has the ticket that shows its
price.   *Marcel Proust*

When a new book is published, read an old one.
Samuel Rogers

The only reason for being a professional writer
is that you can't help it.   *Leo Rosten*

The road to hell is paved with works-in-
progress.   *Philip Roth*

I hate books; they teach us only to talk about
what we do not know.   *Jean-Jacques Rousseau*

It is part of prudence to thank an author for his book before reading it, so as to avoid the necessity of lying about it afterwards.
George Santayana

Of course, literati are almost in every sense of the word nastier than peasants.
Martin Seymour-Smith

What a heartbreaking job is trying to combine authors for their own protection! I had ten years of it on the Committee of Management of the Society of Authors; and the first lesson I learned was that when you take the field for the authors you will be safer without a breastplate than without a backplate. *G. B. Shaw*

The road to ignorance is paved with good editions. *G. B. Shaw*

A great many people now reading and writing would be better employed in keeping rabbits.
Edith Sitwell

A best-seller is the gilded tomb of a mediocre talent. *Logan P. Smith – 'Afterthoughts' (1931)*

Every author, however modest, keeps a most outrageous vanity chained like a madman in the padded cell of his breast. *Logan P. Smith – ibid.*

The writer is either a practising recluse or a delinquent, guilt-ridden one, or both. Usually both. *Susan Sontag*

Perversity is the muse of modern literature.
Susan Sontag

If you are getting the worst of it in an argument with a literary man, always attack his style. That'll touch him if nothing else will.
J. A. Spender

Those big-shot writers could never dig the fact that there are more salted peanuts consumed than caviar. *Mickey Spillane*

Writers are a little below clowns and a little above trained seals. *John Steinbeck*

Satire lies about literary men while they live, and eulogy lies about them when they die.
Voltaire

The 'Literary Digest' says that books have a curative power. Yes: there are some which cure insomnia. *'Washington Post'*

I was never allowed to read the popular American children's books of my day because, as my mother said, the children spoke bad English without the author's knowing it.
Edith Wharton

If we should ever inaugurate a hall of fame, it would be reserved exclusively and hopefully for authors who, having written four bestsellers, still refrained from starting out on a lecture tour. *E. B. White*

I'm never disappointed in literary men. I think they're perfectly charming. It's their works I find so disappointing. *Oscar Wilde*

I quite admit that modern novels have many good points. All I insist on is that, as a class, they are quite unreadable. *Oscar Wilde (1889)*

The difference between journalism and literature is that journalism is unreadable and literature is not read. *Oscar Wilde*

I hate vulgar realism in literature. The man who would call a spade a spade should be compelled to use one. It is the only thing he is fit for. *Oscar Wilde – 'The Picture of Dorian Gray' (1891)*

Literature is the orchestration of platitudes.
Thornton Wilder

Every author really wants to have letters printed in the papers. Unable to make the grade, he drops down a rung of the ladder and writes novels. *P. G. Wodehouse*

On accepting the Nobel Prize – The profession of book writing makes horse racing seem like a solid, stable business. *John Steinbeck (1962)*

CRITICISM

The reviewer's job is to read a novel, find out what the author has set out to do, estimate how far he has succeeded, decide whether his intentions were worthwhile, and report his conclusions to his readers. *Walter Allen*

The one thing I most emphatically do not ask of a critic is that he tells me what I ought to approve or condemn. I have no objection to his telling me what works and authors he likes and dislikes.

W. H. Auden - 'The Dyer's Hand' (1962)

One cannot attack a bad book without showing off. *W. H. Auden - ibid.*

There is nothing like a good negative review to sell a book. *Hugh Barbour*

A good writer is not per se a good book critic. No more than a good drunk is a good bartender.

Jim Bishop - 'New York American-Journal' (1957)

No one is fit to judge a book until he has rounded Cape Horn in a sailing vessel, until he has bumped into two or three icebergs, until he has been lost in the sands of the desert, until he has spent a few years in the House of the Dead.

Van Wyck Brooks

A critic is at best a waiter at the great table of literature. *Louis Dudek*

An author ought to write for the youth of his own generation, the critics and the next, and the schoolmasters of ever afterwards.

F. Scott Fitzgerald

Some reviews give pain. This is regrettable, but no author has the right to whine. He was not obliged to be an author. He invited publicity, and he must take the publicity that comes along. *E. M. Forster*

Sweet, bland commendations fall everywhere upon the scene. A book is born into a puddle of treacle; the brine of hostile criticism is only a memory. *Elizabeth Hardwicke*

Reviewers are forever telling authors they can't understand them. The author might often reply: Is that my fault?

J. C. & A. W. Hare - 'Guesses at the Truth'

Critics are coroners literary. *Ernest Hemingway*

What the mulberry leaf is to the silkworm, the author's book, treatise, essay, poem, is to the

criticial larvae that feed upon it. It furnishes them with food and clothing.

Oliver Wendell Holmes Sr - 'Over the Tea-cups'

Mediocrity is more dangerous in a critic than in a writer. *Eugene Ionescu (1966)*

More and more people think of a critic as an indispensable middle man between writer and reader, and would no more read a book alone, if they could help it, than have a baby alone.

Randall Jarrell

It is advantageous to an author that his book should be attacked as well as praised. Fame is a shuttlecock. If it be struck at only one end of the room, it will soon fall to the ground. To keep it up, it must be struck at both ends.

Samuel Johnson

The man who is asked by an author what he thinks of his work is put to the torture and is not obliged to speak the truth. *Samuel Johnson*

The opinion of a great body of the reading public is very materially influenced even by the unsupported assertions of those who assume a right to criticise.

Thomas Macaulay - 'Essays: Montgomery's Papers'

I can imagine nothing more distressing for a critic than to have a writer see accurately into his own work. *Norman Mailer*

The besetting weakness of criticism, when faced with a new writer, is to define his work too narrowly, and then to keep applying that definition like a label. *F. O. Matthiessen*

The savage review is a too easy form of fun. Far too many worthless books are published every year: why pick out one for attack, unless it is likely to win more respect than it deserves?

Raymond Mortimer - 'Reviewing'

Criticism can be instructive in the sense that it gives readers, including the author of the book, some information about the critic's intelligence, or honesty, or both. *Vladimir Nabokov*

Prolonged indiscriminate reviewing of books involves constantly inventing reactions towards books for which one has no spontaneous feeling, whatever.   *George Orwell - 'Confessions of a Book Reviewer'*

A book reviewer is usually a barker before the door of a publisher's circus.   *Austin O'Malley*

On her last 'Constant Reader' column – I am about to leave literature flat on its face. I don't want to review books any more. It cuts in too much on my reading.
Dorothy Parker - 'New Yorker'

The actual definition of 'reviewmanship' is now, I think stabilised. In its shortest form it is 'how to be one-up on the author without actually tampering with the text'. In other words, how, as a critic, to show that it is really yourself who should have written the book, if you had had the time, and since you hadn't you are glad that someone else has, although obviously it might have been done better.
Stephen Potter

The balance sheets of our great publishing houses would not be materially affected if they ceased from tomorrow the publication of poetry and literary criticism, and most publishers would rejoice to be relieved of the unprofitable burden of vain solicitations which such publication encourages.   *Herbert Read*

As a bankrupt thief turns thief-taker, so an unsuccessful author turns critic.
Percy B. Shelley - 'Adonais'

The critics will say as always that literature is decaying. From the time of the first critic up to now they have said nothing else.
Sir Osbert Sitwell

Lovers of literature will look for the remains of the golden treasure in that shipwreck on the bottom of the sea of criticism.   *Josef Skovorecky*

Book critics are such a weird subspecies. We may pull all-nighters, but they tend to take place at home, where page 648 leads inexorably to page 649.   *Jean Strouse (1980)*

I have long felt that any book reviewer who expresses rage and loathing for a novel is preposterous. He or she is like a person who has just put on full armour and attacked a hot fudge sundae or banana split.   *Kurt Vonnegut Jr*

Professional reviewers read so many bad books in the course of duty that they get an unhealthy craving for arresting phrases.   *Evelyn Waugh*

No publisher should ever express an opinion of the value of what he publishes. That is a matter entirely for the literary critic to decide.
Oscar Wilde (1890)

Nothing induces me to read a novel except when I have to make money by writing about it. I detest them.   *Virginia Woolf*

BIOGRAPHY

One of the new terrors of death.   *John Arbuthnot*

Biographies of writers, whether written by others or themselves, are always superfluous and usually in bad taste. A writer is a maker, not a man of action.   *W. H. Auden*

It is one of the ironies of biographical art that some details are more relevant than others, and many details have no relevance at all.
Paul Bailey (1985)

In writing biography, fact and fiction shouldn't be mixed. And if they are, the fiction parts should be printed in red ink, the fact parts in black ink.   *Catherine D. Bowen (1958)*

A biography, at best, is a series of photographs, taken from a limited number of positions, on a selectively sensitive plate, by a photographer whose presence affects the expression of the sitter in a characteristic way.
C. D. Broad - 'Ethics and the History of Philosophy'

Biography is the most universally profitable, universally pleasant of all things; especially biography of distinguished individuals.
Thomas Carlyle - 'Sartor Resartus'

Once the implicit aim of biography was to uplift – now it is to unveil.
Mark Feeney - 'Boston Globe' (1987)

Biography is history seen through the prism of a person.   *Louis Fischer*

There never was a good biography of a good novelist. There couldn't be. He is too many people, if he's any good. *F. Scott Fitzgerald*

Biography, like big-game hunting, is one of the recognised forms of sport, and it is unfair as only sport can be. *Philip Guedella*

Biography is a region bounded on the north by history, on the south by fiction, on the east by obituary, and on the west by tedium.
Philip Guedella

One of the most arrogant undertakings, to my mind, is to write the biography of a man which pretends to go beyond the external facts and gives the innermost motives. One of the most mendacious is autobiography.
Theodore Haecker - 'Journey in the Night' (1950)

More knowledge can be gained of a man's real character by a short conversation with one of his servants than from a formal and studied narrative, begun with his pedigree and ended with his funeral. *Samuel Johnson*

A biographer must be as ruthless as a board meeting smelling out embezzlement, as suspicious as a secret agent riding the Simplon-Orient Express, as cold-eyed as a pawnbroker viewing a leaky concertina.
Paul M. Kendall - 'The Art of Biography' (1965)

A writer [of biographies] is always going to betray somebody; if you're going to be honest with your subject, you can't be genteel.
Ted Morgan

Never use the word 'gossip' in a pejorative sense. It's the very stuff of biography and has to be woven in. To suggest that the personal life is not an essential element in the creative life is absurd. *Joan Peyser*

Voyeurism embellished with footnotes.
Robert Skidelsky (1987)

Discretion is not the better part of biography.
Lytton Strachey

Biographies are but the clothes and buttons of the man – the biography of the man himself cannot be written. *Mark Twain*

The lives of great men rarely remind us of anything sublime. *Lord Vansittart*

The work of writing fiction is exceedingly tedious. It is like making wallpaper for the Sistine Chapel. *Kurt Vonnegut*

Just how difficult it is to write biography can be reckoned by anybody who sits down and considers just how many people know the real truth about his or her love affairs. *Rebecca West*

The best way to approach a manuscript is on all fours, in utter amazement. *E. B. White*

Every great man nowadays has his disciples, and it is always Judas who writes his biography.
Oscar Wilde (1887)

Formerly we used to canonise our heroes. The modern method is to vulgarise them. Cheap editions of great books may be delightful, but cheap editions of great men are absolutely detestable. *Oscar Wilde - 'The True Function and Value of Criticism' (1890)*

A biography is considered complete if it merely accounts for six or seven selves, whereas a person may well have as many as a thousand.
Virginia Woolf

A biography is to give a man some kind of shape after his death. *Virginia Woolf*

BIOGRAPHERS

Peter Ackroyd
'T. S. Eliot' – But for a few phrases from his letters and an odd line or two of his verse, the poet walks gagged through his own biography.
John Updike - 'New Yorker' (1985)

John James Audubon
Audubon biographers and scholars have noted, by various euphemisms, that all great men have their flaws, and their man's principal flaw was that he, well, he lied a lot.
Bil Gilbert - 'Sports Illustrated' (1985)

Thomas Boswell - *Dr Johnson's biographer*
Silly, snobbish, lecherous, tipsy, given to high-
flown sentiments and more than a little of a
humbug . . . he needed Johnson as ivy needs an
oak.   *Cyril Connolly - 'The Evening Colonnade'*

You have a light head, but a damned heavy a—
——; and, to be sure, such a man will run easily
down hill, but it would be severe work to get
him up. *Lord Eglinton - 'London Journal' (1763)*

You have but two topics, yourself and me, and
I'm sick of both.   *Samuel Johnson*

Biographers, translators, editors, all, in short,
who employ themselves in illustrating the lives
or writings of others, are peculiarly exposed to
the 'Lues Boswelliana' or disease of admiration.
Thomas Macaulay (1834)

Servile and impertinent, shallow and pedantic,
a bigot and a sot, bloated with family pride, and
eternally blustering about the dignity of a born
gentleman, yet stooping to be a talebearer, and
eavesdropper, a common butt in the taverns of
London.   *Thomas Macaulay*

That he was a coxcomb and a bore, weak, vain,
pushing, curious, garrulous, was obvious to all
who were acquainted with him. That he could
not reason, that he had no wit, no humour, no
eloquence, is apparent from his writings.
Nature had made him a slave and an idolater.
His mind resembled those creepers which the
botanists call parasites and which can subsist
only by clinging round the stems and imbibing
the juices of stronger plants. *Thomas Macaulay*

Baron John Campbell - *(1779–1861)*
'Lives of Lord Chancellors' - His biographies
added another sting to death.
Sir Charles Wetherall

Lytton Strachey - *(1880–1932)*
The man who brilliantly ruined the art of
biography.   *George Sherburn*

AUTOBIOGRAPHY

An autobiography is a boast seller.   *Anon*

An autobiography is an I-witness report.   *Anon*

Autobiography is now as common as adultery,
and hardly less reprehensible.
Lord Altrincham - 'Sunday Times' (1962)

Autobiography is a suffering, a weakness, which
cannot be expressed as an aphorism, and should
not be mentioned.   *W. H. Auden*

Literary confessors are contemptible, like
beggars who exhibit their sores for money, but
not so contemptible as the public that buys
their books.   *W. H. Auden*

Most autobiographies are written by corpses.
Daniel Behrman

Just as there is nothing between the admirable
omelette and the intolerable, so with
autobiography.   *Hilaire Belloc*

There is no hiding place so impenetrable as
autobiography. The man who hides in silence is
never so puzzling as the man who hides in a
perpetual flow of talk . . . and any man who is
in danger of attention from posterity, and
wishes to hide certain things, will find no better
hiding place than under the arc-lights of
autobiography.   *Thomas Burke*

A modest or inhibited autobiography is written
without entertainment to the writer and read
with distrust by the reader.
Neville Cardus - 'Autobiography' (1947)

A well-written life is almost as rare as a well-
spent one.   *Thomas Carlyle*

An autobiography is an obituary in serial form
with the last instalment missing.
Quentin Crisp - 'Naked Civil Servant' (1968)

All autobiography is self-indulgent.
Daphne du Maurier (1977)

All good writers of their confessions, from
Augustine on, remain a little in love with their
sins.   *Anatole France*

Autobiography is the last refuse of scoundrels.
Henry Gray

Autobiography is an unrivalled vehicle for

telling the truth about other people.
Philip Guedella

Next to the writer of real estate advertisements, the autobiographer is the most suspect of all prose artists.
Donal Henahan – 'New York Times' (1977)

An autobiography usually reveals nothing bad about its writer except his memory.
Franklin P. Jones

It is not human nature to write the truth about itself.
Rudyard Kipling

When a person starts writing his memoirs it's a sure sign he's washed up.
Groucho Marx

Published memoirs indicate the end of a man's activity, and that he acknowledges the end.
George Meredith

Autobiography is probably the most respectable form of lying.
'New York Times' (1982)

No autobiography ever written went deeper than the author's Sunday clothes.
Austin O'Malley

All those writers who write about their childhood! Gentle God, if I wrote about mine you wouldn't sit in the same room with me.
Dorothy Parker

There's nothing a man can do to improve himself so much as writing his memoirs.
Maynard Printing

Autobiography – when you put down the good things you ought to have done, and leave out the bad ones you did do – that's memoirs!
Will Rogers – 'Autobiography' (1949)

Autobiographies ought to begin with Chapter Two.
Ellery Sedgwick

It is often stupefying to read a piece about somebody one knew intimately and to discover its extraordinary inaccuracy. A good reason for writing one's autobiography is that it may prevent some jerk from writing one's biography!
Preston Sturges

The time to write memoirs is when total recall has not yet invaded the cavities of the mind left empty by the inaction of retirement.
Peter Ullman

Only when one has lost all curiosity about the future has one reached the age to write an autobiography.
Evelyn Waugh

Hiring someone to write your autobiography is like paying someone to take a bath for you.
Mae West

Wherefore do the critics rage?
'Tis the Biographic Age.
Every dolt who duly died
In a book is glorified,
Uniformly with his betters;
All his unimportant letters
Edited by writers gifted,
Every scrap of MS sifted,
Classified by dates and ages,
Pages multiplied on pages,
Till the man is – for their pains –
Buried 'neath his own remains.
Israel Zangwill

COMIC BOOKS

Comic books are illiterature.
Anon

The marijuana of the nursery, the bane of the bassinet, the horror of the home, the curse of the kids, and a threat to the future.
John Mason Brown

DETECTIVE NOVELS

It is always a misfortune to be taken seriously in a field of writing where quality is not expected or desired.
Raymond Chandler

The beginner who submits a detective novel longer than 80 000 words is courting rejection.
Howard Haycraft

I am devoted to detective novels. They make such a nice change from my work.
Richard L. Jackson – President of Interpol (1961)

Detective stories are the art-for-art's-sake of yawning Philistinism.
V. S. Pritchett

MYSTERY NOVELS

At least half the mystery novels published violate the law that the solution, once revealed, must seem to be inevitable.   *Raymond Chandler*

SCIENCE FICTION

Science fiction is no more written for scientists than ghost stories for ghosts.   *Brian Aldiss*

Don't read science fiction books. It'll look bad if you die in bed with one on the nightstand. Always read stuff that will make you look good if you die in the middle of it.
P. J. O'Rourke – 'National Lampoon' (1979)

SHORT STORIES

A collection of short stories is generally thought to be a horrendous clinker; an enforced courtesy for the elderly writer who wants to display the trophies of his youth, along with his trout flies.   *John Cheever*

OTHER

'Debrett'
'Baronetage of England' – The best thing in English fiction ever written.   *Oscar Wilde*

'New York Review of Books'
The last court of appeal for highbrow screwballs.
William F. Buckley Jr – 'On the Right' (1969)

The dominant rhetoric is academese relieved by flashes of cliché.   *Dwight MacDonald*

'Webster's Dictionary'
'Webster III', behind its front of passionless objectivity, is in truth a fighting document. And the enemy it is out to destroy is every obstinate vestige of linguistic punctilio, every surviving influence that makes us for upholding of standards, every criterion for distinguishing between better usages and worse. In other words, it has gone bodily to the school that construes traditions as enslaving, the rudimentary principles of syntax as crippling and taste as irrelevant.   *Wilson Follett (1962)*

'Who's Who in America'
From which the truly interesting people in this world are rigorously excluded.
William F. Buckley Jr – 'On the Right' (1969)

LITERARY CIRCLES

Algonquin Round Table
A road company of the Last Supper.
Dorothy Parker

REVIEWS
(Listed by author)

Anon
We have read your manuscript with boundless delight. If we were to publish your paper, it would be impossible for us to publish any work of lower standard. And as it is unthinkable that in the next thousand years we shall see its equal, we are, to our regret, compelled to return your divine composition, and to beg you a thousand times to overlook our short sight and timidity.   *Anon Chinese Journal*

A first edition of his work is a rarity, but a second is rarer.   *Franklin P. Adams*

You should read it, though there is much that is skip-worthy.   *Herbert Asquith*

The covers of this book are too far apart.
Ambrose Bierce

That trees should have been cut down to provide paper for this book was an ecological affront.   *Anthony Blond – 'Spectator' (1983)*

'Bunk' – One of the very latest books is named *'Bunk'*. We had thought our fiction writers frank, but this takes the prize.   *'Boston Traveler'*

That passage is what I call the sublime dashed to pieces by cutting too close with the fiery four-in-hand round the corner of nonsense.
S. T. Coleridge

I read part of it all the way through.
Sam Goldwyn

This book fills a much-needed void.
Moses Hadas

Thank you for sending me a copy of your book. I'll waste no time reading it. *Moses Hadas*

I fell asleep reading a dull book, and I dreamed that I was reading on, so I awoke from sheer boredom. *Heinrich Heine*

This book is Number One on my Best Smeller list. *Irving Hoffman*

To read between the lines was easier than to follow the text. *Henry James*

On returning a manuscript – Your manuscript is both good and original; but the part that is good is not original, and the part that is original is not good. *Samuel Johnson*

People who like this sort of thing will find this the sort of thing they like. *Abraham Lincoln*

There are books that are at once interesting and boring. Those that at once leap to the mind are Thoreau's 'Walden', Emerson's 'Essays', George Eliot's 'Adam Bede' and Landors 'Dialogues'. *W. Somerset Maugham*

This is not a novel to be tossed aside lightly. It should be thrown away with great force. *Dorothy Parker*

He is a man of letters – all of them lower case. *Dale Roberts*

His words leap across rivers and mountains, but his thoughts are still only six inches long. *E. B. White*

Edward Abbey – *(b 1927)*
'Abbey's Road' – If you want to read 200 pages of Edward Abbey's self-flattery buy this smug, graceless book. *'New Republic' (1978)*

'The Monkey Wrench Gang' – The author of this book should be neutered and locked away for ever. *'San Juan County Record' (1975)*

Clover Adams
A Voltaire in petticoats. *Henry James*

Amos B. Alcott – *(1799-1888)*
The tedious archangel. *Ralph W. Emerson*

He soared into the infinite and dived into the unfathomable, but never paid cash.
Ralph W. Emerson

Louisa May Alcott – *(1832-88)*
Living almost always among intellectuals, she preserved to the age of fifty-six that contempt for ideas which is normal among boys and girls of fifteen. *Odell Shepherd*

Horatio Alger – *(1834-99)*
Horatio Alger wrote the same novel 135 times and never lost his audience. *George Jurgens*

Nelson Algren – *(1909-81)*
'A Walk on the Wild Side'– My, how this boy needs editing. *'San Francisco Chronicle' (1956)*

Aristophanes – *(448-388BC)*
The language of Aristophanes reeks of his miserable quackery: it is made up of the lowest and most miserable puns; he doesn't even please the people, and to men of judgment and honour he is intolerable; his arrogance is insufferable, and all honest men detest his malice. *Plutarch*

Michael Arlen – *(1895-1956)*
For all his reputation, Arlen is not a bounder. He is every other inch a gentleman.
Alexander Woollcott

Margot Asquith – *(1865-1945)*
Dread death alone could place embargo
Upon the tongue and pen of Margot.
Kensal Green

'Lay Sermons' – 'Daddy, what's an optimist?' said Pat to Mike while they were walking down the street together one day.'One who thought that Margot Asquith wasn't going to write any more,' replied the absent-minded professor, as he wound up the cat and put the clock out.

That gifted entertainer, the Countess of Oxford and Asquith, author of '*The Autobiography of Margot Asquith*' (four volumes, ready boxed, suitable for throwing purposes), reverts to tripe in a new book deftly entitled '*Lay Sermons*'.

I think it must be pleasanter to be Margot Asquith than to be any other living human being . . . The affair between Margot Asquith and Margot Asquith will live as one of the

prettiest love stories in all literature.
Dorothy Parker – 'New Yorker' (1927)

'Lay Sermons' – And you know those anecdotes
. . . I find them more efficacious than sheep-
counting, rain on a tin roof, or alanol tablets.
Just begin a story with such a phrase as 'I
remember Disraeli – poor Dizzy! – once saying
to me, in answer to my poke in the eye,' and
you will find me and Morpheus off in a corner,
necking.   *Dorothy Parker – ibid*

'Lay Sermons' – A naive and annoying and an
unimportant book. The author says, 'I am not
sure that my ultimate choice for the name of
this modest work is altogether happy.' Happier
I think it would have been if, instead of the
word 'Sermons', she had selected the word
'Off'.   *Dorothy Parker – ibid*

Francis Atterbury – *(1662–1732)*
'Defence of the Letters of Phalaris' – The best book
ever written by a man on the wrong side of a
question of which the writer was profoundly
ignorant.   *Thomas Macaulay – 'Life of Atterbury'*

Margaret Attwood – *(b 1939)*
'The Handmaid's Tale' – Norman Mailer,
wheezing lewd approval of some graphic images
he encountered in the writing of Germaine
Greer, remarked that a 'wind in this prose
whistled up the kilt of male conceit.' Reading
Margaret Attwood, I don my kilt but the wind
never comes. Just a cold breeze.
'American Spectator'

John Aubrey – *(1626–97)*
About as credulous an old goose as one could
hope to find out of Gotham.
B.G. Johns – 'Gentleman's Magazine' (1893)

He was a shiftless person, roving and magotis-
headed, and sometimes little better than crased.
And being exceedingly credulous, would stuff
his many letters sent to A.W. with fooleries and
misinformations, which sometimes would guld
him into paths of errour.
Anthony à Wood – 'Life and Times'

Louis Auchinloss – *(b 1917)*
He's a second-rate Stephen Birmingham. And
Stephen Birmingham is third-rate.
Truman Capote

Jane Austen – *(1775–1817)*
Aunt Jane for various circumstances was not so
refined as she ought to have been for her talent.
Anon Niece

'Mansfield Park' – What became of that Jane
Austen (if she ever existed) who set out bravely
to correct conventional notions of the desirable
and virtuous? From being their critic (if she
ever was) she became their slave. That is
another way of saying that her judgment and
her moral sense were corrupted. Mansfield
Park is witness of that corruption.
*Kingsley Amis –
'What Became of Jane Austen?'*

Her books are domestic in the sense that
Oedipus Rex is domestic. Her moral dilemmas
are often drawn in precisely oedipal terms.
Brigid Brophy

Jane Austen was a complete and most sensible
lady, but a very incomplete and rather
insensible (not senseless) woman. If this is
heresy, I can't help it.   *Charlotte Brontë*

Too washy; water-gruel for mind and body at
the same time were too bad.
Jane Welsh Carlyle (1843)

I am at a loss to understand why people hold
Miss Austen's novels at so high a rate, which
seems to me vulgar in tone, sterile in artistic
invention, imprisoned in the wretched
conventions of English society, without genius,
wit, or knowledge of the world. Never was life
so pinched and narrow.
Ralph W. Emerson – 'Journal' (1861)

She was the prettiest, silliest, most affected,
husband-hunting butterfly ever.   *Mary Mitford*

Edgar Allan Poe's prose is unreadable – like
Jane Austen's. No, there is a difference. I could
read his prose on a salary, but not Jane's.
Mark Twain

Francis Bacon – *(1561–1626)*
Lord Bacon could as easily have created the
planets as he could have written Hamlet.
Thomas Carlyle

His faults were – we write it with pain –

coldness of heart, and meanness of spirit. He seems to have been incapable of feeling strong affection, of facing dangers, of making great sacrifices. *Thomas Macaulay*

Honoré de Balzac – *(1799–1830)*
A fat little flabby person with the face of a baker, the clothes of a cobbler, the size of a barrelmaker, the manners of a stocking salesman, and the dress of an innkeeper.
Victor de Balabin – 'Diary' (1843)

Little imagination is shown in invention, in creating of character and plot, or in the delineation of passion. M. de Balzac's place in French literature will be neither considerable or high. *Eugene Poitou (1856)*

John Barth – *(b 1930)*
'The End of the Road' – The same road that has been travelled with Kerouac and to an extent Herbert Gold, this is for those schooled in the waste matter of the body and the mind.
'Kirkus Reviews'

Charles Baudelaire – *(1821–67)*
All that is worst in Algernon Swinburne belongs to Baudelaire. The offensive choice of subject, the obtrusion of unnatural passion, the blasphemy, the wretched animalism, are all taken intact out of 'Fleurs de Mal'. Pitiful that any sane man, least of all any English poet, should think this dunghill worthy of importation. *Robert Buchanan (1872)*

'Les Fleurs du Mal' – In a hundred years the histories of French literature will only mention it as a curio. *Emile Zola (1867)*

Anne Beattie – *(b 1947)*
'Love Always' – Beattie's admirable eye for telling detail has unfortunately developed a squint.
'Commonweal' (1985)

Saul Bellow – *(b 1915)*
'The Adventures of Augie March' – All of Those Words, in denominations of from three to five letters, are present. *'Library Journal' (1953)*

'Henderson the Rain King' – The novelist who doesn't like meanings writes an allegory; the allegory means that men should not mean but

be. Ods bodkins. The reviewer looks at the evidence and wonders, if he should damn the author and praise the book, or praise the author and damn the book. And is it possible, somehow or other to praise or damn, both? He isn't sure. *Reed Whittemore*

Arnold Bennett – *(1867–1931)*
A sort of pig in clover: *D. H. Lawrence*

The Hitler of the book-racket.
P. Wyndham Lewis

Nickel cash-register Bennett.
Ezra Pound (1937)

Thomas Berger – *(b 1924)*
'Little Big Man' – A farce that is continually over-reaching itself. Or, as the Cheyenne might put it, Little Big Man Little Overblown.
Gerald Walker – 'New York Times' (1964)

Roy Blount Jr – *(b 1941)*
'FirstHubby' – A reviewer is obligated to point out typographical errors, no matter how trivial. In the 'About the Author' note at the end of the book, we are told 'Roy Blount, Jr is a novelist. Now.' This makes sense only if the errant 'w' at the end of the last word is omitted. Apart from this bit of inadvertent humor; *First Hubby* is flawlessly lame.
L. S. Klepp – 'Entertainment Weekly' (1990)

Edmund Blunden – *(1896–1974)*
Mr Blunden is no more able to resist a quotation than some people are to refuse a drink. *George Orwell (1944)*

Vance Bourjaily – *(b. 1922)*
'The Man Who Knew Kennedy' – The man who knew Kennedy didn't know him very well. I'm almost as intimate with Lyndon Johnson. I met him once.
Webster Schott – 'New York Times' (1967)

Harold Brodkey – *(b. 1930)*
'Women and Angels' – Much of it reads like an extended obituary produced by a team of more than usually fanciful computers.
'New York Review of Books'

Anne Brontë – *(1820–49)*
A sort of literary Cinderella. *George Moore*

Charlotte Brontë - *(1816–55)*
'Jane Eyre' – I wish her characters would talk a little less like the heroes and heroines of police reports. *George Eliot*

Literature cannot be the business of a woman's life because of the sacredness of her duties at home. *Robert Southey*

'Jane Eyre' – Trivial personalities decomposing in the eternity of print.
Virginia Woolf – 'The Common Reader'

Emily Brontë - *(1818–48)*
'Wuthering Heights' – All the faults of *'Jane Eyre'* are magnified a thousand fold, and the only consolation which we have in reflecting upon it is that it will never be generally read.
James Lorimer – 'North British Review' (1849)

Edward Bulwer - *Earl of Lytton (1831–91)*
He never wrote an invitation to dinner without an eye on posterity. *Benjamin Disraeli*

Anthony Burgess - *(b 1917)*
'A Clockwork Orange' – 'The holy bearded veck all nagoy hanging on a cross' is an example of the author's language and questionable taste. The author seems content to use a serious social challenge for frivolous purposes, but himself to stay neutral. *'The Times' (1963)*

William Burroughs - *(b 1914)*
'Nova Express' – This book is unnecessary.
Granville Hicks (1964)

'Naked Lunch' – The merest trash, not worth a second look. *'New Republic' (1963)*

The works of William Burroughs add up to the world's pluperfect put-on. *'Time'*

Hall Caine - *(1853–1931)*
Mr Hall Caine, it is true, aims at the grandiose, but then he writes at the top of his voice. He is so loud that one cannot hear what he says.
Oscar Wilde

Truman Capote - *(1924–84)*
'In Cold Blood' – One can say of this book – with sufficient truth to make it worth saying; 'This isn't writing. It's research'.
Stanley Kauffmann – 'New Republic' (1965)

At his worst Capote has less to say than any good writer I know. *Norman Mailer (1959)*

On seeing Capote for the first time – For God's sake! What is that! *Harold Ross (1945)*

Truman Capote has made lying an art. A minor art. *Gore Vidal*

Capote should be heard, not read. *Gore Vidal*

He thinks he is a very rich Society Lady, and spends a great deal of money. *Gore Vidal*

He is a sweetly vicious old lady.
Tennessee Williams

I always said Little Truman had a voice so high it could only be detected by a bat.
Tennessee Williams

Thomas Carlyle - *(1795–1881)*
That anyone who dressed so very bad as did Thomas Carlyle should have tried to construct a philosophy of clothes has always seemed to me one of the most pathetic things in literature.
Max Beerbohm – 'Works'

It was very good of God to let Carlyle and Mrs Carlyle marry one another and so make two people miserable instead of four. *Samuel Butler*

Carlyle has led us all into the desert, and he has left us there. *A. H. Clough*

'Sartor Resartus' is quite unreadable, and to me that always sort of spoils a book. *Will Cuppy*

The same old sausage, fizzing and sputtering in its own grease. *Henry James*

Here is a man who beats a big drum under my windows, and when I come running downstairs, has nowhere for me to go. *Douglas Jerrold*

A poet to whom nature has denied the faculty of verse. *Lord Tennyson (1870)*

Lewis Carroll - *(1832–98)*
'Alice's Adventures in Wonderland' – We fancy that any real child might be more puzzled than enchanted by this stiff, overwrought story.
'Children's Books' (1865)

'Alice in Wonderland' – Nothing but a pack of lies.   *Damon Runyon*

G. K. Chesterton – *(1874 – 1936)*
Chesterton is like a vile scum on a pond. All his slop – it is really modern catholicism to a great extent, the never taking a hedge straight, the mumbojumbo of superstitition dodging behind clumsy fun and paradox. I believe he creates a milieu in which art is impossible. He and his kind.   *Ezra Pound (1917)*

Chesterton's resolute conviviality is about as genial as an auto de fe of teetotallers.
                                    G. B. Shaw

Cicero – *(106–43BC)*
His style bores me. When I have spent an hour reading him and try to recollect what I have extracted I usually find it nothing but wind.
                                    Michel de Montaigne

Dame Ivy Compton-Bennett – *(1884–1969)*
Though her novels are not in themselves works of art, the rules of the puzzle are allusions to literary forms and conventions. Reading them is like playing some Monopoly for Intellectuals, in which you can buy, as well as houses and hotels, plaques to set up on them recording that a great writer once lived there.
                                    Brigid Brophy – 'Don't Never Forget'

Evan Connell – *(b 1924)*
'Mr Bridge' – A novel should be something more than an X-ray of a dull life.
                                    'Bridgeport Post' (1969)

'Notes From a Bottle Found On the Beach at Carmel' – Almost pure gingerbread. It has bite, a certain flavour, but it turns into a gluey mass when chewed.   *'San Francisco Examiner' (1963)*

'Son of Morning Star' – This do-it-yourself kit will appeal to those who think confusion is a narrative strategy.
                                    J.O. Tate – 'National Review' (1985)

Joseph Conrad – *(1857–1924)*
Conrad spent a day finding the 'mot juste', and then killed it.   *Ford Madox Ford*

We could pardon his cheerless themes were it not for the imperturbable solemnity with which he piles the unnecessary on the commonplace.
                                    'Literature' (1898)

'Youth' and *'Heart of Darkness'* – It would be useless to pretend that they can be very widely read.   *'Manchester Guardian' (1902)*

What is Conrad but the wreck of Stevenson floating about in the slip-slop of Henry James?
                                    George Moore

'An Outcast of the Islands' – Mr Conrad is wordy; his story is not so much told as seen intermittently through a haze of sentences. His style is like river-mist; for a space things are seen clearly, and then comes a great grey bank of printed matter, page on page, creeping round the reader, swallowing him up. You stumble, you protest, you blunder on, for the drama you saw so cursorily has hold of you; you cannot escape until you have seen it out. You read fast, you run and jump, only to bring yourself to the knees in such mud as will presently be quoted.
                                    H. G. Wells – 'Saturday Review' (1896)

One could always baffle Conrad by saying 'humour'. It was one of our damned English tricks he had never learned to tackle.
                                    H. G. Wells

James Fenimore Cooper – *(1789–1851)*
'Deerslayer' – In one place in Deerslayer, and in the restricted space of two-thirds of a page, Cooper has scored 114 offences against literary art out of a possible 115. It breaks the record.
                                    Mark Twain – 'How to Tell a Story and other Essays' (1897)

Robert Coover – *(b 1932)*
'The Origin of the Brunists' – An explosion in a cesspool.   *Bruno McAndrew (1966)*

'Gerald's Party' – The Novel should develop the reader's sensitivities, not deaded them with risible comic-strip.   *'New Statesman' (1986)*

Marie Corelli [Mary McKay] – *(1855–1924)*
Review while he was in prison – Now don't think I've written anything against her moral character, but from the way she writes she ought to be in here.   *Oscar Wilde*

LITERARY

Stephen Crane - *(1871-1900)*
I had thought that there could only be two worse writers than Stephen Crane, namely two Stephen Cranes. *Ambrose Bierce*

Quentin Crisp [Dennis Pratt] - *(b 1908)*
If Quentin Crisp had never existed it is unlikely that anyone would have had the nerve to invent him. *'The Times' (1977)*

Edward Dahlberg - *(1900-77)*
Dahlberg wrote 18 books and one masterpiece that will endure; at the end of his long life he had less than six people he would have called friends. *William O'Rourke*

Daniel Defoe - *(1661-1731)*
A true malignant, arrogant and sour,
And ever snarling at establish'd power. *Anon*

With the single exception of his Moll [Flanders] all Defoe's characters are completely invisible and utterly, not so much dead, as unalive in the sense that tailors' dummies are unalive.
Ford Madox Ford -
'The March of Literature'

So grave, sententious, dogmatical a Rogue, that there is no enduring him. *Jonathan Swift*

He belongs, indeed, to the school of the great plain writers, whose work is founded upon a knowledge of what is most persistent, though not most seductive, in human nature.
Virginia Woolf - 'The Common Reader'

Thomas de Quincey - *(1785-1859)*
De Quincey, the Opium Eater and that abstruse thinker in logic and metaphysics XYZ.
John Clare -
'Fragment on the Londoners'

Bernard de Voto - *(1897-1955)*
I denounce Mr Bernard De Voto as a fool and a tedious and egotistical fool, as a liar and a pompous and boresome liar . . . his screaming, his bumptiousness, his conviction that he was a combination of Walter Winchell and Erasmus grew hard to take. *Sinclair Lewis*

Charles Dickens - *(1812-70)*
My own experience in reading Dickens, and I doubt whether it is an uncommon one, is to be

bounced between violent admiration and violent distaste almost every couple of paragraphs, and this is too uncomfortable a condition to be much alleviated by an inward recital of one's duty not to be fastidious, to gulp down the stuff in gobbets like a man.
Kingsley Amis

We were put to Dickens as children but it never quite took. That unremitting humanity soon had me cheesed off. *Alan Bennet*

Dickens was the incarnation of cockneydom, a caricaturist who aped the moralist, he should have kept to short stories. If his novels are read at all in the future people will wonder what we saw in him. *George Meredith (1909)*

Fifty years hence, most of his allusions will be harder to understand than the allusions in The Dunciad, and our children will wonder what their ancestors could have meant by putting Mr Dickens at the head of the novelists of his day.
'Saturday Review' (1858)

'Little Nell' - One must have a heart of stone to read the death of Little Nell without laughing.
Oscar Wilde

Sir Kenelm Digby - *(1603-65)*
The very Pliny of our age for lying.
Henry Stubbes

J. P. Donleavy - *(b 1926)*
'The Ginger Man' - This rather nasty, rather pompous novel gives us, in all, a precocious small boy's view of life, the boy having been spoiled somehow and allowed to indulge in sulks and tantrums and abundant self-pity.
'Chicago Tribune' (1958)

Feydor Dostoyevsky - *(1821-81)*
They are great parables, the novels, but false art. They are only parables. All the people are fallen angels - even the dirtiest scrubs. This I cannot stomach. People are not fallen angels, they are merely people. *D. H. Lawrence (1916)*

Theodore Dreiser - *(1871-1945)*
With his proverbial slovenliness, the barbarisms and incongruities whose notoriety has preceded him into history, the bad grammar, the breathless and painful clutching

at words, the vocabulary dotted with 'trig' and
'artistic' that may sound like a salesman's effort
to impress, the outrageous solecisms that give
his novels the flavour of sand, he has seemed
the unique example of a writer who remains
great despite himself.
Alfred Kazin - 'On Native Grounds'

Theodore Dreiser
Should ought to write nicer.
Dorothy Parker - 'New Yorker' (1931)

If we can imagine an old-fashioned ladies'
sewing circle, decorously exchanging local
gossip over cakes and tea, suddenly invaded by
an iceman in his working clothes, who enters
without embarrassment, plants himself
massively in the middle of the sofa, and begins
to regale the company with anecdotes of the
gashouse district, we may form some notion of
the effect produced by Dreiser's first novels.
George F Whicher

His style is atrocious, his sentences are chaotic,
his grammar and syntax faulty; he has no
feeling for words, no sense of diction. His
wordiness and his repetitions are unbearable,
his cacophonies incredible.
T. K. Whipple - 'Spokesman'

Tom Driberg - *(1905-76)*
To have published an obituary of Tom Driberg
without mentioning homosexuality would have
been like publishing an obituary of Maria
Callas without mentioning opera.
William Rees-Mogg - 'The Times' (1980)

George Eliot [Mary Ann Evans] - *(1819-80)*
'*Adam Bede*' - I found out in the first two pages
that it was a woman's writing - she supposed
that in making a door, you last of all put in the
panels! *Thomas Carlyle*

The overdone reputation of the Evans-Eliot-
Lewes-Cross woman (poor creature! one ought
not to speak slightly, I know), half real power,
half imposition. *Gerald M. Hopkins (1886)*

George Eliot had the heart of Sappho; but the
face, with the long proboscis, the protruding
teeth of the Apocalyptic horse, betrayed
animality. *George Meredith*

Judith Exner - *(b 1934)*
'*My Story*' - Hell hath no fury like a hustler
with a literary agent. *Frank Sinatra (1977)*

William Faulkner - *(1897-1962)*
He uses a lot of big words, and his sentences
are from here back to the airport.
Carolyn Chute - 'New York Times' (1985)

Even those who call Mr Faulkner our greatest
literary sadist do not fully appreciate him, for it
is not merely his characters who have to run
the gauntlet but also his readers.
Clifton Fadiman - 'New Yorker' (1934)

'*Absalom, Absalom*' - The final blow-up of what
was once a remarkable, if minor, talent.
Clifton Fadiman - 'New Yorker' (1936)

Poor Faulkner. Does he really think big
emotions come from big words?
Ernest Hemingway

Old Corndrinking Mellifluous.
Ernest Hemingway

Faulkner's work abounds in humbled time
sequences, involuted narrative structures,
mangled syntax, and tortuous diction.
Irving Howe

'*As I Lay Dying*' - The critic can hardly be
blamed if some categorical imperative which
persists in the human condition (even at this
late date) compels him to put this book in a
high place in an inferior category.
'New York Times Book Review'

Edna Furber - *(1887-1968)*
She squares off at her job as in workmanlike
fashion and turns out a nationally advertised
product that looks as sound as this year's model
always does, until next year's model comes
along. *T. S. Matthews - 'New Republic' (1935)*

Henry Fielding - *(1707-54)*
Whose work it has long been the fashion to
abuse in public and to read in secret.
George Borrow

What I mean by his being a blockhead is, that
he was a barren rascal. *Samuel Johnson*

'Amelia' – I have not been able to read any more than the first volume of *'Amelia'*. Poor Fielding! I could not help telling his sister, that I was equally surprised at and concerned for his continued lowness. It is beyond my conception, that a man of family, and who had some learning, and who really is a writer, should descend so excessively low, in all his pieces.
Samuel Richardson (1752)

Fielding had as much humour as [Thomas] Addison but, having no idea of grace, is perpetually disturbing. *Horace Walpole (1785)*

F. Scott *(1896–1940) and*
Zelda Fitzgerald *(1900–57)*
Mr Fitzgerald is a novelist. Mrs Fitzgerald is a novelty. *Ring Lardner – 'The Other Side'*

If F. Scott and Zelda are Class
Cellini made things out of brass,
  And Dacron is fur,
Air-Wick smells like myrrh,
And Plastic's as good as stained glass.
Michael O'Donoghue (1973)

F. Scott Fitzgerald
Fitzgerald never got rid of anything; the ghosts of his adolescence, the failures of his youth, the doubts of his maturity plagued him to the end. He was supremely a part of the world he described, so much a part that he made himself its king and then, when he saw it begin to crumble, he crumbled with it and led it to death. *John Aldridge*

He couldn't distinguish between innocence and social climbing.
Saul Bellow – 'Paris Review'

Mr Fitzgerald – I believe that is how he spells his name – seems to believe that plagiarism begins at home. *Zelda Fitzgerald*

The first American to formulate his own philosophy of the absurd. *Wright Morris*

Gustav Flaubert – *Physician and Author (1821–80)*
You love to diagnose and prescribe for your characters who are obviously your patients. And like every good physician you end in putting all of them to death. *Honoré de Balzac*

'Madame Bovary' – Monsieur Flaubert is not a writer. *'Le Figaro' (1857)*

Ian Fleming – *(1908–64)*
'Dr No' – I am willing to accept the centipede, the tarantulas, the land crabs, the giant squid. I am even willing to forgive your reckless use of invented verbs – 'I inch, Thou inches, He snakes, I snake, We palp, They palp', etc, but what I will neither accept nor forgive is the highly inaccurate statement that when it is eleven a.m. in Jamaica, it is six a.m. in dear old England. This, dear boy, to put not too fine a point on it, is a f***ing lie. When it is eleven a.m. in Jamaica, it is four p.m. in dear old England, and it is carelessness of this kind that makes my eyes steel slits of blue. *Noël Coward*

The trouble with Ian is that he gets off with women because he can't get on with them.
Rosamond Lehmann

'Goldfinger' – I had been told that it was as good as Simenon. This is nonsense . . . Fleming is so fantastic as to arouse disbelief. This story is too improbable to arouse interest, nor do I like the underlying atmosphere of violence, luxury and lust. I regard it as an obscene book, 'liable to corrupt'. *Harold Nicolson 'Diary' (1959)*

Bernard de Fontenelle – *(1657–1757)*
Fontenelle was but the shadow of a man with but the shadow of a voice. You could hear no more, however carefully you listened. He was like an old Titan who had been turned into a grasshopper. *Joseph Joubert*

Ford Madox Ford [Herman Hueffer] – *(1873–1939)*
An animated adenoid. *Anon*

His mind was like a Roquefort cheese, so ripe that it was palpably falling to pieces.
Van Wyck Brooks

His forlorn attempts to throw a smoke-screen round himself produced through the distorted haze, the apparition of a monster, like a pink elephant, absurd, bizarre, immense.
Edward Crankshaw –
'National Review' (1948)

So fat and Buddhistic and nasal.
Norman Douglas

A flabby lemon and pink giant, who hung his mouth open as though he were an animal at a Zoo inviting buns – especially when ladies were present.   *Percy W. Lewis*

Master, mammoth mumbler.   *Robert Lowell*

Ford Madox Ford only lied when he was very tired.   *Ezra Pound*

Freud Madox Fraud.   *Osbert Sitwell*

E. M. Forster – *(1879–1970)*
'Howard's End' – If I were asked to point to a passage which combined all that prose fiction should not be – lurid, sentimentality, preposterous morals, turgid and sticky style – I do not think I could point to anything worse than the closing chapters of *'Howard's End'*. And I am now going to rad a few chapters of Mrs Gaskell to take the taste of *'Howard's End'* out of my mouth.   *Edmund Gosse*

E. M. Forster never gets any further than warming the teapot. He's a rare fine hand at that. Feel this teapot. Is it not beautifully warm? Yes, but there ain't going to be no tea.
Katherine Mansfield

He's a mediocre man – and knows it, or suspects it, which is worse; he will come to no good, and in the meantime he's treated rudely by waiters and is not really admired even by middle-aged dowagers.   *Lytton Strachey (1914)*

He is limp and damp and milder than the breath of a cow.   *Virginia Woolf*

James Froude – *(1818–94)*
Froude informs the Scottish youth
That parsons do not care for truth.
The Reverend Canon Kingsley cries
   History is a pack of lies.
What cause for judgments so malign?
A brief recollection solves the mystery –
   Froude believes Kingsley a divine,
And Kingsley goes to Froude for history.
William Stubbs (1871)

A desultory and theoretical litterateur who wrote more rot on the reign of Elizabeth than Gibbon required for all the Decline and Fall.
Algernon Turner (1878)

William Gaddis – *(b 1922)*
'The Recognitions' – An evil book, a scurrilous book, a profane book, a scatalogical book and an exasperating book. What this squalling overwritten book needs above all is to have its mouth washed out with lye soap. It reeks of decay and filth and perversion and half-digested learning.   *'Chicago Sun-Times' (1955)*

'JR' – To produce an unreadable text, to sustain this foxy purpose over 726 pages, demands rare powers. Mr William Gaddis has them.   *George Steiner – 'New Yorker' (1976)*

Hamlin Garland – *(1860–1940)*
One follows the progress of the man with the constant sense that he is steering by faulty compasses, that fate is leading him into paths too steep and rocky – nay too dark and lonely – for him.   *H. L. Mencken*

Henry George – *(1839–97)*
'Progress and Poverty' – Did you ever read Henry George's *'Progress and Poverty'*? It's more damneder nonsense than poor Rousseau's blether.   *Thomas Huxley (1889)*

Edward Gibbon – *(1737–94)*
Gibbon is an ugly, affected , disgusting fellow, and poisons our literary club for me. I class him among infidel wasps and venomous insects.
James Boswell (1779)

Sapping a solemn creed with solemn sneer.
Lord Byron

Gibbon's style is detestable; but it is not the worst thing about him.

Samuel Taylor Coleridge –
'Complete Works' (1853)

There is no Gibbon but Gibbon and Gibbon is his prophet.
Philip Guedella – 'Supers and Supermen'

Gibbon lived out most of his sex life in his footnotes.   *Philip Guedella*

'A History of the Decline and Fall of the Roman Empire' – Another damned, thick, square book! Always scribble, scribble, scribble! Eh! Mr Gibbon?   *William Henry*

The calumniator of the despised Nazarene, the
derider of Christianity. Awful dispensation! . . .
How many souls have his writings polluted?
Lord preserve others from their contamination!
Hannah More – 'Diary' (1774)

In some passages he drew the thread of his
verbosity finer than the staple of his argument.
Richard Porson

George Gissing – *(1857–1903)*
When I admit neglect of Gissing,
They say I don't know what I'm missing.
Until their arguments are subtler,
I think I'll stick to Samuel Butler.
Dorothy Parker – 'Sunset Gun'

Ellen Glasgow – *(1974–1945)*
Southern romance is dead. Ellen Glasgow has
murdered it. *Carl Van Doren*

Elinor Glyn – *(1864–1943)*
*Passing judgement on a copyright dispute involving
'Three Weeks'* – Copyright cannot exist in a
work of a tendency so grossly immoral as this.
Justice Younger (1915)

Gail Godwin – *(b 1937)*
'A Mother and Two Daughters' – Godwin
earnestly sticks by her characters. The only
trouble is, she likes the people next door, they're
nice but not very interesting.
'Saturday Review' (1981)

William Golding – *(b 1911)*
'Lord of the Flies' – Completely unpleasant.
'New Yorker' (1955)

Gunter Grass – *(b 1927)*
'The Tin Drum' – Bewildered by the torrent of
fantastic incident, mystified by what Gunter
Grass intends by it all, one feels like a zoologist
who discovers some monstrous unrecorded
mammal gobbling leaves: it may have beautiful
horns, but what is it? *'New Statesman' (1963)*

Andrew Greeley – *(b 1928)*
'The Cardinal Sins' – Enough to give trash a bad
name. *'Chicago Sun-Times' (1982)*

Charles Greville – *(1794–1865)*
'Memoirs' – No, I do not feel attracted to them. I
remember the author, and he was the most

conceited person with whom I have ever been
brought into contact, although I have read
Cicero and known Bulwer Lytton.
Benjamin Disraeli (1875)

For fifty years he listened at the door,
He heard some secrets and invented more.
These he wrote down, and women, statesmen,
   kings
Became degraded into common things.
Lord Winchilsea

Zane Grey – *(1875–1939)*
You've wasted enough of our time with your
junk. Why don't you go back to filling teeth?
You can't write, you never could write, and you
never will be able to write. *Anon Publisher*

If Zane went out with a mosquito net to catch
minnows, he could make it sound like a Roman
gladiator setting forth to slay whales in the
Tiber. *Robert H. Davies*

The 20th Century heir of the dime novel.
James D. Hart

Francesco Guicciardini – *(1483–1540)*
'Storia d'Italia' – Compared with the labour of
reading through these volumes all other labour,
the labour of thieves on the treadmill, of
children in factories, of negroes in sugar
plantations is an agreeable recreation. There
was, it is said, a criminal in Italy, who has
suffered to make his choice between
Guicciardini and the galleys. He chose the
history. But the war of Pisa was too much for
him. He changed his mind and went to the oar.
*Thomas Macaulay –
'Critical and Historical Essays'*

H. Rider Haggard – *(1856–1925)*
Even your imagination is out of the fifth form.
Andrew Lang

Like so many popular best sellers, he was a
very sad and solemn man who took himself too
seriously and his art not seriously enough:
*V. S. Pritchett –
'The Tale Bearers' (1980)*

Radclyffe Hall – *(1886–1943)*
'The Well of Loneliness' – It's worse than

throwing acid in a young person's eyes.
Anon Judge (1928)

Thomas Hardy - *(1840–1928)*
Thomas Hardy went down to botanise in the
swamps, while George Meredith climbed
toward the sun. Meredith became, at his best, a
sort of daintily dressed Walt Whitman; Hardy
became a sort of village atheist brooding and
blaspheming over the village idiot.
G. K. Chesterton –
'The Victorian Age in Literature'

He claimed his modest share of the general
foolishness of the human race.   *Irving Howe*

A provincial manufacturer of gauche and heavy
fictions that sometimes have corresponding
values.   *F. R. Leavis*

No one has written worse English than Mr
Hardy in some of his novels – cumbrous,
stilted, ugly, and inexpressive – yes.
Virginia Woolf – 'The Moment'

Frank Harris - *(1856–1931)*
I tell you, you are a ruffian exactly as an oculist
might tell you that you are astigmatic.
G. B. Shaw

Frank Harris is invited to all of the great
houses in England – once.   *Oscar Wilde*

Joel Harris - *(1848–1908)*
In reality his stories are only alligator pears –
one eats them merely for the sake of the
dressing.   *Mark Twain (1881)*

Barbara Grizzuti Harrison - *(b 1934)*
'Foreign Bodies' – Aphorisms are bad for teeth.
They stick in the reader's throat.
Anatole Broyard (1984)

Bret Harte - *(1836–1902)*
Harte, in a mild and colourless way, was that
kind of man – that is to say, he was a man
without a country; no, not a man – man is too
strong a term; he was an invertebrate without a
country.   *Mark Twain*

He hasn't a sincere fibre in him. I think he was
incapable of emotion for I think he had nothing
to feel with.   *Mark Twain*

He was an incorrigible borrower of money: he
borrowed from all of his friends; if he ever
repaid a loan the incident failed to pass into
history.   *Mark Twain (1924)*

Nathaniel Hawthorne - *(1804–64)*
His reputation as a writer is a very pleasing
fact, because his writing is not good for
anything, and this is a tribute to the man.
R. W. Emerson

Hawthorne – the half man of genius who never
could carry out an idea or work it through to
the full result.   *Algernon Swinburne (1875)*

There never surely was a powerful, active,
continually effective mind less round, more lop-
sided, than that of Nathaniel Hawthorne.
Anthony Trollope

Hawthorne can be casual, desultory, even
pedagogic in his method; he can be pale and
dull. At his worst, he has much feeble and
conventional allegory and much that is fanciful
rather than truly imaginative, and he had a
tiresome weakness for dioramas, processions,
and exhibits.   *Edward Wagenknecht*

He never seemed to be doing anything, and yet
he did not like to be disturbed at it.
John G. Whittier

Heinrich Heine - *(1797–1856)*
Blackguard Heine is worth very little.
Thomas Carlyle (1836)

Joseph Heller
'Catch 22' – Heller wallows in his own laughter
and finally drowns in it. What remains is a
debris of sour jokes, stage anger, dirty words,
synthetic looniness, and the sort of antic
behaviour the children fall into when they
know they are losing our attention.
Whitney Balliett – 'New Yorker' (1961)

'God Knows' – It even looks exactly like a real
book, with pages and print and dust jacket and
everything. This disguise is extremely clever,
considering the contents; the longest lounge act
never performed in the history of the Catskills.
Paul Gray – 'Time' (1984)

'Good as Gold' – Heller operates as if he were a

jewel thief wearing boxing gloves.
'Newsweek' (1979)

'We Bombed in New Haven' – A dud of the first
magnitude. *'Saturday Review' (1968)*

Lillian Hellman – *(1907-84)*
'Toys in the Attic' – It is curious how incest,
impotence, nymphomania, religious mania and
real estate speculation can be so dull.
Richard Findlater – 'Time and Tide' (1961)

Every word she writes is a lie, including 'and'
and 'the'. *Mary McCarthy (1979)*

'Toys in the Attic' – Lillian Hellman has chosen
to write on a Tennessee Williams theme in an
Agatha Christie style. *'The Times'*

Ernest Hemingway – *(1898-1961)*
He is the bully on the Left Bank, always ready
to twist the milksop's arm.
Cyril Connolly – 'The Observer' (1964)

It is of course a commonplace that Hemingway
lacks the serene confidence that he is a full-
sized man.
Max Eastman – 'New Republic' (1933)

A literary style of wearing false hair on the
chest. *Max Eastman*

Always willing to lend a helping hand to the
one above him. *F. Scott Fitzgerald*

When his cock wouldn't stand up he blew his
head off. He sold himself a line of bullshit and
he bought it. *Germaine Greer*

Editing Hemingway was like wrestling with
God. *Tom Jenks*

He's the original Limelight Kid, just you watch
him for a few months. Wherever the limelight
is, you'll find Ernest with his big lovable boyish
grin, making hay. *Robert McAlmon*

Hemingway was a jerk. *Harold Robbins*

Remarks are not literature. *Gertrude Stein*

To her dog – Play Hemingway, be fierce.
Gertrude Stein

'A Moveable Feast' – This book was apparently
completed in Cuba in 1960 and, for all the good
it is likely to do Hemingway's reputation, it
could very well have stayed there –
permanently.
Geoffrey Wagner – 'Commonweal' (1964)

Baron John Hervey – *(1696-1743)*
Yet let me flap this bug with gilded wings,
This painted child of dirt, that stinks and sings.
Alexander Pope

Richard Hildreth – *(1807-65)*
As venomous and deaf as an adder.
Richard H. Dana

Oliver Wendell Holmes Sr – *(1807-94)*
Fat as a balloon – he weighed as much as three
hundred, and had double chins all the way
down to his stomach.

William D. Howells – *(1837-1920)*
The lousy cat of our letters. *Ambrose Bierce*

The truth about Howells is that he really has
nothing to say, for all the charm he gets into
saying it. His psychology is superficial,
amateurish, often nonsensical; his irony is
scarcely more than a polite facetiousness; his
characters simply refuse to live.
H. L. Mencken – 'Prejudices'

If he had been as thorough-going as his
programme demanded, he would have been the
American Zola; he became instead our
masculine Jane Austen. *George Snell*

Victor Hugo – *(1802-85)*
A glittering humbug. *Thomas Carlyle (1840)*

Fannie Hurst – *(1889-1968)*
'A President is Born' – I can find in *'A President Is
Born'* no character nor any thought to touch or
excite me. I am awfully sorry, but it is to me a
pretty dull book.
Dorothy Parker – 'New Yorker' (1928)

Aldous Huxley – *(1894-1963)*
The stupid person's idea of the clever person.
Elizabeth Bowen – 'Spectator' (1936)

The great Mahatma of all misanthropy.
Roy Campbell

'*Crome Yellow*' – He has an utterly ruthless habit of building up an elaborate and sometimes almost romantic structure and then blowing it down with something too ironic to be called satire and too scornful to be called irony.
F. Scott Fitzgerald (1922)

I don't like his books, even if I admire the sort of desperate courage of repulsion and repudiation in them. But again, I feel only half a man writes the books – a sort of precocious adolescent. *D. H. Lawrence (1929)*

'*Brave New World*' – There are no surprises in it; and even if he had no surprises to give us, why should Mr Huxley have bothered to turn this essay of indignation into a novel?
'*New Statesman*'

'*Ape and Essence*' – It is awful. And do you notice that the more holy he gets, the more his books sting with sex? He cannot get off the subject of flagellating women. *George Orwell*

You could tell by his conversation which volume of the Encyclopaedia Britannica he'd been reading. One day it would be Alps, Andes and Apennines, and the next it would be the Himalayas and the Hippocratic Oath.
Bertrand Russell (1965)

'*Point Counter Point*' – All raw, uncooked, protesting. *Virginia Woolf (1935)*

Washington Irving – *(1783–1859)*
Excellent for an acquaintance but for a bosom friend – no! *Thomas Carlyle*

The pursuit of the picturesque lured him away into the sterile waters, and when the will-o'-the-wisp was gone it left him empty.
Vernon Parrington –
'*Main Currents in American Thought*'

Henry James – *(1843–1916)*
It's not that he 'bites off more than he can chew' but he chews more than he bites off.
Clover Adams

Few writers have had less journalistic talent than James, and this is his defect, for the supreme masters have one trait in common with the childish scribbling mass, the vulgar curiosity of a police-court reporter.
W. H. Auden – 'The Dyer's Hand'

He is tremendously lacking in emotional power. Also his sense of beauty is over-sophisticated and wants originality. Also his attitude towards the spectacle of life is at bottom conventional, timid and undecided. Also he seldom chooses themes of first class importance, and when he does choose such a theme he never fairly bites it and makes it bleed. Also his curiosity is limited. It seems to me to have been specially created to be admired by super-dilettanti.
Arnold Bennett – 'New Age' (1910)

Henry James had a mind so fine that no idea could violate it. *T. S. Eliot*

One of the nicest old ladies I ever met.
William Faulkner

The work of Henry James had always seemed divisible by a simple dynastic arrangement into three reigns; James I, James II and the Old Pretender. *Philip Guedella – 'Men of Letters'*

Poor Henry James! He's spending eternity walking round and round a stately park and the fence is just too high for him to peep over and he's just too far away to hear what the countess is saying. *W. Somerset Maugham*

Henry James's fiction are like the cobwebs which a spider may spin in the attic of some old house, intricate, delicate and even beautiful, but which at any moment the housemaid's broom with brutal common sense may sweep away. *W. Somerset Maugham*

An idiot, and a Boston idiot, to boot, than which there is nothing lower in the world.
H. L. Mencken – 'The American Scene'

It is becoming painfully evident that Mr James has written himself out as far as the international novel is concerned, and probably as far as any kind of novel-writing is concerned.
William M. Payne – 'The Dial' (1884)

'*The Bostonians*' – And as for '*The Bostonians*', I would rather be damned to John Bunyan's heaven than read that. *Mark Twain (1885)*

James's denatured people are only the equivalent in fiction of Japanese colour-prints.
H. G. Wells (1915)

Mr Henry James writes fiction as if it were a painful duty. *Oscar Wilde*

James is developing, but he will never arrive at passion, I fear. *Oscar Wilde (1899)*

I am reading Henry James and feel myself entombed in a block of smooth amber.
Virginia Woolf

Soame Jenyns - *(1704–89)*
Soame Jenyns was an old woman and his vocabulary was as trite as could be.
A. E. Housman

Ruth P. Jhabvalar - *(b 1927)*
'Out of India' - Muffled lives explode in understatements. *Paul Gray (1986)*

James Jones - *(1921–77)*
'From Here to Eternity' - Certainly America has something better to offer the world, along with its arms and its armies, than such a confession of spiritual vacuum as this.
'Christian Science Monitor'

Erica Jong - *(b 1942)*
'Any Woman's Blues' - Always adept at sniffing the zeitgeist, Jong ransacked the self-help books on the best-seller list and produced a novel that managed to combine *'Beyond Codependency'* and *'Women Who Love Too Much'*.
'Entertainment Weekly' (1990)

James Joyce - *(1882-1941)*
'Ulysses' - Written by a man with a diseased mind and soul so black that he would even obscure the darkness of hell. *Anon US Senator*

On his letters - An account of some of these acts makes Henry Miller's crudest imaginations seem as chaste as a nun's diary. *James Atlas*

'Ulysses' - The key to reading *'Ulysses'* is to treat it like a comedian would - as a sort of gag book.
Brendan Behan

I am inclined to think that Mr Joyce is riding

his method to death.
Ford Madox Ford - 'Thus to Revisit'

'Ulysses' - A dogged attempt to cover the universe with mud, an inverted Victorianism, an attempt to make crossness and dirt succeed where sweetness and light failed, a simplification of the human character in the interests of Hell. *E. M. Forster -*
'Aspects of the Novel' (1927)

'Ulysses' - I have difficulty in describing the character of Mr Joyce's morality. He is a literary charlatan of the extremist order. His principal book *'Ulysses'* is an anarchical production, infamous in taste, in style in everything. He is a sort of M. de Sade, but does not write so well. There are no English critics of weight or judgement who consider Mr Joyce an author of any importance.
Edmund Gosse (1924)

'Ulysses' - I never got very much out of *'Ulysses'* ... so much of it consists of rather lengthy demonstrations of how a novel ought not to be written. *Aldous Huxley - 'Paris Review'*

Why don't you write books people can read?
Mrs Nora Joyce

'Finnegans Wake' - As one tortures one's way through *Finnegans Wake* an impression grows that Joyce has lost his hold on human life. Obsessed by a spaceless and timeless void, he has outrun himself. We begin to feel that his very freedom to say anything has become a compulsion to say nothing.
Alfred Kazin - 'New York Herald-Tribune'

James Joyce's ultimate works are like a man who is too shy to write a love-letter except in the form of a crossword puzzle.
Constant Lambert - 'Music Ho!'

'Ulysses' - The last part of it is the dirtiest, most indecent, most obscene thing ever written. Yes, it is ... it is filthy. *D. H. Lawrence*

My God, what a clumsy 'olla putrida' James Joyce is! Nothing but old fags and cabbage-stumps of quotation from the Bible and the rest, stewed in the juice of deliberate

journalistic dirty-mindedness.
D.H. Lawrence (1928)

He has sunk a shaft down into the welter of
nonsense which lies at the bottom of the mind,
and pumping up this stuff (it is an astounding
hydraulic feat) presented it as criticism of life.
Desmond McCarthy - 'Criticism'

'Finnegan's Wake' - Considered as a book
'Finnegan's Wake' must be pronounced a
complete fiasco. *Malcolm Muggeridge (1939)*

In Ireland they try to make a cat clean by
rubbing its nose in its own filth. Mr Joyce has
tried the same treatment on the human subject.
G. B. Shaw (1921)

An essentially private man who wished his total
indifference to public notice to be universally
recognised. *Tom Stoppard*

He started off writing very well, then you can
watch his going mad with vanity. He ends up a
lunatic. *Evelyn Waugh - 'Paris Review' (1962)*

The work of a queasy undergraduate scratching
his pimples. *Virginia Woolf*

'Ulysses' - It is a mis-fire. The book is diffuse. It
is brackish. It is pretentious. It is underbred,
not only in the obvious sense but in the literary
sense. A first-rate writer, I mean, respects
writing too much to be tricky.
Virginia Woolf - 'Diary' (1922)

'Ulysses' - The first 200 pages of 'Ulysses' . . .
Never have I read such tosh. As for the first 2
chapters we will let them pass, but the 3rd, 4th,
5th, 6th - merely the scratching of pimples on
the body of the bootboy at Claridges.
Virginia Woolf (1922)

Susan Kenney - *(b 1941)*
'In Another Country' - The catalogue of miseries
seems to cry out for commercial spots and a
station break: the stuff of noon-day soap-operas.
Stefan Kanfer - 'Time' (1984)

Jack Kerouac - *(1922-69)*
'On the Road' - That's not writing, that's
typing. *Truman Capote*

Charles Kingsley - *(1819-75)*
He has attempted (as I may call it) to poison
the wells.
Cardinal Newman - 'Apologia Pro Vita Sua'

Froude informs the Scottish youth
That parsons do not care for truth.
The Reverend Canon Kingsley cries
History is a pack of lies.
What cause for judgments so malign?
A brief recollection solves the mystery -
Froude believes Kingsley a divine,
And Kingsley goes to Froude for history.
Bishop William Stubbs (1871)

Rudyard Kipling - *(1865-1936)*
There are some poets, Kipling for example,
whose relation to language reminds one of a
drill sergeant; the words are taught to wash
behind the ears, stand properly to attention and
execute complicated manoeuvres, but at the
cost of never being allowed to think for
themselves. *W. H. Auden - 'The Dyer's Hand'*

The arrival of a new book of his verse is not
likely to stir the slightest ripple on the surface
of our conversational intelligentsia.
T. S. Eliot - 'Athenaeum' (1919)

I doubt that the infant monster has any more to
give. *Henry James*

The one great fault in Mr Kipling's work is, not
its 'brutality', nor its fondness for strong
effects, but a certain taint of bad manners, from
the literary point of view. He insists upon
spicing his stories with an ill-flavoured kind of
gossip, wholly irrelevant, and very offensive.
Lionel Johnson - 'Academy' (1891)

This pickle has a peculiar mordant quality
which distinguishes it from all others. The chief
ingredient is unwashed English, chopped,
broken, broken and bruised with a brazen
instrument. Then work in chips and fragments
of cynicism, 'B.V.' poems, the seven cardinal
sins, the 'Soldier's Pocket Book', the 'Civil
Service Regulations', Simla manners, profanity,
an Ekka pony, the Southern Cross, and genius.
E. V. Lucan - 'Kipling Chutnee' (1892)

From a letter of rejection - I'm sorry, Mr Kipling,

but you just don't know how to use the English
language.   *'San Francisco Examiner' (1889)*

Mr Kipling stands for everything in this
cankered world which I would wish were
otherwise.   *Dylan Thomas (1933)*

Lady Caroline Lamb - *(1785-1828)*
Keep clear of her - she is a villainous
intriguante - in every sense of the word - mad
and malignant - capable of all and every
mischief.   *Lord Byron (1815)*

Charles Lamb - *(1775-1834)*
Charles Lamb I sincerely believe to be in some
considerable degree insane. A more pitiful,
rickety, gasping, staggering, Tomfool, I do not
know. Poor Lamb! Poor England! when such a
despicable abortion is named genius.
        Thomas Carlyle (1831)

A clever fellow certainly, but full of villainous
and abortive puns which he miscarries every
minute.   *Thomas Moore (1823)*

Francois Duc de La Rochefoucauld -
(1613-80)
La Rochfoucauld who . . . was a master of self-
love . . . in real life was nothing but a silly man
of letters.   *Henri-Marie Stendhal*

D. H. Lawrence - *(1885-1930)*
'Lady Chatterly's Lover' - Mr Lawrence has a
diseased mind. He is obsessed by sex and we
have no doubt that he will be ostracised by all
except the most degenerate coteries in the
world.   *'John Bull' (1928)*

'Lady Chatterley's Lover' - The pictorial account
of the day-to-day life of an English game-keeper
is full of considerable interest to outdoor
readers. Unfortunately, one is obliged to wade
through many pages of extraneous material. In
this reviewer's opinion, the book cannot take
the place of J R. Miller's *'Practical Game-
keeping'.'*   *Field and Stream'*

'The Rainbow' - It is more hideous than
imaginable reality. The thing is done so coldly,
so pompously, so gravely, that it is like a savage
rite. There is no gleam of humour in the fog of
eloquent lubricity. The thud-thud-thud of
hectic phrases is intolerably wearisome. They

pound away like engines, grinding out a dull
monotonous tune of spiritless sensuality.
        James Douglas - 'Star' (1919)

In the work of D. H. Lawrence is found the
most erratic and uneven writing, by any writer
of our generation.
        T. S. Eliot - 'Vanity Fair' (1923)

Your novel has every fault that the English
novel can have - a rotten work of genius.
        Ford Madox Ford

'Sons and Lovers' - It is not good enough to
spend time and ink in describing the
penultimate sensations and physical
movements of people getting into a state of rut,
we all know them too well.
        John Galsworthy (1914)

For Lawrence, existence was one continuous
convalescence; it was as though he were newly
re-born from a mortal illness every day of his
life.   *Aldous Huxley*

We know what sort of picture D. H. Lawrence
would paint if he took to the brush instead of
the pen. For he did so, and even held
exhibitions. As one might have expected, it
turned out to be incompetent Gaugin.
        Percy W. Lewis - 'Men Without Art'

'Women in Love' - Justly merits the fate of its
predecessor [*'The Rainbow'*]. I do not claim to
be a literary critic, but I know dirt when I smell
it and here it is in heaps - festering, putrid
heaps which smell to high Heaven.
        Charles Pilley - 'John Bull' (1921)

Lawrence is a long line of people, beginning
with Herclitus and ending with Hitler, whose
ruling motive is hatred derived from
megalomania, and I am sorry to see that I was
once so far out in estimating him.
        Bertrand Russell (1937)

Mr Lawrence looked like a plaster gnome on a
stone toadstool in some suburban garden. At
the same time he bore some resemblance to a
bad self-portrait by Van Gogh. He had a rather
matted, dank appearance. He looked as if he
had just returned from spending an
uncomfortable night in a very dark cave,

hiding, perhaps in the darkness, from something which, at the same time, he on his side was hunting.
Edith Sitwell – 'Taken Care Of'

T. E. Lawrence [of Arabia] – *(1888– 1935)*
Arabian Lawrence, who whatever his claims as a man, was surely a sonorous fake as a writer.
Kingsley Amis

A bore and a bounder and a prig. He was intoxicated with his own youth, and loathed any milieu which he couldn't dominate. Certainly he had none of a gentleman's instincts, strutting about Peace Conferences in Arab dress.   *Henry Channon – 'Diary' (1935)*

T. E. Lawrence was an adventurer with a genius for backing into the limelight.
Lowell Thomas

Sir Roger L'Estrange – *(1616–1704)*
The pattern of bad writing.
Henry Hallam – 'Literature of Europe'

Percy Wyndham Lewis – *(1884–1957)*
That lonely old volcano of the Right.
W. H. Auden

He is like a maddened elephant which, careering through a village, sometimes leans against a house and carelessly demolishes the most compact masonry, trumpeting defiance to the inhabitants within, sometimes pursues a dog or a chicken or stops to uproot a shrub or bang a piece of corrugated iron.
Cyril Connolly – 'Enemies of Promise'

I don't think I have ever seen a nastier-looking man. Under the black hat, when I had first seen them, the eyes had been those of an unsuccessful rapist.
Ernest Hemingway – 'A Moveable Feast'

You, like the mills of God, grind slow, and I might add, grind exceedingly small.   *Paul Nash*

It would be a very heavy labour to read one of his novels right through. Some indefinable quality, a sort of literary vitamin, is absent from them.   *George Orwell – 'Tribune' (1937)*

A buffalo in wolf's clothing.   *Robert Ross*

Sinclair Lewis – *(1885–1951)*
'Babbit' – As a humorist, Mr Lewis makes valiant attempts to be funny; he merely succeeds in being silly. In fact it is as yellow a novel as novel can be.
'Boston Evening Transcript' (1922)

He has weighed down his novels with a heavy burden of unreal and exaggerated jargon, palmed off as common speech, with unfunny topical jokes, passed on as native humour, and the weight of that dated mockery grows heavier every year.   *Robert Cantwell*

'The Man Who Knew Coolidge' – Mr Lewis's latest work is as heavy-handed, clumsy, and as dishonest as burlesque as it has been my misfortune to see in years . . . I wish I could say 'rotten'. You don't know how much I need to say it.   *Dorothy Parker – 'New Yorker' (1928)*

He was one of the worst writers in modern American literature.   *Mark Schorer – 'Sinclair Lewis: An American Life'*

'Main Street' – It is a bulky collection of scenes, types, caricatures, humorous episodes, and facetious turns of phrase; a mine of comedy from which the ore has not been lifted.
'The Weekly Review' (1920)

He is a master of that species of art to which belong glass flowers, imitation fruit, Mme Tussaud's waxworks, and barnyard symphonies, which aims at deceiving the spectator into thinking that the work in question is not an artificial product but the real thing.   *T. K. Whipple – 'Spokesman'*

Thomas Lodge – *(1558–1625)*
In wit, simple; in learning, ignorant; in attempt, rash; in name, Lodge.   *Stephen Gosson*

Jack London – *(1876–1916)*
Like Peter Pan, he never grew up, and he lived his own stories with such intensity that he ended by believing them himself.
Ford Madox Ford

Easy to criticise, easy to deplore him, impossible to avoid him.   *Fred L. Pattee*

LITERARY

Anita Loos – *(1893–1981)*
'Kiss Hollywood Goodbye' – On her pages sacred cows become blustering pachyderms.
Mel Gussow – 'New York Times' (1974)

Malcolm Lowry – *(1909–57)*
'Under the Volcano' – Mr Lowry is passionately in earnest about what he has to say concerning human hope and defeat, but for all his earnestness he has succeeded only in writing a rather good imitation of an important novel.
'New Yorker' (1947)

Mabel Dodge Luhan – *(1879–1962)*
'Background' – *'Background'* is to me as dull, and with that same stuffy, oppressive, plush-thick dullness, as an album of old snapshots of somebody else's family.
Dorothy Parker– 'New Yorker' (1931)

Thomas B. Macaulay – *(1800–59)*
The great apostle of the Philistines.
Matthew Arnold – 'Essays'

An ugly, cross-made, splay-footed, shapeless little dumpling of a fellow, with a featureless face too – except indeed a good expansive forehead – sleek, puritanical, sandy hair – large glimmering eyes – and a mouth from ear to ear. He has a lisp and a burr.
'Blackwood's Magazine' (1831)

A poor creature with his dictionary literature and erudition, his saloon arrogance. He has no vision in him. He will neither see nor do any great thing, but be a poor Holland House unbeliever, with spectacles instead of eyes, to the end of him.
Thomas Carlyle

Thomas Macaulay is well for a while, but one couldn't live under Niagara.
Thomas Carlyle

No person ever knew so much that was so little to the purpose.
R. W. Emerson

His speeches are harangues and never replies.
Charles Greville – 'Diary' (1831)

The worst of it is that Macaulay, like Rousseau, talked his nonsense so well that it still passes for gospel with all those who have advanced as far as reading, but have not as yet attained to thinking.
George Hill – 'Footsteps of Dr Johnson'

I wish I was as cocksure of anything as Tom Macaulay is of everything
William Lamb

His conversation was a procession of one.
Florence Nightingale

A sentence of Macaulay's may have no more sense in it than a blot pinched between doubled paper.
John Ruskin

He is like a book in breeches.
Sydney Smith – 'Memoirs' (1855)

His enemies might have said before that he has talked rather too much; but now he has occasional flashes of silence that make his conversation perfectly delightful.
Sydney Smith – ibid

He not only overflowed with learning, but stood in the slop.
Sydney Smith

Norman Mailer – *(b 1923)*
'An American Dream' – Mailer meant to make money with this book. Hollywood should go for it. It should make the Best Seller lists. But it is a book calculated to leave All America holding its nose.
'Best Sellers' (1965)

If only he would take his eyes from the world's genital glands.
William F. Buckley Jr – 'Rumbles' (1963)

Mailer decocts matters of the first philosophical magnitude from an examination of his own ordure, and I am not talking about books.
William F. Buckley Jr –
'National Review' (1968)

'Ancient Evenings' – It's like going for brain dialysis.
D. Keith Mano – 'National Review' (1983)

Thomas Mann – *(1875–1955)*
'Buddenbrooks' – Nothing but two thick tomes in which the author describes the worthless story of worthless people in worthless chatter.
Edward Engel – 'The Art of Folly' (1901)

Ethel Mannin
I do not want Miss Mannin's feelings to be hurt by the fact that I have never heard of her. At the moment I am debarred from the pleasures

of putting her in her place by the fact she has not got one. *Dame Edith Sitwell*

Katherine Mansfield - *(1888-1923)*
I loathe you. You revolt me stewing in your consumption. The Italians were quite right to have nothing to do with you.
D. H. Lawrence (1919)

We could both wish that our first impression of K.M. was not that she stinks like the - well, civet cat that had taken to street walking. In truth, I'm a little shocked by her commonness at first sight; lines so hard and cheap.
Virginia Woolf (1917)

Harriet Martineau - *(1802-76)*
She is an infidel . . . a vulgar and foolish one.
John Ruskin

Suzanne Massie
'Land of the Firebird' - A lollipop speaking bay-talk. *John Leonard*

W. Somerset Maugham - *(1874-1965)*
A half-trashy novelist, who writes badly, but is patronised by half-serious readers, who do not care much about writing.
Edmund Wilson - 'Classics and Commercials'

Herman Melville - *(1819-91)*
'Moby Dick' - A huge dose of hyperbolical slang, maudlin sentimentalism and tragi-comic bubble-and-squeak.
William H. Ainsworth - 'New Monthly Magazine'

'Moby Dick' - *'Redburn'* was a failure, *'Mardi'* was hopelessly dull, *'White Jacket'* was worse than either; and, in fact was such a very bad book that, until the appearance of *'Moby Dick'*, we had set it down as the very ultimatum of weakness to which the author could attain. It seems, however, that we were mistaken. In bombast, in caricature, in rhetorical artifice - generally as clumsy as it is ineffectual - and in low attempts at humour, each of his volumes has been an advance upon its predecessor.
'Democratic Review'

'Moby Dick' - Sad stuff, dull and dreary, or ridiculous. Mr Melville's Quakers are the wretchedest dolts and drivellers, and his Mad Captain is a monstrous bore.
'Southern Quarterly Review' (1851)

His vocabulary was large, fluent, eloquent, but it was excessive, inaccurate and unliterary. He wrote too easily, and at too great length, his pen sometimes running away from him, and from his readers. *Richard Stoddard*

Menippe - *(c 300BC)*
Menippe is the bird in borrowed plumes. He does not speak; he does not feel. He repeats sentiments and speeches and uses the wits of others so naturally that he is himself the first to be deceived, and often believes he is displaying his own taste, or developing his own thoughts, when he is but the echo of someone he has just left off. He is bearable for quarter of an hour, after that he falls off, losing what little brightness his memory gave him, and showing threadbare condition. *Jean de la Bruyère*

George Meredith - *(1828-1909)*
At best, a sort of daintily dressed Walt Whitman. *G. K. Chesterton - 'The Victorian Age in Literature'*

By the side of George Eliot, Meredith appears as a shallow exhibitionist (his famous 'intelligence' a laboured and vulgar brilliance).
F. R. Leavis - 'The Great Tradition'

'Tragic Comedians' - In George Meredith there is nothing but crackjaw sentences, empty and unpleasant in the mouth as sterile nuts. I do not know any book more tedious than Tragic Comedians, more pretentious, more blatant, it struts and screams, stupid in all its gaud and absurdity as a cockatoo. *George Moore (1888)*

Meredith is, to me, chiefly a stink. I should never write on him as I detest him too much to trust myself as a critic of him.
Ezra Pound (1918)

His style is chaos illumined by flashes of lightning. As a writer he has mastered everything except language. As a novelist he can do everything except tell a story. As an artist he is everything except articulate.
Oscar Wilde - 'The Decay of Living' (1889)

Meredith is only a prose Browning - and so was Browning. *Oscar Wilde*

Henry Miller - *(1891-1980)*
He is not really a writer, but a non-stop talker
to whom someone has given a typewriter.
Gerald Brenan - 'Thought in a Dry Season'

'Tropic of Capricorn' - A gadfly with delusions of
grandeur. *'Time' (1962)*

A. A. Milne - *(1882-1956)*
*'The House at Pooh Corner' [which on page five
contains the 'hum': The more it Snows-tiddely-pom,
The more it Goes-tiddely-pom, The more it Goes-
tiddely-pom On Snowing . . .]*
*Final six paragraphs of her 'Constant Reader'
review - 'Far From Well'* - . . . 'That's a very
good idea, Piglet,' said Pooh. 'We'll practise it
now as we go along. But it's no good going
home to practise it, because it's a special
Outdoor Song which Has To Be Sung In The
Snow.'

'Are you sure?' asked Piglet anxiously.

'Well, you'll see, Piglet, when you listen.
Because this is how it begins. The more it
Snows-tiddely-pom –'

'Tiddely what?' said Piglet. (He took, as you
might say, the very words out of your
correspondent's mouth.)

'Pom!' said Pooh. 'I put it in to make it
hummy.'

And it is that word 'hummy', my darlings,
that marks the first place in 'The House at
Pooh Corner' at which Tonstant Weader
Fwowed up.
Dorothy Parker - 'New Yorker' (1928)

George A. Moore - *(1852-1933)*
We should really be much more interested in
Mr Moore if he were not quite so interested in
himself. We feel as if we were being shown
through a gallery of really fine pictures, into
each of which, by some useless and discordant
convention, the artist had represented the same
figure in the same attitude. 'The Grand Canal
with a distant view of George Moore', 'Effect of
Mr Moore through a Scotch Mist', 'Mr Moore
by Firelight', 'Ruins of Mr Moore by
Moonlight'. *G. K. Chesterton - 'Heretics'*

That old pink petulant walrus.
Henry Channon - 'Diary' (1941)

The technical perfection of the novels of Mr
George Moore does not prevent them from

being faultlessly dead. *Q. D. Leavis*

Some men kiss and do not tell, some kiss and
tell; but George Moore told and did not kiss.
Susan Mitchell

George Moore looked like a preposterous
Mellon's Food baby.
Gertrude Stein - 'Alice B. Toklas'

He leads his readers to the latrine and locks
them in. *Oscar Wilde*

Know him? I know him so well that I haven't
spoken to him for ten years. *Oscar Wilde*

That vague formless obscene face.
Oscar Wilde (1899)

He wrote brilliant English until he discovered
grammar. *Oscar Wilde*

Mopse
A dog makes his way into a church; and if you
drive him from the king's seat, the chances are
he will mount the pulpit, from which eminence
he will look upon the congregation without
being in any way embarrassed or ashamed. He
feels no more cause for blushing than Mopse.
Jean de la Bruyère

Flannery O'Connor - *(1925-64)*
Her characters are almost all fantastic,
suffering from what we might diagnose as an
acute sense of dislocation of place.
Mervyn J. Friedman

John O'Hara - *(1905-70)*
'Sermons and Soda-water' - O'Hara normally
puts everything into a novel, including the
kitchen sink complete with stopped drain,
plumber, and plumber's mate, and does this not
once but four or five times per book. The
novella form has merely limited the author in a
statistical way; one kitchen sink is all he can fit
into his predetermined space.
'Atlantic Monthly' (1960)

Hard to lay down, but easy not to pick up.
Malcolm Cowley

Mr O'Hara can write like a streak, but he just

won't think, or any rate he won't think in his novels. *Clifton Fadiman*

He lives in a perpetual state of just having discovered it's a lousy world. *F. Scott Fitzgerald*

George Orwell – *(1903-50)*
I often feel that I will never pick up a book by Orwell again until I have read a frank discussion of the dishonesty and hysteria that mar some of his best work. *Kingsley Amis*

'The Road to Wigan Pier' – I think his data was derived much more from the *'News of the World'* and seaside picture postcards – two of his ruling passions – and even from Dickens, than from direct observation. *Malcolm Muggeridge*

Thomas Paine – *(1737-1809)*
'Common Sense' – What a poor ignorant, malicious, short-sighte, crapulous mass, is Tom Paine's *'Common Sense'*. *John Adams*

John Dos Passos – *(1896-1970)*
He is like a man who is trying to run in a dozen directions at once, succeeding thereby merely in standing still and making a noise.
V.S. Pritchett – 'The Spectator'

Samuel Pepys – *(1633-1703)*
In S. Pepys, the Understanding is hypertrophied to the necrosis or marasmus of the Reason and Imagination, while far-sighted (yet Oh! how short-sighted) Self-interest fills the place of Conscience. *Samuel T. Coleridge*

Walker Percy – *(1916-90)*
'The Moviegoer' – Mr Percy's prose needs oil and a good check-up. *'New Yorker' (1961)*

Sidney J. Perelman – *(1904-79)*
Before they made S. J. Perelman they broke the mould. *Anon*

'Dawn Ginsbergh's Revenge' – From the moment I picked up your book until I laid it down I was convulsed with laughter. Someday I intend reading it. *Groucho Marx (1929)*

This is a man who has not let success go to his head – a man who is humble and unspoiled. He

is just as unassuming, as comfortable to be with as an old glove – and just about as interesting.
Groucho Marx

Pliny the Younger – *(62-113)*
Pliny the Younger took great care over his words, but none over his thoughts.
Joseph Joubert

Edgar Allan Poe – *(1809-49)*
I've got an idea that if Poe had been an exemplary, conventional, tax-oppressed citizen like Longfellow, his poems, as striking as they are, would not have made so great a stir.
Thomas B. Aldrich (1900)

An unmanly sort of man whose love-life seems to have been largely confined to crying in laps and playing mouse. *W. H. Auden*

Three-fifths of him genius, and two-fifths sheer fudge. *J. R. Lowell – 'A Fable for Critics'*

Poe is a kind of Hawthorne with delirium tremens. *Leslie Stephens*

Marcel Proust – *(1871-1922)*
Letter of rejection for 'Remembrance of Things Past" – I may be dead from the neck up, but rack my brains as I may I can't see why a chap should need thirty pages to describe how he turns over in bed before going to sleep.
Marc Humbolt (1912)
I was reading Proust for the first time. Very poor stuff. I think he was a mentally defective.
Evelyn Waugh (1948)

Reading Proust is like bathing in someone else's dirty water. *Alexander Woolcott*

François Rabelais – *(1494-1553)*
His book, whatever may be said, is an inexplicable enigma. It is a chimera; it has the face of a beautiful woman, with the feet and tail of a reptile, or some still more unsightly creature. It is an incongruous collection of refined and ingenious moral teaching and of what badness – garbage which can please none but the most depraved tastes.
Jean de la Bruyère

Ann Radcliffe – *(1764-1823)*
Her descriptions of scenery, indeed, are vague

and wordy to the last degree – her characters are insipid, the shadows of a shade, continued on, under a different name, through all her novels: her story comes to nothing.

William Hazlitt

Jean Rhys – *(1894–1979)*
Her novels read now like a single continuing work with the same heroine and the same single, persistent, disconnected disaster of a life in which only four things can be relied on: loneliness, fear, booze and lack of money.

A. Alvarez – 'The Observer' (1979)

Samuel Richardson – *(1689–1761)*
His mind is so vile a mind, so cosy, hypocritical, praise-mad, canting, envious, concupiscent.

Samuel T. Coleridge

Lord Patrick Robertson – *(1794–1855)*
Here lies that peerless paper peer Lord Peter,
    Who broke the laws of God and man and
metre.

Sir Walter Scott

Philip Roth – *(b 1933)*
'The Great American Novel' – Roth has, most unfortunately, got into such a shouting match with his readers that some of us are going to have to start shouting back.   *'Encounter' (1973)*

'Portnoy's Complaint' – Philip Roth is a good writer, but I wouldn't want to shake hands with him.   *Jacqueline Susann*

George Sand [Madame Dudevant] – *(1904–76)*
George Sand is one of those old ingenues who wish never to leave the boards. Lately I read a preface in which she maintains that a true Christian cannot believe in Hell. She has good reasons for wishing to suppress Hell.

Charles Baudelaire

In the world there are fewer sadder, sicklier phenomena for me than George Sand and the response she meets with. A new Phallus worship . . . and Madame Sand for a virgin.

Thomas Carlyle

Carl Sandburg – *(1878–1967)*
He is submerged in adolescence. Give Sandburg a mind, and you perhaps destroy him.   *Sherwood Anderson (1919)*

Under close scrutiny Sandburg's verse reminds us of the blobs of living jelly or plankton brought up by deep-sea dredging; it is a kind or protoplasmic poetry, lacking higher organisation.   *George F. Whicher – 'The Twentieth Century'*

'Lincoln' – The cruelest thing that has happened to Lincoln since he was shot by Booth has been to fall into the hands of Carl Sandburg.

Edmund Wilson – 'Time' (1972)

May Sarton – *(b 1912)*
'Crucial Conversations' – May Sarton's book reads like an unsuccessful attempt to make a Montaigne out of a molehill.   *'Listener' (1976)*

I think her lack of greater popularity is due to her habit of dissecting her bowels and displaying for public observation.

'Maine Life' (1977)

'The Magnificent Spinster' – The long experience of the book, personally speaking, was like a long hike home in wet socks and gym shoes, uncomfortable and unnecessary.   *'Out' (1986)*

Dorothy L. Sayers – *(1893–1957)*
Her slickness in writing has blinded many readers to the fact that her stories, considered as detective stories, are very bad ones. They lack the minimum of probability that even a detective story ought to have, and the crime is always committed in a way that is incredibly tortuous and quite uninteresting.

George Orwell – 'New English Review' (1936)

For her warm-hearted admirers she is still the finest detective writer of the century, to those less enthusiastic her work is long-winded and ludicrously snobbish.   *Julian Symons*

Really, she does not write very well . . . In any serious department of fiction, her writing would not appear to have any distinction at all.

Edmund Wilson – 'Classics and Commercials'

Sir Walter Scott – *(1771–1832)*
I do not care for him, and find it difficult to understand his continued reputation.

When we fish him out of the river of time. . . he is seen to have a trivial mind and a heavy style. He cannot construct. He has neither artistic detachment nor passion, and how can a writer who is devoid of both, create characters who will move us deeply?

He only has a temperate heart and gentlemanly feelings, and an intelligent affection for the countryside: and this is not enough for great novels.

E. M. Forster – 'Aspects of the Novel'

He dotes on all well-authenticated superstitions, he shudders at the shadow of innovation . . . Sir Walter would make a bad hand of a description of 'Millennium', unless he could lay the scene in Scotland some five hundred years ago. *William Hazlitt*

Sir Walter Scott, when all is said and done, is an inspired butler. *William Hazlitt*

Scott appears hemmed in, his prose is curiously fatigued – the clumsy, unrealised descriptions of thrilling actions, the rhetorical outbursts in 'the language of passion', the conscientious oil-paintings of historical scenes and characters, drag their slow lengths along often ridiculously. *Q. D. Leavis*

Then comes Sir Walter Scott with his enchantments, and by his single might checks this wave of progress, and even turns it back; sets the world in love with dreams and phantoms; with systems of government; with the silliness and emptiness, sham grandeurs, sham gauds, and sham chivalries of a brainless and worthless long-vanished society. He did measureless harm; more real and lasting harm, perhaps, than any other individual that ever wrote. *Mark Twain*

In making amusing stories in verse; he will be superseded by some newer versifier; what he writes in the way of natural description is merely rhyming nonesense.
William Wordsworth (1884)

Hubert Selby – *(b 1929)*
'Last Exit to Brooklyn ' – This is Grove Press's extra special dirty book for fall. *'Time' (1965)*

Marquisse Marie de Sevigne – *(1626–96)*
'Letters' – You can gain nothing by reading her. It is like eating snowballs, with which one can

surfeit one's self without satisfying the stomach. *Napoleon Bonaparte*

The Marquisse de Sevigne has the heart of a cucumber, fried in snow. *Ninon de Lenclos*

Anna Seward – *(1747–1809)*
Here is Miss Seward with six tomes of the most disgusting trash, sailing over Styx with a Foolscap over her periwig as complacent as can be – Of all Bitches dead or alive a scribbling woman is the most canine. *Lord Byron (1811)*

Frances Sheridan – *(1724–67)*
I know not, madam, that you have a right, upon moral principles, to make your readers suffer so much. *Samuel Johnson*

Charles Simmons – *(b 1924)*
'Wrinkles' – The epic implications of being human end in more than this: We start our lives as if they were momentous stories, with a beginning, a middle and an appropriate end, only to find that they are mostly middles.
Anatole Broyard (1978)

Albert Smith – *(1816–60)*
On his habit of signing his articles 'A.S.' – Tut, what a pity Smith will tell only two-thirds of the truth. *Douglas Jerrold*

Alexander Solzhenitsyn – *(b 1918)*
He is a bad novelist and a fool. The combination usually makes for great popularity in the U.S. *Gore Vidal (1980)*

Susan Sontag – *(b 1933)*
Miss Sontag, whose sense of humour is about as well developed as King Kong.
William F. Buckley Jr – 'On the Right' (1967)

Theodore C. Sorenson – *(b 1928)*
'Kennedy' – A great American need not fear the hand of his assassin; his real demise begins only when a friend like Mr Sorenson closes the mouth of his tomb with a stone. *Nigel Dennis*

Mickey Spillane – *(b 1918)*
'The Girl Hunters' – A sorry exhibit of toughness gone slimy. *'New Statesman' (1963)*

Anne Louise de Stael – *(1766–1817)*
She has only one fault. She is insufferable.
Napoleon Bonaparte

Arianna Stassinopoulos – *(b 1950)*
So boring you fall asleep halfway through her
name.   *Alan Bennett – 'The Observer' (1983)*

Wallace Stegner – *(b 1909)*
'The Spectator Bid' – It would seem that Stegner
emptied a desk drawer and decided to make a
book out of the contents.
'Monterey Herald' (1976)

John Steinbeck – *(1902–68)*
After a dozen books Steinbeck still looks like a
distinguished apprentice, and what is so
striking in his work is it inconclusiveness, his
moving approach to human life and yet his
failure to be creative with it.   *Alfred Kazin*

His career to date has the shape of a suggestive,
a representative, and a completely honourable
failure.   *R. W. Lewis*

'Of Mice and Men' (1937) – Readers less easily
thrown off their trolley will still prefer Hans
Andersen.   *'Time'*

Laurence Sterne – *(1713–68)*
'Tristram Shandy' – It may perhaps go on a little
longer, but we will not follow him. With all his
drollery there is a sameness of extravagance
which tires us. We have just a succession of
Surprise, surprise, surprise.   *David Hume*

'Tristram Shandy' – Nothing odd will do long.
Tristram Shandy did not last.   *Samuel Johnson*

Harriet Beecher Stowe – *(1812–96)*
A blatant Bassarid of Boston, a rampant
Maenad of Massachusetts.   *Algernon Swinburne*

Lytton Strachey – *(1880–1932)*
Incapable of creation in life or literature, his
writings were a substitute for both.
T. R. Barnes

Eugene Sue [Marie Joseph] – *(1804–57)*
'Arthur' – It's indescribable, enough to make
you vomit. You have to read this to realise the
pitifulness of money, success and the public.
Literature has become consumptive. It spits

and slobbers, covers all its blisters with salve
and sticking-plaster, and has grown bald from
too much hair-slicking. It would take Christs of
art to cure this leper.   *Gustave Flaubert*

Jacqueline Susann – *(1926–74)*
'Valley of the Dolls' – For the reader who has put
away comic books, but isn't ready for editorials
in the Daily News.
Gloria Steinem – 'New York Times' (1976)

Jonathan Swift – *(1667–1745)*
'Gulliver's Travels' – The reader of the fourth
part of *'Gulliver's Travels'* is like the hero
himself in this instance. It is Yahoo language, a
monster gibbering shrieks and gnashing
imprecations against mankind – tearing down
all shreds of modesty, past all sense of
manliness and shame; filthy in word, filthy in
thought, furious, raging, obscene.
William M. Thackeray

William M. Thackeray – *(1811–63)*
The Cynic Parasite.
Benjamin Disraeli – 'Reminiscences'

Thackeray settled like a meat-fly on whatever
one had got for dinner, and made one sick of it.
John Ruskin – 'Fors Clavigera'

James Thurber –*(1894–1961)*
A tall, thin, spectacled man with the face of a
harrassed rat.
Russell Maloney – 'Saturday Review'

Alice B. Toklas – *(1877–1967)*
Miss Toklas was incredibly ugly, uglier than
almost anyone I had ever met. A thin, withered
creature, she sat hunched in her chair, in her
heavy tweed suit and her thick lisle stockings,
impregnable and indifferent. She had a huge
nose, a dark moustache, and her dark-dyed hair
was combed into absurd bangs over her
forehead.   *Otto Friedrich – 'Esquire' (1968)*

J. R. R. Tolkien – *(1892–1975)*
He talks in shorthand and then smudges it.
Anon

His was not a true imagination. He made it all
up.   *H. V. Dyson*

Leo Tolstoy - *(1828-1910)*
'War and Peace' - I took a speedy reading course and read *'War and Peace'* in twenty minutes. It involves Russia. *Woody Allen*

Diana Trilling - *(b 1905)*
'The Death of a Scarsdale Diet Doctor' -If you are unhealthily addicted to reading about murder trials, this book may cure you.
John Carey - 'Sunday Times' (1982)

Anthony Trollope - *(1815-72)*
'Orley Farm' - What a pity it is that so powerful and idiomatic a writer should be so incorrect grammatically and scholastically speaking! Robert Browning insists on my putting down such phrases as these: 'The Cleeve was distant from Orley two miles, though it could not be driven under five.' 'One rises up the hill.' 'As good as him.' 'Possessing more acquirements than he would have learned at Harrow.' Learning acquirements! Yes, they are faults, and should be put away by a first-rate writer like Anthony Trollope. It's always worth while to be correct. *Elizabeth Barrett Browning (1861)*

He has a gross and repulsive face and manner, but appears bon enfant when you talk to him. But he is the dullest Briton of them all.
Henry James (1875)

Mark Twain - *(1835-1910)*
'Huckleberry Finn' - If Mr Clemens cannot think of something better to tell our pure-minded lads and lasses, he had better stop writing for them.
Louisa May Alcott (1885)

A hack writer who would not have been considered fourth rate in Europe, who tried out a few of the old proven 'sure-fire' literary skeletons with sufficient local colour to intrigue the superficial and the lazy. *William Faulkner*

Gore Vidal - *(b 1925)*
'Lincoln'- He offers the never-never land of convenient cliches. *Paul Gray - 'Time' (1984)*

'Two Sisters' - He seems to have gone to his icebox, pulled out all the cold obsessions, mixed them in a bowl, beat too lightly and baked too long . . . Aspiring to a souffle, he achieves a pancake at which the reader saws without

much attention . . . There are too many ironies in the fire.
John Leonard - 'New York Times' (1970)

'Myra Breckenridge' - A rather damp fizzle.
'Library Journal' (1968)

'Creation' - Vidal's book is manufactured, not created. *'New Statesman' (1981)*

Kurt Vonnegut - *(b 1922)*
'Breakfast of Champions' - From time to time it's nice to have a book you can hate - it clears the pipes - and I hate this book.
Peter Prescott -'Newsweek' (1973)

Horace Walpole - *(1717-97)*
The conformation of his mind was such that whatever was little seemed to him great, and whatever was great seemed to him little.
Thomas Macaulay

Sir Hugh Walpole - *(1884-1941)*
How coooold he be ainy good? He knows naaaathing about saix! *Robertson Nicoll*

Izaak Walton - *(1593-1683)*
'Compleat Angler' -And angling, too, that
    solitary vice,
Whatever Izaak Walton sings or says:
The quaint, old, cruel coxcomb, in his gullet
Should have a hook, and small trout to pullit.
Lord Byron (1823)

Evelyn Waugh - *(1903-66)*
He looked, I decided, like a letter delivered to the wrong address. *Malcolm Muggeridge - 'Tread Softly for You Tread on My Jokes' (1966)*

Mr Waugh, I always feel, is an antique in search of a period, a snob in search of a class, perhaps even a mystic in search of a beatific vision. *Malcolm Muggeridge - 'The Most of . . .'*

A disgusting common little man - he had never been taught how to avoid being offensive.
Rebecca West

His style has the desperate jauntiness of an orchestra fiddling away for dear life on a sinking ship. *Edmund Wilson*

Noah Webster – *(1758–1843)*
In conversation he is even duller than in
writing, if that is possible.   *Juliana Smith*

H. G. Wells – *(1866–1946)*
The critics have been right. For as one looks
back over Mr Wells's long and honourable
record as a novelist, one fails to recall a single
vivid or credible character. They are all alike
and all alike in being rather colourless
automata, mere puppets by which their
manipulation has sought to demonstrate his
successive attitudes toward a changing world.
        Conrad Aitken – 'Atlantic Monthly' (1926)

'Ann Veronica' – He is the old maid among
novelists; even the sex obsession that lay
clotted on Ann Veronica and the new
Machiavelli like cold white sauce was merely
old maid's mania, the reaction towards the flesh
of a mind too long absorbed in airships and
colloids.   *Rebecca West – 'Freewoman'*

Paul West – *(b 1930)*
'Rat Man of Paris' – All of this would make a
great short story. Unfortunately, this is a 180-
page novel.   *'Bestsellers' (1986)*

Rebecca West – *(1892–1983)*
Rebecca was a busy liar in her distinguished old
age, reinventing her past for gullible biographers.
        Walter Clemons – 'Newsweek' (1984)

She writes like a loom, producing her broad
rich fabric with hardly a thought of how it will
make up into a shape.   *H. G. Wells*

Edith Wharton – *(1862–1937)*
The glittering structure of her cultivation sits
on her novels like a rather showy icing that
detracts from the cake beneath.
        Louis Auchinloss (1965)

Mrs Wharton, do you know what's the matter
with you? You don't know anything about life.
        F. Scott Fitzgerald

P. G. Wodehouse – *(1881–1975)*
Literature's performing flea.   *Sean O'Casey*

Thomas Wolfe – *(1900–38)*
If it must be Thomas, let it be Mann, and if it
must be Wolfe let it be Nero, but let it never be

Thomas Wolfe.   *Peter de Vries*

Thomas Wolfe has always seemed to be the
most overrated, long-winded and boring of
reputable American novelists.   *Edith Oliver*

*'The Kandy-coloured, Tangerine-flake, Streamline
Baby'* – One wants to say to Mr Wolfe; you're
so clever, you can write so well, tell us
something interesting. *'Saturday Review' (1965)*

Anthony à Wood – *(1632–95)*
A little silly fellow who hath an ill designe to
libell honest men.   *Gilbert Burnet*

Just as naturally as cuttle fish ejects poisonous
ink, so did Mr Wood eject spite.
        Llewellyn Powys

Virginia Woolf – *(1882–1941)*
In real estate parlance – a single room.   *Anon*

Replying to the author's dislike of his drawing of her
– Mrs Woolf's complaint should be addressed
to her creator, who made her, rather than me.
        Cecil Beaton

Virginia Woolf's novels are too devastatingly
vague. I lost patience when I discovered (from
the luncheon in *'Between the Acts'* . . .) that she
thought you need a corkscrew to open a bottle
of champagne
        Brigid Brophy – 'Don't Never Forget'

Virginia Woolf herself never got used to the fact
that if you write books, some people are bound
to be rude about them.
        Anthony Powell – 'Daily Telegraph' (1984)

I enjoyed talking to her, but thought nothing of
her writing. I considered her a 'beautiful little
knitter'.   *Edith Sitwell*

Herman Wouk – *(b 1915)*
'The Winds of War' – This is not at all bad,
except as prose.   *Gore Vidal – 'Time' (1984)*

Sir Nathaniel Wraxall – *(1751–1838)*
Misplacing – mistaking –
Misquoting – misdating –
Men, manners, things, facts all,
  Here lies Nathan Wraxall.

        'Epitaph'

Emile Zola – *(1840-1902)*
'La Terre' – His work is evil, and he is one of those unhappy beings of whom one can say that it would be better had he never been born.
Anatole France (1988)

M. Zola is determined to show that, if he has not genius, he can at least be dull.   *Oscar Wilde*

POETRY

A poet is someone who is astonished by everything.   *Anon*

Poetry is the stuff in books that doesn't quite reach the margins.   *Anon*

Poetry is living proof that rhyme doesn't pay.
Anon

More and more I feel bent against the modern English habit of using poetry as a channel for thinking aloud, instead of making things happen.   *Matthew Arnold*

We must get rid of our superstitious valuation of texts and written poetry. Written poetry is worth reading once, and then should be destroyed. Let dead poets make way for others.
Antonin Artaud –
'The Theatre and its Double'

Verse is a special illness of the ear.
W. H. Auden

Poetry is the Devil's wine.   *St Augustine (387)*

I gave up on new poetry myself 30 years ago when most of it began to read like coded messages passing between lonely aliens in a hostile world.   *Russell Baker (1986)*

Anticipating that most poetry will be worse than carrying heavy luggage through O'Hare Airport, the public reads very little of it.
Russell Baker (1986)

Elegy – a composition in verse, in which, without employing any of the methods of humour, the writer aims to produce in the reader's mind the dampest kind of dejection. The most famous English example begins somewhat like this:

The cur foretells the knell of parting day;
The loafing herd winds slowly o'er the lea
  The wise man homeward plods; I only stay
  To fiddle-faddle in a minor key.
Ambrose Bierce

All poets are mad.   *Robert Burton (1621)*

I never saw such work or works. Campbell is lecturing – Moore is idling – Southey twaddling – Wordsworth drivelling – Coleridge muddling – Joanna Baillie piddling – Bowles quibbling, squabbling and snivelling.   *Lord Byron*

Poetry is man's rebellion against being what he is.   *James Cabell*

Modesty is a virtue not often found among poets, for almost every one of them thinks himself the greatest in the world.
Miguel de Cervantes

I know that poetry is indispensable, but to what I could not say.   *Jean Cocteau (1955)*

Some prose writers go from bad to verse.
'Columbia Record'

Idleness, that is the curse of other men, is the nurse of poets.   *D'Arcy Cresswell*

Poetry is what happens when an anxiety meets a technique.   *Lawrence Durrell*

A poet in history is divine; but a poet in the next room is a joke.   *Max Eastman*

In the case of many poets, the most important thing for them to do is to write as little as possible.   *T. S. Eliot*

The immature poet imitates; the mature poet plagiarises.   *T. S. Eliot*

Poetry is ordinary language raised to the nth power.   *Paul Engle*

Poetry is what gets lost in translation.
Robert Frost

A true sonnet goes eight lines and then takes a turn for the better or worse and goes six or eight lines more.   *Robert Frost*

Poetry is the language in which man explores his own amazement. *Christopher Fry*

Modern poets add a lot of water to their ink.
Johann Goethe

Poetry gives no adequate return in money, is expensive to print by reason of the waste of space occasioned by its form, and nearly always promulgates illusory concepts of life. But a better case for the banning of all poetry is the simple fact that most of it is bad. Nobody is going to manufacture a thousand tons of jam in the expectation that five tons may be eatable. Furthermore, poetry has the effect on the negligible handful who read it of stimulating them to write poetry themselves. One poem, if widely disseminated, will breed perhaps a thousand inferior copies.
Myles ná Gopaleen (1968)

There is no money in poetry; but then there is no poetry in money, either. *Robert Graves*

It is indeed a pity that our great public knows so little about poetry; almost as little, in fact, as our poets. *Heinrich Heine*

It's hard to say why writing verse
Should terminate in drink or worse.
A. P. Herbert

A poet is the most unpoetical of anything in existence, because he has no identity; he is continually informing and filling some other body. *John Keats*

The poet ranks far below the painter in the representation of visible things, and far below the musician in that of invisible things.
Leonardo da Vinci – 'Notebooks'

Show me a poet and I'll show you a shit.
A. J. Liebling

Athens had a newspaper written entirely in verse? Why can't some of our poets go to Hellas? *'Little Rock Arkansas Gazette'*

The world, we believe, is pretty well agreed in thinking that the shorter a prize poem is, the better. *Thomas Macaulay*

Publishing a volume of verse is like dropping a rose petal down the Grand Canyon and waiting for the echo. *Don Marquis – 'The Sun Dial'*

A poet more than thirty years old is simply an overgrown child. *H. L. Mencken*

Poets aren't very useful,
Because they aren't consumeful or very
    produceful. *Ogden Nash*

Ninety percent of the worst human beings I know are poets. Most poets these days are so square they have to walk around the block just to turn over in bed. *Kenneth Rexroth*

We now live in the Era of Incompetence; we have painters who can't paint, poets who can't rhyme and composers who whistle dissonance.
Dagobert Runes

The writing of more than seventy-five poems in any fiscal year should be punishable by a fine of $500. *Ed Sanders (1980)*

SALLY: We've been reading poems in school, but I never understand any of them. How am I supposed to know which poems I like?
CHARLIE BROWN: Somebody tells you!
Charles Schulz – 'Peanuts' (1990)

Poetry and consumption are the most flattering of diseases. *William Shenstone*

Poetry is like fish: if it's fresh, it's good; if it's stale, it's bad; and if you're not certain, try it on the cat. *Osbert Sitwell*

Poets tell many lies. *Solon*

A publisher of today would as soon see a burglar in his office as a poet.
Henry de Vere Stacpole

Poets are mysterious, but a poet when all is said and done is not much more mysterious than a banker. *Allen Tate*

Much of our poetry has the very best manners, but no character. *Henry D. Thoreau*

All bad poetry springs from genuine feeling.
Oscar Wilde (1890)

Books of poetry by young writers are usually

promissory notes that are never met.
Oscar Wilde

The poet, no less than the scientist, works on the assumption that inert and live things and relations hold enough interest to keep him alive as part of nature. *Louis Zukovsky*

CRITICISM

I agree with one of your reputable critics that a taste for drawing rooms has spoiled more poets than ever did a taste for gutters.
Thomas Beer – 'The Mauve Decade'

Whenever a poet praises the verses of another poet you may be sure that they are stupid and of no real value. *Jean de la Bruyère.*

It is the business of reviewers to watch poets, not of poets to watch reviewers.
William Hazlitt –
'Lectures on English Poets'

We praise the dramatic poet who possesses the art of drawing tears – a talent which he has in common with the meanest onion.
Heinrich Heine

What is a modern poet's fate?
To write his thoughts upon a slate;
The critic spits on what is done,
Gives it a wipe – and all is gone.
Thomas Hood

I would rather be hissed for a good verse than applauded for a bad one. *Victor Hugo*

The work of criticism is rooted in the unconscious of the critic just as the poem is rooted in the unconscious of the poet.
Randall Jarrell –
'A Sad Heart at the Supermarket' (1905)

Criticism is necessary, I suppose; I know. Yet criticism to the poet is no necessity, but a luxury he can ill afford. *Randall Jarrell – ibid*

It is always hard for poets to believe that one says their poems are bad not because one is a fiend but because their poems are bad.
Randall Jarrell

The one man who should never attempt an explanation of a poem is its author. If the poem can be improved by its author's explanation it never should have been published.
Archibald Macleish

Every critic in the town
Runs the minor poet down;
Every critic – don't you know it?
Is himself a minor poet.
Robert Murray – 'Critic and Poet'

Some have at first for wits, then poets pass'd,
Turn'd critics next, and prov'd plain fools at
last. *Alexander Pope –*
'An Essay on Criticism' (1711)

A poet that fails in writing becomes often a morose critic; the weak and insipid white wine makes a great length excellent vinegar.
Alexander Pope –
'Essays: On Writing and Books'

We do not see that a man to be a critic must necessarily be a poet, but to be a good critic he ought not to be a bad poet. *William Shenstone –*
'Characters of Shakespeare's Plays'

For poems read without a name,
We justly praise, or justly blame;
And critics have no partial views,
Except they know whom they abuse.
And since you ne'er provoke their spite,
Depend upon't their judgement right.
Jonathan Swift

Poetry is nobody's business except the poet's, and everbody else can **** off. *Walt Whitman*

REVIEWS
(Listed by Author)

Anon

Here lies a poet – where's the great surprise!
Since all men know, a poet deals in lies.
'Epitaph'
Rejection slip returned with a poem entitled 'Why Do I Live?' – Because you send your poem by mail.

Eugene Field

Poem - A B C D E F
       G H I J K L
       M N O P Q R
       S T U V W X
          Y Z

Review - 1 2 3 4 5
        6 7 8 9 10

Richard Aldington

Anon couplet - Excellent were it not for its
length. *Sebastian Chamfort*

Anon couplet - Very nice, though there are dull
stretches. *Antoine de Rivarol*

Joseph Addison - *(1672-1719)*

Addison was responsible for many of the evils
from which English prose has since suffered.
He made prose artful and whimsical, he made it
sonorous when sonority was not needed,
affected when it did not require affectation.
Addison had the misuse of an extensive
vocabulary and was so able to invalidate a great
number of words and expressions; the quality
of his mind was inferior to the language which
he used to express it.
Cyril Connolly - 'Enemies of Promise'

Mark Akenside - *(1721-70)*

I see they have published a splendid edition of
Akenside's works. One bad Ode may be
suffered, but a number of them together makes
one sick. *Samuel Johnson*

Matthew Arnold - *(1822-88)*

Arnold is a dandy Isaiah, a poet without
passion, whose verse, written in surplice, is for
freshmen and for gentle maidens who be wooed
in the arms of these future rectors.
George Meredith - 'Fortnightly Review' (1909)

Poor Matt, he's gone to Heaven, no doubt – but
he won't like God. *Robert Louis Stevenson*

Wordsworth's 'Immortality Ode' is no more
than moderately good. I put by its side the
poems of Matthew Arnold and think what a
delightfully loud splash the two would make if I
dropped them into a river.
Dylan Thomas (1933)

W. H. Auden - *(1907-73)*

My face looks like a wedding cake that has been
left out in the rain. *W. H. Auden*

One never steps twice into the same Auden.
*Randell Jarrell - 'The Third
Book of Criticism' (1969)*

An engaging, bookish, American talent, too
verbose to be memorable and too intellectual to
be moving. *Philip Larkin*

He is all ice and wooden-faced acrobatics.
Percy W. Lewis - 'Blasting and Bombardiering'

A sort of gutless Kipling.
George Orwell - 'The Road to Wigan Pier' (1937)

Mr Auden's brand of amoralism is only possible
if you are the kind of person who is always
somewhere else when the trigger is pulled.
George Orwell

Mr Auden himself has presented the curious
case of a poet who writes an original poetic
language in the most robust English tradition
but who seems to have been arrested in the
mentality of an adolescent schoolboy.
Edmund Wilson - 'The Shores of Light' (1952)

Alfred Austin - *Poet Laureate (1835-1913)*

Mr Alfred Austin has a clearly-defined talent,
the limits of which are by this time generally
recognised. *'Daily Telegraph' (1908)*

Mr Austin is neither an Olympian nor a Titan,
and all the puffing in Paternoster Row cannot
set him on Parnassus.
Oscar Wilde - 'Pall Mall Gazette' (1887)

Joel Barlow - *(1754-1812)*

A writer of good doggerel and the author of a
turgid epic couched in gaudy and inane
phraseology. *M. Ray Adams (1937)*

No poet with so little of poetry ever received so
much of glory. *Fred L. Pattee*

William Barnes - *(1801-86)*

In his poems, he is nothing but a poet. He does
not there protest against anything in religion,
politics, or the arrangements of society; nor has
he the advantage of being able to demand the

admiration of the sympathising public on the score that he is a chimney sweep, or a rat catcher, and has never learned to read.

Coventry Patmore

S. Laman Blanchard - *(1804–45)*
'Orient Pearls at Random Strung' - Dear Mr Blanchard - too much string.   *Charles Dickens*

Rupert Brooke -*(1887–1915)*
His verse exhibits something that is rather like Keats's vulgarity with a Public school accent.
F. R. Leavis –
'New Bearings in English Poetry'

Robert Browning - *(1812–89)*
Browning used words with the violence of a horse-breaker, giving out the scent of a he-goat.
Ford Madox Ford –
'The March of Literature'

Shelley is a light, and Swinburne is a sound – Browning alone is a temperature.   *Henry James*

George Meredith is only a prose Browning – and so was Browning.   *Oscar Wilde*

Of all remembered poets the most wanting in distinction of any kind, the most dependent for his effects on the most violent and vulgar resources of rant and cant and glare and splash and splutter.   *Algernon Swinburne*

Lord Byron - *(1788–1824)*
His versification is so destitute of sustained harmony, many of his thoughts are so strained, his sentiments so unamiable, his misanthropy so gloomy, his libertinism so shameless, his merriment such a grinning of a ghastly smile, that I have always believed his verses would soon rank with forgotten things.
John Quincy Adams – 'Memoirs' (1830)

He had not the intellectual equipment of a supreme modern poet; except for his genius he was an ordinary nineteenth-century English gentleman, with little culture and no ideas.
Matthew Arnold – 'Essays in Criticism'

As a thinker he was, as Goethe perceived, childish, and he possessed neither the imaginative vision – he could never invent anything, only remember – nor the verbal

sensibility such poetry demands.   *W. H. Auden*

On his death – The world is rid of Lord Byron, but the deadly slime of his touch remains.
John Constable

The most vulgar minded genius that ever produced a great effect in literature.
George Eliot (1969)

Of Byron one can say, as of no other English poet of his eminence, that he added nothing to the language, that he discovered nothing in the sounds, and developed nothing in the meaning, of individual words. I cannot think of any other poet of his distinction who might so easily have been an accomplished foreigner writing English.   *T. S. Eliot*

He writes with the thoughts of a city clerk in metropolitan clerical vernacular.
Ford Madox Ford – 'The March of Literature'

Mad - bad – and dangerous to know.
Lady Caroline Lamb – 'Journal' (1812)

It was to me offensive, and I can never make out his great power, which his admirers talk of. Why, a line of Wordsworth's is a lever to lift the immortal spirit! Byron can only bore the spleen.   *Charles Lamb*

Byron dealt chiefly in felt and furbelow, wavy Damascus daggers, and pocket pistols studded with paste. He threw out frequent and brilliant sparks; but his fire burnt to no purpose; it blazed furiously when it caught muslin, and it hurried many a pretty wearer into an untimely blanket.   *Walter S. Landor*

From the poetry of Lord Byron they drew a system of ethics compounded of misanthropy and voluptuousness – a system in which the two greatest commandments were to hate your neighbour and to love your neighbour's wife.
Thomas Macaulay

The Coryphaeus of the Satanic School.
Robert Southey – 'London Courier' (1822)

Of all remembered poets the most wanting in distinction of any kind, the most dependent for his effects on the most violent and vulgar resources of rant and cant and glare and splash and splutter. *Algernon Swinburne*

Catallus – *(84–54BC)*
We find in Catallus two things that make the worst blend in the world – sentimentality and grossness. But generally the main idea of each little poem is of a felicitous and simple turn; his airs are pretty, but his instrument is barbarous.
Joseph Joubert

Chaung Tzu
Chaung Tzu was born in the fourth century before Christ. The publication of this book in English, two thousand years after his death, is obviously premature. *Anon*

Thomas Chatterton – *(1752–70)*
An addiction to poetry is very generally the result of 'an uneasy mind in an uneasy body' Chatterton, I think, mad. *Lord Byron (1815)*

Geoffrey Chaucer – *(1340–1400)*
Mr C. had talent, but he couldn't spel. No man has a right to be a lit'rary man onless he knows how to spel. It is a pity that Chawcer, who had geneyus, was so unedicated. He's the wus speller I know of.
Artemus Ward – 'Chaucer's Poems'

Charles Churchill – *(1731–64)*
Churchill was a poor, low, unprincipled, vicious, coarse creature, with smartness that was sometimes almost strength; and what to us must in such a person always be a mystery, he had a command over the English language, as far as his mind enabled him to get in it, which made everything he said tell, far beyond its native power, and has secured him no contemptible place among English satirists.
'Blackwood's Magazine' (1828)

No, Sir, I called the fellow a blockhead at first, and I will call him a blockhead still.
Samuel Johnson

To be sure, he is a tree that cannot produce true fruit. He only bears crabs.
Samuel Johnson

Arthur Clough – *(1819–61)*
There was a bad poet named Clough,
Whom his friends found it useless to puff:

For the public, if dull,
Has not quite such a skull,
As belongs to believers in Clough.
Algernon Swinburne

Samuel Taylor Coleridge – *(1772–1834)*
Never did I see such apparatus get ready for thinking, and so little thought. He mounts scaffolding, pulleys, and tackles, gathers all the tools in the neighbourhood with labour, with noise, demonstration, precept, and sets – three bricks. *Thomas Carlyle*

How great a possibility; how small a realised result. *Thomas Carlyle*

A weak, diffusive, weltering, ineffectual man.
Thomas Carlyle

We cannot name one considerable poem of his that is likely to remain upon the thresh-floor of fame. We fear we shall seem to our children to have been pigmies, indeed, in intellect, since a man as Coleridge would appear great to us.
'London Weekly Review' (1828)

'Ancient Mariner' – A man who would not have taken so well if he had been called the 'Old Sailor'. *Samuel Butler*

He is the man of all others to swim on empty bladders in a sea without shores or soundings; to drive an empty stage-coach without passengers or lading, and arrive behind his time.
William Hazlitt – 'London Magazine' (1820)

Coleridge was a muddle-headed metaphysician who by some strange streak of fortune turned out a few poems amongst the dreary flood on inanity which was his wont.
William Morris (1894)

A huge pendulum attached to a small clock.
Ivan Panin

To tell the story of Coleridge without opium is to tell the story of Hamlet without the ghost.
Leslie Stephens

His misfortune was to appear at a time when there was a man's work to do – and he did it not. He had not sufficient strength of character, but professed doctrines which he had ceased to believe, in order to avoid the trouble of controversy. *John Sterling*

William Cowper - *(1731-1800)*
They say poets never or rarely go mad. Cowper and [William] Collins are instances to the contrary (but Cowper was no poet).
Lord Byron (1813)

George Crabbe - *(1754-1832)*
Mr Crabbe, it must be confessed, is a repulsive writer. He contrives to 'turn diseases into commodities', and makes a virtue of necessity. He puts us out of conceit with this world, which perhaps a severe divine should do; yet does not, as a charitable divine ought, point to another. His morbid feelings droop and cling to the earth, grovel where they should soar; and throw a dead weight on every aspiration of soul after the good or beautiful.
William Hazlitt - 'The Spirit of the Age'

His poems are a sort of funeral dirge over human life, but without pity, without hope. He has neither smiles, nor tears, for his readers.
William Hazlitt

E. E. Cummings - *(1894-1962)*
He replaces the old poetic conventions with equally limited conventions of his own.
Allen Tate

One imagines him giving off poems as spontaneously as perspiration and with as little application of the intellect. *Edmund Wilson*

Dante - *(1265-1321)*
A hyena that wrote poetry in tombs.
Friedrich Nietzsche

A Methodist parson in Bedlam. *Horace Walpole*

Samuel Derrick - *(1724-69)*
On comparing him to Christopher Smart - There is no setting the point of precedency between a louse and a flea. *Samuel Johnson*

Emily Dickinson - *(1830-86)*
An eccentric, dreamy, half-educated recluse in an out-of-the-way New England village (or anywhere else) cannot with impunity set at

defiance the laws of gravitation and grammar.
Thomas B. Aldrich

Of all great poets, she is the most lacking in taste; there are innumerable beautiful lines and passages wasted in the desert of her crudities; her defects, more than those of any other great poet I have read, are constantly at the brink, or pushing beyond the brink, of her best poems.
Yvor Winters - 'Maule's Curse'

John Donne - *(1573-1631)*
With Donne, whose muse on dromedary trots,.
  Wreathe iron pokers into true-love knots.
Samuel T. Coleridge

Of his earlier poems, many are very licentious; the later are chiefly devout. Few are good for much. *Henry Hallam -*
'The Literature of Europe' (1837)

Dr Donne's verses are like the Peace of God, for they pass all understanding. *King James I*

John Dryden - *(1631-1700)*
'The Spanish Friar' - This litter of epithets make the poem look like a bitch over-stocked with puppies, and sucks the sense almost to skin and bone. *Jeremy Collier (1698)*

His imagination resembles the wings of an ostrich. It enabled him to run, though not to soar. *Thomas Macaulay - 'Essays'*

  Read all the prefaces of Dryden,
For these our critics much confide in
(Tho' merely writ at first for filling
To raise the volume's price a shilling).
Jonathan Swift - 'On Poetry'

William Dunbar - *(1465-1530)*
Dunbar writes so scathingly of women that, when he treats them in complimentary vein, doubts have been cast upon his authorship.
J. W. Baxter - 'Dunbar'

T. S. Eliot - *(1888-1965)*
T. S. Eliot is quite at a loss
When clubwomen bustle across
At literary teas
Crying - 'What, if you please,
Did you mean by the Mill on the Floss?'
W. H. Auden

That awful boresome man? You can't be serious! Why he's so stoopid! He's such a bore, don't you know?   *Henry Isherwood*

Eliot fears to abandon an old masquerade;
Pound's one perfect happiness is to parade.
Eliot's learning was won at a very great price;
What Pound calls his learning he got in a trice.
Eliot knows what he knows, though he cannot
    digest it;
Pound knows nothing at all, but has frequently
    guessed it.
Eliot builds his essays by a process of massing;
Pound's are mostly hot air, what the vulgar call
    'gassing'.
Eliot lives like a snail in his shell, pen
    protruding;
Pound struts like a cock, self-adored, self-
    deluding.
                              Amy Lowell

'The Waste Land' – One can only say that if Mr Eliot had been pleased to write in demotic English 'The Waste Land' might not have been, as it is to all but anthropologists, and literati, so much waste-paper.
                    'Manchester Guardian' (1922)

'The Waste Land' – Mr Eliot has shown that he can at moments write real blank verse; but that is all. For the rest he has quoted a great deal, he has parodied and imitated. But the parodies are cheap and the imitations inferior.
                    'New Statesman' (1922)

He is very yellow and glum. Perfect manners. He looks like a sacerdotal lawyer – dyspeptic, ascetic, eclectic.
                    Harold Nicolson – 'Diary' (1932)

Mr Eliot is at times an excellent poet and has arrived at the supreme Eminence among English critics largely through disguising himself as a corpse.   *Ezra Pound*

A company of actors inside one suit, each twitting the others.   *V. S. Pritchett*

'Ara Vus Prec' – Mr Eliot does not convince us that his weariness is anything but a habit, an anti-romantic reaction, a new Byronism which he must throw off if he is not to become a recurring decimal in his fear of being a mere

vulgar fraction.
                    'Times Literary Supplement' (1920)

The cold douche of T. S. Eliot had not washed over the warm and previous velvet of those lawns, still less the outlandish flotsam of Ezra Pound.   *Laurence Whistler –*
                    'The Laughter & the Urn'

Ralph Waldo Emerson – *(1803–82)*
Like most poets, preachers and metaphysicians, he burst into conclusions at a spark of evidence.
                    Henry S. Canby – 'Classical Americans'

That everlasting rejector of all that is, and seeker for he knows not what.
                    Nathaniel Hawthorne

I could readily see in Emerson a gaping flaw. It was the insinuation that had he lived in those days when the world was made, he might have offered some valuable suggestions.
                    Herman Melville

One of the seven humbugs of Xtiandom.
                    William Morris

Emerson is one who lives instinctively on ambrosia – and leaves everything indigestible on his plate.   *Friedrich Nietzsche*

The best answer to his twaddle is cui bono? – a very little Latin phrase very generally mistranslated and misunderstood – cui bono? to whom is it a benefit? If not to Mr Emerson individually, then surely to no man.
                    Edgar Allan Poe – 'Autobiography' (1842)

Waldo is one of those people who would be enormously improved by death.
                    Saki – 'The Forest of Nemesis'

He was like a young god making experiments in creation. He botched the work and always began on a new and better plan.
                    George Santayana

A foul mouth is so ill-matched with a white beard that I would gladly believe the newspaper-scribes alone responsible for the bestial utterances which they declare to have dropped from a teacher whom such disciples as these exhibit to our disgust and compassion as performing on their obscene platform the last tricks of tongue now possible to a gap-toothed and hoary ape, carried at first notice on the shoulder of [Thomas] Carlyle, and who now in his dotage spits and chatters from a dirtier perch of his finding and fouling: coryphaeus or choragus of his Bulgarian tribe of auto-coprophagous baboons, who make the filth they feed on.   *A. G. Swinburne (1874)*

[*Swinburne later recalled his words, for the benefit of Edmund Gosse*] – I merely informed him, in language of the strictest reserve, that he was a hoary-headed and toothless baboon, who, first lifted into notice on the shoulder of Carlyle, now spits and splutters from a filthier platform of his own finding and fouling.

Elijah Fenton – *(1683–1730)*
Fenton's productions are more characterised by indecency than wit. He is said to have been a moral man. What must have been the morality of an age when a moral man could write such poems?   *Robert Southey – 'Specimens'*

Robert Frost – *(1874–1963)*
If it were thought that anything I wrote was influenced by Robert Frost I would take that particular piece of mine, shred it and flush it down the toilet, hoping not to clog the pipes.
                    James Dickey

Allen Ginsberg – *(b 1926)*
'Howl' – It is only fair to Allen Ginsberg to remark on the utter lack of decorum of any kind in his dreadful little volume. 'Howl' is meant to be a noun, but I can't help taking it as an imperative.
        John Hollander – 'Partisan Review' (1956)

Oliver Goldsmith – *(1728–74)*
Poor fellow! he hardly knew an ass from a mule, nor a turkey from a goose, but when he saw it on the table.   *Richard Cumberland*

Here lies Nolly Goldsmith, for shortness call'd Noll,
Who wrote like an angel, but talk'd like Poll.
                    David Garrick – 'Epitaph'

To Oliver Goldsmith, poet, physician and historian, who in the range of his writing scarcely left a style untouched, and touched

nothing that he did not adorn.   *Samuel Johnson*

The misfortune of Goldsmith in conversation is this: he goes on without knowing how he is to get off.   *Samuel Johnson*

It is amazing how little Goldsmith knows. He seldom comes where he is not more ignorant than anyone else.   *Samuel Johnson*

Goldsmith's mind was entirely unfurnished. When he was engaged in a work, he had all his knowledge to find, which when he found, he knew how to use, but forgot immediately after he had used it.   *Sir Joshua Reynolds*

Thomas Gray – *(1716–71)*
No man ever walked down to posterity with so small a book under his arm.   *Charles Dickens*

'Odes' – They are forced plants, raised in a hot-bed, and they are poor plants; they are but cucumbers after all.   *Samuel Johnson*

He was dull in company, dull in his closet, dull everywhere. He was dull in a new way, and that made many people think him GREAT. He was a mechanical poet.   *Samuel Johnson*

Thomas Gray walks as if he had fouled his small-clothes and looks as if he smelt it.
                    Christopher Smart

I do not profess to be a person of various reading; nevertheless, if I were to pluck out of Gray's tail all the feathers which I know belong to other birds, he would be left very bare indeed.   *William Wordsworth*

William Hayley – *(1746–1820)*
Behold – ye tarts! – one moment spare the text –
Hayley's last work, and worst – until his next.
                    Lord Byron

Robert Herrick – *(1591–1674)*
Of all our poets this man appears to have had the coarsest mind. Without being intentionally obscene, he is thoroughly filthy, and he has not the slightest sense of decency. In an old writer, and especially one of that age. I never saw so large a proportion of what may truly be called either trash or ordure.   *Robert Southey*

A. E. Housman – *(1859–1936)*
A prim, old-maidish, rather second-rate, rather
tired, rather querulous person.   *A. C. Benson*

Ted Hughes – *Poet Laureate (b 1930)*
Ted Hughes has been appointed Poet Laureate
to succeed Sir John Betjeman, which is a bit
like appointing a grim young crow to replace a
cuddly old teddy bear.
            Philip Howard – 'The Times' (1984)

Samuel Johnson – *(1709–84)*
'Lives of the English Poets' – Johnson wrote the
lives of the poets and left out the poets.
                Elizabeth Barrett Browning –
                'The Book of the Poets' (1842)

John Keats – *(1795–1821)*
A tadpole of the Lakes.
            Lord Byron – 'Journal' (1820)

Johnny Keats's piss-a-bed poetry.
            Lord Byron (1820)

That dirty little blackguard. *Lord Byron (1820)*

Such writing is a sort of mental masturbation –
he is always f**gging his imagination. I don't
mean he is indecent, but viciously soliciting his
own ideas into a state, which is neither poetry
nor anything else but a Bedlam vision produced
by raw pork and opium.   *Lord Byron (1820)*

'Isabella' – Almost any young gentleman with
such a sweet tooth might be expected to write
such things. Isabella might have been written
by a seamstress who had eaten something too
rich for supper and slept upon her back.
                    Jane Carlyle

Keats is a miserable creature; hungering after
sweets which he can't get.   *Thomas Carlyle*

'Endymion' – It is a better and wiser thing to be
a starved apothecary than a starved poet; so
back to the shop, Mr John, back to the 'plasters,
pills and ointment boxes,' etc. But for Heaven's
sake, young Sangrado, be a little more sparing
of extenuatives and soporifics in your practice
than you have been with your poetry.
                John Gibson Lockhart

Joyce Kilmer – *(1886–1918)*
'Trees' – One of the most annoying pieces of
verse within my knowledge. Surely the Kilmer
tongue must not have been very far from the
Kilmer cheek when she wrote, 'Poems are made
by fools like me.'   *Heywood Broun*

Carolyn Kizer – *(b 1925)*
'Midnight Was My Cry' – Like most poets, she
teaches, and like most teachers, she isn't very
good.   *'Esquire' (1971)*

Walter Savage Landor – *(1775–1864)*
Upon the work of Walter Landor
I am unfit to write with candor.
If you can read it, well and good;
But as for me, I never could.   *Dorothy Parker*

Sidney Lanier – *(1842–81)*
His language, too often over-wrought, was
sometimes silly or namby-pamby, with too
much of the mawkish adolescent in the quality
of the feeling and there were elements in his
writing too of the feverish exaltation of
tuberculosis.   *Van Wyck Brooks*

Never simple, never easy, never in one single
lyric natural and spontaneous for more than
one stanza, always concealing his barrenness
and tameness by grotesque violence to language
and preposterous storm of sound, Lanier
appears to me to be as conclusively not a poet
of genius as any ambitious man who ever lived,
laboured, and failed.   *Walt Whitman*

He is at once insipid and florid. He is noble, to
be sure, but his nobility is boring; his eloquence
comes to seem empty.   *Edmund Wilson*

Ligurinus
I don't know whether Phoebus fled from the
dinner table of Thyestes: at any rate, Ligurinus,
we fell from yours. Splendid, indeed, it is, and
magnificently supplied with good things, but
when you recite you spoil it. I don't want you
to set before me a turbot or a two-pound
mullet: I don't want your mushrooms or your
oysters. I want you to keep your mouth shut!
                        Martial

Henry W. Longfellow – *(1807–82)*
His didactics are all out of place. He has
written brilliant poems, by accident, that is to

say, when permitting his genius to get the better of his conventional habit of thinking, a habit deduced from German study.
Edgar Allan Poe

John Masefield – *(1878-1967)*
He's a horrible sentimentalist – the cheap Byron of the day.   *D. H. Lawrence (1913)*

Edna St Vincent Millay – *(1892-1950)*
The career of Edna Millay presented the still sadder spectacle of a poet who withered on the stalk before attaining fruition.
George F. Whicher

John Milton – *(1608-74)*
Our language sunk under him.   *Joseph Addison*

Read not Milton, for he is dry.   *C. S. Calverly*

'Paradise Lost' – Indeed, the whole of Milton's poem is such barbarous trash, so outrageously offensive to reason and to common sense that one is naturally led to wonder how it can have been tolerated by a people, amongst who astronomy, navigation, and chemistry are understood.   *William Cobbett*

'Paradise Lost' – So far as I perceive anything, it is a glimpse of theology that I find in large part repellent, expressed through a mythology which would have been better left in the Book of Genesis, upon which Milton has not improved.
J.S. Diekhoff

Many people will agree that a man may be a great artist, and yet be a bad influence. There is more of Milton's influence in the badness of the bad verse of the eighteenth century than of anybody else's; he certainly did more harm than Dryden and Pope. It was an influence against which we still have to struggle.
T. S. Eliot – 'Essays and Studies'

'Paradise Lost' – One of those books which the reader admires and lays down and forgets to take up again. Its perusal is a duty rather than a pleasure.   *Samuel Johnson*

Milton was a genius that could cut a Colossus from a rock; but he could not carve heads upon cherry-stones.   *Samuel Johnson*

Having never had any mental vision, he has now lost his bodily sight; a silly coxcomb, fancifying himself a beauty; an unclean beast, with nothing more human about him than his guttering eyelids; the fittest doom for him would be to hang him on the highest gallow, and set his head on the Tower of London.
Claudius Salmasius

'Paradise Lose' – If its length be not considered a merit, it hath no other.   *Edmund Waller*

His fame is gone out like a candle in a snuff and his memory will always stink.
William Winstanley – Diary' (1687)

Robert Montgomery – *(1807-55)*
Satan Montgomery.   *Caroline Bowles (1832)*

His writing bears the same relation to poetry which a Turkey carpet bears to a picture. There are colours in the Turkey carpet out of which a picture might be made. There are words in Mr Montgomery's writing which, when disposed in certain orders and combinations, have made, and will make again, good poetry. But, as they now stand, they seem to be put together on principle in such a manner as to give no image of anything 'in the heavens above, or in the earth beneath, or in the waters under the earth'.   *Thomas Macaulay – 'Essays' (1830)*

Thomas Moore – *(1779-1852)*
'LALLA ROOKH' –
Is a naughty book
By Tommy Moore,
Who has written four,
Each warmer
Than the former,
So the most recent
Is the least decent.   *Anon*

William Morris – *(1834-96)*
Of course, we all know that Morris was a wonderful all-round man, but the act of walking round him has always tired me.
Max Beerbohm

Wilfred Owen – *(1893-1918)*
A revered sandwich-board . . . He is all blood, dirt and sucked sugar stick.   *W. B. Yeats (1936)*

Ambrose Phillips - *(1674-1749)*
A good Whig and a middling poet.
Thomas Macaulay - 'Essays'

Alexander Pope - *(1688-1744)*
Let us take the initial and final letters of his
Surname, viz., A. P--E, and they give you the
Idea of an Ape. - Pope comes from the Latin
word Popa, which signifies a little wart; or from
Poppysma, because he was continually popping
out squibs of wit, or rather Po–pysmata, or Po–
piams. *John Dennis - 'Daily Journal' (1728)*

Who is this Pope that I hear so much about? I
cannot discover what is his merit. Why will not
my subjects write in prose? *King George II*

'Translations of Homer' - A portrait endowed
with every merit excepting that of likeness to
the original. *Edward Gibbon*

Europe has not as yet recovered from the
Renaissance nor has English poetry recovered
from Alexander Pope. *Oliver St J. Gogarty -*
'As I Was Going Down Sackville Street'

He hardly drank tea without a stratagem.
Samuel Johnson

His more ambitious works may be classified as
careless thinking carefully versified.
James R. Lowell

The verses, when they were written, resembled
nothing so much as spoonfuls of boiling oil,
ladled out by a fiendish monkey at an upstairs
window upon such of the passers-by whom the
wretch had a grudge against. *Lytton Strachey*

The sublime and the pathetic are the two chief
nerves of all genuine poetry. What is there
transcendently sublime or pathetic in Pope?
Joseph Warton

There are two ways of disliking poetry; one way
is to dislike it, the other is to read Pope.
Oscar Wilde

Ezra Pound - *(1885-1972)*
Mr Pound is humane, but not human.
e. e. cummings

To me Pound remains the exquisite showman

minus the show. *Ben Hecht - 'Pounding Ezra'*

An idiosyncracy on a monument.
Randall Jarrell

A genuine naif, a sort of revolutionary
simpleton. *Percy W. Lewis*

A village explainer, excellent if you were a
village, but if you were not, not. *Gertrude Stein*

I remember only one thing about Pound. He
had a beard, and it looked false.
'Times Literary Supplement'

The cold douche of T. S. Eliot had not washed
over the warm and precious velvet of those
lawns, still less the outlandish flotsam of Ezra
Pound. *Laurence Whistler -*
'The Laughter & the Urn'

Matthew Prior - *(1664-1721)*
His Muse is, in fact, a giddy wanton flirt, who
spends her time in playing snap-dragon and
blind man's buff, who tells what she should not,
and knows more than she tells. *William Hazlitt*

Most of his faults brought their excuse with
them. *Samuel Johnson*

Is not Prior the most indecent of story-tellers,
not even excepting la Fontaine; and how often
do we see his works in female hands!
Sir Walter Scott

James W. Riley - *(1849-1916)*
His pathos is bathos, his sentiment sediment,
his 'homely philosophy' brute platitudes -
beasts of the field of thought. *Ambrose Bierce*

The unctuous, over-cheerful, word-mouthing,
flabby-faced citizen, who condescendingly tells
Providence, in flowery and well-founded
periods, where to get off. *Hewitt Howland*

Lord Patrick [Peter] Robertson - *(1794-1855)*
Here lies the Christian, judge, and poet Peter,
Who broke the laws of God, and man, and
metre. *Sir Walter Scott*

Samuel Rogers - *(1763-1855)*
Your poetry is bad enough, so pray be sparing
of your prose. *Lady Holland*

Dante Rossetti – *(1828–82)*
Rossetti was a man without any principles at
all, who earnestly desired to find some means of
salvation along the lines of least resistance.
Ford Madox Ford

Rossetti, dear Rossetti – I love your work
But you were really a bit of a jerk.
George MacBeth

Jean B. Rousseau – *(1671–1741)*
'Ode to Posterity' – I do not think this poem will
reach its destination. *Voltaire*

Carl Sandburg – *(1878–1967)*
The Poet lariat of Chicago.
Richard Daley (1960)

Richard Savage –*(1697–1743)*
Hack, spendthrift, starveling, duellist in turn;
Too cross to cherish, yet too fierce to spurn;
Begrimed with ink or brave with wine or blood;
Spirit of fir and manikin of mud;
Now shining clear, now fain to starve and
skulk;
Star of the cellar, pensioner of the bulk;
At once the child of passion and the slave;
Brawling his way to an unhonoured grave –
That was DICK SAVAGE.
W. E. Henley

Friedrich von Schiller – *(1759–1805)*
Schiller's blank verse is bad. He moves in it as
a fly in a glue bottle. His thoughts have their
connections and variety, it is true, but there is
no sufficiently corresponding movement in the
verse. *Samuel T. Coleridge – 'Table-talk' (1834)*

Thomas Shadwell – *(1642–92)*
He never was a Poet of God's making;
The Midwife laid her hand on his Thick Skull,
With this Prophetick blessing – Be Thou Dull.
John Dryden

William Shakespeare – *(1564–1616)*
Never did any author precipitate himself from
such heights of thought to so low expressions,
as he often does. He is the very Janus of poets;
he wears, almost everywhere two faces: and you
have scarce begun to admire the one, e'er you
despise the other. *John Dryden*

'Sonnets' – Not a single one is very admirable.

They are hot and pothery; there is much
condensation, little delicacy; like raspberry jam
without cream, without crust, without bread.
Walter S. Landor

Percy B. Shelley – *(1792–1822)*
A beautiful and ineffectual angel, beating in the
void his luminous wings in vain.
Matthew Arnold – 'Essays'

Shelley is a poor creature, who has said or done
nothing worth a serious man being at trouble of
remembering. *Thomas Carlyle*

He always was, and is, a kind of ghastly object;
colourless, pallid, tuneless, without health or
warmth or vigour. *Thomas Carlyle*

Shelley I saw once. His voice was the most
obnoxious squeak I ever was tormented with.
Charles Lamb (1822)

'Prometheus Unbound' – His principles are
ludicrously wicked, and his poetry a melange of
nonsense, cockneyism, poverty and pedantry.
'Literary Gazette' (1819)

Shelley's mind was like a statue by Phidias that
had lost its head. *Robert Southey (1830)*

He was a liar and a cheat; he paid no regard to
truth, nor to any kind of moral obligation.
Robert Southey (1830)

Dame Edith Sitwell – *(1887–1964)*
I am fairly unrepentant about her poetry. I
really think that three quarters of it is
gibberish. However, I must crush down these
thoughts otherwise the dove of peace will shit
on me. *Noël Coward – 'Diary' (1962)*

She is genuinely bogus. *Christopher Hassall*

The Sitwells belong to the history of publicity
rather than of poetry. *F. R. Leavis*

Edith is a bad loser. When worsted in an
argument, she throws Queensberry Rules to the
winds. She once called me Percy.
Percy Wyndham Lewis –
'Blasting and Bombardering'

An evening at Arnold Bennet's house – Then Edith

Sitwell appeared, her nose longer than an anteater's, and read some of her absurd stuff.
Lytton Strachey (1921)

So you've been reviewing Edith Sitwell's latest piece of virgin dung, have you? Isn't she a poisonous thing of a woman, lying, concealing, flapping, plagiarising, misquoting, and being as clever a literary publicist as ever.
Dylan Thomas – 'Letter to Glyn Jones' (1934)

In full regalia, she looked like Lyndon B. Johnson dressed up like Elizabeth I.
'Time' (1965)

Edith wholly ignorant. She said that port was made with methylated spirit: she knew this for a fact because her charwoman told her.
Evelyn Waugh – 'Diary' (1930)

I am appreciatively indifferent to Edith Sitwell as I am to the quaint patterns of old chintzes, the designs of dinner plates, or the charm of nursery rhymes. *H. G. Wells – 'Experiments in Autobiography' (1934)*

Christopher Smart – *(1722-71)*
Comparing him to Samuel Derrick – There is no setting the point of precedency between a louse and a flea. *Samuel Johnson*

Robert Southey – *Poet Laureate (1774-1843)*
He had sung against all battles, and again
In their high praise and glory: he had call'd
Reviewing 'the ungentle craft' and then
Became as base a critic as ever crawled –
Fed, paid, and pamp'd by the very men
By whom his muse and morals had been maul'd
He had written much blank verse, and blanker prose,
And more of both than anybody knows.
Lord Byron

The living undertaker of epics. *William Hazlitt*

Beneath these poppies buried deep,
The bones of Bob the Bard lie hid;
Peace to his manes; and may he sleep
As soundly as his readers did! . . .
Death, weary of so dull a writer,
Put to his books a finis thus.
Oh! May the earth on him lie lighter

Than did his quartos upon us!
Thomas Moore – 'Epitaph'

Mr Southey wades through ponderous volumes of travels and old chronicles, from which he carefully selects all that is false, useless and absurd, as being essentially poetical; and when he has a common-place book full of monstrosities, strings them into an epic.
Thomas Peacock – 'Four Ages of Poetry'

His work will be read after Shakespeare and Milton are forgotton – and not until then.
Richard Porson

Stephen Spender – *(b 1909)*
'World Within World' – To see him fumbling with our rich and delicate language is to experience all the horror of seeing a Sevres vase in the hands of a chimpanzee.
Evelyn Waugh (1951)

Edmund Spenser – *(1552-99)*
'Faerie Queen' – Spenser maintains his place upon the shelves, among our English classics, but he is seldom seen on the table.
David Hume – 'The History of Great Britain' (1759)

'Faerie Queen' – The quotation of two or three lines of a stanza from Spenser's 'Faerie Queen' is probably as good an all-round silencer as anything. *Stephen Potter – 'Lifemanship' (1950)*

Gertrude Stein – *(1874-1946)*
There is a famous family named Stein –
There's Gert, and there's Epp, and there's Ein;
Gert's poems are bunk,
Epp's statues are junk,
And no one understands Ein. *Anon*

Reading Gertrude Stein at length is not unlike making one's way through an interminably and badly printed game-book. *Richard Bridgeman – 'Gertrude Stein in Pieces'*

While she believed that most writers failed to allow writing to express all that it could, in her own practice she scrupulously saw to it that writing expressed less than it would.
John M. Brinnan – 'The Third Rose' (1959)

The supreme egocentric of the most perfect

clique of egocentrics.   *Oscar Cargill*

Gertrude Stein was masterly in making nothing happen very slowly.
Clifton Fadiman - 'Puzzlements'

Editor's rejection (imitating her repetitive style) – I am only one, only one, only one. Only one being, one at the same time. Not two, not three, only one. Only one life to live, only sixty minutes in one hour. Only one pair of eyes. Only one brain. Only one being. Being only one, having only one pair of eyes, having only one time, having only one life, I cannot read your MS three or four times. Not even one time. Only one look, only one look is enough. Hardly one copy would sell here. Hardly one, hardly one.   *A. J. Fifield*

What an old covered wagon she is.
F. Scott Fitzgerald

It's a shame you never knew her before she went to pot. You know a funny thing, she never could write dialogue. It was terrible. She learned how to do it from me.
Ernest Hemingway – 'Green Hills of Africa' (1935)

Her prose-song is a cold, black suet-pudding. We can represent it as a cold suet roll of fabulously reptilian length. Cut it at any point, it is the same thing; the same heavy, sticky, opaque mass all through and along. It is mournful and monstrous, composed of dead and inanimate material.   *Percy W. Lewis*

Elias Stoeber - *(1719–78)*
Stoeber's mind, though that is no name to call it by, turns unswervingly to the false, the meaningless, the unmetrical, as the needle to the pole.   *A. E. Housman*

Algernon Swinburne - *(1837–1909)*
As to Swinburne's verses – they are 'florid impotence' to my taste, the minimum of thought and idea in the maximum of words and phraseology. Nothing said and nothing done with, left to stand alone and trust for its effect in its own worth.   *Robert Browning (1870)*

All that is worst in Mr Swinburne belongs to Baudelaire. The offensive choice of subject, the obtrusion of unnatural passion, the blasphemy, the wretched animals, are all taken intact out of the Fleures du Mal. Pitiful! that any sane man, least of all an English poet, should think this dunghill worthy of importance.
Robert Buchanan

I attempt to describe Mr Swinburne; and lo! the Bacchanal screams, the sterile Dolores sweats, serpents dance, men and women wrench, wriggle, and foam in an endless alliteration of heated and meaningless words.
Robert Buchanan

I have no wish to know anyone sitting in a sewer and adding to it.   *Thomas Carlyle*

He mastered his technique, which is a great deal, but he did not make it to the extent of being able to take liberties with it, which is everything.
T. S. Eliot - 'Reflections of Vers Libre'

A perfect leper, and a mere sodomite.
Ralph W. Emerson

He was certainly an odd, scarcely human figure.   *Richard le Gallienne*

'Poems and Ballads' – A mind all aflame with the feverish carnality of a schoolboy over the dirtiest passages in Lempriere.
John Morley - 'Saturday Review' (1866)

'Poems and Ballads' – Having Mr Swinburne's defence of his prurient poetics, 'Punch' hereby gives him his royal licence to change his name to what is evidently its true form – Swine-born.
'Punch' (1866)

Isn't he the damnedest simulacrum!
Walt Whitman

Alfred, Lord Tennyson - *Poet Laureate (1809–92)*
'Maud' – It has one vowel too many in the title, and it makes sense no matter which is deleted.
Anon

The real truth is that Tennyson, with all his temperament and artistic skill, is deficient in intellectual power; and no modern poet can make very much of his business unless he is pre-eminently strong in this.

Matthew Arnold (1860)

In youth he looked like a gypsy; in age like a dirty old monk; he had the finest ear, perhaps, of any English poet; he was also undoubtedly the stupidest; there was little about melancholia that he didn't know; there was little else that he did.

W. H. Auden

Let school-miss Alfred vent her chaste delight
On 'darling little rooms so warm and light';
Outbaying Wordsworth and out-glittering
Keats.

E. Bulwer-Lytton

We agreed that Blake was no good because he learned Italian at 60 in order to study Dante, and we knew Dante was no good because he was so fond of Virgil, and Virgil was no good because Tennyson ran him, and as for Tennyson – well, Tennyson goes without saying.

Samuel Butler

Tennyson is a beautiful half of a poet.

Ralph W. Emerson

'Idylls of the King' – You cannot read 'Idylls of the King' except in minute doses because of the sub-nauseating sissiness – there is no other convenient word – of the points of view of both Lord Tennyson and the characters that he projects . . . and because of the insupportable want of skill in the construction of sentences, the choice of words and the perpetual ampliation of images.

Ford Madox Ford – 'The March of Literature'

Should Heaven send me any son,
I hope he's not like Tennyson.
  I'd rather have him play a fiddle
Than rise and bow and speak an idyll.

Dorothy Parker

Brahms is just like Tennyson, an extraordinary musician with the brains of a third-rate village policeman.

G. B. Shaw

Tennyson . . . never produced a success that will bear reading after Poe's failures.

G.B. Shaw – 'Pen Portraits and Reviews'

Dylan Thomas – *(1914–53)*

His poems were strewn with wild, organic, telescoped images underneath which, perhaps, ran a submerged stream of poetic thought.

Robert Graves – 'The Long Weekend'

Henry D. Thoreau – *(1817–62)*

Behind a mask of self-exaltation Thoreau performed as before a mirror – and first of all for his own edification. He was a fragile Narcissus embodied in a homely New Englander.

Leon Edel

The nullifier of civilisation, who insisted on nibbling his asparagus at the wrong end.

Oliver Wendell Holmes Sr.

He was imperfect, unfinished, inartistic, he was worse than provincial – he was parochial.

Henry James (1879)

He seems to me to have been a man with so high a conceit of himself that he accepted without question, and insisted on our accepting, his defects and weaknesses of character as virtues and powers peculiar to himself.

James Lowell

Joan Ludwig Uhland – *(1787–1862)*

Uhland's poetry is like the famous war horse, Bayard; it possesses all possible virtues and only one fault – it is dead.

Heinrich Heine

Louis Untermeyer – *(1885–1977)*

Upon meeting the poet – And you're 'Required Reading'!

Anon college student

Virgil – *(70–19 BC)*

A crawling and disgusting parasite, a base scoundrel, and a pander to unnatural passion.

William Cobbett

Phillis Wheatley – *(1753–84)*

Beneath the dignity of criticism.

Thomas Jefferson

She sings like a canary in a cage, a bird that forgets its native melody and imitates only what it hears.

William Long

Walt Whitman – *(1819–92)*

'Leaves of Grass' – To call it poetry, in any

sense, would be mere abuse of language,
William Allingham (1857)

Incapable of true poetical originality, Whitman had the cleverness to invent a literary trick, and the shrewdness to stick to it.
Peter Bayne – 'Contemporary Review' (1875)

His lack of sense of poetic finesse, his failure to understand the business of a poet, is clearly astounding.
Francis F. Browne – 'The Dial' (1882)

He had the bad taste bred in bone of all missionaries and palmists, the sign-manual of a true quack. This bad taste is nothing more than the offensive intrusion of himself and his mission into the matter in hand.
John Jay Chapman

Mr Whitman's muse is at once indecent and ugly, lascivious and gawky, lubricious and coarse.   *Lafcadio Hearn (1881)*

This awful Whitman. This post-mortem poet. This poet with the private soul leaking out of him all the time. All his privacy leaking out in a sort of dribble, oozing into the universe.
D. H. Lawrence – 'Studies'

Whitman is as unacquainted with art, as a hog with mathematics.   *'The London Critic'*

'Leaves of Grass' – No, no, this kind of thing won't do. The good folks down below (I mean posterity) will have none of it.
James Lowell (1855)

He was a vagabond, a reprobate, and his poems contain outbursts of erotomania so artlessly shameless that their parallel in literature could hardly be found with the author's name attached.   *Max Nordau – 'Degeneration' (1895)*

Poe played on one key-bank of a church organ, Whittier on a meeting-house melodeon, Walt Whitman on a Salvation Army bass drum.
Austin O'Malley

Under the dirty clumsy paws of a harper whose plectrum is a muck-rake, any tune will become a chaos of dischords . . . Mr Whitman's Eve is a drunken apple-woman, indecently sprawling in

the slush and garbage of the gutter amid the rotten refuse of her overturned fruit-stall: but Mr Whitman's Venus is a Hottentot wench under the influence of catharides and adulterated rum.   *Algernon Swinburne*

John G. Whittier – *(1807–92)*
His technical methods were stereotyped. The simplest and most conventional ballad metres, the sentiments, phrases and rhymes of other poets served him to the last. He had no pride of artistry. When editors revised his manuscripts, Whittier accepted their changes without remark.   *Van Wyck Brooks*

A sort of minor saint in outmoded Quaker dress.   *Robert P. Warner*

Oscar Wilde – *(1854–1900)*
Of his poems not one has survived, for he was totally lacking in a poetic voice of his own; what he wrote was an imitation of a poetry-in-general.
W. H. Auden – 'Forewards and Afterwords'

He festooned the dung heap on which he had placed himself with sonnets as people grow honey-suckle around outdoor privies.
Quentin Crisp

John Wilmot, Earl of Rochester – *(1647–80)*
Mean in action, lewd in every limb,
Manners themselves are mischievous in him.
John Sheffield

Lord Rochester's poems have much more obscenity than wit, more wit than poetry, more poetry than politeness.   *Horace Walpole*

William Wordsworth – *(1770–1850)*
When Wordsworth tries to write according to his theories, the result is nearly always flat.
W. H. Auden

One finds also a kind of sincerity in his speech. But for prolixity, thinness, endless dilation, it excels all the other speeches I had heard from mortals. A genuine man, which is much, but also essentially a small genuine man.
Thomas Carlyle

I cannot help thinking that there is in Wordsworth's poems something of a spirit of

withdrawal and seclusion from, and even evasion of, the actual world . . . This gives to his writings, compared with those of Scott or Byron, an appearance of sterility and unreality.
A. H. Clough

A bell with a wooden tongue. *Ralph W. Emerson*

He has no fancy, no wit, no humour, little descriptive power, no dramatic power, great occasional elegance, with the continual rusticity and boldness of allusion: but he is sublime without the Muse's aid, pathetic in the contemplation of his own and man's nature.
William Hazlitt

This will never do. The case of Mr Wordsworth is manifestly hopeless; and we give him as altogether incurable and beyond the power of criticism. *Francis Jeffrey (1814)*

A modern Moses who sits on Pisgah with his back obstinately turned to that promised land, the Future; he is only fit for those old maid tabbies, the Muses. *Douglas Jerrold*

The surface of Wordsworth's mind, the poetry, has a good deal of staple about it, and will bear handling, but the inner, the conversational and private, has many coarse intractable dangling threads, fit only for the flocked equipage of grooms. *William S. Landor*

Dank, liber verses, stuft with lakeside sedges,
And propt with rotten stakes from rotten
     hedges. *William S. Landor*

He keeps one eye on a daffodil and the other on a canal-share. *William S. Landor*

Mr Wordsworth, a stupid man, with a decided gift for portraying nature in vignettes, never yet ruined anyone's morals, unless, perhaps, he has driven some susceptible persons to crime in a very fury of boredom.
Ezra Pound – 'Future' (1913)

In his youth, Wordsworth sympathised with the French Revolution, went to France, wrote good poetry and had a natural daughter. At this period, he was a 'bad' man. Then he became 'good', abandoned his daughter, adopted correct principles, and wrote bad poetry.
Bertrand Russell

What a beastly and pitiful wretch that Wordsworth is! I can compare him with no one but Simonides, that flatterer of the Sycillian tyrants. *Percy B. Shelley*

'*Immortality Ode*' – It is no more than moderately good. I put by its side the poems of Matthew Arnold and think what a delightfully loud splash the two would make if I dropped them into a river. *Dylan Thomas*

Wordsworth was a tea-time bore, the great Frost of literature, the verbose, the humourless, the platitudinary reporter of Nature in her dullest moods. Open him at any page; and there lies the English language not, as George Moore said of Pater in a glass coffin, but in a large, sultry, and unhygienic box.
Dylan Thomas (1933)

W. B. Yeats – *(1865–1939)*
I am too old for Yeats, just as I am too old to hear the cry of a bat. *G. W. Lyttleton (1955)*

Yevegeny Yevtushenko – *(b 1933)*
He is a ham actor, not a poet. *Allen Tate*

Edward Young – *(1683–1765)*
A sort of cross between sycophant and a psalmist.
George Eliot – 'Westminster Review' (1857)

FREE VERSE [VERS LIBRE]

I have read some free verse and wonder who set it free. *John Barrymore*

Writing free verse is like playing tennis with the net down. *Robert Frost (1935)*

Free verse is the triumph of mind over metre.
'Life'

Vers libre – a device for making poetry easier to read and harder to write. *H. L. Mencken (1916)*

It is said that free verse poets lack humour. It might also be said the too many of them lack poetry. *'New York Evening Post'*

The worst indictment against free verse is that it is not only free, but free and easy.
'New York Morning Telegraph'

DRAMATIC

THEATRE

Long experience has taught me that in England nobody goes to the theatre unless he or she has bronchitis. *James Agate*

The theatre is the devil's own territory. *Edward Allyn*

The theatre is an industry that doesn't have the common cold. It has cholera. *Emanuel Azenberg*

I don't see why people want new plays all the time. What would happen to concerts if people wanted new music all the time? *Clive Barnes*

There is something about seeing real people on a stage that makes a bad play more intimately, more personally offensive than any other art form. *Anatole Broyard - 'New York Times' (1976)*

A play is like a cigar. If it is a failure no amount of puffing will make it draw. It is is a success everybody wants a box. *Henry J. Bryan*

The modern theatre is a skin disease, a sinful disease of the cities. It must be swept away with a broom; it is unwholesome to love it. *Anton Chekhov (1888)*

'Don't put your daughter on the stage, Mrs Worthington.' *Noël Coward*

I don't like propaganda in the theatre unless it is disguised so brilliantly that the audience mistakes it for entertainment. *Noël Coward*

Why should anyone write for the theatre? The theatre is a necropolis of ideas. One goes there to mourn the loss of life, and to numb the backside. Occasionally we hear laughter, but only because an old man in the street has slipped on a banana peel. *Rosalyn Drexler*

A play should give you something to think about. When I see a play and understand it the first time, then I know it can't be much of a play. *T. S. Eliot - 'New York Post' (1963)*

The theatre is the aspirin of the middle-classes. *Wolcott Gibbs*

Watching my plays performed in London is like seeing them in translation. *Lillian Hellman*

Much of the contemporary English polite comedy writing suggests a highly polished and very smooth billiard table with all the necessary brightly polished cues, but without balls. *George J. Nathan (1940)*

The average modern play has three acts. Its contact with life generally ends with the first. *George J. Nathan*

Opening night is the night before the play is ready to open. *George J. Nathan*

Opening night - you will find a sizeable number of people with severe respiratory infections who have, it appears, defied their doctors, torn aside oxygen tents, evaded the floor nurses at various hospitals and courageously made their way to the theatre to enjoy the play. *Mike Nicholls - 'New York Times' (1977)*

What are the plays of today? They're either so chockful of intellect that they send you to sleep, or they reek of sentiment till you yearn for the smell of a cabbage. *Alfred Sutro*

Contemporary English drama is the measuring out of life in tepid teacups. *'Time' (1965)*

A good many inconveniences attend playgoing in any large city, but the greatest of them all is usually the play itself. *Kenneth Tynan - 'New York Herald Tribune' (1957)*

There is a total extinction of all taste; our authors are vulgar, illiberal; the theatre swarms with wretched translations, and ballad operas, and we have nothing new but improving abuse. *Horace Walpole*

DRAMATIC

CRITICISM

A dramatic critic is a person who gives a
theatre the best jeers of his life.   *Anon*

Those who have free seats at a play hiss first.
                                    Chinese Proverb

When a play is crashingly dull the critic has
only two resources. One is sleep, in justification
whereof I shall quote William Archer's dictum
that the first qualification for a dramatic critic
is the capacity to sleep while sitting bolt
upright.   *James Agate*

You cannot dispose of a play by saying it is
either rotten or not rotten. A piece of writing by
a playwright calls for a piece of writing by the
critic.   *James Agate – 'Ego 1' (1932)*

The Four Periods of a Dramatic Critic –
In the first he is boundless in confidence, crying
lo here and lo there, as world geniuses swim
into his ken.
In the second period he wearisomely reiterates
that there were great players before Alexander.
The third is the critic's mellow period in which,
finding nobody to hold up in his arms, he tires
of maintaining the standard and desists from
giving battle. He murmurs that today's
everything and everybody are magnoperative
and pre-eminent, and will somebody pass the
port, please!
In the fourth period . . . he is gaga, and then
only is that which he writes believed!
              James Agate – 'Sunday Times' (1933)

Only two rules of dramatic criticism matter.
One. Decide what the playwright was trying to
do, and pronounce how well he has done it.
Two. Determine whether the well-done thing
was worth doing at all.
                    James Agate – 'Ego 8' (1945)

Dramatic criticism has three functions. The
first is to let the world know what the previous
night's play has been about. There's no reason
why a report of this kind should not be written
by the same man who describes how in the
afternoon he saw a man knocked down in
Oxford Street trying to stop a runaway horse.
The second function is to tell the public
whether the new play is good, bad or

indifferent. This means that the critic must
know his job. That is if you hold with my
dictionary, which defines criticism as 'The art
of judging with knowledge and propriety of the
beauties and faults of art'. The third function is
to report the theatre in terms of the art of
writing.   *James Agate – 'Ego 9' (1946)*

[*J. B. Fagan, on being told that Agate was dozing,
during the first night of his 'The Improper Duchess'*
– Don't wake him. Agate's always very good
when he's asleep.]

Critics are forever discovering homosexual
references in my plays where they don't exist.
                              Edward Albee (1983)

If Attila the Hun were alive today, he'd be a
dramatic critic.   *Edward Albee*

One of the first and most important things for a
critic to learn is how to sleep undetected in the
theatre.   *William Archer*

A critic was a man with a wee foot-rule who
measured plays with it, and if it was five by
four it was a good play, and if it was no' five by
four it was no' a play.   *J.M. Barrie*

The fact is, though nobody has perceived it,
that a professional play-critic is a monstrosity –
a sow with five legs or a man with four thumbs.
Nature did not intend him, and that is why we
have to conceal our repulsion when he
confronts us.   *Clifford Bax*

I find that when I dislike what I see on the
stage that I can be vastly amusing, but when I
write about something I like, I find I am
appallingly dull.   *Max Beerbohm*

Critics should be searched for certain adjectives
at the door of the theatre. Irreverent, probing
and (above all) satirical. I would have all such
adjectives left with their coats in the foyer, only
to be redeemed when their notices are written.
                                 Alan Bennett

To many people dramatic criticism must be like
trying to tattoo soap bubbles.
                           James Mason Brown

On the critical reception for his play – 'Look

After Lulu' – If enough people told enough people to put their heads under trucks, I'm sure they would do. I wonder why no one has thought of that. *Noël Coward (1959)*

The day I shall begin to worry is when the critics declare, "This is Noël Coward's greatest play.' But I know they bloody well won't. *Noël Coward*

If the critics unanimously take exception to one particular scene it is advisable to move that scene to a more conspicuous place in the programme. *Noël Coward*

Five rules for dramatic critics –
a] Never take any notice whatever of the author of the play, or the play itself, unless it be a new one.
b] Indulge an acquaintance with every dramatic writer and with every actor.
c] Say it would have been infinitely more entertaining if a little had been added or a little had been taken away, a probability which few will dispute with you.
d] If you do not exactly understand how to conceal your evil opinion of men's writing or performances always say the direct contrary of what you think.
e] Never exceed six or seven lines, but be sure to notice by name the fashionable in the boxes.
Leigh Hunt – 'Critical Essays on the Performers of the London Theatre'

Reviewers must normally function as huff-and-puff artists blowing laggard theatre-goers stageward. *William Kerr (1975)*

The dramatic critic who is without prejudice is on the same plane with the general who does not believe in the taking of life.
George J. Nathan – 'Comedians All'

There are two kinds of dramatic critics – destructive and constructive. I am destructive. There are two kinds of gun – Krupp and pop.
George J. Nathan – 'The World in Falseface'

Five ways to spot a 'bad' play –
1. When, as the curtain goes up, you hear newsboys shouting, 'Extra! Extra!'
2. As soon as you hear the line, 'If a man kills a man, that's murder. Why isn't it then also murder if a man in uniform does the same thing? War is murder.'
3. Any mystery in which, at the very start, someone remarks that the nearest house is two miles away.
4. The moment anyone puts anything into a drawer with a furtive look.
5. Any translation from the Hungarian in which the heroine is called Countess Katinka. *George J. Nathan*

It is common knowledge that the leading newspapers employ as dramatic critics journalists who are excellent on a racecourse or a football field but who are hopelessly astray – or asleep – in the stalls of the Gaiety or the Abbey. *Lennox Robinson – 'A Young Man from the South'*

A drama critic is a man who leaves no turn unstoned. *G. B. Shaw*

Reviewing has one advantage over suicide; in suicide you take it out on yourself; in reviewing you take it out on other people. *G. B. Shaw*

The true critic is the man who becomes your personal enemy on the sole provocation of a bad performance, and will only be appeased by good performances.
G. B. Shaw – 'Music in London'

You don't expect me to know what to say about a play when I don't know who the author is, do you? If it's by a good author, it's a good play, naturally. That stands to reason.
G. B. Shaw – 'Fanny's First Play'

[*Eric Bentley disagreed with Shaw* – It is all very well to believe, as Shaw did, that all criticism is prejudiced, but, with Shaw's dramatic criticism, the prejudice is more important than anything else.]

The sheer complexity of writing a play always had dazzled me. In an effort to understand it, I became a critic.
Kenneth Tynan – 'New York Mirror' (1963)

A good drama critic is one who perceives what is happening in the theatre of his time. A great drama critic is one who perceives what is not happening. *Kenneth Tynan*

DRAMATIC

A year to write a play, a year before it's
produced, then those unassailable reviews,
claiming the right to be unfair. Two years of
work wiped out, two more years to wait.
Arnold Wesker – 'The Listener' (1983)

The critic leaves at curtain fall
To find, in starting to review it,
  He scarcely saw the play at all
  For watching his reaction to it.
E. B. White – 'Critic'

Ideal dramatic criticism is unqualified
appreciation. *Oscar Wilde*

After being mugged in Florida – Maybe they
weren't punks, but New York drama critics.
Tennessee Williams (1979)

Has anybody seen a dramatic critic in the
daytime? Of course not. They come out after
dark, up to no good.
P. G. Wodehouse – 'New York Mirror' (1955)

It is probably not necessary for a critic to be
insane to survive all those opening nights but I
assure you it helps. *Alexander Woollcott*

PLAYWRIGHTS

There are no dull subjects, only dull
playwrights. *Robert Anderson*

A dramatist is one who adapts plays from the
French. *Ambrose Bierce*

When a playwright tells you that the reviews of
his new show were 'mixed', he means they were
'good' and 'rotten'. *George S. Kaufman*

All playwrights should be dead for three
hundred years. *Joseph L. Mankiewicz*

To be able to write a play a man must be
sensitive, imaginative, naïve, gullible,
passionate: he must be something of an
imbecile, something of a poet, something of a
liar, something of a damn fool.
Robert E. Sherwood

A playwright is a lay preacher peddling the
ideas of his time in popular form.
August Strindberg

Show me a congenital eavesdropper with the
instincts of a Peeping Tom and I will show you
the makings of a dramatist.
Kenneth Tynan (1957)

By increasing the size of the keyhole, today's
playwrights are in danger of doing away with
the door. *Peter Ustinov –
'Christian Science Monitor' (1962)*

Playwrights are like men who have been dining
for a month in an Indian restaurant. After
eating curry night after night, they deny the
existence of asparagus. *Peter Ustinov – ibid*

PLAYWRIGHTS (BY NAME)

Anon
That poor man. He's completely unspoiled by
failure. *Noël Coward*

Go on writing plays, my boy. One of these days
a London producer will go into his office and
say to his secretary, 'Is there a play from Shaw
this morning?' and when she says 'No,' he will
say 'Well, then we'll have to start on the
rubbish.' And that's your chance, my boy.
G. B. Shaw

James M. Barrie – *(1860–1937)*
The cheerful clatter of Sir James Barrie's cans
as he went round with the milk of human
kindness. *Philip Guedella – 'Some Criticisms'*

Barrie struck twelve once – with Peter Pan – a
subtly unwholesome sweetmeat, like most of his
books. *Florence Becker Lennon*

Mr Barrie is a born storyteller; and sees no
further than his stories – conceives any
discrepancy between them and the world as a
shortcoming on the world's part, and is only too
happy to be able to rearrange matters in a
pleasanter way. *G.B. Shaw*

Francis Beaumont – *(1584–1616)*
The blossoms of Beaumont's imagination draw
no sustenance from the soil, but are cut and
slightly withered flowers stuck into sand.
T. S. Eliot

Samuel Beckett – *(b 1906)*
I suspect that Beckett is a confidence trick

perpetrated on the Twentieth century by a theatre-hating God. He remains the only playwright in my experience capable of making forty minutes seem like an eternity and the wrong kind of eternity at that.

Sheridan Morley - 'Punch' (1973)

In attempting to depict the boredom of human existence, he has run the very grave risk of thoroughly boring his reader.

'San Francisco Chronicle'

The suggestion that something larger is being said about the human predicament won't hold water any more than Beckett's incontinent heroes can. *'Spectator' (1959)*

Robert Bird - *(1806-54)*
He had so many irons in the fire that he was never able to forge any single one into a weapon with which to conquer his world. *Curtis Dahl*

Bertol Brecht - *(1898-1956)*
He has neither good manners nor elementary decency. He is like Dubedat in 'The Doctor's Dilemma' - a scoundrel but an artist.

Eric Bentley

I don't regard Brecht as a man of iron-grey purpose and intellect, I think he is a theatrical whore of the first quality. *Peter Hall*

Noël Coward - *(1899-1973)*
'Memoirs' - A triptych in which the presiding deities are Mother, England and Me.

Peter Ackroyd - 'The Times' (1986)

One can't read any of Noël Coward's plays now, they are written in the most topical and perishable way imaginable, the cream in them turns sour overnight. *Cyril Connolly (1937)*

Sir George Etherege - *(1635-91)*
    Grammar and Rules of Art, he knows 'em not,
Yet writ two Talking plays without one Plot.

John Wilmot

Euripides - *(c 500 BC)*
A cliché anthologist and maker of ragamuffin manikins. *Aristophanes*

George Feydeau - *(1862-1921)*
Without the right timing Feydeau falls flat on his farce. *Alexander Woollcott*

John Fletcher - *(1579-1625)*
Though he treated love in perfection, yet Honour, Ambition, Revenge, and generally all the stronger Passions, he either touch'd not, or not masterly. To conclude all; he was a Limb of Shakespeare. *John Dryden*

John Gay - *(1685-1732)*
Gay is a great eater. As the French Philosopher used to prove his existence by 'Cogito ergo sum', the greatest proof of Gay's existence is 'Edit, ergo est.' *William Congreve*

Robert Greene - *(1560-92)*
A rakehell: a makeshift: A scribbling foole:
    A famous Bayrd in Citty, and Schoole.
Now sicke as a dog: and ever Brainesick:
Where such a raving, and desperate Dick?

Gabriel Harvey

Lady Isabella Gregory - *(1852-1932)*
Now that the Abbey Players are world-renowned, I begin to realise that with such an audience and such actors an author is hardly needed. Good acting covers a multitude of defects. It explains the success of Lady Gregory's plays. *Oliver St J. Gogarty*

Henrik Ibsen - *(1828-1906)*
'Peer Gynt' - Written by a mad poet. One goes crazy oneself if reading this book.

Hans Christian Andersen (1870)

Henry A. Jones - *(1851-1929)*
The first rule for a playwright is not to write like Henry Arthur Jones. The second and third rules are the same. *Oscar Wilde*

Ben Jonson - *(1573-1673)*
He was not only a professed imitator of Horace, but a learned plagiary of all the others; you track him everywhere in their snow.

John Dryden - 'Essay of Dramatic Poesy'

I can't read Ben Jonson, especially his comedies. To me, he appears to move in a wide sea of glue. *Alfred, Lord Tennyson*

George S. Kaufman - *(1889–1961)*
He was like a dry cracker. Brittle.   *Edna Ferber*

Clare Booth Luce - *(b 1903)*
No woman of our time has gone further with
less mental equipment.   *Clifton Fadiman*

Alfred Lunt - *(1893–1977)*
He has his head in the clouds and his feet in the
box office.   *Noël Coward*

Maurice Maeterlinck - *(1862–1949)*
The joy of every parodist.   *G. B. Shaw*

Moliere [Jean Baptiste Poquelin] - *(1622–73)*
He should be burned at a stake as a foretaste of
the fires of Hell.   *Pierre Roulle*

Eugene O'Neill - *(1888–1953)*
Though he possesses the tragic vision, he
cannot claim the tragic tongue.
    John Mason Brown

Sir Arthur Pinero - *(1855–1934)*
His eyebrows look like the skins of some small
mammal just not large enough to be used as
mats.   *Max Beerbohm*

Thomas Shadwell - *(1642–92)*
The rest to some faint meaning make pretence,
But Shadwell never deviates into sense.
    John Dryden

William Shakespeare - *(1564–1616)*
Shakespeare's name, you may depend on it,
stands absurdly too high and will go down. He
had no invention as to stories, none whatever.
He took all his plots from old novels, and threw
their stories into a dramatic shape, at as little
expense of thought as you or I could turn his
plays back again into prose tales.
    Lord Byron (1814)

I have tried lately to read Shakespeare, and
found it so intolerably dull that it nauseated
me.   *Charles Darwin*

A sycophant, a flatterer, a breaker of marriage
vows, a whining and inconstant person.
    Elizabeth Forsyth

I cannot read him, he is a bombast fellow.
    King George II

The remarkable thing about Shakespeare is
that he really is very good, in spite of all the
people who say he is very good.   *Robert Graves*

Playing Shakespeare is very tiring. You never
get to sit down, unless you're a king.
    Josephine Hull – 'Time' (1953)

A quibble is to Shakespeare what luminous
vapours are to the traveller: he follows it at all
adventures; it is sure to lead him out of his way
and sure to engulf him in the mire.
    Samuel Johnson

Shakespeare never has six lines together
without a fault. Perhaps you may find seven,
but this does not refute my general assertion.
    Samuel Johnson (1769)

Shakespeare boasted that as a country school
master he had never blotted out a line. I wish
he'd blotted out a thousand.   *Samuel Johnson*

Shakespeare generally used to stiffen his style
with high words and metaphors for the
speeches of his Kings and great men. He
mistook it for a mark of greatness. This is
strongest in his early plays, but in his very
latest play, his *'Othello'*, what a forced language
has he put into the mouth of the Duke of
Venice!   *Alexander Pope*

Shakespeare is like a picture full of
anachronisms – geographical blunders,
forgetfulness of his plot, and even sometimes of
character.   *Sir Joshua Reynolds*

With the single exception of Homer, there is no
eminent writer, not even Sir Walter Scott,
whom I can despise so entirely as I despise
Shakespeare when I measure my mind against
his. The intensity of my impatience with him
occasionally reaches such a pitch, that it would
positively be a relief to me to dig him up and
throw stones at him.   *G. B. Shaw*

Even when Shakespeare, in his efforts to be a
social philosopher, does rise for an instant to
the level of a sixth-rate Kingsley, his solemn
self-complacency infuriates me.   *G. B. Shaw*

Shakespeare is to me one of the Towers of the Bastille, and down he must come.   *G. B. Shaw*

I think Shakespeare is shit. Absolute shit! He may have been a genius for his time, but I just can't relate to that stuff. 'Thee' and 'Thou' – the guy sounds like a faggot.   *Gene Simmons*

Crude, immoral, vulgar and senseless.
Leo Tolstoy

The undisputed fame enjoyed by Shakespeare as a writer, is like every other lie, a great evil.
Leo Tolstoy

Shakespeare is obscene, and, thank God, we are sufficiently advanced to have found out.
Frances Trollope

This enormous dunghill.   *Voltaire (1776)*

Shakespeare – what trash are his works in the gross.   *Edward Young*

Who knows if Shakespeare might not have thought less if he had read more? *Edward Young*

George Bernard Shaw – *(1856-1950)*
I really enjoy only his stage directions; the dialogue is vortical, and I find, fatiguing. It is like being harangued. He uses the English language like a truncheon.   *Max Beerbohm*

The first man to have cut a swathe through the theatre and left it strewn with virgins.
Frank Harris

Shaw's works make me admire the magnificent tolerance and broadmindedness of the English.
James Joyce

Shaw writes his plays for the ages, the ages between five and twelve.   *George J. Nathan*

He writes like a Pakistani who has learned English when he was twelve years old in order to become a chartered accountant.
John Osborne

Shaw is the most fraudulent, inept writer of Victorian melodrama ever to gull a timid critic or fool a dull public.   *John Osborne*

The absence of fine shades and atmosphere explains why repertory companies, in a hurry, so often choose a Shaw play. You have only to learn the lines, slam them across, and the piece comes to life.
J. B. Priestley – 'Thoughts in the Wilderness'

Sherard Blaw, the dramatist who had discovered himself, and who had given so ungrudgingly of his discovery to the world.
Saki [H. H. Munro]

Richard B. Sheridan – *(1751-1816)*
Every man has his element. Sheridan's is hot water.   *John Eldon*

Sherry is dull, naturally dull; but it must have taken him a great deal of pain to become what we now see him. Such an excess of stupidity is not in nature.   *Samuel Johnson*

His work is like burning a farthing candle at Dover, to shew light at Calais.   *Samuel Johnson*

Fox outlived his vices; those of Sheridan followed him to the tomb.
Sir Nathaniel Wraxall

John Synge– *(1871-1909)*
He was the only man I have ever known incapable of a political thought or of a humanitarian purpose.   *William Yeats*

Voltaire – *(1694-1778)*
The godless arch-scoundrel! Voltaire is dead – dead like a dog, like a beast.
Wolfgang A. Mozart (1778)

Oscar Wilde – *(1854-1900)*
From beginning to end Wilde performed his life and continued to do so even after fame had taken the plot out of his hands.   *W. H. Auden*

The sovereign of insufferables.
Ambrose Bierce (1882)

Paradox with him was only truth standing on its head to attract attention.
Richard le Gallienne

He was, on his plane, as insufferable as a Methodist is on his.   *H. L. Mencken*

Oscar Wilde's talent seems to me essentially rootless, something growing in a glass in a little water. *George Moore (1918)*

Oscar and George Bernard
  Cannot be reconciled.
When I'm Wilde about Shaw
I'm not Shaw about Wilde. *Freddie Oliver*

Too many of Wilde's paragraphs are perforations. *Arthur Ransome*

When Oscar came to join his God,
Not earth to earth, but sod to sod,
It was for sinners such as this
  Hell was created bottomless.
Algernon Swinburne

His manner had hardened to meet opposition and at times he allowed one to see an unpardonable insolence. His charm was acquired and systemised, a mask, which he wore only when it pleased him.
William B. Yeats

Tennessee Williams – *(1911–83)*
Mr Williams's problem is not a lack of talent. It is, perhaps, an ambiguity of aim; he seems to want to kick the world in the pants and yet be the world's sweetheart, to combine the glories of martyrdom with the comforts of success.
Eric Bentley – 'New Republic'

He sometimes ran a purple ribbon through his typewriter and gushed where he should have damned. *T. E. Kalem – 'Time' (1983)*

If a swamp alligator could talk, it would sound like Tennessee Williams. *Rex Reed (1972)*

William Wycherley – *(1640–1716)*
He appears to have led, during a long course of years, that most wretched life, the life of a vicious old boy about town.
Thomas Macaulay – 'Essays'

In truth, Wycherley's indecency is protected against the critics as a skunk is protected against the hunters. It is safe because it is too filthy to handle, and too noisome even to approach. *Thomas Macaulay – ibid*

DIRECTORS AND PRODUCERS

A theatre director is a person engaged by the management to conceal the fact that the players cannot act. *James Agate – 'Sunday Times'*

There are two kinds of directors in the theatre. Those who think they are God and those who are certain of it. *Rhetta Hughes*

An actor-manager is one to whom the part is greater than the whole. *Ronald Jeans*

The theatre got along very nicely without directors for approximately two thousand and thirty-five years. *Walter Kerr*

DIRECTORS AND PRODUCERS (BY NAME)

H. Greville Barker – *(1877–1946)*
Oh, G. B., you are a very clever and interesting youth of 30; but you are an atrocious manager. You don't know where to put your high light and where to put your smudge. *G. B. Shaw*

Peter Hall – *Director of the National Theatre, London (b 1930)*
Graffiti on the walls of the National Theatre – The trouble with God is he thinks he's Peter Hall.

Jed Harris – *(1906–76)*
When I die, I want to be cremated and have my ashes thrown in Jed Harris's face.
George S. Kaufman

Lynn Loesser
On the theatrical couple, Lynn and her lyricist husband, Frank –
Lynn is the evil of two Loessers. *Harry Kurnitz*

David Merrick – *(b 1911)*
He displayed a sneaky knack for extending the life of a production beyond the reasonable expectations of the playwright's mother.
Walter Kerr

If there is any serious doubt that David Merrick is one of the greatest showmen in Broadway history, it can be dispelled by the fact that his flops are as fabled as his hits.
Frank Rich – 'New York Times' (1990)

REVIEWS (Listed by reviewer)

Anon

'Anon' – A vast improvement can be made in the third act. Instead of the hero dying on the scaffold he should be shot by a firing squad. It would not only wake up the audience but it would let them know the show is over.

'Dreadful Night' – Sure is.

'A Good Time' (1900) – No!

G. B. Shaw's *'Mrs Warren's Profession' (1905)* – Smells to high high heaven. It is a dramatised stench.

George S. Kaufman's 'The Solid Gold Cadillac' opening night in Washington D.C. (1953) – Drag this tin Lizzie out of town.

Noël Coward's 'Vortex' (1924) – A dustbin of a play.

James Agate

J. M. Barrie's 'Peter Pan' – The ideal audience for this would be a house composed entirely of married couples who never had any children, or parents who have lost them all. *'Ego 3' (1937)*

On hearing the line – 'Methinks you did wrong to come' – Methought this was addressed to me. Me took the hint.

William Archer

G. B. Shaw's *'Arms and the Man' (1894)* – Shaw may one day write a serious and even artistic play, if he will only repress his irreverent whimsicality, try to clothe his character conceptions in flesh and blood, and realise the difference between knowingness and knowledge. *'World'*

G. B. Shaw's *'Major Barbara' (1905)* – There are no human beings in Major Barbara; only animated points of view. *'World'*

Brooks Atkinson

Anon play – The play opened last night. Why?

Anon play – Beautiful, if you are deaf and dumb.

'Halfway to Hell' (1934) – When Mr Wilbur calls his play 'Halfway to Hell' he underestimates the distance.

Tallulah Bankhead

Aside whispered to Alex Woollcott during a revival of Maurice Maeterlinck's 'Algavine and Selysette' – There is less in this than meets the eye.

W. Somerset Maugham's 'The Constant Wife' (1975) – Dialogue more tame than Wilde.
'New York Times'

Max Beerbohm

William Shakespeare's 'Henry V' (1900) – Speech after speech was sent spinning across the boundary, and one was constantly inclined to shout, 'Well played, sir! Well played, sir!' As a branch of university cricket, the whole performance was, indeed, beyond praise. But, as a form of acting, it was not impressive. Not one of the parts was played with any distinction.

William Shakespeare's 'As You Like It' (1907) – Perhaps if the players weren't munching apples quote so assiduously the verse and the prose would stand a better chance.

William Shakespeare's 'Macbeth' – To mankind in general, Macbeth and Lady Macbeth stand out as the supreme type of all that a host and hostess should not be.

Brendan Behan

'Anon' – The play's impact was like the banging together of two damp dish-cloths.

Robert Benchley

'Perfectly Scandalous' – One of those plays in which all of the actors unfortunately enunciated very clearly.

'Abie's Irish Rose' –

1. People laugh at this every night, which explains why democracy can never be a success.
2. Where do people come from who keep this going? You don't see them out in the daytime.
3. In another two or three years, we'll have this play driven out of town.
4. And that, my dears, is how I came to marry your grandfather.
5. Don't ask.

6. See 'Hebrews 13:8'.
   [Jesus Christ, the same yesterday, and
   today, and forever.]

'Bet Your Life' (1937) – There must have been a
play called Bet Your Life which opened last
week, for I have it on my list. However, as I
can't find it anywhere in the advertisements
and nobody seems to know anything about it
now, we might as well let the whole thing drop.
'New Yorker'

'Bitter Oleander' (1937) – Designed by Cleon
Throckmorton from sketches by Santiago
Ontanon of an old Spanish intestinal tract.

Arnold Bennett
G. B. Shaw's 'The Academy' (1901) – One might
still be hopeful for Mr Shaw's future as a
dramatist, despite his present incompetence, if
there were any hint in his plays of creative
power. But there is no such hint.

Katherine Brisbane
William Shakespeare's 'Othello' (1967) – My
companion had a point when, listening to one
of the bursts of noise off stage from time to
time, she remarked that there was obviously a
better play going on back there.   *'Australian'*

Heywood C. Broun
'Anon' – It opened at 8.40 sharp and closed at
10.40 dull.

'Abie's Irish Rose' – So cheap and offensive that
it might serve to unite all the races of the world
in a common hymn of hate.

John Mason Brown
William Shakespeare's 'Julius Caesar' – Brutus
seems no more than a resounding set of vocal
chords wrapped up in a toga.

Robert Brustein
Arthur Miller's 'After the Fall' – A three-and-a-
half-hour breach of taste . . . wanton invasion
of privacy . . . shameless piece of tabloid gossip,
an act of exhibitionism, which makes us all
voyeurs . . . wretched, shapeless and tedious.

Donald Bryden
John Webster's 'Duchess of Malfi' (1971) – I
suppose you could define a pessimist as a man
who thinks John Webster's *'Duchess of Malfi'* a
great play; an optimist as one who believes it
actable.   *'The Observer'*

Mrs Patrick Campbell
*To Noël Coward, on the first night of his 'The
Vortex' (1924)* – Your characters all talk like
typewriters, and you yourself talk like a
telegram.

John Chapman
'Last Stop' – It is enough to make your flesh
crawl – right out of Ethel Barrymore Theatre.
'New York Daily News'

'Who's Afraid of Virginia Woolf?' (1962) – It is
three and a half hours long, four characters
wide, and a cesspool deep.
'New York Daily News'

William Collier
Anon play – The play was a success, but the
audience was a failure.

Gary Cooper
Arthur Miller's 'Death of a Salesman' – Sure there
are fellows like Willie Loman, but you don't
have to write plays about them.

Richard Corliss
'Tom and Viv' (1985) – Mausoleum air and
anguished pauses; if this production were a
poem, it would mostly be white space.

Noël Coward
Anon play with a child actor – Two things should
be cut: the second act and the child's throat.

*On the New York production of his 'This Was A
Man' (1926)* – If the writing of *'This Was A
Man'* was slow, the production by Basil Dean
was practically stationary. The second act
dinner scene between Francine Larrimore and
Nigel Bruce made *'Parsifal'* in its entirety seem
like a quick-fire vaudeville sketch.

Samuel Beckett's 'Waiting for Godot' (1960) – It is
pretentious gibberish, without any claim to
importance whatsoever. It is nothing but
phoney surrealism with occasional references to
Christ and mankind. It has no form, no basic
philosophy and absolutely no lucidity. It's too
conscious to be written off as mad. It's just a

waste of everybody's time and it made me
ashamed to think that such balls could be taken
seriously for a moment.

*On the male nude scenes in David Storey's 'The
Changing Room' (1972)* – I didn't pay three
pounds fifty just to see half a dozen acorns and
a chipolata.

Cheryl Crawford
Arthur Miller's 'Death of a Salesman' (1948) –
Who would want to see a play about an
unhappy travelling salesman? Too depressing.

Kyle Crichton
Adaptation of Henry Fielding's 'Tom Jones' – Good
Fielding. No Hit.

'Daily Mirror'
'The Force of Habit' – It is said that the quickest
way to empty a theatre is to yell 'Fire!' Another
method, slightly slower, is to put on the current
National Theatre production of 'The Force of
Habit'.

'Daily Telegraph'
Henrik Ibsen's 'Ghosts' – The play performed last
night is 'simple' enough in plan and purpose,
but simple only in the sense of an open drain;
of a loathsome sore unbandaged; of a dirty act
done publicly.

W. A. Darlington
*Tom Stoppard's 'Rosencrantz and Guilderstein are
dead' (1967)* – It is the kind of play that one
might enjoy more at a second hearing, if only
the first time through hadn't left such a strong
feeling that once is enough.   *'Daily Telegraph'*

Alan Dent
J. B. Priestley's 'An Inspector Calls' – The week
after – as well as the morning after – I take it to
be nothing but a finely acted piece of
flapdoodle.   *'News Chronicle' (1946)*

Richard Findlater
Lillian Hellman's 'Toys in the Attic' (1960) – It is
curious how incest, impotence, nymphomania,
religious mania and real estate speculation can
be so dull.   *'Time and Tide'*

Robert Garland
Clifford Odets' 'Clash by Night' – Odets, where is
thy sting?

Anton Chekov's 'Uncle Vanya' (1949) – If you
were to ask me that *'Uncle Vanya'* is about, I
would say about as much as I can take.
     'Journal American'

'Victory Belles' – Must be seen to be depreciated.

Wolcott Gibbs
'Anon' – The plot of this play was intended to
be in a light vein, but the vein became varicose.

'Anon' – This is a fine sample of what happens
when somebody just goes out of his way to
write a play.

Gilbert W. Gabriel
'The World' – More like a Henderson Seed Co.
catalogue than an honest-to-living drama.

'De Luxe' – An ornamentally dull play about a
lot of dull people.

Brendan Gill
Eugene O'Neill's 'The Iceman Cometh' (1985) –
Of plays by authors with high reputations and
of the most serious dramaturgic intentions, this
is the most boring play ever written.

Edmund Gosse
Anon Algernon Swinburne play – We were as
nearly bored as enthusiasm would permit.

Lionel Hale
Lady Longford's 'Anything But the Truth' (1937) –
a 'tale' of Irish homosexuality – Marks the
beginning of the Sodom-and-Begorra School.

Don Herold
'Uncle Tom's Cabin' – There were fifty in the
cast and ten real bloodhounds. The dogs were
poorly supported by the rest of the cast.

Harold Hobson
Lillian Hellman's 'Toys in the Attic' (1960) –
Lillian Hellman has chosen to write on a
Tennessee Williams theme in an Agatha
Christie style.   *'Sunday Times'*

Irving Hoffman
'Mrs January and Mr Ex' – We're sorry, but it's
not our cup of tee-hee.

DRAMATIC

Anthony Hope
J. M. Barrie's 'Peter Pan' – Oh, for an hour of
Herod!

Phillip Hope-Wallace
John Osborne's 'Inadmissible Evidence' (1964) –
Before the end a feeling obtrudes that a
bulldozer is being used where a trowel would
have done.   *'The Guardian'*

Stanley Kauffman
*American Conservatory Theater's 'The Taming of
the Shrew' (1973)* – If a director doesn't really
want to do the Shrew, this is a pretty good way
not to do it.

George S. Kaufman
Anon play – I don't like the play, but then I saw
it under adverse conditions – the curtain was
up.

Anon play – There was scattered laughter in the
rear of the theatre, leading to the belief that
somebody was telling jokes back there.

'Someone in the House' (1918)
Beware of flu
Avoid crowds
See 'Someone in the House'
[*Kaufman referred to his own play, whose audiences
had been hit by a flu epidemic that had swept New
York. The play also caught a cold.*]

To Howard Dietz on his 'Between the Sheets' – I
understand your new play is full of single
entendre.

Walter Kerr
'Hook and Ladder' – It's the sort of play that
gives failure a bad name.

'I am a Camera' (1951) – Me no Leica.

'The Seventh Trumpet' – 'The Seventh Trumpet'
opened last night on Broadway and blew its last
blast.

Dane and Addinsell's 'Come of Age' – The
authors did explain that they had written the
play in doggerel as being the most suitable
verse form for our time. Our time may not be a
happy one, but I am still not convinced that it
deserves a play written on the artistic level of
the Burma-Shave ads.

'Illya Darling' (1967) – I think they've made a
mistake. They've left the show in Detroit, or
wherever it was last warming up, and brought
in the publicity stills.

Jeremy Kingston
Edward Bond's 'Saved' (1965) – The production
is painstaking, the writing often powerful, the
acting meticulously naturalistic. Barbara Ferris
gave a frighteningly exact performance as the
girl and I don't want to see the play again.
                                              'Punch'

John David Klein
'Three Guys Naked from the Waist Down' (1985) –
I saw this show under adverse circumstances –
my seat was facing the stage.

Steward Klein
'Break a Leg' (1979) – I have seen stronger plots
in a cemetery.

Mimi Kramer
Arthur Miller's 'Death of a Salesman' – She saw
'Death of a Salesman' from the balcony. From
the evidence of her essay, it was close enough.
                                      Helen Dudar (1984)

Herbert Kretzmer
Harold Pinter's 'The Homecoming' (1965) – We
have all come to recognise these Pintermimes a
mile off – with these long, unblinking pauses,
the aura of something horrific behind the
humdrum action, the sense of suppressed
violence beneath the banal utterance.
                                         'Daily Express'

Harold Pinter's 'Betrayal' (1978) – A woman's
magazine romance that goes backwards until it
disappears up its own pauses.   *'Daily Express'*

Charles Lamb
William Shakespeare's 'Hamlet' (1811) – I confess
myself utterly unable to appreciate that
celebrated soliloquoy in 'Hamlet', beginning 'To
be or not to be,' and tell whether it be good, bad
or indifferent, it has been handled and pawed
about by declamatory boys and men, and torn
so inhumanly from its living place and principle
of continuity in the play, till it has become to
me a perfect dead number.

D. H. Lawrence
G. B. Shaw's 'The Intelligent Woman's Guide'

(1928) – I'm afraid *'The Intelligent Woman's Guide'*. I shall have to leave to the intelligent woman: it is too boring for the intelligent man, if I'm any sample. Too much gas-bag.

Bernard Levin
'The World of Suzie Wong' *(1959)* – . . . a lot of Chinese junk . . . In wise old Lee Vin's opinion, if you want more of China than wide sleeves and more of a play than romantic twaddle, to pay it a visit would be to enter the world of choosy wrong.   *'Daily Express'*

'The Amorous Prawn' *(1959)* – I think *'The Amorous Prawn'* is perhaps the most grisly, glassy-eyed thing I haveencountered in the theatre for a very long time, and even outside the theatre its like is rarely met except on a fishmonger's slab, and now I feel very ill indeed, and would like to lie down. Before doing so I should say that *'The Amorous Prawn'* is a farce made out of cobwebs and mothballs, my old socks, empty beer bottles, copies of the *'Strand Magazine'*, dust, holes, mildew, and Mr Ben Travers's discarded typewriter ribbons . . . And now I really must go and lie down and hope I shall feel better in the morning.

Marotti's 'Out of This World' *(1960)* – Strictly speaking, I cannot swear that being kicked in the stomach by a horse would be an experience preferable to seeing this play by Signor Guiseppe Marotti because I have never been kicked in the stomach by a horse.

But I have seen this play, and I can certainly say that if a kick in the stomach by a horse would be worse, I do not wish to be kicked in the stomach by a horse.

And I can certainly add that, unpleasant though the prospect of being kicked in the stomach by a horse may be, I would certainly rather be kicked in the stomach by a horse than see the play again.   *'Daily Express'*

'The Gazebo' *(1960)* – A placebo . . . is a pill which looks impressive but is, in fact, quite inefficacious. It is given by doctors to hypochondriacs, who need nothing more than reassurance. Its etymology is from the Latin; placebo means 'I will please.' *'The Gazebo'* is a placebo and it doesn't.   *'Daily Express'*

Eugene O'Neill's 'Mourning Becomes Electra' *(1961)* – *'Mourning Becomes Electra'* is hollow.   *'Daily Express'*

'Dazzling Prospect' *(1961)* – The pitiful little thing has to do with horse-racing, and you might perhaps say that it is by Imbecility out of Staggering Incompetence.   *'Daily Express'*

William Shakespeare's 'Richard III' *(1962)* – There is a learned man at present trying to discover whether dolphins can talk. When he has finished this study, he might consider investigating whether producers can think. On the evidence of this disastrous production by Mr Colin George, it seems unlikely.   *'Daily Express'*

Camoletti's 'Boeing Boeing' – I think I'll go by boat.   *'Daily Express' (1963)*

'Sons of Light' *(1973)* – The play is certainly obscure enough to satisfy the most tenacious holder of the belief that being bored in the theatre is good for you.   *'Daily Express'*

Donald Malcolm
'Little Mary Sunshine' *(1959)* – A genuine delight to those amiable qualities that thrive best when the critical senses are out to lunch.   *'New Yorker'*

'Manchester Guardian'
Harold Pinter's 'The Birthday Party' *(1958)* – If the author can forget Beckett, Ionesco and Simpson he may do much better next time.

Lady Mansfield
G. B. Shaw's 'The Devil's Disciple' – Why on earth did such a good play have to be written by Bernard Shaw?

Harpo Marx
'Abie's Irish Rose' – No worse than a bad cold.

Tom Masson
William Shakespeare's 'Hamlet' – The tragedy of tackling a family problem too soon after college.

Sheridan Morley
Samuel Beckett's 'Not I' *(1973)* – A seventeen-minute speech of mind-bending inconsequence unless you happen to have a morbid interest in

amateur psychiatry. *'Punch'*

'Mistress of Novices' (1973) – The hills are alive with the sound of clichés; *'Mistress of Novices'* by John Kerr is one of those truly bad plays that, if seen in sufficient quantity, drive dramatic critics to drink. *'Punch'*

Goldoni's *'Il Campiello' (1976)* – There is a number of possible explanations for the presence of *'Il Campiello'* in the repertoire of the National Theatre at the Olivier. The one I like best is that it represents a complete and never-to-be-repeated mental, physical and theatrical breakdown on the part of all concerned. *'Punch'*

George Jean Nathan
'The Flashing Stream' (1938) – Margaret Rawlings, ordinarily an actress of distinction, further succumbed to the fault of confusing intonation with lyricism, in which confusion Godfrey Tearle handsomely backed her up with the inference that he must have had a Wurlitzer for dinner.

'The Cat Screams' (1942) – The majority of mystery plays, with their disappointing last-minute solutions, are like sitting nervously around for two hours waiting for a telephone call from one's best girl and then at long length suddenly hearing the bell ring, jumping up eagerly to answer it, and finding that it is her mother. This was no exception.

Stanley Young's *'Ask My Friend Sandy' (1943)* – It is alleged that one of the most deplorable aspects of contemporary play-reviewing is its habit of either condemning a presentation outright and with no modifications or eulogising it to the skies, also with no modifications. Something, in short, is either totally excellent or totally awful. By way of giving further support to the allegation, which hasn't much basis in fact, let me say, with no reservations whatever, that this farce-comedy of Mr Young's is totally awful.

William Shakespeare's *'Richard III' (1943)* – To the multiplicity of the play's murders, Mr Coulouris and his company added another: that of the play itself. Under the species of acting which they visited upon it, Shakespeare's tragedy was for the most part transformed into

something vaguely resembling *'Dr Jekyll and Mr Hyde'*, without Mr Hyde.

'Tonight or Never' – Very well then: I say Never.

'The Righteous are Bold' – A cheap, marked-down bargain basement type of a play.

T. S. Eliot's *'The Cocktail Party'* – Bosh sprinkled with mystic cologne.

'Newsweek'
Edward Albee's *'Counting the Ways' (1977)* – The play sounds like George Burns and Gracie Allen trying to keep up a dinner conversation with Wittgenstein. I have never seen such desperately ingratiating smiles on the faces of actors.

'New Yorker'
Neil Simon's *'Biloxi Blues' (1985)* – A comedy that verges on autohagiography, the hero being the author.

Benedict Nightingale
Edward Albee's *'Counting the Ways' (1976)* – It lasts one hour only, but that hour left me feeling I had spent an evening fidgeting in an expensive and pretentious restaurant while a peculiarly snooty waiter insisted on serving me, with impeccable sloth, elaborate objects that turned out to be British Rail buns in disguise.

William Inge's *'Come Back, Little Sheba' (1984)* – Inge handles symbolism rather like an Olympic weight-lifter, raising it with agonising care, brandishing it with a tiny grunt of triumph, then dropping it with a clang.
'New York Times'

Dorothy Parker
Leo Tolstoy's *'Redemption' (1918)* – It isn't what you might call sunny. I went into the Plymouth Theatre a comparatively young woman and I staggered out of it three hours later, twenty years older, haggard and broken with suffering.
'Vanity Fair'

'The Admirable Crichton' (1931) – The all-star cast, as is the manner of all-star casts, held hams' holiday, and did every line, every bit of business, for all it was worth and just that little touch more. I have happily for me, never seen

upon one stage so many discourteous, patronising and exaggerated performances. [*As she had been filling in for the absent Robert Benchley she added a PS* – Robert Benchley, please come home. A joke's a joke.] *'New Yorker'*

'The Barretts of Wimpole Street' (1931) – Now that you've got me right down to it, the only thing I didn't like about *'The Barretts of Wimpole Street'* was the play.   *'The New Yorker'*

'The House Beautiful' – 'The House Beautiful' is play lousy.   *'Life'*

'The Greeks Had a Word for It' – So did the Hebrews – lousy.

Samuel Pepys

William Shakespeare's 'A Midsummer Night's Dream' – It is the most insipid, ridiculous play that ever I saw in my life.   *'Diary'*

First performance of Shakespeare's 'Romeo and Juliet' (1662) – It is a play of itself the worst that ever I heard in my life, and worst acted that ever I saw these people do.   *'Diary'*

Norman Phelps

Michael Langham's production of 'A Midsummer Night's Dream' (1960) – Michael Langham could not make his mind up apparently, whether this was a funny play or an office party.   *'Daily Post'*

'Punch'

William Shakespeare's 'King Lear' (1951) – The Old Vic's *'King Lear'* is not helped by a set which suggests a corner of a geological museum, occasionally cut off by a slide of old portcullises, like a feudal trap for heffalumps.

Frank Rich – *'The Butcher of Broadway'*
'La Cage au Follies' (1983) – As synthetic and padded as the transvestite's cleavage.
'New York Times'

Lee Breur's 'Gospel at Colonus' (1988) – A superficial Ivy League bull-session. *'New York Times'*

Eleanor Roosevelt

On a play about her family, 'Sunrise at Campobello' (1958) – It had no more to do with me than the man in the moon.

Bertrand Russell

G. B. Shaw's 'Man and Superman' (1904) – I think Shaw, on the whole, is more bounder than genius; and though, of course, I admit him to be 'forcible', I don't admit him to be 'moral' . . . I couldn't get on with *'Man and Superman'*: it disgusted me.

Clement Scott

Henrik Ibsen's 'A Doll's House' (1889) – It was as though someone had dramatised the cooking of a Sunday dinner.   *'Sporting and Dramatic News'*

Henrik Ibsen's 'The Wild Duck' (1894) – Commonplace and suburban, bald and unconvincing.   *'Daily Telegraph'*

George Bernard Shaw

William Shakespeare's 'Romeo and Juliet' (1895) – Mrs Patrick Campbell's dresses, says the programme, carried out by Mrs Mason of New Burlington Street. I can only say that I wish they had been carried out and buried.

William Shakespeare's 'Cymbeline' (1896) – For the most part stagey trash of the lowest melodramatic order, in parts abominably written, throughout intellectually vulgar, foolish, offensive, indecent, and exasperating beyond all tolerance.

William Shakespeare's 'Othello' (1897) – To anyone capable of reading the play with an open mind as to its merits, it is obvious that Shakespeare plunged through it so impetuously that he had finished it before he had made his mind up as to the character and motives of a single person in it.   *'Saturday Review'*

Robert E. Sherwood

After reading a typically in-depth foreign play script – I prefer the plays of Robert Emmett Sherwood. He hasn't much to say but at least he does not try to say anything else.

Anon G. B. Shaw play – It is disappointing to report that George Bernard Shaw appearing as George Bernard Shaw is sadly miscast in the part. Satirists should be heard and not seen.

Milton Shulman

J. B. Priestley's 'A Severed Head' (1963) – Co-written with Iris Murdoch this is not a black comedy, but a black-and-white comedy, striped in much the same way as those humbugs one sued to suck at school and with just as much nutritious and sticky content.

'Evening Standard'

Leopold Lewis's 'The Bells' (1970) – Clang!

'Evening Standard'

John Simon

Rolf Hochhuth's 'The Deputy' (1964) – On Broadway it is like one of those comic-strip versions of a literary classic and as the characters bestride the stage you can virtually see the balloons coming out of their mouths.

'Hudson Review'

'La Cage aux Follies' (1983) – For homosexuals, this play, even more so than *'Torch Song Trilogy'*, is from the Broadway legitimisation of their modus vivendi, all the way from respectably bourgeois to outrageously transvestite, via a budget of $5 million.

Madame de Stael

Voltaire's 'Candide' – It seems to have been written by a creature of a nature wholly different from our own, indifferent to our lot, rejoicing in our sufferings, and laughing like a demon or an ape at the misery of the human race with which he has nothing in common.

'De L'Allemagne'

Hannan Swaffer

'Yes and No' (1938) – No!

James Thurber

'Anon' – It had only one fault. It was kind of lousy.

'The Times'

On the review of his play 'French without Tears' – I don't believe it. Even the Times likes it!

Terence Rattigan

Kenneth Tynan

'Quadrille' (1952) – The excuse for this monstrously over-loaded tea-trolley of a play is, of course, the presence in it of Alfred Lunt and Lynn Fontaine who play together as, the millionaire and the marchioness, like sandpaper on diamond.

Terence Rattigan's 'The Sleeping Prince' (1953) specially written for Laurence Olivier and Vivien Leigh – Among the select group of plays written for eminent husband-and-wife teams in coronation years, it ranks very high.

'Daily Sketch'

'The Glorious Days' (1953) – There was a heated diversion of opinion in the lobbies during the interval but a small conservative majority took the view that it might be as well to remain in the theatre.

Ronald Culver's 'A River Breeze' (1956) – A theatrical coelacanth; a thing we had long thought extinct, now surfacing unexpectedly in semi-fossilised form. It is a Loamshire comedy.

'The Observer'

Queen Victoria

William Shakespeare's 'King Lear' – A strange, horrible business, but I suppose good enough for Shakespeare's day.

Gore Vidal

G. B. Shaw's 'Heartbreak House' – Shaw's improvisatory genius breaks down; he keeps marching into conversational cul-de-sacs.

Voltaire

William Shakespeare's 'Hamlet' (1748) – It is a vulgar and barbarous drama, which would not be tolerated by the vilest populace of France, or Italy . . . one would imagine this piece to be the work of a drunken savage.

Wilella Waldorf

Anon – At first we thought the actors were making it up as they went along.

Irving Wardle

'What's Got Into You?' (1981) – I left the show feeling very keen to get home to the washing up.   'The Times'

Earl Wilson

Anon play – I've seen more excitement at the opening of an umbrella.

Walt Winchell

At the Broadway opening of 'The Admirable Crichton' (1931) – For Crichton out loud!

'The Hero in Man' – Most of the heroes are in the audience.

'The Bishop Misbehaves' – A new high for misleading titles.

After being banned from all Shubert Theater opening nights – A certain columnist has been barred from all Shubert openings. Now he can wait three days and go to their closings.

P. G. Wodehouse
Anon play – It's one of those avant-garde plays which bring the scent of boiling cabbage across the footlights and in which the little man in the bowler hat turns out to be God.

Alexander Woollcott
Anon play – The scenery was beautiful, but the actors got in front of it. The play left a taste of lukewarm parsnip wine.

Anon play – In the first act 'she' becomes a lady. In the second act 'he' becomes a lady.

'The Lake' – If this play lasts overnight it should not only be considered a long run but a revival as well.

'Mourning Becomes Electra' (1931) – That glum three-decker.

'Number Seven' – 'Number Seven' opened last night. It was misnamed by five.

'Wham' – Ouch!

'Yorkshire Post'
Harold Pinter's 'The Homecoming' (1965) – He is more cruel, gruesome and deliberately offensive in this two act horror than in his previous plays. On its face value, it is callous and empty enough; what lies in its Freudian depths one dreads to think.

THEATRELAND

Broadway, New York
Broadway, a branch of the narcotics world run by actors.   *Bertol Brecht*

What a glorious garden of wonders the lights of Broadway would be to anyone lucky enough to

be unable to read.   *G. K. Chesterton – 'What I Saw in America' (1923)*

When St Genesius, the patron saint of actors, refused to act in a Roman play that ridiculed Christianity, the legend goes, the producers executed him. It reminds some people of Broadway today.   *Samuel G. Freedman – 'New York Times' (1983)*

Things are so bad on Broadway today an actor is lucky to be miscast.   *George S. Kaufman*

After a brief assignment as drama critic to the 'New York Times' – I never quite managed to find the New York theatre. It always seemed to be out when I called.   *Benedict Nightingale (1984)*

West End, London
To my mind there is no sadder spectacle of artistic debauchery than a London theatre; the overfed inhabitants of the villa in the stalls hoping for gross excitement to assist them through their hesitating digestions; an ignorant mob in the pit and gallery forgetting the miseries of life in imbecile stories reeking of the sentimentality of the backstairs.

George Moore – 'Confessions of a Young Man' (1888)

MUSICALS

Musicals – a series of catastrophes ending with a floor show.   *Oscar Levant*

Musicals are to the theatre what wines are to a substantial dinner.   *George J. Nathan*

It seems that the moment anyone gets hold of an exclamation mark these days, he promptly sits down and writes a musical show around it.   *George J. Nathan*

REVIEWS
(Listed by reviewer)

Martin Amis
'Elvis – The Musical' (1981) – It may indeed be the case that Elvis [Presley] was no more than a horrible and highly uncomplicated embodiment of American Success, but 'Elvis' leaves us none the wiser.   *'The Observer'*

Clive Barnes
'Oh! Calcutta' – The sort of show that gives pornography a bad name.

Max Beerbohm
'Anon' W. S. Gilbert Show – Verse is not the only thing it ought to have been written in; it ought also to have been written in the [eighteen] seventies.

Leonard Bernstein
'Anon' – I walked out infuriated after the first act. The lyrics are just laundry lists.

Michael Billington
'Godspell' (1981) – Heralded by a sprinking of glitter-dust and much laying on of microphones, *'Godspell'* is back . . . For those who missed it the first time, this is your golden opportunity: you can miss it again.
'The Guardian'

Robert Brustein
'Cats' – This spectacle could have been manufactured by Disney World, using audio-animatronics instead of actors; I perceived no sign of flesh-and-blood behaviour beneath the glitter and flash.

Noël Coward
'Camelot' – It's like *'Parsifal'* without the jokes.

T. S. Eliot
'My Fair Lady' adapted from G. B. Shaw's 'Pygmalion' – I must say Bernard Shaw is greatly improved by music.

Peter Hall
'Sweeney Todd' – Gilbert and Sullivan out of Leonard Bernstein – no balls, New York chic.

Percy Hammond
'Anon' – I have knocked everything in this play except the chorus girls' knees, and there God anticipated me.

On female revues – The Messrs Shubert seem to forget that the female knee is a joint and not an evening's entertainment.

Irving Hoffman
'Follow the Girls' (1944) – Boston liked *'Follow the Girls.'* Boston also likes baked beans. It is

like one of those books found in library dens. When opened, they turn out to be a cigarette case.

Stanley Kauffman
'Jesus Christ Superstar' (1971) – It will flow on, if only at a syrup's pace. Religion and atheism will both survive it.

Louis Kronenberger
'Anon' (1946) – Irving Berlin's score is not musically exciting – of the real songs, only one or two are tuneful.
'PM'

Tom Lehrer
On Gilbert and Sullivan – One can always count on Gilbert and Sullivan for a rousing finale, full of words and music, signifying nothing.

Bernard Levin
'Flower Drum Song' (1960) – An American musical, so bad that at times I longed for the boy-meets-tractor theme of Soviet drama.
'Daily Express'

'Evita' (1978) – It's best tune, the already famous 'Don't Cry For Me Argentina', is inferior as a melody to the ones I used to hear improvised on a saxophone outside the Albert Hall by a busker with only three fingers on his left hand.
'Daily Express'

Groucho Marx
'Hair' – Why should I pay ten dollars for something I can see in the bathroom for nothing?

Johnny Mercer
'Anon' (1975) – I could eat alphabet soup and SHIT better lyrics!

Sheridan Morley
'Jesus Christ Superstar' (1972) – *'Jesus Christ Superstar'* is by *'Godspell'*, out of *'Hair'*. In terms of taste it is as unimpeachable as vanilla ice-cream and every bit as bland.
'Punch'

'Tom Brown's Schooldays' (1972) – The score (by Chris Andrews) has a ghastly Radio Two mid-morning jollity about it and also a Muzakish oblivion so that one left the theatre humming only the National Anthem.
'Punch'

Anthony Newley's 'The Good Old Bad Old Days' (1973) – As a musical it desperately needs the discipline of a different scriptwriter and director and of a less docile cast (outside of Mr Newley the actors have the uneasy air of those assembled for an understudy rehearsal on a stage suddenly larger than the one they had anticipated). *'Punch'*

'Pippin' (1973) – There is nothing like a good Broadway musical and Pippin is alas not like a good Broadway musical. *'Punch'*

Robert Muller

'The Sound of Music' (1960) – It is the final fruit of Rodgers and Hammerstein's collaboration, and an over ripe, not to say soggy, old plum it is.

George Jean Nathan

'Tickets Please!' (1950) – Another of the revues with a titular exclamation point which may be taken in either of two ways. I prefer to take it in the other.

Maureen Paton

Andrew Lloyd Webber's 'Aspects of Love' – A second-rate musical based on a third-rate novel. *'Daily Express' (1989)*

Frank Rich - 'The Butcher of Broadway'

Andrew Lloyd Webber's 'Starlight Express' (1987) – A confusing jamboree of piercing noise, routine roller-skating, misogyny and Orwellian special effects, *'Starlight Express'* is the perfect gift for the kid who has everything except parents. *'New York Times'*

Andrew Lloyd Webber's 'Phantom of the Opera' (1988) – Mr Lloyd Webber has again written a score so generic that most of the songs could be reordered and redistributed among the characters (indeed, among other Lloyd Webber musicals) without altering the show's story or meaning. *'New York Times'*

[*Leading lady Sarah Brightman* – . . . reveals little competence as an actress. After months of playing *'Phantom'* in London, she still simulates fear and affection alike by screwing up her face into bug-eyed, chipmunk-cheeked poses more appropriate to the Lon Chaney film version.]

Trevor Nunn's 'Chess' (1988) – The show is a suite of temper tantrums, all amplified to a piercing pitch that would not be out of place in a musical about one of chess's somewhat noisier fellow sports, like stock-car racing. *'New York Times'*

Segovia and Orezzoli's 'Black and Blue' (1989) – While bursting with talent worthy of the Cotton Club or the Apollo or Birdland, *'Black and Blue'* looks like the bloated nightclub floor shows that used to flourish in decadent Latin American capitals just before dictatorships collapsed. *'New York Times'*

John Dexter's adaptation of Bertolt Brecht's 'Threepenny Opera' (1989) – After emerging from the inert grey mass that is Broadway's *'Threepenny Opera'*, the first thing you want to do – assuming you don't drink – is run home and listen to any available recording of its score. The reason is not to revisit the evening's high points – there are none – but to make sure you are still living . . . As it happens, nearly any *'Threepenny Opera'* recording (Bobby Darin's possibly excepted) will resuscitate the spirit absent at the theatre. *'New York Times'*

[*Not escaping the critic's eye was Sting, who played Macheath* – A plausible actor in the films *'Plenty'* and *'Stormy Monday'*, Sting is a stiff onstage. He seems to hope that a large cane and a smug, insistent pout will somehow convey the menace of a character who is a murderer, rapist, thief and arsonist.
And – Julius Rudel's onstage band, sitting on top of the squat and cluttered playing area, renders the familiar orchestrations with a lassitude more appropriate to a hotel-lobby tea-service than a Weimar cabaret.
Rich concluded his review – Not for the first time does Brecht get the last – and, in this production, the only – laugh.]

George Bernard Shaw

Jerome K. Jerome's 'Biarritz' (1896) Two minutes of *'Biarritz'* would reconcile a Trappist monk to his monastery for life. *'Saturday Review'*

Ian Shoales

'Annie' – I had to hit myself on the head afterward with a small hammer to get that stupid 'Tomorrow' song out of my head.

John Simon

'No, No Nannette' – What about the songs? 'Tea for Two' is almost as simple-minded as the sound of train wheels nocturnal travellers cannot get out of their insomniac brains. One does not come out humming 'Tea for Two' – one runs out pursued, bugged, hummed by it.

'Singing in the Rain' (1985) – Like springs, adaptations can only go downhill.   *'New York'*

Mervyn Stockwood

'Oh! Calcutta' (1980) – As boring as a boarding school on bath night.   *'Sunday Times'*

Virgil Thomson

'Porgy and Bess' – Falsely conceived and rather clumsily executed . . . crooked folklore and halfway opera.

Michael Todd

'Oklahoma' (1943) – No legs, no jokes, no chance.

Kenneth Tynan

'Anon' – It contains a number of tunes one goes into the theatre humming.

'Flower Drum Song' – Perhaps as a riposte to Joshua Logan's *'The World of Suzie Wong'*. Rodgers and Hammerstein have given us what, if I had any self-control at all, I would refrain from describing as a world of woozy song.

Willela Waldorf

'Take a Bow' – The Murtah Sisters murtahed several songs.   *'New York Post'*

VAUDEVILLE

With the collapse of vaudeville new talent has no place to stink.   *George Burns*

Vaudeville is a species of entertainment derived from the dregs of drama and musical comedy assembled in such wise that they shall appeal to the dregs of the drama and musical comedy audiences.   *George J. Nathan – 'American Mercury' (1929)*

DANCE

Dancing is the perpendicular expression of a horizontal desire.   *Anon*

Good dancers have mostly better heels than heads.   *Proverb*

Dancing? Oh, how dreadful! How it was ever adopted in a civilised country I cannot find out; 'tis certainly a barbarian exercise, and of savage origin.   *Fanny Burney – 'Cecilia' (1782)*

Down with the modern dance!
    That craze we'll quickly smother,
    It looks all right
If your coat's on tight
And you really do love each other.
Down with the Shimmie Shake
    That makes poor Auntie hot!
We'll see that every dance club fails,
    And slap Pavlova till she wails.
What about Salome and her seven veils?
Down with the whole damn lot!
         Noël Coward – 'Co-optimists' (1928)

Dancers ennoble what is vulgar; but they degrade what is heroic.   *Joseph Joubert*

Dance today is terrifying.   *Agnes de Mille*

The man who doesn't know which way to turn is probably learning the latest dance.
         Bert H. Kruse

DANCERS

Anon

An an eighteenth-century dancer from the Paris Opera – It's too bad she broke her arm not her leg, that wouldn't have interfered with her dancing.   *Sophie Arnold*

Fred Astaire *(1899–1987)*

Can't act. Slightly bald. Can dance a little.
         Anon screen test

On his performance in 'The Gay Divorcé' – To the dull, dotish, imperceptient male eye it would appear that Mr Astaire is neither a stage-shaking dancer nor a world-shaking dancer. As a dancer he is not in the Nijinsky class. When he mounts into the air it is by means of a chair and a table, and his descents are similarly accomplished.

James Agate – 'Sunday Times' (1933)

Watching the nondancing, nonsinging Astaire is like watching a grounded skylark.

Vincent Canby

Isadora Duncan *(1878–1927)*
On her performance – Made me think of Grant's Tomb in love.   *Peter Finlay Dunne*

A woman whose face looked as if it had been made out of sugar and someone had licked it.

G. B. Shaw

In less inspired moments Isadora Duncan followed the music as a bear might pursue a mouse.   *Adrian Stokes*

Martha Graham *(b 1894)*
I'm afraid she is going to give birth to a cube.

Stark Young

Hot Gossip
The black male dancers in Hot Gossip have always been a dead bore, mainly because of their humourless frowns of concentration while making movements with their hips which suggest a doomed, no-hands attempt to scratch their groins against an invisible tree.

Clive James – 'The Observer'

Rodulf Nureyev *(b 1938)*
Anon – During one modern ballet . . . Nureyev and a drowsily sexy ballerina engaged in a long attempt to pull each other's tights off without using fingers, toes, or teeth. It sounds difficult, but was fun to watch, although probably not as much fun as it was to do.

Clive James – 'The Observer' (1980)

'Oh Calcutta!'
The trouble with nude dancing is that not everything stops when the music stops.

Robert Helpman

Anna Pavlova *(1882–1931)*
She had bad taste and chose dreadful music. She liked the Hungarian composers and dainty tippety-toe dances. And her feet were ugly. Such large, lumpy shoes. And her dresses! It

was terrible but the audience loved it. They didn't know any better in those days.

George Balanchine

STYLES

Ballet
Most ballet teachers in the United States are terrible. If they were in medicine, everyone would be poisoned.

George Ballanchine – 'Newsweek' (1964)

On the cost of ballet tickets – That's a lot to see buggers jump.   *Nigel Bruce*

I'm a guy who likes to keep score. With ballet I can't tell who's ahead.   *Fiorello la Guardia*

Transplanting ballet to the USA is like trying to raise a palm tree in Dakota. *Leonard Kirstein*

All those great swans chasing that absurd young man!   *Terence Rattigan*

Ballroom dancing
An art which is compounded equally of the lithe, sinuous panther, the lissom, supple gigolo, and the light-shod, look-slippy waiter who can steer a tray and twenty glasses through a crowd without spilling.

James Agate – 'Sunday Times' (1933)

Disco dancing
Disco dancing is really for people who hate dancing, since the beat is so monotonous that only champions can find interesting ways of reacting to it. There is no syncopation, just the steady thump of a giant moron knocking in an endless nail. *Clive James – 'The Observer' (1978)*

A seventies sedative: music to look in the mirror by.   *Billy Joel (1978)*

It is like a musical iron lung for a culture in respiratory distress.

Jack Kroll – 'Newsweek' (1978)

Disco is a period of McDonald's music.

Melba Moore (1979)

Folk dancing
Try everything once except incest and folk-dancing.   *Sir Thomas Beecham*

Foxtrot

The Englishman foxtrots as he fox-hunts, with
all his being through thickets, through ditches,
over hedges, through chiffons, through waiters,
over saxophones, to the victorious finish; and
who goes home depends on how many the
ambulance will accommodate.

Nancy Boyd [aka Edna St Vincent Millay]

Non-stop [Marathon]

The long-distance dancing craze is still further
evidence that the theory of evolution is a libel
on the ape.   *'Nashville Banner'*

These non-stop dancers must be strong and
vigorous people – from the neck down.

'Nashville Tennessean'

Those who trip the 'light fantastic toe' in one of
those marathon dances appear to have the same
kind of heads.   *'Tampa Tribune'*

Rhumba

A dance where the front of you goes along nice
and smooth like a Cadillac, and the back of you
makes like a jeep.   *Anon*

A foxtrot with the backfield in motion.   *Anon*

CINEMA

In case of an air raid, go directly to RKO – they
haven't had a hit there in years.   *Anon*

Making a funny film provides all the enjoyment
of getting your leg caught in the blades of a
threshing machine. As a matter of fact, it's not
even that pleasurable; with the threshing
machine the end comes much quicker.

Woody Allen – 'Esquire' (1975)

Movies are fun, but they're not a cure for
cancer.   *Warren Beatty*

They've made everybody like the girl next door.
And you're not going to the movies to see the
girl next door – if you can go next door.

Joan Bennett

The making of a motion picture is an endless
contention of tawdry egos, almost none of them
capable of anything more than credit stealing
and self-promotion.   *Raymond Chandler*

Filming is like a long air journey; there's so
much hanging around and boredom that they
keep giving you food.   *John Cleese*

What do you see now when you go to the
movies? A terrified girl being raped by four or
five idiots on a beach. They make burlesque
look like 'Rebecca of Sunnybrook Farm'.

Ann Corio

French cinema – Mediocrity shuffles after
banality in an unending process.

Alice Demoree (1968)

Cinema is an old whore, like circus and variety,
who knows how to give many kinds of pleasure.
Besides, you can't teach an old flea new dogs.

Federico Fellini – 'Atlantic' (1965)

I have yet to be convinced that the film
business is a profession for adults.

Frederick Forsyth

Most horror movies are certainly that.

Brendan Francis

Filmmaking has now reached the same stage as
sex – it's all technique and no feeling.

Penelope Gilliatt

I don't care for modern films. Cars crashing
over cliffs and close-ups of people's feet.

Lillian Gish

Cinema is the most beautiful fraud in the
world.   *Jean-Luc Godard*

Movies are just another form of merchandising
– we have our factory, which is called a stage;
we make a product, we colour it, we title it and
we ship it out in cans.   *Cary Grant*

A movie is never any better than the stupidest
man connected with it.   *Ben Hecht*

Movies are one of the bad habits that have
corrupted our century. They have slipped into
the American mind more misinformation in one
evening than the Dark Ages could muster in a
decade.   *Ben Hecht*

The movies are an eruption of trash that has tamed the American mind and retarded the Americans from being cultured people.
Ben Hecht

Film is not an art of scholars but of illiterates.
Werner Herzog

An epic is the easiest kind of picture to make badly.
Charlton Heston

The length of a film should be directly related to the endurance of the human bladder.
Alfred Hitchcock

Most of us would like to see a good movie, but there are so many 'super-films' it's hard to find a good movie.
Elsie Janis

My reaction to porno films is as follows:
After the first ten minutes, I want to go home and screw.
After the first twenty minutes, I never want to screw again as long as I live.
Erica Jong

The words 'Kiss Kiss Bang Bang', which I saw on an Italian movie poster, are perhaps the briefest statement imaginable of the basic appeal of the movies.
Pauline Kael (1968)

Movies are so rarely great that if we cannot appreciate great trash we have very little reason to be interested in them.
Pauline Kael

The movie is a toupee made up to look like honest baldness.
Pauline Kael – 'New Yorker' (1986)

Films nowadays suffer two debits:
Too short on art, too long on credits.
Mimi Kay

Film-making has become a kind of hysterical pregnancy.
Richard Lester

You can fool all the people all the time if the advertising is right and the budget is big enough.
Joseph E. Levine

The reformers need not worry. The movies are never as wicked as the advertisements promise.
'Long Beach Telegram'

Film is a dog: the head is commerce, the tail is art. And only rarely does the tail wag the dog.
Joseph Losey

Damn it! Can't they realise that most movie-goers are sick to death of the dingy sexpot who lives next door and the hairy oaf who's screwing her?
Ray Milland

A double-feature is a show that enables you to sit through a picture you don't care to see, so you can see one you don't like.
Henry Morgan

My interest in the cinema has lapsed since women began to talk.
George J. Nathan

There aren't any real movie-makers any more. The business is run by the cornflakes men and they are only in it for the girls.
Peter O'Toole

I attend no movies, for any motion-picture theatre is as an enlarged and a magnificently decorated lethal chamber to me.
Dorothy Parker

What puzzles most of us are the things which have been left in the movies rather than the things which have been taken out.
Agnes Repplier

This isn't exactly a stable business. It's like trying to stand up in a canoe with your pants down.
Cliff Robertson

There is only one thing that can kill the movies – and that is education.
Will Rogers – 'Autobiography' (1949)

A man can make more money with less effort in the movies than in any other profession.
George Sands

There might have been good movies if there had been no movie industry.
David O. Selznick

Some films could only have been cast in one way: screen tests were given and the losers got the parts.
Gene Shalit (1971)

Film, called the Seventh Lively Art, all too often usurps its title after the fashion of the Holy Roman Empire: it is generally not in the least lively, not seventh but seventh-rate, and decidedly not art.
John Simon – 'Acid Test' (1963)

I love film, but the film business is shit.
Oliver Stone

A film is never really good unless the camera is an eye in the head of a poet.   *Orson Welles*

A movie without sex is like a candy bar without nuts.   *Earle Wilson*

CRITICISM

The criterion for judging whether a picture is successful or not is time.   *Peter Bogdanovich*

I make my pictures for people, not critics.
Cecil B. de Mille

Every time I make a picture the critics' estimate of American public taste goes down ten per cent.   *Cecil B. de Mille*

The first words of film criticism I ever heard were 'terrific' and 'great'.   *David Frost*

It is my indignant opinion that ninety per cent of the moving pictures exhibited in America are so vulgar, witless and dull that it is preposterous to write about them in any publication not intended to be read while chewing gum.   *Woolcot Gibbs*

Critics have never been able to discover a unifying theme in my films. For that matter, neither have I.   *John Huston*

Cinema criticism, in the main, is a total waste of everybody's time.   *Glenda Jackson*

Is there a cure for film criticism?   *Pauline Kael*

I wouldn't take the advice of a lot of critics on how to shoot a close-up of a teapot.   *David Lean*

A reason for his retirement – One finds that as the years go by one has already reviewed, under another title, almost every new film one sees.
Dwight MacDonald (1966)

I never take any notice of reviews – unless a critic has thought of some new way of describing me. That old one about my lizard eyes and anteater nose and the way I sleep my way through my pictures is so hackneyed now.
Robert Mitchum (1959)

This review has the place of honour in my lavatory.   *David Niven*

Those who can't – teach.
And those who can't do either – review.
Burt Reynolds

Film critics are writers, and they are hostile and uneasy in the presence of a visual phenomenon.   *Jack Smith*

Film review of 'Sentimental Journey' (1946) – It may not be for the critics, but who are the critics? Just a bunch of Joes, with passes.
'Variety'

What critics call dirty in our movies they call lusty in foreign films.   *Billy Wilder*

On critics who praise foreign movies – They get excited about the sort of stuff I could get shooting through a piece of Kleenex.
Billy Wilder

DIRECTORS & PRODUCERS

The producer is a man who gives the public what they want – and then hopes they want it.
Anon

On movie moguls – They were monsters and pirates and bastards right down to the bottom of their feet but they loved the movies. Some of the jerks running the business today don't even have faces.   *Richard Brooks (1970)*

Many directors are just pedestrian workmen, who couldn't direct you to a cheap delicatessen.
James Cagney

On a film set the only person less important than a director is a talent agent.
John Cassavetes

I would take a bad script and a good director any day against a good script and a bad director.   *Bette Davis*

Directors bite the hand that lays the golden egg.   *Sam Goldwyn*

Directors are people too short to be actors.
Josh Greenfeld

If big film directors are to get credit for doing badly what others have been doing brilliantly for years with no money, just because they've put it on a big screen, the businessmen are greater than poets, and theft is an art.
Pauline Kael – 'Movies as an Opera' (1968)

The big studios were each headed by a Big Daddy who reigned supreme. *Evelyn Keyes*

German movie directors are like airplanes always circling the airport, but never landing.
Alexander Kluge

The millionaire movie directors can thank their lucky stars. *'Newspaper Enterprise Association'*

Studio heads have foreheads by dint of electrolysis. *S. J. Perelman*

A producer is a clever man whose brain starts working the moment he wakes up in the morning and doesn't stop working until he gets to the studio. *Martin Rugway*

Who invented 'hokum'? Think how much money he'd have made from the film producers if he'd sold his invention on a royalty basis.
Robert Sherwood

The director is the most overrated artist in the world. He is the only artist who, with no talent whatsoever, can be a success for 50 years without his lack of talent ever being discovered.
Orson Welles – 'Time' (1982)

Most directors couldn't earn twopence in any other business and I wouldn't trust any of them to book me a bus from Green Park to Piccadilly. They're inept, arrogant, foolish and totally uncaring for the artist.
Michael Winner – 'Sunday Times' (1970)

REVIEWS
(Listed by reviewer)

Anon
'Lost in a Harem' (1944) – But with Abbott and Costello.

'Mr Parkinson' – It's two hours too long.
[*The film ran for 121 minutes!*]

'Love Story' (1970) – Not since Walt Disney made 'Bambi' has a courtship like it been seen on the screen.

'The Poseidon Adventure' (1972) – All hull broke loose.

'Howard the Duck' (1986) – Howard lays an egg!

Charles Addams
'Cleopatra' (1963) – I only came to see the asp.

James Agate
'Victoria the Great' (1937) – The effect of the final colour reel is to make the picture look like something enamelled on pottery and labelled 'A present from Blackpool'.

'The Man in Grey' (1943) – There was not a moment when I would not gladly have dived for my hat.

James Agee
'King Kong' (1933) – amusing nonsense punctuated by such reflections as why, if the natives wanted to keep the monster on the other side of the wall, they built a door big enough to let him through.

'Random Harvest' (1942), starring Ronald Colman – I would like to recommend this film to those who can stay interested in Ronald Colman's amnesia for two hours and who could with pleasure eat a bowl of Yardley's shaving soap for breakfast.

'Star-Spangled Rhythm' (1942) – A variety show including everyone at Paramount who was not overseas, in hiding or out to lunch.

'The Miracle at Morgan's Creek' (1943) – Like taking a nun on a roller-coaster.

'Mission to Moscow' (1943) – A mishmash: of Stalinism with New Dealism with Hollywoodism with opportunism with shaky experimentalism with mesmerism with onanism, all mosaicked into a remarkable portrait of what the makers of the film think the Soviet Union is like – a great glad two-

115

million-dollar bowl of canned borscht, eminently approvable by the Institute of Good Housekeeping.

'So Proudly We Hail' (1943) – Probably the most deadly accurate picture ever made of what war looks like through the lenses of a housewives' magazine romance.

'Frenchman's Creek' (1944) – Masturbation fantasy triple distilled.

'The Jolson Story' (1946) – I have nothing in the world against this picture except that at least half of it seemed to be enormously tiresome.

'Till the Clouds Roll By' (1946) – A little like sitting down to a soda fountain de luxe atomic special of maple walnut on vanilla on burnt almond on strawberry on butter pecan on coffee on raspberry sherbert on tutti frutti with hot fudge, butterscotch, marshmallow, filberts, pistachios, shredded pineapple, and rainbow spirals on top, go double on the whipped cream.

'Bill and Coo' (1947) – By conservative estimate, one of the God-damnedest things ever seen.

'I Walk Alone' (1947) – The picture deserves, like four out of five other movies, to walk alone, tinkle a bell, and cry, 'Unclean, unclean!'

'The Paradine Case' (1947) – One of the wordiest scripts since the death of Edmund Burke.

'This Time for Keeps' (1947) – The money spent on this production might easily have kept Mozart and Schubert alive and busy to the age of sixty, with enough left over to finance five of the best movies ever made. It might even have been invested in a good movie musical.

'Tycoon' (1947) – Several tons of dynamite are set off in this picture – none of it under the right people.

'Fort Apache' (1948) – There is enough Irish comedy to make me wish Cromwell had done a more thorough job.

'You Were Meant for Me' (1948) – That's what you think.

Richard Sheridan Ames
'100 Men and a Girl' (1937) – Deanna Durbin's name precedes the title in the billing, so you know that a nymphomaniac is not on the loose.

Tim Appelo
'Young Einstein' (1990), written and directed by and starring Yahoo Serious – Yahoo Serious shouldn't be blamed because the hype that preceded *'Young Einstein'* cast him as the Second Coming of Paul Hogan. Yahoo Serious should be blamed for making *'Young Einstein'* in the first place . . . Crocodile Dundee was a gas: *'Young Einstein'* is merely gaseous.

Lew Ayres
'Fingers at the Window' (1942) – The kind of picture actors do when they need work.

John Barbour
'At Long Last Love' (1975) – If this film were any more of a dog, it would shed.

Michael Billington
'Rooster Cogburn' (1975), starring John Wayne and Katharine Hepburn – Like one of those infuriating exhibition bouts in which two resilient old pros bob, weave and spar without ever landing any punches.

'From Noon Till Tnree' (1976) – It squanders its early sparkle for a pot of message.

'The Man Who Fell to Earth' (1976) – Once you have pierced through its glittering veneer, you find only another glittering veneer beneath.

'Murder by Death' (1976) – Plenty of scene-stealing actors but not many scenes worth stealing.

Alan Brien
'The Stud' (1978) – Watching it is rather like being buried alive in a coffin stuffed with back numbers of 'Men Only'.

Geoff Brown
'Robin and Marion' (1976) – Surface realism only hides a core of mush, suddenly revealed

when the hero and heroine settle down for love-making in a field of corn.

Michael Buckley
'Spaceballs' (1987) – Spaceballs is nine years too late and light years unfunny.   'Films in Review'

Vincent Canby
'Song of Norway' (1970) – Watching 'Song of Norway' is like being trapped in an aerial tramway with nothing to read.

'Heaven's Gate' (1980), directed and produced by Michael Cimino – It fails so completely that you might suspect Michael Cimino sold his soul to the devil to obtain the success of 'The Deer Hunter', and the devil has just come around to collect.

Charles Champlin
'1776' (1972) – 1776 is as American as turkey, which it closely resembles.

'Lucky Lady' (1975) – The simple secret of Lucky Lady's plot is that if at first you don't menage à trois, trois again.

'The Missouri Breaks' (1976), starring Marlon Brando and Jack Nicholson – A pair of million-dollar babies in a five and ten cent flick.

'Death on the Nile' (1978) – The cobra at least has a plot to hiss in.

'Health' (1979) – Health has easily won this year's Listerine Prize for lousy word of mouth.

Judith Crist
'Blind Terror' (1971) – For those who like to watch folks pull the wings off flies.

'Lost Horizon' (1972) – Only Ross Hunter would remake a 1937 film into a 1932 one.

'King Kong' (1976) – The story of a dumb blonde who falls for a huge plastic finger.

Bosley Crowther
Walt Disney's 'Song of the South' (1946) – The ratio of live to cartoon action is approximately two to one, and that is the ratio of the film's mediocrity to its charm.

'Underwater' (1955), starring Jane Russell – This presentation of Miss Russell is like one of those fountain pens guaranteed to write under water – novel, but impractical.

'Daily Herald'
'One Way Street' (1950) – It is reported that James Mason chooses his own parts, and if this is true I have to report that he is a glutton for punishment.

'Daily Mail'
'Grease 2' (1982) – It's like being cooped up for two hours inside a combination of a juke box and a pin-ball machine, with you as the ball.

Paul Dehn
'Richard III' (1955) – Wherever the play was loose-jointed or ill-fitting, Sir Laurence [Olivier] has been its tinker and its tailor, but never once its butcher.

Peter John Dyer
'That Kind of Woman' (1959), starring Sophia Loren and Tab Hunter – The romantic reunion of Hunter and Loren resembles nothing so much as a sea scout given a luxury liner for Christmas.

Roger Ebert
'Fatal Attraction' (1987) – A grown-up 'Friday the 13th'.   'New York Post'

'Ishtar' (1987) – This movie is a long, dry slog. It's not funny, it's not smart, it's interesting only in the way a traffic accident is interesting.   'New York Post'

Gabe Essoe
'Boom' (1968) – This fuzzy Joseph Losey adaptation of a Tennessee Williams play should have been called 'Plop' for the pile it resembles.

'Myra Breckenridge' (1970) – As bad as any movie ever made, this tasteless garbage about a sex change operation should have been sent to Sweden for more surgery.

Otis Ferguson
'Anne of Green Gables' (1934) – Made up and monotonous – tragedy having its breakfast in bed.

'*Mary of Scotland*' *(1936)* – Events are walked through as though they were rooms in a museum, and closing time at three.

'*The Adventures of Tom Sawyer*' *(1938)* – Should make Mark Twain circulate in his grave like a trout in a creel.

'*Seven Sinners*' *(1940)* – Nothing to worry about, unless you happen to be in the theatre watching it go from fairly good to worse than worse.

'*Sergeant York*' *(1941)* – There are too many hold-ups and too many people out of step, and your residue of opinion on the matter is that it will be nice to get home and get your shoes off.

Gene Fowler
'*Intolerance*' *(1916)* – The greatest commercial anticlimax in film history.

Philip French
'*Carry on Emmanuelle*' *(1978)* – Put together with an almost palpable contempt for its audience, this relentless sequence of badly written, badly timed dirty jokes is surely one of the most morally and aesthetically offensive pictures to emerge from a British studio.

'*The Sure Thing*' *(1985)* – Two sounds clash: old wine being poured into new bottles, and familiar barrels being scraped.

Joseph Gelmis
'*Live and Let Die*' *(1973)* – A Bond movie is not made. It is packaged. Like an Almond Joy. So much coconut to this much chocolate and a dash of raisins.

Penelope Gilliatt
'*Goldfinger*' *(1964)* – A dazzling object lesson in the principle that nothing succeeds like excess.

'*The Green Berets*' *(1968)* – A film best handled from a distance and with a pair of tongs.

Owen Gleiberman
'*Born on the Fourth of July*' *(1990)* – . . . so inflated with purpose and 'good intentions' it doesn't breathe. It's a new-style mutant – a message on steroids.

'*Joe Versus the Volcano*' *(1990)* – All the show-stopping whammy of a '*Love Boat*' rerun.

'*Predator 2*' *(1990)* – Predator is an alien warrior who looks like a cross between Whoopi Goldberg and RoboCop.

'*Texasville*' *(1990)* – It's like one of those 20-years-after reunion episodes of baby-boomer TV shows – all you can do is stare at the screen and count the wrinkles.

'*Wild Orchid*' *(1990)* – A sort-of-sequel to 9½ weeks, this soft-core extravaganza wants to be a kind of '*Last Samba in Rio*'. It's really just a racy perfume commercial posing as movie.

Benny Green
'*The Return of the Pink Panther*' *(1974)* – The first film to be upstaged by its own credit titles.

'*The Texas Chainsaw Massacre*' *(1974)* – An absolute must for all maniacs and blood drinkers in need of a few tips.

'*Logan's Run*' *(1976)* – It puts the future back two thousand years.

'*The Sailor Who Fell from Grace*' *(1976)* – Required viewing for timorous kamikaze pilots.

Graham Greene
'*Rhythm on the Range*' *(1936)* – Bing Crosby as a cowboy; Bing Crosy crooning a prize bull to sleep on a freight car; Bing Crosby more than ever like Walt Disney's Cock Robin; it needs some stamina to be a film reviewer.

'*The Road Back*' *(1937)* – They call it an all-star cast and that means there isn't a single player of any distinction to be picked out of the herd.

Philip T. Hartung
'*War and Peace*' *(1956)* – The film has no more warmth than pictures in an art gallery.

Frank Hauser
'*Another Man's Poison*' *(1951)* – Like reading Ethel M. Dell by flashes of lightning.

A. P. Herbert
'*The Terror*' *(1928)* – The characters speak as if they were dictating important letters.

Don Herold
'*The Bride Walks Out*' *(1936)* – You've seen this

a million times on the screen, but they keep making it, and folks keep asking me why I am so dyspeptic regarding the cinema. Because I have judgement, is the answer.

'Modern Times' (1936) – Merely an elaboration of an old joke about the man in the Ford production line who laid down his wrench to scratch his ear and threw the whole factory out of gear.

'Things to Come' (1936) – The existence pictured is as joyless as a squeezed grapefruit.

Margaret Hinxman
'Eureka' (1982) – No one will convince me that it isn't just the poshest kind of tosh.

'The World According to Garp' (1982) – Rather like watching a puppy chase its own tail – engaging, touching, but pointless.

Clive Hirschorn
'Footsteps in the Dark' (1941) – The footsteps were those of restless patrons on their way to buy popcorn.

J. Hoberman
'Empire of the Sun' (1987) – Light spectacle in the sense of light opera (or lite beer), *'Empire of the Sun'* packs the wallop of a fading shadow boxer. *'Village Voice'*

'Hollywood Reporter'
'Tarantula' (1955) – It's a great children's picture . . . particularly for bad children. It'll scare hell out of the little monsters.

Frankie Howerd
'The Cool Mikado' – I can say without equivocation that not only was it the worst film ever made, but the only production in show business that I'm positively ashamed of having appeared in.

Clive James
'Grease' (1978) – A movie of such grubbiness that after seeing it I felt like washing my skull out with soap.

Pauline Kael
'The Appaloosa' (1966) – A dog of a movie about a horse.

'Fantastic Voyage' (1966) – The actors look as if a child has cut them out with blunt scissors.

'The Naked Runner' (1967) – It might be a good film to read by if there were light in the theatre.

'Ulysses' (1967), based on James Joyce's novel – An act of homage in the form of readings from the book plus illustrated slides.

'The Night They Raided Minsky's' (1968) – It has a wonderful seedy chorus line – a row of pudgy girls with faces like slipped discs.

'Goodbye Mr Chips' (1969) – An overblown version with songs where they are not needed (and Leslie Bricusse's songs are never needed). *'New Yorker'*

'Marooned' (1969) – A space epic with a horse-and-buggy script.

'The Wild Bunch' (1969), directed by Sam Peckinpah – Pouring new wine into the bottle of Western, Peckinpah explodes the bottle.

'Mary Queen of Scots' (1971) – Without a better script, Hercules couldn't lift this story off the ground.

'Alex and the Gypsy' (1976) – Off the beaten track, but that's just about the only thing you can give it points for.

'Oh, God' (1977) – Basically a single-joke movie: George Burns is God in a baseball cap. *'New Yorker'*

'All That Jazz' (1979) – High cholesterol hokum. Enjoyable, but probably not good for you.

Stanley Kanfer
'The Thomas Crown Affair' (1968) – A glimmering, empty film reminiscent of an haute-couture model – stunning on the surface, concave and undernourished beneath.

Stanley Kauffman
Otto Preminger's 'In Harm's Way' (1965) – Lacks even a touch of the [Preminger] touch.

'Isadora' (1968) – This long but tiny film.

'The Owl and the Pussycat' (1970) – If computers ever turn out romantic comedies, the results will look like this.

'The Way We Were' (1973) – Garbage under the gravy of false honesty.

'The Godfather' (1974) – It was made from a best-seller, a lot of money was spent on it, and it runs over three hours. Therefore, it's important.

Pamelo Kellino
'The Egyptian' (1954) – One of those great big rotten pictures Hollywood keeps turning out.

Arthur Knight
'Walk, Don't Run' (1966) – Too long, as are most comedies today, it seems to take its title far too seriously.

Jack Kroll
'Inchon' (1981) – The worst movie ever made, a turkey the size of Godzilla.

Burt Lancaster
'Concorde – Airport 1979' – The biggest piece of junk ever made.

David Lardner
'Panama Hattie' (1942) – This film needs a certain something. Possibly burial.

Mike McGrady
'Less Than Zero' (1987) – Moviemakers hate to use a title like *'Less Than Zero'* because it makes life too easy for the critical fraternity. Noble, indeed, is the critic able to shun this kind of temptation. *'Less Than Zero'*, in fact, stands right up there with 1965's *'Rotten to the Core'* and such other all-time critics' favourite titles as *'The Bad One'*, *'Not So Dumb'* and *'What Have I Done to Deserve This?'*   *'Newsday'*

Groucho Marx
'Samson and Delilah' (1949), starring Victor Mature and Hedy Lamarr – You can't expect the public to get excited about a film where the leading man's tits are bigger than the leading lady's.

'The Last Tango in Paris' (1976) – Saddest movie I've ever seen – I cried all the way through. It's sad when you're 82.

Janet Maslin
'The Sentinel' (1976) – A perfect film – for those who like to slow down and look at traffic accidents.   *'Newsweek'*

'Suspiria' (1977) – . . . is really quite funny, during those isolated interludes when nobody is bleeding.   *'New York Times'*

Leonard Matlin
'My Blood Runs Cold' (1965) – Not all that bad, but not worth missing *'I Love Lucy'* for either.

Harry and Michael Medved
'Hello Dolly' (1969) – Goodbye budget! [*The musical cost $24 million and recouped less than $10 million.*]

Tom Milne
'The Carpetbaggers' (1964) – One of those elaborate conjuring tricks in which yards and yards of coloured ribbon are spread all over the stage merely to prove the conjurer has nothing up his sleeve.

'When Time Ran Out' (1980) – Disaster movies don't come any more disastrous than this.

'Rocky III' (1982) – The time has surely come for Rocky Balboa to take the final count.

'Monthly Film Bulletin'
'Walk on the Wild Side' (1962) – Since the film prides itself in calling a spade a spade, it is surprising to find all concerned reacting to their material as though they were up to their waists in a quagmire.

'To Sir With Love' (1967) – The sententious script sounds as if it has been written by a zealous Sunday school teacher after a particularly exhilarating boycott of South African oranges.

'New York Times'
'Kiss the Boys Goodbye' (1941) – The producers have kept the boys and kissed the script goodbye.

Frank Nugent
'Woman Chases Man' (1937) – A pleasant warm weather fabrication – lightweight, attractively tailored and not meant to withstand the rigours of wear or the chill blasts of the critics.

Philip Oakes
'Time Without Pity' (1957) – It hammers home its effects with the concentration of a heavyweight out for the kill.

'The Observer'
'Re-animator' (1985) – A cheap smell of excess.

Robert Orben
Anon film – Yesterday I saw a movie so embarrassing, I asked the woman in front of me to put her hat back on again.

William S. Petcher
'Jaws' (1975) – Shark stew for the stupefied.

Rex Reed
'The Chase' (1966) – The worst thing that has happened to movies since Lassie played a war veteran with amnesia.

'Women in Love' (1969) – They should take all the pretentious dialogue off the soundtrack and call it 'Women in Heat'.

'Personal Best' (1982) – According to this movie, lesbianism is just something you catch in the locker room, like athlete's foot.

'Blue Velvet' (1986) – In the brain-damaged garbage department, Blue Velvet gives pretentiousness new meaning. It should score high with the kind of sickos who like to smell dirty socks and pull the wings off butterflies . . . Blue Velvet opens today at the Baronet. Bring a barf bag. *'New York Post'*

'Cobra' (1986), starring Sylvester Stallone – 'Rambo Goes To Hollywood'. It is 90 minutes of unrelievedly nauseous, imbecilic swill, custom-tailored for the star's pecs, and cheaply packaged to appeal to the lowest animal instincts . . . It's playing all over town. Just follow the odour to your nearest neighbourhood showcase. *'New York Post'*

'Reporter Magazine'
'Guess Who's Coming to Dinner?' (1967) – Abie's Irish Rose in blackface.

Frank Rich
'The Hindenburg' (1975) – A cheap and chaotic collage of painted props, wooden actors and not-so-special effects that manages to make one of the century's most sensational real-life catastrophes seem roughly as terrifying as a stubbed toe.

David Robinson
'Fort Ti' in 3-D (1953) – The lack of restraint is remarkable. To the injury of tomahawks, rifle shots, cannon balls, flaming arrows, broken bottles and blazing torches is added the insult of grubby redskins hurled judo style into one's lap.

'The Bible' (1966) – An Old Testament spectacular like any other.

Will Rogers
'The Ten Commandments' (1923) – A fine film up to the point where God finishes and the script writer takes over.

Richard Roud
'A Walk in the Spring Rain' (1969), directed by Guy Green – The direction is so lazy it appears to have been mailed in during the postal strike.

Mort Sahl
'Ben Hur' (1959) – Loved Ben, hated Hur.

'Saturday Evening Post'
'Macabre' (1958) – It plods along from its opening scene in a funeral parlour to its denouement in a graveyard, unimpeded by the faintest intrusion of good taste, literacy, or sense.

'Saturday Review'
'Sincerely Yours' (1955) – Given sufficient intoxication you could find this movie amusing.

Steven H. Scheuer
'The Loves of Hercules' (1960) – The most Herculean labour there is for the audience to sit though it with a straight face.

Robert Schickel
'Hooper' (1978) – Burt Reynolds's annual Kleenex of a movie; something to use and throw away without any thought beyond a certain gratitude for the conveniences of the thing.

Gene Shalit
'Bring Me the Head of Alfredo Garcia' (1974) – Bring me the head of the studio that released this one.

Wilfrid Sheed
'Harry Sundown' (1967) – To criticise it would be like tripping a dwarf.

Robert E. Sherwood
'Anazol' (1921), adapted from Arthur Schnitzler's play – Should be enormously popular, especially with those who think Schnitzler is a cheese.

'Sunday Times'
'The Blue Lagoon' (1980) – A Sunday school fairy tale which makes the story of Adam and Eve seem like hard porn, as hygienically sanitized as a Hilton Hotel lavatory seat.

'One from the Heart' (1982) – If this is the essence of cinema, then Salvador Dali is the essence of painting.

Lowell Thomas
'Lawrence of Arabia' (1962) – They only got two things right – the camels and the sand. [*Won four Oscars including Best Picture*]

'Time Magazine'
'Circus World' (1964) – To sit through this film is something like holding an elephant on your lap for two hours and fifteen minutes.

'Myra Breckenridge' (1970) – About as funny as a child molester.

Barry Took
Walt Disney's 'The Rescuers' (1977) – If you are going to put this amount of effort into a movie, shouldn't you have more at the end than a snappy collection of 330 000 drawings and a bill for six million dollars?

'Interiors' (1978) – As dull as toothache and as predictable as a metronome.

Peter Travers
'Bird on a Wire' starring Goldie Hawn and Mel Gibson (1990) – Dumb Dee Dumb Dumb Dumb. *'Rolling Stone'*

'Variety Magazine'
'Kiki' (1931) – What was to have been a cocktail has turned out to have been a soda.

'Tillie and Gus' (1933) – Very funny in spots, but not enough spots.

'The Strange Woman' (1946) starring Hedy Lamarr – Hedy bit off more than she could chew, so the chewing was done by the rest of the cast, and what was chewed was the scenery.

'Executive Action' (1973) – A dodo bird of a movie, the winner of the Tora, Tora, Tora prize.

'Can't Stop the Music' (1980) – Some scenes could pulp and solve the paper shortage, they are so wooden.

'Eureka' (1982) directed by Nicolas Roeg – A Roeg elephant film.

'Silver Bullet' (1985) – It's a Stephen King filmette from his novelette which may sell some tickettes but not without regrettes.

'Young Sherlock Holmes' (1985) – Another Steven Spielberg version of those lamps made from driftwood and coffee tables from redwood burl. It's not art but they all serve their purpose and sell by millions.

'Lonesome Cowboy' (1968) – Andy Warhol's best movie to date, which is like saying a three-year-old has graduated from smearing faeces on the wall to the occasional use of finger-paints.

'Village Voice'
'A Star Is Born' (1976), starring Barbra Streisand – A bore is starred.

Rob Wagner
'Frankenstein' (1931) – All the old Mack Sennet scare-sequence gags are used to give us the creeps – a goofy windmill atop a mountain of rocks (windmills are always in the valleys!) . . .

The only thing omitted is the comedy relief of a frightened coon.

'I am a Fugitive from a Chain Gang' (1932) – Talk about roast beef cut thick; this picture is sorghum and sowbelly, and your enjoyment (!) of it will depend upon your film dietary strength.
[*Nominated for an Oscar as Best Film.*]

'Duck Soup' (1933) starring the Marx Brothers – The basis of homoeopathy is that 'like cures like', and in a world that has gone completely haywire I can suggest no better medicine than *'Duck Soup'.*

'Flying Down to Rio' (1933) – The trouble with 'big smash numbers' is that they are likely to smash not only the picture – if any – but everybody that gets in their way.

'Of Human Bondage' (1934) – This is a picture of English roast beef, cut thick with lots of gravy – a grim story of an over-sensitive, club-footed fellow love-bound to a 'sow's ear', who under no circumstance could ever rise to even the splendour of rayon silk.

'Mutiny on the Bounty' (1935) – If you like your roast beef rare, cut thick with lots of gravy, this is your meat.

'A Night at the Opera' (1935) – Did you ever try to shoot swallows in a cyclone? It's easy compared with reviewing a Marx Brothers film.

Alexander Walker
'A Place for Lovers' (1969) – One of those costly, empty films that look as if they've been made with somebody else's blank chic.

'Love Story' (1970) starring Ali McGraw – Ali McGraw plays 'Camille' with bullshit.

'Ryan's Daughter' (1970) – Instead of looking like the money it cost to make, the film feels like the time it took to shoot.
[*Oscar for Best Photography*]

'Sunflower' (1970) – A story that an illiterate chamber-maid might consider a bit beneath her customary standards. It moves along with the pace of a scene-shifter from La Scala.

'Beneath the Valley of the Dolls' (1971) – The kind of movie that a maladroit Mack Sennett might have made if he had worked in a sex-shop, not a fun factory.

'Mahler' (1974) – A film for the kind of people who want to 'see' symphonies the way 'The Forsyte Saga' was a telly serial for the kind of people who want to 'watch' a book.

Bruce Williamson
'Fritz the Cat' (1971) – A bitter and snarling satire that refuses to curl up in anyone's lap.

'Godspell' (1973) – A patch of terra incognita somewhere between *'Sesame Street'* and the gospel according to Laugh-In.

Michael Wilmington
'Ernest Goes to Camp' (1987) – The kind of movie that could drive you to Chinese Checkers, or Saturday nights at the laundromat. A few more on this level might help bring back radio drama or flea circuses . . . it makes movies like *Meatballs* look like models of dry, sophisticated, urbane wit.
'Los Angeles Times'

'Lethal Weapon' (1987) – It's a big, shallow, flashy, buddy-buddy cop thriller; it attacks you like a stereophonic steamroller, flattening everything behind it. Snatches of *'Hustle'*, *'Magnum Force'* and *'48 Hrs'* float above this plot like scum on a polluted lake.
'Los Angeles Times'

Walter Winchell
'Wake Up and Live' (1937) starring Walter Winchell – The title should be changed to 'Wake Up and Leave'.

Richard Winnington
'Pandora and the Flying Dutchman' (1950) – An air of third-degree decadence hangs about it. This is an Anglo-American co-production and one of the occasions, I think, when we might be generous and let Hollywood have all the credit.

Archer Winsten
'The Doughgirls' (1944) – There's nothing so good in it that you must attend, just as there is nothing bad enough to keep you away.

Basil Wright

'The Wages of Fear' (1953) – It has some claim to be the greatest suspense thriller of all time; it is the suspense not of mystery but of Damocles' sword.

Paul D. Zimmermann

'The Cocoanuts' (1929) – The camerawork showed all the mobility of a concrete fire hydrant caught in winter freeze.

'Papillon' (1973) – It offers torture as an entertainment but winds up making entertainment a form of torture.

CELEBRITIES

A celebrity is a person whose name is in everything except the phone directory. *Anon*

Man dreads fame as a pig dreads fat.
Chinese proverb

A celebrity is a person who works hard all his life to become well known, and then wears dark glasses to avoid being recognised. *Fred Allen*

Fame always brings loneliness. Success is as ice cold and lonely as the North Pole.
Vicki Baum - 'Grand Hotel'

You're not a star until they can spell your name in Karachi. *Humphrey Bogart*

Being well known for their well-knownness, celebrities intensify their celebrity images simply by being well known for relations among themselves. By a kind of symbiosis, celebrities live off each other. *Daniel J. Boorstin*

A sign of celebrity is often that his name is worth more than his services. *Daniel J. Boorstin*

The celebrity is usually nothing greater than a more publicised version of us. He has been fabricated on purpose to satisfy our exaggerated expectations of human greatness. They are nothing but ourselves seen in a magnifying mirror. *Daniel J. Boorstin*

Celebrity is the advantage of being known to those who do not know you.
Nicholas de Chamfort

That's what fame is: solitude. *Coco Chanel*

Fame is proof that the people are gullible.
Ralph Waldo Emerson

The plain fact is that a celebrity is anyone 'People' writes about. *Nora Ephron*

Show business is sincere insincerity. *Benny Hill*

Interviewing celebrities is just a step above calling the morgue. *Garrison Keiller*

Being a celebrity is like rape. *John McEnroe*

A celebrity is one who is known to many persons he is glad he doesn't know.
H. L. Mencken

Celebrities are intellectual fast food.
Lance Morrow

ACTING - SPECIFIC
(Listed by Actor)

Anon
He isn't the kind of performer who stops a show; he is content to merely slow it up. *Anon*

British actress, named April, performing in the USA - Oh, to be in England, now April's here.
Brooks Atkinson

She had the assurance of a woman who has swum the Channel against a rip-tide.
Tallulah Bankhead

To an aspiring actress - If you really want to help the American theatre, don't be an actress, dahling. Be an audience.
Tallulah Bankhead (1951)

She is the great lady of the American stage. Her voice is so beautiful that you won't be able to understand a word she says.
Mrs Patrick Campbell

Actress playing Queen Victoria - Her Victoria made me feel that Albert had married beneath his station. *Noël Coward*

She's the original good time that was had by all. *Bette Davis*

He played Hamlet last night. He played it until one o'clock. *Eugene Field*

He has delusions of adequacy. *Walter Kerr*

Young girl suffering from starlet fever.
'New York Daily News'

That girl speaks eighteen languages and she can't say no in any of them. *Dorothy Parker*

He had never acted in his life and couldn't play the pin in 'Pinafore'.
P. G. Wodehouse – 'The Luck of the Bodkins' (1935)

Max Adrian – *(1903–73)*
Feste in 'Twelfth Night' – Max Adrian's Feste astonishingly transported that really fine actor to a kind of cloud cuckoo garden for aged psychos. *Caryl Brahms (1961)*

Henry Ainley – *(1879–1945)*
'The Tempest' – He played the old codger like a toastmaster celebrating his golden wedding.
James Agate – 'Sunday Times' (1934)

Jane Alexander – *(b 1939)*
'Goodbye Fidel' – She's about as Latin as a New England boiled dinner.
Douglas Watt – 'New York Daily News' (1980)

Patrick Allen – *(b 1927)*
The Ghost in 'Hamlet' – Clad in complete steel and a flying panel of what looked like tulle, Patrick Allen, voice-over in a thousand [TV] commercials, was a good ghost, although you would not have been stunned to hear him recommend Danish bacon.
Clive James – 'The Observer' (1980)

Harry Andrews – *(b 1911)*
'Hamlet' – Harry Andrews' well-spoken King looked like a futuristic cinema commissionaire.
'Bristol Evening News' (1956)

Julie Andrews – *(b 1934)*
'The Sound of Music' (1965) – She is like a nun with a switchblade. *Anon*

'The Tamarind Seed' (1974) – One wishes Miss Andrews didn't always give the impression that she had just left her horse in the hallway.
Michael Billington

'The Sound of Music' (1965) – Working with her is like being hit over the head with a Valentine card. *Christopher Plummer*

Carroll Baker – *(b 1931)*
More bomb than bombshell. *Judith Crist*

Lucille Ball – *(1910–89)*
Try another profession. Any other.
John Murray Anderson Drama School (1927)

Tallulah Bankhead – *(1903–68)*
More of an act than an actress. *Anon*

The longer she plays in something the less you see of the play, the more you see of Tallulah.
Anon

After a series of poor performances in 'The Exciters' – Don't look now, Tallulah, but your show's slipping. *Heywood Broun*

'Antony and Cleopatra' – Tallulah Bankhead barged down the aisle as Cleopatra and sank. As the serpent of the Nile she proves to be no more dangerous than a garter snake.
John Mason Brown

Tallulah was sitting in a group of people, giving the monologue she always thought was conversation. *Lillian Hellman*

'Antony and Cleopatra' – Miss Bankhead played the Queen of the Nil.
George J. Nathan

'Antony and Cleopatra' – Miss Bankhead seemed more a serpent of the Suwannee than of the Nile. *Richard Watts Jr – 'New York Tribune'*

Watching Tallulah on stage is like watching someone skating on thin ice – everybody wants to be there when it breaks. *Mrs Patrick Campbell*

Miss Bankhead isn't well enough known nationally to warrant my imitating her.
Bette Davis

A day away from Tallulah Bankhead is like a month in the country. *Howard Dietz*

She was always a star, but only intermittently a good actress. *Brendan Gill*

Few actresses can portray more convincingly than Miss Bankhead the difficult part of a pretty girl. *Percy Hammond*

I've just spent an hour talking to Tallulah for a few minutes. *Fred Keating*

Tallulah who?   *Beatrice Lillie*

The screen had just started talking when Miss
Bankhead interrupted in 1930.   *Richard Maney*

T is for Tallulah. She was rightly annoyed
When a journalist called her the 'Helen of
Freud'
          Humbert Wolfe – 'The A.B.C. of Theatre'

Theda Bara – *(1890–1955)*
Theda Bara was another dream-world figure.
Surrounded by potted palms, silken hangings
and blackamoors and other dust collectors,
Miss Bara was Pestilence herself, her
monumental wickedness would not have been
tolerated by Caligula in his beatnik depths for
one moment. She was divinely, hysterically,
insanely malevolent. The public fell at Miss
Bara's feet. She climbed from option to option
while thousands cheered.
               Bette Davis – 'The Lonely Life'

Miss Bara made voluptuousness a common
American commodity, as accessible as chewing
gum.   *Lloyd Morris – 'Not So Long Ago'*

H. Greville Barker – *actor/manager (1877–1946)*
Oh, G.B., you are a very clever and interesting
youth of 30; but you are an atrocious manager.
You don't know where to put your high light
and where to put your smudge.   *G. B. Shaw*

Ethel Barrymore – *(1879–1959)*
'Captain Jinks of the Horse Marines' – If the
young lady who plays Madame Trentoni had
possessed beauty, charm or talent, this play
might have been a success.   *Anon*

John Barrymore – *(1882–1942)*
'Magda' – He walked about the stage as if he
had been all dressed up and forgotten.
                                  Anon (1903)

'My Dear Children' – I always said that I'd like
Barrymore's acting till the cows came home.
Well, ladies and gentlemen, last night the cows
came home.   *George J. Nathan*

Warren Beatty – *(b 1937)*
You're so vain. You probably think this song is
about you.
          Carly Simon – 'You're So Vain' (1972)

William Bendix – *(1906–64)*
Neanderthal man reincarnated in Brooklyn.
                              David Shipman

Dirk Benedict – *(b 1945)*
'Scavenger Hunt' (1979) – You thought Dirk
Benedict had problems in TV's *'Battlestar
Galactica'?* In *'Scavenger Hunt'*, he really had
problems – in one mercifully brief scene, he
was out-acted by a jock-strap.   *Rona Barrett*

Robbie Benson – *(b 1956)*
Cute as Bambi and twice as smarmy.   *Anon*

Candice Bergen – *(b 1946)*
'The Group' (1966) – She doesn't know how to
move, she cannot say her lines so that one
sounds different from the one before. As an
actress her only flair is her nostrils.
                      Pauline Kael – 'Life'

Ingrid Bergman – *(1915–82)*
'The Visit' (1964) – The vengeful hag is played
by Ingrid Bergman, which is like casting
Eleanor Roosevelt as Lizzie Borden.
                      Dame Margaret Kendal

Sarah Bernhardt – *(1844–1923)*
A great actress, from the waist down.
                      Dame Margaret Kendal

Thomas Betterton – *(1635–1710)*
For who can hold to see the Foppish Town
Admire so bad a Wretch as Betterton?
Isn't for his Legs, his Shoulders or his face,
His formal Stiffness, or his awkward Grace.
          Anon – 'Satyr on the Players' (1684)

Master Betty – *(1791–1874)*
Betty is performing here, I fear, very ill; his
figure is that of a hippopotamus, his face like
the bull and mouth on the panels of a heavy
coach, his arms are fins fattened out of shape,
his voice gargling of an alderman with the
quinsy, and his acting altogether ought to be a
natural, for it certainly is like nothing that Art
has ever yet exhibited on stage.   *Lord Byron*

The popularity of that baby-faced boy, who
possessed not even the elements of a good actor,
was a hallucination in the public mind, and a
disgrace to our theatre history.
                          Thomas Campbell

'Richard III' – Nature has denied him the first and simplest materials of theatrical excellence; and art has not given him even the humblest compensation that art can give.   *'The Times'*

Claire Bloom – *(b 1931)*
Viola in 'Twelfth Night' – Claire Bloom played Viola like a wistful little Peter Pan who is worried to death about Tinkerbell.
'Time and Tide' (1953)

Humphrey Bogart – *(1899–1957)*
He was playing Bogart all the time, but he was really just a big sloppy bowl of mush.
Stanley Kramer

You can't kill Jimmy Stewart, Gary Cooper or Gregory Peck in a picture. But you can kill off Bogart. The audience doesn't resent it.
Raoul Walsh

John Wilkes Booth – *(1838–65)*
He was mad with his own ego, possessed of a theatrical vanity that gnawed incessantly for fame.   *Jay Robert Nash*

Clara Bow – *(1905–65)*
Her life and career still seem to have been dreamed up by one of her scriptwriters.
David Shipman

Anne Bracegirdle – *(1663–1748)*
She seems to have been a cold, vain and interested coquette, who perfectly understood how much the influence of her charms was increased by the fame of a severity which cost her nothing, and who could venture to flirt with a succession of admirers in the just confidence that no flame which she might kindle in them would thaw her own ice.
Thomas Macaulay – 'History of England'

Marlon Brando – *(b 1924)*
'Mutiny on the Bounty' (1962) – Brando is a yawn again Fletcher Christian.   *Graffiti*

An angel as a man, a monster as an actor.
Bernardo Bertolucci

Most of the time he sounds like he has a mouth full of wet toilet paper.   *Rex Reed*

'The Freshman' (1990) – Brando's craft is less an actor's than a taxidermist's.
John Simon – 'National Review'

Richard Briers – *(b 1933)*
'Hamlet' – Richard Briers last night played Hamlet like a demented typewriter.
W. A. Darlington – 'Daily Telegraph'

Madge Brindley
'A Dead Secret' – A deadly aim with her saliva.
Roger Spate – 'New Statesman' (1957)

Charles Bronson – *(b 1922)*
His popularity within the movie industry is not legendary.   *David Shipman*

Pamela Brown – *(1917–75)*
Millament in 'The Way of the World' – Millament must be the empress of her sex, and her words, whether tinkling like a fountain or cascading like Niagara, must always flow from a great height. From Miss Brown's mouth they do not flow at all; they leak.   *Kenneth Tynan (1953)*

Richard Burton – *(1925–84)*
'Hamlet' – A trumpet blares and on to the stage struts Richard Burton as Hamlet. But he only looks like a film-star with the sulks.
John Barber – 'Daily Express'

Who could take that scruffy arrogant buffoon seriously?   *Eddie Fisher*

'Hamlet' – A rugger-playing Hamlet.
David Lewin

'Where Eagles Dare' (1969) – Playing a British spy dressed up as a German officer, he added to the confusion by sporting a pageboy hairstyle and giving his usual impersonation of a Welsh rugby-forward who has just been told that he has been dropped from the team.
Clive James – 'The Observer' (1979)

Caliban in 'The Tempest' – He looked like a miner with a tail coming up from the coal face.
'Sunday Express' (1954)

James Cagney – *(b 1899)*
Cagney rolled through the film like a belligerent barrel.   *Noel Coward*

Mrs Patrick Campbell – *(1865-1940)*
She has a Siamese forehead and a mouth like a
galosh.   *James Agate – 'Ego 3' (1937)*

Juliet in 'Romeo and Juliet' – As for the final
stabbing scene, she might as well have tickled
herself with a straw and died o' laughing.
'Punch' (1895)

'Fedora' – It is greatly to Mrs Patrick
Campbell's credit that, bad as the play was, her
acting was worse. It was a masterpiece of
failure.   *G. B. Shaw (1895)*

Bah! You have no nerve; you have no brain:
you are the caricature of an 18th-century male
sentimentalist, a Hedda Gabler titivated with
odds and ends from Burne-Jones' rag-bag. You
are an owl sickened by two days of my
sunshine.   *G. B. Shaw (1913)*

If only you could write a true book, entitled
'Why, though I was a wonderful actress, no
manager or author would ever engage me twice
if he could possibly help it', it would be a
bestseller. But you couldn't. Besides, you don't
know how. I do.   *G. B. Shaw (1938)*

'Aunt Jeannie' – Mrs Campbell as an elderly
siren was effective, but neither bewitchment
nor singularity makes a great actress.
William Winter

An ego like a raging tooth.   *W. B. Yeats*

Richard Chamberlain – *(b 1935)*
*'Allan Quartermain and the Lost City of Gold'
(1987)* – Chamberlain has none of the breezy
irreverence that made Harrison Ford's Indiana
Jones such a delightful hero. In his Banana
Republic khaki duds and a bulletproof
undershirt, he exudes the dashing spirit of a
game-show host.
Patrick Goldstein – 'Los Angeles Times'

Charlie Chaplin – *(1889-1977)*
When Chaplin found a voice to say what was
on his mind, he was like a child of eight writing
lyrics for Beethoven's Ninth.   *Billy Wilder*

Creston Clarke – *(1865-1910)*
Last night Mr Creston Clarke played King Lear
at the Tabor Grand. All through the five acts of

the Shakespearian tragedy he played the King
as though under the premonition that someone
was about to play the Ace.
Eugene Field – 'Denver Post/Tribune'

John Cleese – *(b 1939)*
He emits an air of overwhelming vanity
combined with some unspecific nastiness, like a
black widow spider on heat. But nobody seems
to notice. He could be reciting Fox's *'Book of
Martyrs'* in Finnish and these people would be
rolling out of their seats.
Roger Gellert – 'New Statesman'

Joan Collins – *(b 1933)*
She looks like she combs her hair with an egg-
beater.   *Louella Parsons*

Sean Connery – *(b 1929)*
On meeting the leading man in his '007' films – I'm
looking for Commander James Bond, not an
overgrown stunt man.   *Ian Fleming*

Diana Cooper
A blank, helpless sort of face, rather like a rose
just before you drench it with DDT.
John Carey – 'Sunday Times' (1981)

Gary Cooper – *(1901-61)*
He's got a reputation as a great actor just by
thinking hard about the next line.   *King Vidor*

Sofia Coppola – *(b 1962)*
'Godfather III' (1990) – Her gosling
gracelessness comes close to wrecking the
movie.   *Richard Corliss – 'Time'*

Cherry Cottrell – *(b 1909)*
Ophelia in 'Hamlet' – As Ophelia, Miss Cherry
Cottrell strikes me as being unripe.
James Agate (1937)

Noël Coward – *(1899-1973)*
'The Scoundrel' (1935) – Noël Coward is a busy
and talented young man, but when it comes to
acting I believe he belongs in the will-power
class. His notion of acting is to hold his body
rigid and bite out cutting remarks.
Don Herold – 'Life'

Forty years ago he was Slightly in *'Peter Pan'*,
and you might say he has been in *'Peter Pan'*
ever since.   *Kenneth Tynan*

Joan Crawford - *(1906-77)*
The best time I had with Joan Crawford was when I pushed her down the stairs in 'Whatever Happened to Baby Jane'. *Bette Davis*

On her biographies [by Christina Crawford and Bob Thomas] - On closing these two books, a reader senses that Joan Crawford, idol of an age, would have made an exemplary prison matron, possible at Buchenwald. She had the requisite sadism, paranoia and taste for violence.
Harriet van Horne - 'New York Post' (1978)

She was a mean, tipsy, powerful, rotten-egg.
Mercedes McCambridge

Annette Crosbie - *(b 1934)*
Sarah Davenport in 'My Place' - Annette Crosbie, who is normally an intelligent actress, if nothing else, spent the entire evening chasing her voice about the stage as if it were an escaped canary. *Anon (1962)*

Tony Curtis - *(b 1925)*
The only trouble with Tony Curtis is that he's only interested in tight pants and wide billing.
Billy Wilder

Sinead Cusack - *(b 1948)*
Roxanne in 'Cyrano de Bergerac' - Sinead Cusack plays this role and plays it poorly. It's not just that she's too old for Roxanne and a little too frumpy, but that her hoarse simpering delivery substitutes winsomeness for character - an attention to diction rather than depth that makes her sound like Liza Doolittle wheezing over phonetics. *Robert Brustein*

Jim Dale - *(b 1935)*
Bottom in 'A Midsummer Night's Dream' - Jim Dale's ton-up Bottom rushes on to the stage like an ex-pirate radio station disc jockey late for his stint on Radio One. *Peter Ansorge (1967)*

Paul Daneman - *(b 1925)*
'Richard III' - Clearly little thought has gone into Mr Paul Daneman's Richard. He seems to think that the more he sends up the lines, the funnier the part will be, which is true.
Bernard Levin - 'Daily Express' (1962)

Marion Davies - *(1897-1961)*
She has two expressions - joy and indigestion.
Dorothy Parker

Bette Davis - *(b 1908)*
Publicity for 'Beyond the Forest' (1949) - Nobody's as good as Bette when she's bad.

Her career has been recycled more often than the average tyre. *Vincent Canby*

I can't imagine any guy giving her a tumble.
Carl Laemmle

She has as much sex appeal as Slim Summerville. *Carl Laemmle*

After failing to win the 1935 Oscar for 'Of Human Bondage' - You were good playing a bitch-heroine, but you shouldn't win an award for playing yourself. *Jack Warner*

Doris Day - *(b 1924)*
Just about the remotest person I know.
Kirk Douglas

'Romance on the High Seas' - This was Doris Day's first picture; before she became a virgin.
Oscar Levant

She is as wholesome as a bowl of cornflakes and at least as sexy. *Dwight MacDonald*

The only real talent Miss Day possesses is that of being absolutely sanitary: her personality untouched by human emotions, her brow unclouded by human thought, her form unsmudged by the slightest form of femininity.
John Simon (1967)

James Dean - *(1931-55)*
Another dirty shirt-tail actor from New York.
Hedda Hopper

He was a hero to the people who saw him only as a little waif, when actually he was a pudding of hatred. *Elia Kazan*

Frances de la Tour - *(b 1944)*
'Duet for One' - Frances de la Tour, looking astonishingly like James Coburn's twin sister.
Michael Billington - 'The Guardian' (1980)

'Hamlet' – She speaks most of the poetry on a one-note nasal pitch and, in her final death throes, she tottered about so long I thought she was in danger of being given a breathalyser test.
Milton Shulman (1979)

Dame Judi Dench – *(b 1934)*
Michael Langham's production of 'A Midsummer Night's Dream' – Mr Langham has decided that something must be done to brighten the misunderstandings of the lovers in the forest, and so turns the tussle between Hermia and Helena into a rugger movement, the two men as hard-working backs keeping them apart. It's clear that, had she been a man, Judi Dench with her astonishing speed and agility would have been an England fly-half. I grant it is amusing, but I have an old-fashioned feeling that it is not quite Shakespeare.
Eric Keown – 'Punch' (1961)

Sandy Dennis – *(b 1937)*
She has made an acting style out of a postnasal drip.   *Pauline Kael*

'The Fox' (1968) – Pauline Kael has aptly observed that Miss Dennis 'has made an acting style out of postnasal drip'. It should be added that she balanced her postnasal condition with something like a prefrontal lobotomy, so that when she is not a walking catarrh she is a blithering imbecile.   *John Simon*

Bo Derek – *(b 1957)*
She turned down the role of Helen Keller because she couldn't remember the lines.
Joan Rivers

She is so stupid she returns bowling balls because they've got holes in them.   *Joan Rivers*

Vittorio de Sica – *(1901–74)*
A fine actor, a polished hack, and a flabby whore – not necessarily in that order.
Stanley Kauffmann

Marlene Dietrich – *(b 1901)*
Age cannot wither her, nor custom stale her infinite sameness.   *David Shipman*

Kirk Douglas – *(b 1916)*
He's wanted to be Burt Lancaster all of his life.
John Frankenheimer

Donald Duck – *('born' 1934)*
There is nothing on land or sea, nothing in the air or in the bowels of the earth, that bores me so abysmally as the later pictures of Walt Disney. Which goes for Donald Duck too. I would rather sit at the bottom of a coal-mine, in the dark, alone, and think of nothing, than go to see any of the successors to Fantasia. I would rather listen to Bloch's String Quartet played in a goods-yard, with shunting operations in full swing and all the Jews trying to get into or out of Palestine (I never know which) wailing up against the walls – there is no noise known to me, including the road drill and the later compositions of Bela Bartok, that I execrate so deeply as the squawking of that abominable fowl.   *James Agate – 'Ego 9' (1946)*

Eleonora Duse – *(1859–1924)*
'Hedda' – It was not the only performance of Hedda. There was another and, in some ways, a better. While Signora Duse walked through her part, the prompter threw himself into it with a will. A more raucous whisper I have never heard than that which preceded Signora's every sentence. It was like the continuous tearing of very thick silk.
Max Beerbohm – 'Saturday Review'

'Hedda' – In this as in every other part that she plays she behaved like a guardian angel half-asleep at her post over humanity.
Max Beerbohm – 'Saturday Review'

Shelley Duvall – *(b 1949)*
The worst and homeliest thing to hit the screens since Liza Minnelli.   *John Simon*

Clint Eastwood – *(b 1930)*
On running for Mayor of Carmel – What makes him think a middle-aged actor, who's played with a chimp, could have a future in politics?
Ronald Reagan

Robert Eddison
Mephistopheles in 'Dr Faustus' – Mr Eddison's haunted Mephistopheles has a fine melancholy. So had his recent Feste, so had Hamlet. I expect that this rising actor will shortly give us a finely melancholy Charley's Aunt.
Harold Hobson – 'Sunday Times' (1948)

Nelson Eddy - *(1901-67)*
The ham of hams. *Allan Dwan*

Anita Ekberg - *(b 1931)*
I thought there was something more
worthwhile in life than acting with an ex-
Beauty Queen. *Trevor Howard*

Robert W. Ellston - *(1774-1831)*
His feelings follow each other like the buckets
on a water-wheel, full one instant and empty
the next. *Leigh Hunt*

A wretched Tragedian . . . his attempts at
dignity are ludicrous. He is a fine bustling
comedian but he bustles in tragedy too.
Henry C. Robinson - 'Diary' (1811)

Dame Edith Evans - *(1888-1976)*
To me, Edith looks like something that would
eat its young. *Dorothy Parker*

'All's Well That Ends Well' - The role of the
Countess . . . is played by Dame Edith in her
characteristic later manner - tranquillized
benevolence cascading from a great height, like
royalty opening a bazaar.
Kenneth Tynan (1959)

Maurice Evans - *(b 1901)*
A great actor must include the forbidding in his
facial range: when I last saw Maurice he could
do no better in this line than stave off with
impudence. *James Agate - 'Sunday Times'*

Douglas Fairbanks - *(1883-1939)*
Douglas always faced a situation the only way
he knew how, by running away from it.
Mary Pickford

Thomas Edison devoted his life to machines
intended to make thinking unnecessary for the
masses. Fairbanks is devoting his to pictures
calculated to keep their minds off the fact that
they do not think. *Terry Ramsaye*

Frances Farmer - *(1914-70)*
The nicest thing I can say about Frances
Farmer is that she is unbearable.
William Wyler

Farrah Fawcett - *(b 1947)*
'Sunburn' (1979) - The only thing tinier than

the bikini Farrah Fawcett wore in this comedy-
thriller was La Farrah's talent. *Rona Barrett*

She is uniquely suited to play a woman of
limited intelligence. *Harry and Michael Medved*

Maybe it's the hair. Maybe it's the teeth.
Maybe it's the intellect. No, it's the hair.
Tom Shales

Elsie Ferguson - *(1883-1961)*
*Telegram to George S. Kaufman, on his fifth
wedding anniversary* - I have been looking
around for an appropriate wooden gift and am
pleased hereby to present you with Elsie
Ferguson's performance in her new play.
Alexander Woollcott

Albert Finney - *(b 1936)*
'Hamlet' - More of a Spamlet really.
Jason Hillgate - 'Theatre' (1975)

Errol Flynn - *(1909-59)*
His life was a fifty-year-old trespass against
good taste. *Leslie Mallory*

He had a mediocre talent. *Jack Warner*

Jane Fonda - *(b 1937)*
Today's heroines are all like Jane Fonda.
Anita Loos

Samuel Foote - *(1720-77)*
Thou Mimic of Cibber - of Garrick, thou Ape!
Thou Fop in Othello! thou Cypher in Shape!
Thou trifle in Person! thou Puppet in Voice!
Thou Farce of a Player! thou Rattle for Boys!
Thou Mongrel! thou dirty face Harlequin
 Thing!
Thou Puff of bad Past! thou Ginger-bred King!
Anon

Foote is quite impartial, for he tells lies of
everybody. *Samuel Johnson*

Harrison Ford - *(b 1942)*
'Hanover Street' (1979) - Co-star Harrison
Ford, as Lesley-Anne Down's G.I. lover, gets
our Ryan O'Neal Underacting Award for 1979
. . . and '80 . . . and '81. *Rona Barrett*

'Presumed Innocent' (1990) – Harrison Ford looks more and more like an Edsel.
John Simon – 'National Review'

Clark Gable – *(1901–60)*
Clark Gable has the best ears of our lives.
Milton Berle

He's the kind of guy who, if you say, 'Hiya Clark, how are yah?', is stuck for an answer.
Ava Gardner

His ears make him look like a taxi-cab with both doors open.
Howard Hughes

You're only a big ape.
Jack Warner

What can you do with a guy like that?
Jack Warner

His ears are too big. They make him look like an ape.
Darryl F. Zanuck

Zsa Zsa Gabor – *(b 1919)*
Zsa Zsa Gabor got married as a one-off and it was so successful she turned it into a series.
Bob Hope

Zsa Zsa Gabor not only worships the Golden Calf – she barbecues it for lunch.
Oscar Levant

She has discovered the secret of perpetual middle age.
Oscar Levant

Marriage is for bores – I mean Gabors.
Oscar Levant

Zsa Zsa Gabor is an expert house-keeper. Every time she gets divorced, she keeps the house.
Henny Youngman

Greta Garbo – *(1905–90)*
If Greta really wants to be alone, she should come to a performance of one of her films in Dublin.
Anonymous Irish critic

She'd make you eat a mile of her shit, just to get a whiff of her asshole.
John Gilbert

Boiled down to essentials, she is a plain mortal with large feet.
Herbert Kretzmer

A deer in a body of a woman, living resentfully in the Hollywood zoo.
Clare Booth Luce

Judy Garland – *(1922–69)*
I didn't know her well, but after watching her in action I didn't want to know her well.
Joan Crawford

An Angel – with spurs.
Joe Pasternak

'I Could Go On Singing' – Miss Garland plays herself, which is horrifying.
John Simon (1967)

'A Child Is Waiting' – Her figure resembles the giant economy-size tube of toothpaste in girls' bathrooms; squeezed intemperately at all points, it acquires a shape that defies definition by the most resourceful solid geometrician.
John Simon

David Garrick – *(1717–79)*
On the stage he was natural, simple, affecting;
'Twas only that when he was off he was acting.
Oliver Goldsmith

Garrick's conversation is gay and grotesque. It is a dish of all sorts, but all good things. There is no solid meat in it: there is a want of sentiment in it.
Samuel Johnson

Greer Garson – *(b 1908)*
One of the most richly syllabled queenly horrors of Hollywood.
Pauline Kael

I gave up being serious about making pictures about the time I made a film with Greer Garson and she took 125 takes to say no.
Robert Mitchum

Sir John Gielgud – *(b 1904)*
Romeo in 'Romeo and Juliet' – Mr Geilgud has the most meaningless legs imaginable.
Ivor Brown (1924)

Sir John Gielgud is the finest actor in the world from the neck up.
Kenneth Tynan (1959)

Lillian Gish – *(b 1893)*
She comes on stage as if she'd been sent for to sew rings on the new curtains.
Mrs Patrick Campbell

'Camille' – One has the illusion of watching Camille being played by a small town high school girl. This is part of an abiding immaturity which one finds difficult to describe in such words as will distinguish it from arrested development.

Alexander Woollcott – 'New Yorker' (1932)

Jackie Gleason – *(1916–87)*
Jackie's consistent – he's got a fat mouth and a big belly. *Joe Namath*

Ruth Gordon – *(1896–1985)*
'Mrs Warren's Profession' – It is a generous role for womanly and impassioned actresses, and many performers have essayed it. I can think of four, however, who have not: Totie Edwards, W. C. Fields, Tutankhamen's mummy, and a trained monkey. Not until now, that is; Miss Gordon's performance combines elements of all four. *John Simon*

Betty Grable – *(1916–73)*
Miss Grable's beauty – if that is the word for it – was of the common sort. Nor did she offer much in the way of character maturity. She was, at best, a sort of great American floozie, and her appeal to lonely GIs was surely that of every hash-house waitress with whom they ever flirted. *Richard Schickel*

Farley Granger – *(b 1925)*
'Pride and Prejudice' – He played Mr Darcy with all the flexibility of a telegraph pole.
Brooks Atkinson (1956)

Cary Grant – *(1904–86)*
You're too bow-legged and your neck is far too thick.
Anonymous Paramount executive at his screentest

Cary Grant, born Archie Leach, was a poor boy who could barely spell 'posh'. That's acting for you – or maybe Hollywood.
Melvin Maddocks – 'Christian Science Monitor' (1986)

His suntan looks like it was done on a rotisserie. *Tom Wolfe*

Hugh Griffiths – *(1916–80)*
It is hard to think of a role for which Mr Griffiths would not be Too Much, with his piercing glare, his insanely dominant nose, his beetling eye-brows and cavernous mouth, his over-ripe diction. Perhaps, God.
Dwight MacDonald

Charles Grodin – *(b 1935)*
He keeps threatening to be funny but he rarely makes it. *Pauline Kael*

Kay Hammond – *(1909–80)*
'The Way of the World' – Here is no imperious beauty commanding universal masculine respect, but an eighteenth-century dumb blonde. *Frank Grenville-Barker*

Sir Cedrick Hardwicke – *(1893–1964)*
'Dr Faustus' – He conducted the soul-selling transaction with the thoughtful dignity of a grocer selling a pound of cheese.
Hubert Griffith – 'Sunday Graphic' (1948)

Robert Hardy – *(b 1925)*
Ariel in 'The Tempest' – Mr Hardy was for some unexplained reason painted the colour of an auk's egg, and postured throughout like a stone hatstand in a Second Empire Turkish bath.
Anon (1954)

Jean Harlow – *(1911–37)*
There is no sign that her acting would ever have progressed beyond the scope of the restless shoulders and protuberant breasts, her technique was the gangster's technique – she toted a breast like a man totes a gun.
Graham Greene

Mark Harmon – *(b 1951)*
'Dillinger' [*ABC TV*] – Harmon must be the stiffest, sexiest-man-alive imaginable; he always looks somewhat annoyed, and when he wants to show that Dillinger is thinking, he frowns ferociously and stops talking. This does not make for exciting TV.
Ken Tucker – 'Entertainment Weekly' (1991)

Richard Harris – *(b 1932)*
'Cymbeline' – Cymbeline is an unrewarding part, but surely he is more than a testy Father Christmas in cricket pads.
Felix Barker – 'Evening News' (1957)

He's something of a f***-up, no question.
Charlton Heston

Laurence Harvey – *(1928-73)*
Acting with Harvey is like acting by yourself –
but worse.   *Jane Fonda*

Goldie Hawn – *(b 1945)*
'Wildcats' – It's hate at first sight.
                                        Rex Reed (1986)

Helen Hayes – *(b 1900)*
Cleopatra in 'Caesar and Cleopatra' – Fallen
Archness.   *Franklin P. Adams (1925)*

Susan Hayward – *(1918-75)*
'The Marriage Go Round' (1961) – A bargain
basement Bette Davis, whose lightest touch as
a comedienne would stun a horse.   *'Time'*

Rita Hayworth – *(1918-87)*
The audience was reserved and quietly
attentive – until Rita Hayworth danced on to
the screen in a flaming red dress, cut to show a
major part of her acting ability.
                                    Gerald Lieberman

Sir Robert Helpmann – *(1909-86)*
Shylock in 'The Merchant of Venice' – His voice
has all the finesse of a ventriloquist's doll.
                                        'The Bulletin'

Paul Henreid – *(b 1907)*
He looks as if his idea of fun would be to find a
cold, damp grave and sit in it.
                                    Richard Winnington

Audrey Hepburn – *(b 1929)*
A walking X-ray.   *Oscar Levant*

Not an actress . . . a model with her stiff
meagre body and her blank face full of Good
Bone Structure.   *Dwight MacDonald*

Katharine Hepburn – *(b 1907)*
A cross between Donald Duck and a
Stradivarius.   *Anon*

She has a cheekbone like a death's head allied
to a manner as sinister and aggressive as
crossbones.   *James Agate*

She has a face that belongs to the sea and the
wind, with large rocking-horse nostrils and
teeth that you just know bite an apple a day.
                                        Cecil Beaton

'Without Love' – You know she can't act, yet you
do not particularly mind. In this respect she
resembles a child's toy choo-choo. You know
that it is only a poor imitation of the big, real
article but it none the less exercises a
fascination even for a paternal locomotive
engineer.   *George J. Nathan (1942)*

'The Lake' – Go to the Martin Beck Theatre
and watch Katharine Hepburn run the gamut
of emotion from A to B.
                        Dorothy Parker – 'Life' (1933)
[*Hepburn replied* – 'Extremely funny and
accurate']

Katharine of Arrogance.
                            R.K.O. studio nickname

Charlton Heston – *(b 1924)*
'Ben Hur' (1959) – Charlton Heston throws all
his punches in the first 10 minutes (3 grimaces
and 2 intonations) so that he has nothing left
long before he stumbles to the end, 4 hours
later, and has to react to the Crucifixion. (He
does make it clear, I must admit, that he
disapproves of it.)   *Dwight MacDonald (1964)*

Anthony Hopkins – *(b 1941)*
'Macbeth' – This cocky genial fellow sometimes
sweats apprehensively and occasionally bellows,
but frequently he gives the impression that he
is a Rotarian pork butcher about to tell the
stalls a dirty story.
                    Felix Barker – 'Evening News' (1973)

Miriam Hopkins – *(1902-72)*
The least desirable companion on a desert
island.   *'Harvard Lampoon'*

Sir Michael Hordern – *(b 1911)*
'Macbeth' – Half his time on the stage he cringes
like an Armenian carpet-seller in an ankle-
length black dressing gown of fuzzy candlewick
while his ruched gold-cloth sleeves sag like
concertinas around the tips of his fingers.
                                    Alan Brien (1959)

Cassius in 'Julius Caesar' – This Cassius watches
John Phillips' alarmingly tall Brutus like an
insurance agent estimating how much life cover
he can offer without insisting on a medical
examination.   *'Sunday Times' (1958)*

Malvolio in 'Twelfth Night' – His smile, when it came, reminded one of a crumpled tray after a lorry has ground over it.

J. Trewin – 'The Lady' (1953)

Rock Hudson – *(1925–85)*
I called him Ernie because he's certainly no Rock.   *Doris Day*

Gayle Hunnicutt – *(b 1942)*
Viola in 'Twelfth Night' – Miss Hunnicutt's Viola was not 'Patience on a Monument' – it was a monument of patience!   *Bernard Levin*

Angelica Huston – *(b 1952)*
She has the face of an exhausted gnu, the voice of an unstrung tennis racket, and a figure of no describable shape.   *John Simon*

Lady June Inverclyde
Appearing in New York – Oh, to be in England, now that June's here.   *Robert Garland*

Sir Henry Irving – *(1838–1905)*
Ungoverned rage, sorrow, dread, he can depict, but not pure mental force. He well expresses the emotion of a mind acted on but not of a mind acting on others. He lacks what one may call the muscle and sinew of the brain.

James Albrey (1873)

'Hamlet' – Funny without being vulgar.

W. S. Gilbert

Upon being asked if he had seen Irving in 'Faust' – I go to the pantomime only at Christmas.

W. S. Gilbert

I wish they wouldn't make such a white-winged angel of father. He was never that.

Laurence Irving

'Romeo & Juliet' – How little Mr Irving is Romeo it is not worth while even to attempt to declare.

Henry James – 'Atlantic Monthly' (1882)

Sir Henry Irving would ere this have expiated his acting versions on the scaffold. He does not merely cut plays, he disembowels them.

G. B. Shaw

Of the theatre at large he knew almost nothing; for he never left his own stage.   *G. B. Shaw*

He has never in his life conceived or interpreted the characters of any author except himself. He is really as incapable of acting another man's play as Wagner was of setting another man's libretto.

G. B. Shaw – 'Saturday Review' (1896)

'King Lear' – His Lear was an impertinent intrusion of a quite silly conceit of his own into a great play.

G. B. Shaw – 'Pen Portraits and Reviews'

On refusing to attend the actor's funeral – I return the ticket for the Irving funeral. Literature, alas, has no place in his death as it had no place in his life. Irving would turn in his coffin if I came, just as Shakespeare will turn in his coffin when Irving comes.   *G. B. Shaw (1905)*

He has an ugly ear! Large, flabby, ill-cut, and pasty looking, pale and lumpy.

Ellen Terry – 'Notes on Irving'

Glenda Jackson – *(b 1923)*
Cleopatra in 'Antony and Cleopatra' – Glenda Jackson meanwhile is still Elizabeth I.

Robert Cushman – 'The Observer' (1978)

Gudrun in 'Women in Love' – She has a face to launch a thousand dredgers.   *Jack De Manio*

She has the look of an asexual harlequin.

John Simon

Joseph Jefferson – *(1829–1905)*
'The Heir-in-Law' – Nervous, fidgety young man by the name of Jefferson appeared as Dr Pangloss, into which character he infused a number of curious interpolations, occasionally using the text prepared by the author.

Anon (1857)

Van Johnson – *(b 1916)*
Van Johnson does his best: appears.

Caroline A. Lejeune

James Earl Jones – *(b 1931)*
'Coriolanus' – James Earl Jones sounded like a one-stringed double-bass with a faintly Calypso accent, and rolled about like a huge barrel set in motion by a homunculus within. *John Simon*

Boris Karloff - *(1887-1969)*
Like Lon Chaney, he reached stardom with the
sole assistance of the make-up man.
Graham Greene

Charles Kean - *(1811-68)*
His tone somewhat dogmatic but I prefer him
in the dining room to him on the stage.
Henry Robinson - 'Diary' (1856)

Edmund Kean - *(1787-1833)*
I know of no more irksome noises than those
which issue from his breast.   *Anon*

Kean is original; but he copies from himself.
His rapid descents from the hyper-tragic to the
infracolloquial though sometimes productive of
great effect are often unreasonable. To see him
act is like reading Shakespeare by flashes of
lightning. I do not think him thorough-bred
gentleman enough to play Othello.
Samuel T. Coleridge - 'Table Talk'

He had no gaiety; he could not laugh; he had
no playfulness that was not the playfulness of a
panther showing her claws every moment.
George H. Lewes - 'On Actors and Acting'

'Romeo & Juliet' - A rotationary movement of
the hand, as if describing the revolution of a
spinning jenny; multiplied slaps upon his
forehead, and manual elevation of his fall hair;
repeated knocking upon his own breast, and
occasional rapping at the chests of others; the
opening of his ruffles, like a schoolboy run riot
from the playground, and a strange indistinct
groping inside of his shirt, as if in search of
something uncommonly minute, filled up the
round of his action, while a voice most
unmusical, exerted to a harsh and painful
screech, afforded the finishing touch to a
Romeo decidedly the worst we have ever
witnessed on the London boards.
'The Sun' (1815)

Diane Keaton - *(b 1946)*
In real life, Keaton believes in God. But she
also believes that the radio works because there
are tiny people inside it.   *Woody Allen (1975)*

An acting style that's really a nervous
breakdown in slow-motion.   *John Simon*

John Kemble - *(1757-1823)*
Frogs in a marsh, flies in a bottle, wind in a
crevice, a preacher in a field, the drone of the
bagpipe, all yielded inimitable soporific
monotony of Mr Kemble.   *George Coleman*

Alan Ladd - *(1913-64)*
Alan Ladd is hard, bitter and occasionally
charming, but he is, after all, a small boy's idea
of a tough guy.   *Raymond Chandler*

No one ever pretended that he could act. He
got to the top, therefore, by a combination of
determination and luck.   *David Shipman*

Dinsdale Landen - *(b 1931)*
Beethoven in 'The Copyist' - Let's face it, Mr
Dinsdale Landen was not born to play
Beethoven. However, last night he took a
running jump at it and landed up as Lon
Chaney.   *Nancy Banks-Smith (1978)*

Jessica Lange - *(b 1949)*
'King Kong' (1976) - A dumb blonde who falls
for a huge plastic finger.
Judith Crist - 'Saturday Review'

Charles Laughton - *(1899-1962)*
He was a big, brazen, show-off actor. He went
overboard sometimes and, in some of the poor
films he made, he got near to chewing the
scenery.   *David Shipman*

He had a face that faintly resembled a large
wad of cotton wool.   *Joseph von Sternberg*

Gertrude Lawrence - *(1898-1952)*
'Skylark' - A bad play saved by a bad
performance.   *George S. Kaufman*

Vivien Leigh - *(1913-67)*
'Macbeth' - Her Lady Macbeth is more niminy-
piminy than thundery-blundery, more viper
than anaconda, but still quite competent in its
small way.   *Kenneth Tynan (1955)*

Margaret Leighton - *(1922-76)*
Rosalind in 'As You Like It' - This Rosalind was
a gay and giddy creature - loads of fun, game
for any jape, rather like a popular head girl -
but a tiring companion, I felt, after a long day.
Kenneth Tynan (1952)

Jack Lemmon - *(b 1925)*
'The Front Page' (1974) - Jack Lemmon's Hildy
Johnson is like a mortuary assistant having a
wild fling. *'New Yorker'*

He has a gift for butchering good parts while
managing to look intelligent, thus constituting
Hollywood's abiding answer to the theatre.
Wilfrid Sheed

Jerry Lewis - *(b 1926)*
This arrogant, sour, ceremonial, pious,
chauvinistic egomaniac. *Elliot Gould*

Moira Lister - *(b 1923)*
'The Gazebo' - Miss Moira Lister speaks all her
lines as if they are written in very faint ink on a
tele-prompter slightly too far away to be read
with comfort. *Bernard Levin (1960)*

John Lodge - *(1903-85)*
'The Tenth Man' - Mr John Lodge continues to
suffer from a kind of lockjaw, an inability to
move the tight muscles of his mouth, to do
anything but glare with the dumbness and
glossiness of an injured seal.
Graham Greene (1936)

Sophia Loren - *(b 1934)*
She is quite impossible to photograph, too tall,
too big-boned, too heavy all around. The face is
too short, the mouth is too wide, the nose is too
long. *Anonymous screentest cameraman*

Bela Lugosi - *(1882-1956)*
For some people, he was the embodiment of
dark, mysterious forces, a harbinger of evil
from the world of shadow. For others he was
merely a ham actor appearing in a type of film
unsuitable for children and often unfit for
adults. *Arthur Lennig*

Ida Lupino - *(b 1914)*
'The Hard Way' - His familiar expression of
strained intensity would be less quickly relieved
by a merciful death than by Ex-Lax.
James Agee (1942)

Ali MacGraw - *(b 1938)*
'Players' (1979) - A multi-million-dollar tennis
movie - that didn't score. Maybe it was just the
fact that (1) Ali MacGraw can't act, (2) Dean-
Paul Martin can't act, or (3) nobody really

gives a fig about Ali MacGraw. *Rona Barrett*

'The Getaway' (1972) - Miss MacGraw cannot
act at all . . . her delivery of lines is rather like
a grade-school pupil asking to be excused to go
to the bathroom. *John Simon*

Geraldine McEwan - *(b 1932)*
'Edward II' - Geraldine McEwan, powdered
white like a clownish whey-faced doll,
simpered, whined and groaned to such an effect
as the Queen, that Edward's homosexuality
became both understandable and forgivable.
Milton Shulman (1968)

Virginia McKenna - *(b 1931)*
Rosalind in 'As You Like It' - In an attempt to be
boyish she raises her voice so loudly at times
that I had the impression she was a desperate
auctioneer trying to sell the lines.
Milton Shulman - 'Evening Standard' (1954)

Steve McQueen - *(1930-80)*
His features resembled a fossilised wash-rag.
Alan Brien

His face had that look people get when they
ride in elevators. *Anatole Broyard (1976)*

I can honestly say he's the most difficult actor I
ever worked with. *Norman Jewison*

You've got to realise that a Steve McQueen
performance lends itself to monotony.
Robert Mitchum

Jayne Mansfield - *(1932-67)*
Dramatic art in her opinion is knowing how to
fill a sweater. *Bette Davis*

Miss United Dairies herself. *David Niven*

Frederic March - *(1897-1975)*
'The Buccaneer' (1958) - He came in like a lion
and went out like a ham.
Frank Nugent

Dean-Paul Martin - *(b 1951)*
'Players' (1979) - A multi-million-dollar tennis
movie - that didn't score. Maybe it was just the
fact that (1) Ali MacGraw can't act, (2) Dean-
Paul Martin can't act, or (3) nobody really
gives a fig about Ali MacGraw. *Rona Barrett*

Mary Martin - *(1913-90)*
She is O.K., if you like talent. *Ethel Murman*

Ilona Massey - *(1912-74)*
'Ziegfeld Follies Revue' - Miss Ilona Massey, the
blonde film actress who is making her
Broadway debut in this production, is doubtless
very good in films.
Willela Waldorf - 'New York Post'

Raymond Massey - *(1896-1983)*
'Abe Lincoln in Illinois' (1938) - Massey won't
be satisfied until he's assassinated.
George S. Kaufman

Walter Matthau - *(b 1920)*
He looked like a half-melted rubber bulldog.
John Simon

He is about as likely a candidate for superstardom
as the neighbourhood delicatessen man. *'Time'*

A. E. Matthews - *(1869-1960)*
'This Was a Man' - A. E. Matthews ambled
through 'This Was a Man' like a charming
retriever who has buried a bone and can't quite
remember where. *Noël Coward (1926)*

Victor Mature - *(b 1915)*
Hollywood's self-acclaimed disciple of conceit
and vulgarity. *William Mooring*

To which Mature replied - Actually, I'm a
golfer. That is my real occupation. I never was
an actor, ask anybody, particularly the critics.

Eleanora Mendelssohn - *(1900-51)*
Miss Mendelssohn, as the demented governess,
gave a notable display of the continental acting
technique, which seems to have quite a bit in
common with professional wrestling.
Wolcott Gibbs

Melina Mercouri - *(b 1923)*
Her blackly mascaraed eye-sockets gape like
twin craters, unfortunately extinct.
John Simon

Bette Midler - *(b 1944)*
'The Divine Miss M' - Her eyebrows are clipped
parentheses, and she paints her face for the last
days of the Weimar Republic. Frizzy orange
curls grow in her wild hair like snapdragons
pleading for water.
Paul Gardner - 'New York Times' (1972)

Liza Minnelli - *(b 1946)*
She has only two things going for her - a father
and a mother. *John Simon*

I always thought Miss Minnelli's face deserving
- of first prize in the beagle category.
John Simon

Tom Mix - *(1880-1940)*
They say he rides like a part of the horse, but
they don't say which part. *Robert E. Sherwood*

Marilyn Monroe - *(1926-62)*
A broad with a big future behind her.
Constance Bennett

It's like kissing Hitler. *Tony Curtis*

She was good at being inarticulately abstracted
for the same reason that midgets are good at
being short.
Clive James - 'At the Pillars of Hercules'

As far as talent goes, Marilyn Monroe was so
minimally gifted as to be unemployable, and
anyone who holds to the opinion that she was a
great natural comic identifies himself
immediately as a dunce.
Clive James - 'Commentary' (1973)

A natural phenomenon like Niagara Falls or the
Grand Canyon. You can't talk to it. It can't talk
to you. All you can do is stand back and be
awed by it. *Nunnally Johnson*

I don't think she could act her way out of a
paper script. She has no charm, delicacy or
taste. She is just an arrogant little tail-twitcher
who learned to throw sex in your face.
Nunnally Johnson

A vacuum with nipples. *Otto Preminger*

You'd better learn secretarial work or else get
married. *Emmeline Snively - Blue Book
Modelling Agency (1944)*

On her marriage to playwright Arthur Miller -
Egghead marries Hourglass. *'Variety'*

Is Marilyn a person at all or is she one of the
greatest DuPont products ever invented? She
has breasts like granite and a brain like Swiss
cheese. *Billy Wilder*

Hollywood didn't kill Marilyn Monroe; it's the Marilyn Monroes who are killing Hollywood. Marilyn was mean. Terribly mean. The meanest woman I have ever met around this town. I have never met anyone as mean as Marilyn Monroe.   *Billy Wilder*

Dudley Moore – *(b 1935)*
A grubby cherub.   *Jonathan Miller*

Eddie Murphy – *(b 1961)*
'Another 48 Hours' (1990) – He skulks through the picture like a pasha who has been ordered to perform for his slaves.   *Owen Gleiberman –*
'Entertainment Weekly' (1990)

Stephen Murray – *(1912–83)*
'King Lear' – He maintains a gravelly, rasping note, hammering at you until – after two hours without an interval – you rush out thankfully to listen to the traffic.
John Barber – 'Daily Mail' (1951)

Guido Nazzo
Guido Nazzo is nazzo guido!   *George S. Kaufman*
[*This review was much copied and plagued Nazzo's career. Kaufman apologised and offered the hard-done-by actor a part in one of his musicals.*]

Pola Negri – *(1897–1987)*
She had a blind and uncritical admiration of her own genius in the blaze of which her sense of humour evaporated like a dew-drop on a million-watt arc lamp.   *Rodney Ackland*

Paul Newman – *(b 1925)*
'The Color of Money' – Newman . . . is an aristocrat of sleaze.   *David Ansen (1986)*

'The Silver Chalice' (1954) – He delivered his lines with the emotional fervor of a conductor announcing local stops.   *'New Yorker'*
[*A. H. Weiler felt Newman was . . . Rarely better than wooden.*]

He has the attention span of a lightning bolt.
Robert Redford (1986)

David Niven – *(1909–83)*
'Dodsworth' (1936) – In this picture we are privileged to see Mr Samuel Goldwyn's latest 'discovery'. All we can say about this actor is

that he is tall, dark and not the slightest handsome.   *'Detroit Free Press'*

Kim Novak – *(b 1933)*
Trying to hide what Kim Novak has got is like trying to hide an elephant in a phone booth.
Joshua Logan

Ivor Novello – *(1893–1951)*
'King's Rhapsody' – He plays the King with all the assurance of a man who has gauged public taste down to the last emotional millimetre.
Milton Shulman – 'Evening Standard' (1949)

Margaret O'Brien – *(b 1937)*
If this child had been born in the Middle Ages, she'd have been burned as a witch.
Lionel Barrymore (1943)

Carroll O'Connor – *(b 1922)*
'Home Front' – His Texas accent doesn't come closer than Perth Amboy.   *Joel Siegel (1985)*

Maureen O'Hara – *(b 1920)*
She looks as though butter wouldn't melt in her mouth – or anywhere else for that matter.
Else Lanchester (1950)

Laurence Olivier – *(1907–89)*
'Othello' (1964) – Sir Laurence is elaborately at ease, graceful and suave, more like a seducer than a cuckold. But as the jealousy is transfused into his blood, the white man shows through more obviously. He begins to double and treble his vowels, to stretch his consonants to stagger and shake, even to vomit, near the frontiers of self-parody. His hips oscillate, his palms rotate, his voice skids and slides so that the Othello music takes on a Beatle beat.
Alan Brien – 'Sunday Telegraph'

'Hamlet' (1948) – Olivier's idea of introspection was to hood his eyes, dentalise his consonants and let the camera circle his blondined head like a sparrow looking for a place to deposit its droppings.
Robert Brustein – 'New Republic' (1986)

Shylock in 'The Merchant of Venice'– Any fan of Walt Disney comics could . . . see that he had modelled his appearance on Scrooge McDuck.
Clive James – 'Observer' (1974)

Ryan O'Neal - *(b 1941)*
'What's Up, Doc?' (1972) - He is so stiff and clumsy that he can't even manage a part requiring him to be stiff and clumsy.   *Jay Cocks*

Cliff Osmond
After he had auditioned for a singing role - He has Van Gogh's ear for music.   *Billy Wilder*

Peter O'Toole - *(b 1932)*
'Macbeth' - He delivers every line with a monotonous tenor bark as if addressing an audience of deaf Eskimos. It was P. G. Wodehouse who memorably said that the 'Tomorrow and tomorrow and tomorrow' speech has got a lot of spin on it but, as delivered by Mr O'Toole, it is hit for a six like a full toss.
Michael Billington - 'The Guardian' (1980)

The very prototype of a ham.   *Omar Sharif*

Ronald Pickup - *(b 1940)*
Cassius in 'Julius Caesar' - He plays Cassius like a malignant ferret snapping at the air.
Michael Billington (1977)

Harve Presnell - *(b 1933)*
London stage version of 'Gone with the Wind' - He was so wooden that they should have used him for kindling in the burning of Atlanta.   *Anon*

Basil Radford - *(1897-1953)*
'The Innocent Party' - Mr Basil Radford imitates an American so inadequately that I arranged to take the next boat to New York to lay my apologies at the feet of that continent.
James Agate - 'Sunday Times' (1938)

Robert Redford - *(b 1936)*
He has turned almost alarmingly blond - he's gone past platinum, he must be plutonium; his hair is coordinated with his teeth.
Pauline Kael (1976)

Poor little man, they made him out of lemon Jello and there he is. He's honest and he's hard-working. But he's not great.
Adela Rogers St John

Vanessa Redgrave - *(b 1937)*
'The Bostonians' (1984) - This is a soul under perpetual migraine attack.
Richard Schickel - 'Time'

Natasha Richardson
'The Handmaid's Tale' (1990) - She is singularly unappealing: hard-featured, frozen, cocky, stolidly invulnerable.   *John Simon*

Ralph Richardson - *(1902-83)*
'An Inspector Calls' - Mr Richardson, looking for something to act in a nebulous part, paraded like some dummy in the Tailoring Section of a 'Britain Used to Make It' exhibition.
Anon (1947)

A year or two ago Richardson had the habit of acting all his parts with his buttocks.
James Agate - 'Ego 1' (1932)

'Othello' (1938) - Richardson killed himself from the start with a disastrous make-up; no man looking like a golliwog can persuade us that he is talking like a god.   *Harold Hobson*

'Macbeth' - His Macbeth is slovenly; and to go further into it would be as frustrating as trying to write with a pencil whose point has long since worn down to the wood.
Kenneth Tynan (1952)

'The White Carnation' - He has taken to ambling across our stages in a spectral, shell-shocked manner, choosing odd moments to jump and frisk, like a man through whom an electric current is being intermittently passed.
Kenneth Tynan (1953)

Diana Rigg - *(b 1938)*
After appearing nude in 'Abelard and Heloise' - Diana Rigg is built like a brick mausoleum with insufficient flying buttresses.
John Simon (1970)

Mickey Rooney - *(b 1920)*
His favourite exercise is climbing tall people.
Phyllis Diller

Mrs Ruppert
Mrs Ruppert is unfortunately not an actress at all . . . but her pathos is deliciously comic.
R. E. Golding Bright

Dame Margaret Rutherford - *(1892-1972)*
'Murder, She Says' (1962) - A British comedienne whose appearance suggests an overstuffed electric chair.   *'Time'*

George Sanders - *(1906-72)*
He had a face, even in his twenties, which
looked as though he had rented it on a long
lease and had lived in it so long he didn't want
to move out.
David Niven - 'Bring On the Empty Horses'

Prunella Scales - *(b 1938)*
'Anatol' - Her face . . . is that of a worried
hamster.   *Anon*

Arnold Schwarzenegger
'Running Man' (1987) - He's hilariously cast as
someone called 'the running man'; he's so
muscle-bound he can hardly walk.
David Edelstein - 'Village Voice'

Paul Scofield - *(b 1922)*
'Othello' (1980) - He comes with the stiff
swagger of a peacock and an equally awkward
accent, which makes him sound less like a
Moor and more like a man wrestling with a new
set of National Health teeth.   *'The Field'*

Sir Thomas More in 'A Man for All Seasons'
(1960) - Towards the end, when he is bowed
and grey but unbroken, Mr Scofield comes into
his own, for greyness is then needed. But until
then, his playing bores the doublet and hose off
me.   *Bernard Levin - 'Daily Express'*

George C. Scott - *(b 1926)*
'Exorcist III' (1990) - Since no Exorcist sequel
would be complete without a name actor
making a fool of himself, this one had George
C. Scott popping his eyes and grimacing into
the camera as though someone had put a gun to
his head and said, 'Overact, or else!'
Owen Gleiberman - 'Entertainment Weekly'

Omar Sharif - *(b 1932)*
'The Tamarind Seed' (1974), co-starring with Julie
Andrews - Very believably playing an English
secretary, Julie fell for Omar, who had been
cast as a Russian spy because there was no role
available as a date-picker.
Clive James - 'Observer' (1979)

Norma Shearer - *(1900-83)*
A face unclouded by thought.   *Lillian Hellman*

Cybill Shepherd - *(b 1949)*
She comes across like one of those inanimate

objects, say, a cupboard or a grandfather clock,
which is made in certain humorous shorts to
act, through trick photography.   *John Simon*

Simone Signoret - *(1921-85)*
Lady Macbeth in 'Macbeth' - Simone Signoret's
Lady Macbeth, a conical, bell-tented matron
who moves on wheels like a draped Dalek
surmounted by a beautiful Medusa head, speaks
with a monotous French accent punctuated by
American vowels.
Alan Brien - 'Sunday Telegraph' (1966)

Cornelia Otis Skinner - *(1901-79)*
On her one-woman show - A woman talking
steadily for two hours is hardly my idea of
entertainment whether in the theatre or in
private.   *George J. Nathan*

Sylvester Stallone - *(b 1946)*
'Over the Top' (1987) - It's time to put an All
Points Bulletin on Sylvester Stallone. Not for
artistic crimes but for grossly abusing his
license to pander.
David Elliot - 'San Diego Union'

Maureen Stapleton - *(b 1925)*
'The Emperor's Clothes' - Miss Stapleton played
the part as though she had not yet signed the
contract with the producer.
George J. Nathan (1953)

Rod Steiger
'Waterloo' (1970) - One cannot direct an
explosion. Rod Steiger is an explosion.
Sergei Bondarchuk

Yorke Stephens
'The Sorrows of Satan' - Mr Yorke Stephens
fulfils his obligations to Miss Corelli and the
audience most scrupulously but with the air of
a man who has resolved to shoot himself the
moment the curtain is down.
G. B. Shaw - 'Saturday Review' (1897)

Barbra Streisand - *(b 1942)*
She ought to be called 'Barbra Strident'.
Stanley Kaufmann

On the set of 'Hello Dolly' (1969) - I have more
talent in my smallest fart than you have in your
entire body.   *Walter Matthau*

I would love to work with Barbra Streisand again in something appropriate, perhaps Macbeth. *Walter Matthau*

I have no disagreement with Barbra Streisand. I was merely exasperated by her tendency to megalomania. *Walter Matthau*

The most pretentious woman the cinema has ever known. *Ryan O'Neal*

She looks like a cross between an aardvark and an albino rat surmounted by a platinum-coated horse bun. *John Simon*

Her acting consists entirely of fishily thrusting out her lips, sounding like a cabbie bellyaching at breakneck speed, and throwing her weight around. *John Simon*

Dudley Sutton - *(b 1933)*
Jacko in 'Incident at Vichy' - Peter Woods' efficient production has some odd lapses, such as casting Dudley Sutton as the one Jew who was identified by the size of his nose, though everyone knows Mr Sutton's nose, which gives his face that fascinating look of a squashed car-seat, is non-existent.
Alan Brien - 'Sunday Telegraph' (1966)

Elizabeth Taylor - *(b 1932)*
'Cleopatra' (1963) - Elizabeth Taylor is the first Cleopatra to sail down the Nile to Las Vegas.
Anon

She has an insipid double chin, her legs are too short and she has a slight potbelly.
Richard Burton (1967)

If I'd had a face like Elizabeth Taylor's I would never have won my two Oscars. *Bette Davis*

When Elizabeth Taylor meets a man she takes him and squeezes the life out of him and then throws away the pulp. *Eddie Fisher's mother*

'Private Lives' - Miss Taylor lists about, her hands fluttering idly, like a wind-up doll in need of a new mainspring.
'New York Times' (1983)

She is short, with a large head and an anvil-shaped torso, which, when clothed, seems to

have been stuffed into a quality holdall.
Deborah Norton - 'The Observer' (1977)

'The Taming of the Shrew' (1967) - Just how garish her commonplace accent, her squeakily shrill voice, and the childish petulance with which she delivers her lines are, my pen is neither scratchy nor leaky enough to convey.
John Simon

'The Sandpiper' (1965) - On the few occasions when she does reveal her bosom (or part thereof), one breast (or part thereof) proves sufficient to traverse an entire wide-screen frame - diagonally. *John Simon*

She has grown so ample that it has become necessary to dress her almost exclusively in a variety of ambulatory tents. *John Simon*

'The Mirror Crack'd' (1980) - A pharaonic mummy, moving on tiny castors, like a touring replica of the Queen Mother.
'Sunday Times' (1980)

The way things are going I'd be more interested in seeing Cleopatra play the life of Elizabeth Taylor. *Earl Wilson (1962)*

Lou Tellegen - *(1881-1934)*
'Women Have Been Kind' - Mr Tellegen has recently seen fit to write his memoirs; though it is at least debatable that it would have been more public-spirited of him to have sent the results to the zoo.
Dorothy Parker - 'New Yorker' (1931)
[*Dorothy Parker's review was titled - 'Kiss and Tellegen'*]

Shirley Temple - *(b 1928)*
She wasn't very good. She was fine when she was 6 or 7. But did you notice how she couldn't act when she was 14? *Tatum O'Neal*

Ellen Terry - *(1847-1928)*
'Anon' - She was an extremely beautiful girl and as innocent as a rose. When Watts kissed her she took it for granted that she was going to have a baby. *G. B. Shaw*

Lady Macbeth in 'Macbeth' - Judging from the banquet, Lady Macbeth seems an economical housekeeper and evidently patronises local industries for her husband's clothes and the servants' liveries, but she takes care to do all her own shopping in Byzantium.

Oscar Wilde (1888)

Rip Torn – *(b 1931)*
'Daughter of Silence' – Mr Torn allows words to revolve wanly in his mouth like a jingling key chain in a bored man's pocket.

John Simon (1961)

John Travolta – *(b 1954)*
Because the Jews killed our Lord, they are forever marked with hair on their shoulders – something that no gentile man has on his shoulders except for John Travolta.

Gore Vidal

Sir Herbert Beerbohm Tree – *(1853–1917)*
'Hamlet' – Funny without being vulgar.

W. S. Gilbert

Do you know how they are going to decide the Shakespeare–Bacon dispute? They are going to dig up Shakespeare and dig up Bacon; they are going to set their coffins side by side, and they are going to get Tree to recite 'Hamlet' to them. and the one who turns in his coffin will be the author of the play. *W. S. Gilbert*

Mr Tree wants one thing to make him an excellent Falstaff and that is to get born again as unlike himself as possible . . . Mr Tree might as well try to play Juliet. *G. B. Shaw (1896)*

He quoted foreign languages to hide his ignorance of life.

Arthur B. Walkley – 'The Times'

Lana Turner – *(b 1920)*
She's a nice girl, but it's like sitting in a room with a beautiful vase. *Judy Garland*

Kenneth Tynan – *(1927–80)*
Responding to Beverley Baxter's review [Evening Standard] on his role of The Player King in 'Hamlet' (1949) – I am quite a good enough critic to know that my performance is not 'quite dreadful'; it is, in fact, only slightly less than mediocre. I do not actually exit through the scenery, or wave to my friends in the audience.

Brenda Vaccaro – *(b 1939)*
A cube-shaped creature who comes across as a dikey Kewpey doll. *John Simon*

Rudolph Valentino – *(1895–1926)*
He had the acting ability of the average wardrobe. *Anon*

Trish Van Devere – *(b 1943)*
Barely more than a smiling hole in the air.

'Sunday Times'

David Warner – *(b 1941)*
'Hamlet' (1965) – He delivers the soliloquies as though he were dictating to the literary pirates jotting down the first-quarto version of the play. *Julian Holland – 'Daily Mail'*

John Wayne – *(1907–79)*
Demonstrating facial isometrics, based on newly discovered manuscripts of Calvin Coolidge. *'Harvard Lampoon'*

Raquel Welch – *(b 1942)*
I have never met anyone so badly behaved.

James Mason

She's silicone from the knees up.

George Masters – make-up artist

Mae West – *(1892–1980)*
A plumber's idea of Cleopatra. *W. C. Fields*

Jane White – *(b 1922)*
'Coriolanus' – Her every look, gesture and move is that of a fishwife, suffering in equal measure from neurasthenia and megalomania.

John Simon (1965)

Billie Whitelaw – *(b 1932)*
'The Dutch Courtesan' – Billie Whitelaw's Dutch accent sounded like a Welsh au pair by way of Calcutta. *Milton Shulman (1964)*

Esther Williams – *(b 1923)*
Wet she's a star – dry she ain't. *Fanny Brice*

Kenneth Williams – *(1926–88)*
'Signed and Sealed' – There is no point in seeing a man reduced to hysterical panic if hysterical panic is his forte.

Michael Billington – 'The Guardian' (1976)

Noel Williams
Claudius in 'Julius Caesar' – At his first entrance
Mr Williams strikes a note of banality from
which he never afterwards departs. To establish
that he is a crafty fellow, he keeps his eyes
roving from side-to-side, like air-pockets in a
pair of spirit-levels; and he clinches the case
against Claudius by eating grapes. It is a rule of
Shakespearean production that men who eat
grapes are definitely voluptuaries and probably
murderers. *Kenneth Tynan*

Nicol Williamson – *(b 1938)*
Williamson is always 'brilliant' and 'dazzling'.
He is brilliant, he is dazzling – yet he's awful
. . . probably the worst major (and greatly
gifted) actor on the English-speaking screen
today. *Pauline Kael – 'New Yorker' (1970)*

'Hamlet' – The voice is a quick twang, the sort
of sound a man might make if he spoke rapidly
while carefully pinching the bridge of his nose.
The performance, as a whole, seems one given
by a museum guide who obviously knows what
he is talking about but is severely crippled by a
blocked sinus.
Walter Kerr – 'New York Times' (1969)

Norman Wisdom – *(b 1918)*
Mr Wisdom, though English, does what most
successful American stars have done: every
look, every gesture, every intonation of his
shrieks (or, perhaps reeks): 'Love me! Love me!
Love me! Look how little, how defenceless, how
lovable I am!' *John Simon (1965)*

Natalie Wood – *(1938-81)*
She is built like a brick dollshouse.
Harry Kurnitz

Edward Woodward
'Cyrano de Bergerac' – As swashbuckling
Cyrano, Mr Woodward's performance buckles
more often than it swashes.
Kenneth Hurren – 'Spectator' (1970)

Monty Woolley – *(1888-1963)*
'The Man Who Came to Dinner' (1942) – These
popping consonants, this practiced roar, this
sarcasm without inner compulsion and ranting
without the fire of rage – these are possibly
necessary where there are people to be tickled
in the back row, where motion needs

overemphasis to keep the front rows awake, and
where an actor has been so long in the same
routine that he has felt it go stale and slipped
into making it louder and busier, hence funnier.
The camera eye picks this all up, shows
relentlessly where it is false, and literally throw
it at your head, back row or front.
Otis Ferguson

Mary Ann Yates – *(1728-87)*
Too much stumping about, and too much
flumping about. *Kitty Clive*

Susannah York – *(b 1941)*
The personification of uninformed arrogance in
youth. *John Huston*

COMEDY

Musical Comedy is where all good jokes go just
before they die. *Anon*

Comedy, like sodomy, is an unnatural act.
Marty Feldman (1969)

A comedian is not an actor. His work bears the
same relation to acting as that of a hangman, a
midwife or a divorce lawyer bears to poetry, or
that of a bishop to religion.
H. L. Mencken (1929)

SPECIFIC
(Listed by Comedian)

Anon Duo
They skunk up their show with immaterial
material. *Irving Hoffman*

Fred Allen – *(1894-1956)*
'The Little Show' – Fred Allen delivers in a flat
voice like the wit of the senior dormitory.
Brooks Atkinson – 'New York Times' (1929)

Steve Allen – *(b 1921)*
When I can't sleep, I read a book by Steve
Allen. *Oscar Levant*

I'm fond of Steve Allen, but not so much as he
is. *Jack Paar*

Jack Benny – *(1894-1974)*
When Jack Benny plays the violin it sounds as
if the strings are still back in the cat. *Fred Allen*

He couldn't ad-lib a belch after a Hungarian meal.   *Fred Allen*

When they asked Jack Benny to do something for the Actors' Orphanage – he shot both his parents and moved in.   *Bob Hope*

When Moshe Dayan heard him play, he took the patch off his eye and put it over his ear.
                                      Zubin Mehta

Jack's TV show did a lot for the image of black people in America. Before Jack came along, everybody thought blacks were only fit to be shoeshine boys and railroad porters. The Jack Benny program proved to Americans that they could also be chauffeurs, dishwashers and houseboys!   *Desmond Wilson*

Milton Berle – *(b 1908)*
He's been on TV for years and I finally figured out the reason for his success – he never improved.   *Steve Allen*

The Thief of Bad Gags.   *Walter Winchell*

Lenny Bruce – *(1926–66)*
Lenny, despite what his cultists and the Hoffman movie said, was dirty and sick. He had no redeeming social values.   *James Bacon*

George Burns – *(b 1896)*
George, you're too old to get married again. Not only can't you cut the mustard, honey, you're too old to open the jar.   *La Wanda Page*

I know George is a great music lover, because a poet once said that every man kills the thing he loves, and I've heard what George does to a song.   *Harry Von Zell*

Chevy Chase – *(b 1943)*
Chevy Chase couldn't ad-lib a fart after a baked-bean dinner.   *Johnny Carson*

Cheech and Chong
If dope smoking doesn't damage your brain, how come so many teenyboppers think Cheech and Chong are funny?   *Tony Hendra*

'Anon Comedy Records' – Unless Cheech and Chong get run over by a truck, the release of

these albums is likely to be the two best pieces of news in the comedy field for a while.
                                'National Lampoon'

Andrew Dice Clay
A rude-boy comedian who lived up to what the critics say about him. Unlike Lenny Bruce, Richard Pryor, George Carlin or Eddie Murphy, Andrew Dice Clay really is a showbiz jerk who uses dirty words and cheap insults for shock value.   *Owen Gleiberman –*
                          'Entertainment Weekly' (1990)

Clay isn't worth arguing about; take away his four letter words and he stands exposed, a dull doofus.   *Ken Tucker (1990)*

Phyllis Diller – *(b 1917)*
Her laugh – Like an old Chevrolet starting up on a below-freezing morning.   *Anon*

When she started to play, Steinway came on personally and rubbed his name off the piano.
                                  Bob Hope (1985)

Phyllis has had so many face lifts, there's nothing left in her shoes.   *Bob Hope*

I treasure every moment that I do not see her.
                                  Oscar Levant

Bob Hope – *(b 1903)*
Bob Hope is still about as funny as he ever was. I just never thought he was that funny in the first place.   *Chevy Chase*

He cannot make me laugh. When I see Hope, I tell him, 'You are the worst comedian I've ever seen in my life.'   *Jackie Gleason*

George Jessel – *(1898–1981)*
Here in nature's arms I nestle,
Free at last from George Jessel.
                        Eddie Cantor – 'Proposed Epitaph'

Oscar Levant – *(1906–72)*
There's nothing wrong with Oscar Levant that a really first-class miracle couldn't cure.
                                  Sam Behrman

A character who, if he had not existed, could not be imagined.   *Sam Behrman*

'The Memoirs of an Amnesiac' – Anybody who doesn't like this book is healthy.   *Groucho Marx*

A tortured man who sprayed his loathing on anyone within range.   *Shelley Winters*

Marx Brothers

At the Majestic Theatre, Chicago – The Marx Brothers and several relatives ran around the stage for about an hour – why, I don't know.
     Percy Hammond

Working for the Marx Brothers was not unlike being chained to a galley car and lashed at ten-minute intervals.   *S. J. Perelman (1965)*

Chico Marx – *(1895-1977)*

Now there sits a man with an open mind. You can feel the draft from here.   *Groucho Marx*

Groucho Marx – *(1890-1977)*

He's a male chauvinistic piglet.   *Betty Friedan*

Eddie Murphy – *(b 1961)*

'Raw' – The material here isn't just raw, it's scraped to the bone.
     Michael Wilmington – 'Los Angeles Times' (1987)

Don Rickles – *(b 1926)*

He looks like an extra in a crowd scene by Hieronymus Bosch.
     Kenneth Tynan – 'New Yorker' (1978)

Will Rogers – *(1879-1935)*

The bosom friend of senators and congressman was about as daring as an early Shirley Temple movie.   *James Thurber*

Robin Williams – *(b 1951)*

A fellow with the inventiveness of Albert Einstein, but the attention span of Daffy Duck.
     Tom Shales

Henny Youngman – *(b 1906)*

He's beautiful. He'll tell thirty jokes and only get laughs with four of them. That kind of heroism is exquisite to me.   *Jackie Gleason*

MUSIC

Music is but a fart that's sent
  From the guts of an instrument.   *Anon*

If music be the breakfast food of love, kindly do not disturb until lunch time.
          James Agee – 'Agee on Film'

The aim and final end of all music should be none other than the glory of God and the refreshment of the soul. If heed is not paid to this, it is not true music but a diabolical bawling and twanging.   *Johann Sebastian Bach*

It is quite untrue that the English people don't appreciate music. They may not understand it but they absolutely love the noise it makes.
          Sir Thomas Beecham

Music hath charm to soothe a savage beast – but I'd try a revolver first.   *Josh Billings*

Respectable people do not write music or make love as a career.   *Alexander Borodin*

A great fondness for music is a mark of great weakness, great vacuity of mind; not of hardness of heart; not of vice, not of downright folly; but of a want of capacity, or inclination, for sober thought.   *William Cobbett –*
          'Advice to Young Men' (1820)

The ear disapproves but tolerates certain musical pieces; transfer them into the domain of our nose, and we will be forced to flee.
          Jean Cocteau

Music is almost as dangerous as gunpowder.
          Jeremy Collier (1698)

I hate music, especially when it's played.
          Jimmy Durante

Music is the most disagreeable and the dearest of all the noises.   *Theophile Gautier*

Music sweeps by me like a messenger carrying a message that is not for me.
          George Eliot (1868)

The worse kind of music is that which is insipid to the ear. Even that which has an aggressively vulgar flavour is preferable to it. And when the former cloaks itself either in cheap morality or in cheap sentiment, it reaches the pinnacle of bad taste.
          Edwin Evans – 'The Margin of Music' (1924)

Song is the licensed medium for bawling in public things too silly or sacred to be uttered in ordinary speech.   *Oliver Herford*

Anybody who has listened to certain kinds of music, or read certain kinds of poetry, or heard certain kinds of performances on the concertina, will admit that even suicide has its brighter aspects.   *Stephen Leacock*

The first thing that music must understand is that there are two kinds of music – good music and bad music. Good music is music that I want to hear. Bad music is music that I don't want to hear.
          Fran Lebowitz – 'Metropolitan Life' (1978)

Every kind of music is good, except the boring kind.   *Gioacchino Rossini*

Music is essentially useless, as life is.
          George Santayana

Hell is full of musical amateurs: music is the brandy of the damned.
          G. B. Shaw – 'Man & Superman' (1903)

Musical people are so absurdly unreasonable. They always want one to be perfectly dumb at the very moment when one is longing to be absolutely deaf.
          Oscar Wilde – 'An Ideal Husband' (1895)

If one hears bad music, it is one's duty to drown it by one's conversation.   *Oscar Wilde –*
          'The Picture of Dorian Gray' (1891)

CLASSICAL MUSIC

A fugue is a piece of music in which the voices

come in one after another and the audience go
out one after another.   *Anon*

A musicologist is a man who can read music
but can't hear it.   *Sir Thomas Beecham*

Composers shouldn't think too much – it
interferes with their plagiarism.   *Howard Dietz*

Bestial cries are heard: neighing horses, the
squeal of a brass pig, crying jackasses, amorous
quacks of a monstrous toad. This excruciating
medly of brutal sounds is subordinated to a
barely perceptible rhythm. Listening to this
screaming music for a minute or two, one
conjures up an orchestra of madmen, sexual
maniacs, led by a man-stallion beating time
with an enormous phallus.
              Maxim Gorky – 'In America' (1906)

Classical music is music written by famous
dead foreigners.   *Arlene Heath*

I occasionally play works by contemporary
composers and for two reasons. First to
discourage the composer from writing any more
and secondly to remind myself how much I
appreciate Beethoven.
              Jascha Heifitz – 'Life' (1968)

The main thing the public demands of a
composer is that he be dead.   *Arthur Honegger*

Classical music is the kind we keep thinking
will turn into a tune.   *Kin Hubbard*

A concert is a polite form of self-imposed
torture.   *Henry Miller – 'Tropic of Cancer'*

The good composer is slowly discovered, the
bad composer is slowly found out.
                        Sir Ernest Newman

The old new music began before our time, in
the incunabula of Satie, Debussy, Schonberg,
and Stravinsky – you may throw in (out)
Bartok (hammer, hammer, hammer) and
Hindemith (no sex?). All art even Hindemith,
even Satie, even Poulenc, is sad, so sad and
lost.   *James Sellars*

Too many pieces finish too long after the end.
                        *Igor Stravinsky –
              'New York Review of Books' (1971)*

CRITICISM

How seldom do we meet with a proper amount
of sympathy, knowledge, honesty and courage
in a critic. It is sad indeed for the world of
music that criticism, in many respect so useful,
should often be the occupation of persons in no
way endowed with these qualities.
      Carl Philipp Bach – 'Autobiography' (1773)

Music critics – drooling, drivelling, doleful,
depressing, dropsical drips.
                        Sir Thomas Beecham (1954)

Criticism of the arts in London, taken by and
large, ends in a display of suburban
ominscience which sees no further than the
next door garden.   *Sir Thomas Beecham*

The trouble with music critics is that so often
they have the score in their hands and not in
their heads.   *Sir Thomas Beecham*

On his critics in Leipzig – As for the oxen from
Leipzig, they may say what they will. They will
make nobody immortal with their talking, and,
likewise, they will not take immortality from
the man whom Apollo has destined for
immortality.   *Ludwig van Beethoven*

Critics! Poor devils! Where do they come from?
At what age are they sent to the slaughter
house? What is done with their bones? Where
do such animals pasture in the daytime? Do
they have females and young? How many of
them handled the brush before being reduced to
the broom?   *Hector Berlioz –
              'Les Grotesques de la Musique' (1859)*

A piece of music is an art work, and trying to
judge it by 'instinct' in four seconds has about
as much validity as trying to evaluate the worth
of a woman by the size of her bust.
                        *Elmer Bernstein –
                  'Film Music Notebook' (1971)*

If a literary man puts together two words about
music, one of them will be wrong.
                        Aaron Copland

Criticism too often takes the form of brilliant
variations on the theme of 'You're wrong
because you didn't do as I did,' or 'You're

talented and I'm not, that can't go on.'
Claude Debussy – 'La Revue Blanche' (1901)

Hardly does a composer appear than people start devoting essays to him and weighing his music down with ambitious definitions. They do far greater harm than even the fiercest detractors. *Claude Debussy*

Critics never change; I'm still getting the same notices I used to get as a child. They tell me I play very well for my age. *Mischa Elman*

Critics make pipi on music and think they help it grow. *Andre Gedalge*

I have hitherto nearly always fared badly with the so-called critics. Where there was sympathy there was no comprehension, and for so-called comprehension without sympathy I do not give a penny. *Edvard Grieg (1900)*

A sympathetic critic's disapproval is the most interesting and stimulating experience I know. *Gustav Holst*

The only true criticism of music is the playing thereof. *James Huneker – 'Bedouins' (1920)*

There are three worlds of music – the composer's, the performer's and the critic's. *Eric Leinsdorf*

Keep on good terms with the critics! Visit the gentlemen now and then! Consider that you cannot behave with the 'dignity of man' in a kennel, but that you have only to take care that the watchdogs leave you alone. *Gustav Mahler (1897)*

There is so much talk about music, and yet so little is said. For my part, I believe, that words do not suffice for such a purpose and if I find they did suffice, I would finally have nothing more to do with music. *Felix Mendelssohn*

It is a common grievance of the musical critic that he generally has to do his work with one eye on the clock. Perhaps that is just as well, after all; it may keep him from the too fond vanity of fixing both eyes on eternity.
Sir Ernest Newman – 'New Witness' (1918)

Replying to a review from Rudolf Louis – I am sitting in the smallest room of my house. I have your review before me. In a moment it will be behind me. *Max Reger*

Last year I gave several lectures on 'Intelligence and Musicality in Animals'. Today, I shall speak to you about 'Intelligence and Musicality in Critics'. The subject is very similar.
Eric Satie – 'In Praise of Critics' (1918)

Pay no attention to what the music critics say – no statue has ever been put up to a critic.
Jean Sibelius

I had a dream the other night about music critics. They were small and rodent-like with padlocked ears, as if they had stepped out of a painting by Goya. *Igor Stravinsky*

The immoral profession of musical criticism must be abolished. *Richard Wagner (1848)*

I seriously advise all sensitive composers to die at the age of thirty-seven. I know I've gone through the first halcyon period, and am just about ripe for my critical damnation.
Sir William Walton (1939)

Critics are misbegotten abortions.
Ralph Vaughan Williams (1930)

REVIEWS (Listed by composer)

Anon
It may be music in a hundred years; it is not music now. *H. Krehbiel*

Thomas Arne – *(1710–78)*
Thoughtless, dissipated and careless, he neglected or rather scoffed at all other but musical reputation. *Fanny Burney*

For Dr Arne, who sold me a horse, a very dull one; and sent me a comic opera, ditto.
David Garrick

Johann Sebastian Bach – *(1685–1750)*
All Bach's last movements are like the running of a sewing machine. *Arnold Bax*

Too much counterpoint; what is worse, Protestant counterpoint.
Sir Thomas Beecham (1971)

On being asked if Bach was still composing – No madam, he's decomposing.   *W. S. Gilbert*

His compositions are deprived of beauty, of harmony, and of clarity of melody.
Johann A. Scheibe (1737)

Bela Bartok – *(1881-1945)*
If the reader were so rash as to purchase any of Bela Bartok's compositions, he would find that they each and all consist of unmeaning bunches of notes, apparently representing the composer promenading the keyboard in his boots. Some can be played better with the elbows, others with the flat of the hand. None require fingers to perform nor ears to listen to.
Frederick Corder –
'Musical Quarterly' (1915)

'Fourth Quartet' –The third movement began with a dog howling at midnight, proceeded to imitate the regurgitations of the less refined type of water-closet and concluded with the cello reproducing the screech of an ungreased wheelbarrow.   *Alan Dent*

Ludwig van Beethoven – *(1770–1827)*
Beethoven's last quartets were written by a deaf man and should only be listened to by a deaf man.   *Sir Thomas Beecham*

'Seventh Symphony' – What can you do with it? It's like a lot of yaks jumping about.
Sir Thomas Beecham

'Ninth Symphony' – Even Beethoven thumped the tub; the Ninth Symphony was composed by a sort of Mr Gladstone of music.
Sir Thomas Beecham

'Seventh Symphony' – If Beethoven's 7th Symphony is not abridged by some means, it will soon fall into disuse.   *Philip Hale (1837)*

'Eighth Symphony' – Eccentric without being amusing, and laborious without effect.
'The Harmonican' (1827)

'Fourth Symphony' – He has pleased, at most, his fanatical admirers.   *August von Kotzebue (1807)*

'Ninth Symphony' – What is the Ninth Symphony compared to a Tin Pan Alley hit played on a hurdy-gurdy and a memory?
Karl Kraus

He snarled at everyone . . . a dirty, foul, dark man.   *Frau Meinander*

You can chase a Beethoven symphony all your life and never catch up.   *Andre Previn*

Beethoven always sounds like the upsetting of bags – with here and there a dropped hammer.
John Ruskin (1881)

'Fifth Symphony' – An orgy of vulgar sound.
Louis Spohr

'Ninth Symphony' – The fourth movement is so monstrous and tasteless, and in its grasp of Schiller's Ode, so trivial that I cannot understand how a genius like Beethoven could have written it.   *Louis Spohr (1861)*

'Second Symphony' – A crude monstrosity, a serpent which continues to writhe about, refusing to expire, and even when bleeding to death still threshes around angrily and vainly with its tail.   *'Zeiting Welt' (1828)*

Hector Berlioz – *(1803–69)*
It needs no gift of prophecy to predict that Berlioz will be utterly unknown a hundred years hence to everybody but the encyclopaedists and the antiquarians.
'Boston Daily Advertiser' (1874)

Berlioz composes by splashing his pen over the manuscript and leaving the issue to chance.
Frederick Chopin

Berlioz, musically speaking, is a lunatic; a classical composer only in Paris, the great city of quacks. His music is simply and undisguisedly nonsense.
'Dramatic & Musical Review' (1843)

'Les Francs Juges' – Such an incongruous mess, that one ought to wash one's hands after handling one of his scores.
Felix Mendelssohn (1834)

'Symphonie Fantastique' – What a good thing this isn't music.   *Gioacchini Rossini*

He does not know how to write.

Pierre Scudo (1852)

John Blow - *(1648-1708)*
It does not appear that Purcell, whom he did himself the honour to call his scholar, ever threw notes about at random, in his manner, or insulted the ear with lawless discords, which no concords can render tolerable.

Dr Charles Burney

Pierre Boulez - *(b 1925)*
'Pli Selon Pli' - Pretty monstrous and monstrously pretty. *Igor Stravinsky*

Johannes Brahms - *(1833-97)*
Proposed sign above a door of the Boston Symphony Hall - Exit in case of Brahms. *Philip Hale*

'Requiem' - His Requiem is patiently borne only by the corpse. *G. B. Shaw - 'The Star' (1892)*

'Requiem' - There are some expressions in life which should not be demanded twice from any man, and one of them is listening to the Brahms Requiem. *G. B. Shaw*

Brahms is just like [Alfred, Lord] Tennyson, an extraordinary musician with the brains of a third-rate village policeman. *G. B. Shaw*

The real Brahms is nothing more than a sentimental voluptuary, rather tiresomely addicted to dressing himself up as Handel or Beethoven and making a prolonged and intolerable noise. *G. B. Shaw*

I have played over the music of that scoundrel Brahms. What a giftless bastard! It annoys me that this self-inflated mediocrity is hailed as a genius. Brahms is chaotic, and absolutely empty dried-up stuff.

Peter Tchaikovsky - 'Diary' (1886)

'Piano Concerto No 2' - Anyone who can gulp down this Concerto with appetite can face a famine without concern. It may be taken for granted that his digestive system is enviable, and, in a famine, will function splendidly on the nutritive equivalent of window-panes, corks, stove-pipes and the like. *Hugo Wolf*

Max Bruch - *(1838-1920)*
'Violin Concertos' - Pussycats.

Sir Neville Cardus -
'Manchester Guardian' (1938)

Anton Bruckner - *(1824-96)*
His music has the fragrance of heavenly roses, but it is poisonous with the sulphurs of hell.

Anon (1884)

'Seventh Symphony' - In the first movement alone I took notice of six pregnancies and at least four miscarriages. *Sir Thomas Beecham.*

'Symphonies' - Symphonic boa-constrictors.

Johann Brahms

'Third Symphony' - A vision of Beethoven's Ninth becoming friendly with Wagner's Valkyries and finishing up trampled under their hooves. *Eduard Hanslick*

'Symphonies' - The anti-music ravings of a half-wit. *Hans von Bulow (1888)*

John Bull - *(1563-1628)*
Of all the bulls that live, this hath the greatest ass's ears. *Queen Elizabeth I*

William Byrd - *(1543-1623)*
Byrd's misfortune is that when he is not first-rate, he is so rarely second-rate.

Gustav Holst

Frederick Chopin - *(1810-49)*
Had he submitted music to a teacher, the latter, it is to be hoped, would have torn it up and thrown it at his feet - and that is what we symbolically wish to do.

Ludwig Rellstab (1933)

Claude Debussy - *(1862-1918)*
Debussy played the piano with the lid down.

Robert Bresson

'From Dawn to Noon on the Sea' from 'La Mer' - I liked the bit about quarter to eleven. *Erik Satie*

'La Mer' - The audience seemed rather disappointed; they expected the ocean, something big, something colossal, but they were served instead some agitated water in a saucer. *Louis Schneider - 'Gil Blas' (1905)*

Frederick Delius - *(1862-1934)*
Delius is all intoxication but it is all the same intoxication. Wagner has a hundred ways of making you tight.   *James Agate - 'Ego 7' (1944)*

The musical equivalent of blancmange.
Bernard Levin - 'Enthusiasms' 1983

The ugliness of some of his music is really masterly.   *'The Sun' (1899)*

Gaetano Donizetti - *(1797-1848)*
'La Favorita' - Marionette stage-music!
Robert Schumann (1847)

Edward Elgar - *(1857-1934)*
'Symphony in A Flat' The musical equivalent of St Pancras Station - neo-Gothic, you know.
Sir Thomas Beecham

His music is like the façade of Euston Station.
Sir Thomas Beecham

'Dream of Gerontius' - Holy water in a German Beer Barrel.   *George Moore*

Elgar is one of the Seven Humbugs of Christendom.   *G. B. Shaw*

Cesar Franck - *(1822-90)*
The word progress denotes something moving forward, and in moving forward you must leave something behind. Music is going forward and Cesar Franck is being left behind.
Camille Saint-Saens

Charles Gounod - *(1818-93)*
'La Reine de Saba' - Faust was his Austerlitz; La Reine de Saba will be his Waterloo.
Anon (1862)

'Redemption' - If you will only take the precaution to go in long enough after it commences, and to come out long enough before it is over, you will not find it wearisome.
G. B. Shaw

Edvard Grieg - *(1943-1903)*
'Peer Gynt' - Two or three catch-penny phrases served up with plenty of orchestral sugar.
G. B. Shaw - 'The World' (1892)

Gustav Holst - *(1874-1934)*
'Fugal Concerto for flute, oboe and string orchestra, No. 2' - The little Concerto trots peacefully away until, suddenly getting up and scratching itself it disappears in a trill for the two wind instruments and a rising pizzicato scale in an absurd rhythm.   *Sir Ernest Newman*

Charles Ives - *(1874-1954)*
An Old Testament prophet crying a New Mythology in the American wilderness.
David Woodridge - 'Charles Ives' (1974)

Franz Liszt - *(1851-1919)*
'Piano Concerto No. 2' - Sawdust and spangles.
Neville Cardus -
'Manchester Guardian' (1938)

Composition indeed! Decomposition is the proper word for such hateful fungi, which choke up and poison the fertile plains of harmony, threatening the world with drought.
'Musical World' (1855)

Gustav Mahler - *(1860-1911)*
'Symphony No. 2' - If that was music, I no longer understand anything about the subject.
Hans von Bulow

'Symphony No. 3' - It's all very well, but you can't call 'that' a symphony. *Sir William Walton*

Wolfgang A. Mozart - *(1756-91)*
Ah Mozart! He was happily married - but his wife wasn't.   *Victor Borge*

'Symphony in G minor' -The G-minor Symphony consists of eight remarkable measures - surrounded by a half-hour of banality.   *Glenn Gould (1984)*

Mozart died too late rather than too soon.
Glenn Gould (1984)

It is sobering to consider that when Mozart was my age he had already been dead for a year.
Tom Lehrer

Modest Mussorgsky - *(1835-81)*
An amateur with moments of genius.
Sir Ernest Newman - 'The Nation' (1914)

Jacques Offenbach - *(1819-90)*
He has written nothing that will live, nothing
that has made the world better. His name as
well as his music will soon be forgotten.
'Chicago Tribune' (1880)

Sergei Rachmaninov - *(1873-1943)*
Rachmaninov's immortalising totality was his
scowl. He was a six-and-a-half-foot-tall scowl.
Igor Stravinsky

Maurice Ravel - *(1875-1937)*
'Bolero' - The most insolent monstrosity ever
perpetrated in the history of music. From the
beginning to the end of its 339 measures it is
simply the incredible repetition of the same
rhythm and above all it is the blatant
recurrence of an overwhelmingly vulgar cabaret
tune that is little removed from the wail of an
obstreperous back-alley cat.
*Edward Robinson - 'The American
Mercury' (1932)*

Gioacchino Rossini - *(1792-1868)*
Rossini would have been a great composer if his
teacher had spanked him enough on the
backside.   *Ludwig van Beethoven*

After Rossini dies, who will there be to promote
his music?   *Richard Wagner*

Camille Saint-Saëns - *(1835-1921)*
I'm told that Saint-Saëns has informed a
delighted public that since the war began he
has composed music for the stage, melodies, an
elegy and a piece for the trombone. If he'd been
making shell-cases instead it might have been
all the better for music.   *Maurice Ravel (1916)*

Arnold Schonberg - *(1874-1951)*
He'd be better off shovelling snow.
Richard Strauss

Franz Schubert - *(1797-1828)*
'Symphony No. 5' - Charming music to hear in a
beer-garden, with the right company.
Neville Cardus - 'Manchester Guardian' (1938)

Robert Schumann - *(1810-56)*
A pathological case, a literary man turned
composer.   *James Huneker - 'Old Fogy' (1913)*

Humphrey Searle - *(1915-82)*
He writes music that sounds like the theme

from 'Star Wars' played backwards through a
washing machine.
Clive James - 'The Observer' (1979)

Dmitri Shostakovich - *(1906-75)*
'Symphony No. 5' - Creative reply of a Soviet
artist to just criticism.
Note on the original score (1937)

Dame Ethel Smythe - *(1858-1944)*
She would be like Richard Wagner, if only she
looked a bit more feminine.   *Osbert Sitwell*

Sir Charles Stanford - *(1852-1924)*
The stuff I hate and which I know is ruining
any chance for good music in England is stuff
like Stanford's which is neither fish, flesh, fowl,
nor good red-herring.   *Edward Elgar*

Difficult to please and glad to be pleased.
Ivor Gurney

Stanford is all crotchets and fads and moods.
Gustav Holst

His very facility prevented him from knowing
when he was genuinely inspired and when his
work was routine stuff.
Ralph Vaughan Williams (1957)

Karl-Heinz Stockhausen - *(b 1928)*
When asked if he had heard any Stockhausen - No,
not at all. But, I believe I have stepped in some.
Sir Thomas Beecham

More boring than the most boring of
eighteenth-century music.   *Igor Stravinsky*

Richard Strauss - (1864-1949)
If it must be Richard, I prefer Wagner; if it
must be Strauss, I prefer Johann.   *Anon*

Debussy is like a painter who looks at his
canvas to see what more he can take out;
Strauss is like a painter who has covered every
inch and then takes the paint he has left and
throws it at the canvas.   *Ernest Bloch*

'Till Eulenspiegel' - An hour of original music in
a lunatic asylum.   *Claude Debussy*

'Alpensymphonie' - Better to hang oneself than
ever write music like that.
Paul Hindemith (1917)

Such an astounding lack of talent was never before united to such pretentiousness.

Petr Tchaikovsky (1888)

Igor Stravinsky - *(1882-1971)*
'The Rite of Spring' - Where did these turkeys learn to write music, anyway? *'Comoedia' (1913)*

'The Rite of Spring' - This 'Sacre du printemps', or rather a 'Massacre du printemps'.

H. Moreno - 'Le Menestrel' (1914)

'Le Sacre du Printemps' - The music of Le Sacre du Printemps baffles verbal description. Practically it has no relation to music at all as most of us understand the word.

'Musical Times' (1913)

No one can any longer write in the fat style of Strauss. That was killed by Stravinsky. He stripped the body of much of its clothes. Music is the craft of building structures and that is what Stravinsky represents. *Vladimir Nabokov*

His music used to be original. Now it is aboriginal.

Sir Ernest Newman - 'Musical Times' (1921)

His Symphony for Wood Instruments was written in memory of Debussy; if my own memories of a friend were as painful as Stravinsky's seem to be, I would try to forget him. *Ernest Newman*

Bach on the wrong notes. *Sergey Prokofiev*

While vibro-atmospheric copulations
With mezzo-forte mysteries of noise,
Prelude Stravinsky's statement of the joys
That unify the monkeydom of nations.

Siegfried Sassoon

Sir Arthur Sullivan *(1842-1900)*
He is like a man who sits on a stove and then complains that his backside is burning.

W. S. Gilbert

Peter I. Tchaikovsky - *(1840-93)*
'Slavic March' - One feels that the composer must have made a bet, for all that his professional reputation was worth, that he would write the most hideous thing that had ever been put on paper, and he won it, too.

'Boston Evening Transcript' (1883)

'Piano Concerto No. 1' - A hackneyed battle-scarred work that usually has been hammered by the pugilists of the keyboard into cast-iron vulgarity. *Neville Cardus -*
'Manchester Guardian' (1936)

'Violin Concerto' - it gives us, for the first time, the hideous notion that there can be music that stinks to the ear. *Eduard Hanslick (1881)*

'First Piano Concerto' - Like the first pancake it is a flop. *N. F. Soloviev (1875)*

Ralph Vaughan Williams - *(1872-1958)*
'Fifth Symphony' - Listening to the Fifth Symphony of Ralph Vaughan Williams is like staring at a cow for forty-five minutes.

Aaron Copland

Antonio Vivaldi - *(1675-1741)*
Vivaldi is greatly overrated - a dull fellow who would compose the same form so many times over. *Igor Stravinsky*

Richard Wagner - *(1813-83)*
I love Wagner, but the music I prefer is that of a cat hung up by its tail outside a window and trying to stick to the panes of glass with its claws. *Charles Baudelaire*

Wagner is evidently mad. *Hector Berlioz*

He is endowed with a temper so insolent that criticism cannot touch his heart - even admitting that he has a heart, which I doubt.

George Bizet (1871)

If Bach wriggles, Wagner writhes.

Samuel Butler - 'Notebooks' (1912)

To defend Wagner merely because Saint-Sens attacks him is too simple. We must cry 'Down with Wagner!' together with Saint-Saens. That requires real courage. *Jean Cocteau*

A composer whose music is better than it sounds. *Mark Twain*

A composer who had some wonderful moments, but awful quarter hours. *Gioacchino Rossini*

I like Wagner's music better than any other music. It is so loud that one can talk the whole

time without people hearing what one says.
That is a great advantage.   *Oscar Wilde (1891)*

SINGERS

Anon
That was a voice? She sounds like a garbage
disposal with a butcher knife caught in it.
                                    Anon

Her voice was precisely like a stringed
instrument that one imagined to have fallen
into disuse when the viola came along to
replace it.   *Noël Coward*

She was an ageing singer who had to take any
note above A with her eyebrows.
                            Montague Glass

Her singing was mutiny on the high C's.
                            Hedda Hopper

Musicians have the reputation of being not
overly bright. This happens to be only too
fatally true in the case of singers.
                        Alexander King (1965)

Al Jolson
Al Jolson wouldn't mail a letter for anyone or
do any good to my knowledge, but there isn't
anyone who is even twenty-fourth behind him.
                            George Jessel

Tom Jones
To hear Tom Jones sing Sinatra's 'My Way' is
roughly akin to watching Tab Hunter play
King Lear. Mr Jones is, in the words of his own
hit, not unusual . . . at least not as a singer, as a
sex symbol he is nothing short of inexplicable.
                Sheridan Morley – 'Punch' (1972)

Frankie Laine
His approach to the microphone is that of an
accused man pleading with a hostile jury.
                        Kenneth Tynan (1952)

Mario Lanza
He recognised no authority, no discipline, no
frontiers except his own gigantic appetite
for food, drink and women.   *Hedda Hopper*

Frank Sinatra
He's the kind of guy that, when he dies, he's
going to heaven and give God a bad time for
making him bald.   *Marlon Brando*

Sinatra could be terribly nice one minute and,
well, not so nice the next. I was not impressed
with the creeps and Mafia types he kept around
him.   *Prince Charles*

Barbra Streisand
'A Star is Born' (1977) – I realise with a gasp
that this progressively more belligerent
caterwauling can sell anything – concerts,
records, movies. And I feel as if our entire
society were ready to flush itself down in
something even worse than a collective death
wish – a collective will to live in ugliness and
self-debasement.   *John Simon – 'New York'*

She looks like a cross between an aardvark and
an albino rat surmounted by a platinum-coated
horse bun.   *John Simon*

Mel Torme
Mel Torme is one of those singers whose
success makes me feel that middle-age is not
just around the corner but a long way behind.
            Derek Monsey – 'Sunday Express' (1956)

Margaret Truman
Miss Truman is a unique American
phenomenon with a pleasant voice of little size
and fair quality . . . There are few moments
during her recital when one can relax and feel
confident she will make her goal, which is the
end of the song.
        Paul Hume – 'Washington Post' (1950)
*Replying to the above review of his daughter's
singing* – I have just read your lousy review
buried in the back pages of the paper. You
sound like a frustrated old man who never
made a success, an eight-ulcer man on a four-
ulcer job, and all four ulcers working. I have
never met you, but if I do you'll need a new
nose and plenty of beefsteak and perhaps a
supporter below . . . Westbrook Pegler, a
guttersnipe, is a gentleman compared to you.
You can take that as more of an insult than a
reflection of your ancestry.
                        Harry S. Truman (1950)

ROCK & POP ARTISTS

AC/DC
'*Blow up your Video*' – Some hints on how to enjoy this LP.
1. Give your brain the evening off.
'Smash Hits'

John Adams
'*The Chairman Dances*' – If Mr Adams is playing with a full deck, he's taken pains to include both jokers. *'Q' (1988)*

Ian Anderson of Jethro Tull
There's a challenge within the group, that if Ian Anderson gets back into the charts – with or without Jethro Tull – then we'll split up.
Nick of Westworld (1988)

Angst
As an optimistic high school band auditioning for the first time for a night's work in the local lounge, they'd be hard pushed to get the gig.
'Q'

Rick Astley
'*Whenever You Need Somebody*' produced by Stock, Aitken & Waterman – Churning out sewage, churning out effluent, SAW are fouling the air. Rick's just their little helper.
'Melody Maker' (1988)

Bananarama
They have no pretensions toward anything other than dancing around their plassy bags and making lots of loot. *'Sounds'*

The Beach Boys
'*Still Cruisin*'' – If you've been waiting for the Beach Boys to hit rock bottom, the suspense is over . . . 'Still Cruisin'' is still born.
Jimmy Guterman – 'Rolling Stone' (1989)

The Beatles
The Beatles are not merely awful, I would consider it sacrilegious to say anything less than that they are godawful. They are so unbelievably horrible, so appallingly unmusical, so dogmatically insensitive to the magic of the art, that they qualify as crowned heads of anti-music, even as the imposter popes went down in history as 'anti-popes'.
William F. Buckley Jr – 'On the Right' (1964)

Beatlemania is like the frenzied dancing and shouting of voodoo worshippers and the howls and bodily writhings of converts among primitive evangelical sects in the southern states of America.
Dr F. Casson – 'The Times' (1963)

What are the Beatles? I have never been able to understand what one beat singer is saying. Perhaps I shall fare better with four?
Noël Coward

The real Merseysound is the voice of 80,000 crumbling houses and 30,000 people on the dole. *'Daily Worker'*

Their lyrics are unrecognisable as the Queen's English. *Edward Heath*

I see the Beatles have arrived from England. They were forty pounds overweight, and that was just their hair. *Bob Hope (1964)*
[*Dean Martin felt they didn't have long hair – just smaller foreheads and higher eyebrows.*]

I declare that the Beatles are mutants. Prototypes of evolutionary agents sent by God, endowed with a mysterious power to create a new human species – a young race of laughing freemen. *Timothy Leary*

Do you remember when everyone began analysing Beatle songs? I don't think I understood what some of them were supposed to be about. *Ringo Starr*

They look like shaggy Peter Pans. *'Time'*

Bee Gees
'*ESP*' – Few people know that the CIA are planning to cripple Iran by playing this album on special loudspeakers secretly parachuted into the country. *'Record Mirror' (1988)*

Pat Benatar
She looks like a newscaster.
'New Musical Express'

Big Audio Dynamite
'*Tighten Up Vol 88*' – A shambling bag of half-ideas and rhyming couplets that you wouldn't put your name to even if you were a poet and didn't know it. *'Sounds'*

Jon Bon Jovi

'Blaze of Glory' – In comparison, his earlier 'Dead or Alive' sounds like Aaron Copland's Appalachian Spring'.

'Entertainment Weekly' (1990)

Bon Jovi sounds like bad fourth generation metal, a smudgy Xerox of Quiet Riot.

Jimmy Guterman – 'Rolling Stone'

Boy George of Culture Club

Boy George is all England needs – another queen who can't dress.   *Joan Rivers*

He sounded like a wind-up doll, as he generally dressed.   *'Rolling Stone' (1986)*

Braniac 5

'World Inside' – It sounds like Hawkwind with a limited supply of drugs.   *'New Musical Express'*

Bros

I remember when pop music meant jerking off to pictures of Marc Bolan and duffing up Bay City Rollers' fans in lunch breaks. Being 13 was never as vapid as this. If it had been, we would all be traffic wardens by now.   *'Melody Maker'*

'Push' – This album is an insult to 12-year-olds.
'New Musical Express' (1988)

The Cars

Anyone with a passable voice and access to a bath could come up with a Cars album in a couple of minutes.   *'New Musical Express'*

Cheap Trick

'Busted' –If I were a zit-faced, under-age dude with a spit-polished Camaro and a cooler full of beers, *Busted* would make perfect highway fodder to take my mind off the slow clicking of the odometer.   *Chuck Dean (1990)*

'Luxury' – This album is so cynical it makes Stock, Aitken and Waterman seem naive.
'Sounds' (1988)

Leonard Cohen

He gives you the feeling that your dog just died.
'Q'

Elvis Costello

The man who would love to write songs as moving as those that inspired him.   *'Sounds'*

Roger Daltrey of The Who

He had a face like a police identikit photograph.
Richard Baker – 'Omnibus' BBC TV (1983)

Taylor Dayne

In a world free from financial pressures people like Taylor Dayne wouldn't make albums at all.
'Record Mirror'

Depeche Mode

The 'Mode' make very dubious puffing noises as though they were blowing up a paddling pool.   *'Smash Hits'*

Duran Duran

A baroque art-rock bubble-gum broadcast on a frequency understood only by female teenagers and bred field mice.   *Mark Coleman (1987)*

Eurythmics

'Revenge' – Eurythmics haven't lost their innovative tendencies; they've tied them in neat little packages and made them safe by labelling them. For a group that once managed to subvert new pop formats and still be popular, what kind of revenge is that?
Mark Coleman (1986)

Everything But The Girl

'Idlewild' – Music for young single schoolteachers only.   *'Melody Maker ' (1988)*

Faith No More

'Introduce Yourself' – What they didn't tell you of course was that Michael Ryan had this on the walkman as he strode up the High Street that afternoon.   *'Melody Maker' (1988)*

Fat Boys

They should have been born as Barry White in triplicate.   *'New Musical Express'*

Five Star

Wood Green shopping centre has been committed to vinyl.   *'New Musical Express'*

Frankie Goes To Hollywood

'Frankie Came!' said the badges. To Hollywood, yeah! but in the other sense of the phrase, poor Frankie just couldn't keep it up.
Steve Pond – 'Rolling Stone' (1985)

A remote controlled sham with less depth (not to mention stage presence) than its sloganeering T-shirt.   *Ira Robbins – 'Rolling Stone' (1985)*

Martin Fry of ABC

'Alphabet City' – Fry sings as though he takes all of this nonsense seriously.

'New Musical Express'

Guns 'n' Roses

'Appetite for Destruction' issued with a warning label: *'Contains lyrics which some people may find offensive'* – What kind of people? The kind of codgers that G 'n' R might offend are all relegated to walking frames.

'New Musical Express' (1988)

Morten Harket of A-Ha

'Take on Me' – Morten Harket's croon sailed toward the horizon with abandon of a bright-eyed prep-school grad anticipating great days ahead. But here his unyielding groan suggests something closer to a mid-life crisis. Just what we need: another washed-up art-rock curmudgeon, probably bitter because his hackwork was never taken as seriously as his mom tells him it should have been.

Chuck Eddy – 'Entertainment Weekly' (1991)

George Harrison

The boy The Beatles called in to make up the numbers.

'Melody Maker'

Buddy Holly

The biggest no talent I ever worked with.

Paul Cohen (1956)

Chrissie Hynde of The Pretenders

'Get Close' – This failed musical imperialism undermines Hynde's political theses just as surely as the liner notes proclamation that the album 'was made without cruelty to animals' assumes that Hynde's vegetarianism doesn't contradict her fondness for leather apparel.

Rob Tannenbaum – 'Rolling Stone' (1987)

Michael Jackson

He's a great singer – but he's not the most masculine guy, is he?

Alexander O'Neal

Whacko Jacko!

'The Sun'

Mick Jagger of The Rolling Stones

On the early Rolling Stones – The singer will have to go.

Eric Easton (1963)

He sees all women as tarts.

Bianca Jagger

Jellybean

'Just Visiting the Planet' – His overall effect is that of the playlist from the sort of disco that gives away free tickets outside foreign language schools.

'Q'

Jimi Hendrix Experience

A triptych of smirking simian faces . . . The Experience's destruction is inevitable rather than accidental, the surfacing of a violent streak that has always run through Rock and Roll, the spontaneous violence of the young.

'Newsweek'

Jive Bunny and the Mastermixers

History, it is said, repeats itself: first as tragedy, then as farce. But in the case of Jive Bunny and the Mastermixers, it repeats itself like a bad Spanish dinner.

J. D. Considine (1990)

Johnny Hates Jazz

JHJ make the sort of noises indicative of childhoods spent being chosen last for pick up games of rounders.

'Sounds'

Paul King

'Joy' – It's really like Bananarama singing 'Anarchy in the UK'.

'Record Mirror'

Lynyrd Skynyrd

Playing 'Free Bird', Skynyrd were utterly horrible. Playing anything else they're merely a competent bar-room boogie band.

'New Musical Express'

Paul McCartney

'Give My Regards to Broad Street' (1985) – You didn't have to play this movie backward to know that Paul is dead.

'Washington Post'

Malcolm McLaren

'Round the Outside' – McLaren is a cultural kleptomaniac . . . you should also know that McLaren sings and plays as much on this album as Milli Vanilli did on theirs.

Jim Farber (1991)

Madonna

She is so hairy – when she lifted up her arm, I thought it was Tina Turner in her arm-pit.

Joan Rivers

George Michael

'Faith' – Why do we say 'Oh George Michael . . .

can't say I like him but I respect him. He's a craftsman. He's good at his job'? Do we say 'That milkman's a bloody genius, he's good at his job' or 'I reckon that lollypop lady's a genius because she gets the kids across the road okay'? No, we don't. So it's high time we stopped praising efficiency as if it were inspiration. *'Melody Maker'*

The Mission
'Sweet Smile of Mystery' – The most misguided sonic blunder since the overblown rock operas of the mid-70s. *Bob Mack (1990)*

Morrissey of The Smiths
'Strangeways, Here We Come' – If you've ever considered Morrissey a self-obsessed jerk, *Strangeways, Here We Come* isn't likely to change your mind. *David Browne (1987)*

If Morrissey's a genius then what's he doing in a f****** pop group?
Shane MacGowan of The Pogues (1988)

M.T.V. [Music Television]
A videot's delight. *Anon*

MTV is the lava lamp of the 1980s.
Doug Ferrari

Watching three hours of one type of music, you lose your f****** mind. *Ozzy Osborne (1989)*

Olivia Newton-John
If white bread could sing it would sound like Olivia Newton-John. *Anon*

Olivia will always hold the microphone as if it were a lollipop, sing of love as if it were the mumps, look sultry as if she were about to sneeze. *Clive James – 'The Observer' (1980)*

Gary Numan
He has a voice like David Bowie holding his nose very hard. *'Smash Hits'*

Sinead O'Connor
The female Johnny Rotten of the eighties.
'New Musical Express'

Yoko Ono
Her voice sounded like an eagle being goosed.
Ralph Novak – 'People' (1985)

Marie Osmond
She is so pure, Moses couldn't even part her knees. *Joan Rivers*

Robert Palmer
'Didn't Mean to Turn You On' – Palmer's somnambulant reading of this sexy ballad was about as erotic as a Dr Ruth lecture.
'Rolling Stone' (1986)

Pet Shop Boys
Heralding themselves as prophets of doom for British youth culture, the Pet Shop Boys come across more like crybabies who haven't got their allowance. *Rob Hoeburger (1987)*

The Power Station
Given their lack of wattage, a better name for this band might have been the 'Mild Boys'.
David Fricke (1985)

Elvis Presley
Elvis Presley had nothing to do with excellence, just myth. *Marlon Brando*

You ain't going nowhere son. You ought to go back to drivin' a truck. *Jim Denny (1954)*

He was a silly little country boy who just happened to sing like a nigger. *Albert Goodman*

Mr Presley has no discernible singing ability. His speciality is rhythm songs which he renders in an undistinguished whine; his phrasing, if it can be called that, consists of the stereotyped variations that go with a beginner's aria in a bath-tub. For the ear he is an utterable bore. He is a rock-and-roll variation of one of the most standard acts in show business, the virtuoso of one of the most standard acts in show business, the virtuoso of the hootchy-kootchy. *Jack Gould – 'New York Times' (1956)*

His one speciality is an accented movement of the body that heretofore has been primarily identified with the repertoire of the blonde bombshells of the burlesque runway. The gyration never had anything to do with the world of popular music and still doesn't.
Jack Gould – ibid

The dead son of a gun is still riding on my coat-tails. *Jerry Lee Lewis (1986)*

Elvis Presley wiggled and wiggled with such abdominal gyrations that burlesque bombshell Georgie Southern really deserves equal time to reply in gyrating kind. He can't sing a lick, makes up for vocal shortcomings with the weirdest and plainly planned, suggestive animation short of an aborigine's mating dance.

Jack O'Brien – 'New York Journal/American'

One small town boy, born at the right time, in the right place, in the right environment under the right circumstances represented the convergence of all the musical currents of America's sub-culture: black and white gospel, country and western, and rhythm and blues.

Henry Pleasants (1985)

'Love Me Tender' [The Movie] (1956) – Is it a sausage? It is certainly smooth and damp-looking, but whoever heard of a 172lb, six foot tall sausage? *'Time'*

Prince
Bambi with testosterone. *Owen Gleiberman –*
'Entertainment Weekly' (1990)

Jimmy Pursey of Sham 69
It only takes one prick to make a band, in this case . . . Jimmy Pursey. *'Melody Maker'*

Kenny Rogers
The musical equivalent of a black-velvet Elvis, the embodiment of schlock art.
Alanna Nash (1990)

The Rolling Stones
They look like boys whom any self-respecting mum would lock in the bathroom.
'Daily Express' (1964)

The ugliest pop group in Britain.
'Melody Maker'

A caveman-like quintet. *'New Musical Express'*

A symbol of rebellion against the boss, the clock and the clean-shirt-a-day routine.
'News of the World'

A leering quintet. *'Newsweek'*

After listening to the groans, pants and frankly dirty words of the Rolling Stones, one begins to

wonder where they dig up a DJ to play such garbage. *'Time'*

Linda Rondstadt
'Canciones de mi Padre' – Along comes her album of Mexican folk-songs and ballads, complete with a cover that makes her look like an El Torrito waitress who's been nibbling the guacamole.
David Browne – 'Rolling Stone' (1988)

Diana Ross
She is a piece of liquorice in shoes. She walks into a pool hall and they chalk her head.
Joan Rivers

David Lee Roth
'Skyscraper' – Rather like spending an hour with a neurotic child. *'Q' (1988)*

Roth's croon is a solemn croak; he sounds like Tom Waits after a tracheotomy.
Ken Tucker (1991)

Johnny Rotten of the Sex Pistols
Prince Charmless. *Michael Azzerad (1988)*

I can imagine him becoming a successful hairdresser – a singing Vidal Sassoon.
Malcolm McLaren

Run DMC
'Tougher than Leather' – Run DMC are simply thrashing around with clumsy obesity. This album is as soft as their stomachs.
'Melody Maker'

Todd Rungren
If Rungren ever has anything approaching a major hit, it will be totally by accident.
'New Musical Express'

Sade
She has always been crap!
'Melody Maker' (1988)

Saxon
They sound suspiciously like the purr of a clapped-out rusty scooter rather than the roar of a gleaming chrome Harley Davidson powerslave. *'Record Mirror'*

Sex Pistols
The Sex Pistols do as much for music as World

War Two did for peace.
'Melody Maker' (1976)

The Sex Pistols were the worst thing that's ever happened.   *Cliff Richard*

They wouldn't recognise the Antichrist even if he hit them in the face with a kipper.
Joe Strummer

Simple Minds

'Street Fighting Years' – If the road to hell is paved with good intentions, then Simple Minds have pulled onto Satan's expressway . . . An unfortunate example of politicised rock at its most simple minded.   *Mark Coleman (1989)*

Slayer

'Live: Undead' – Caught here in a retrospectively noisy 1984 tour, Slayer bring you the sound of Thora Hird negotiating a sewage outlet against her will.   *'Melody Maker'*

Grace Slick of Fairport Convention

She is like somebody's mom who's had a few too many drinks at a cocktail party.   *Nick Lowe*

Bruce Springsteen

He is a glorified gutter rat from a dying New Jersey town who walks with an easy swagger that is part residual stage presence, part boardwalk braggadacio.
Jay Cocks – 'Time' (1975)

After allowing '2 Live Crew' to use his 'Born in the USA' for their anti-censorship rap 'Banned in the USA' – Dear Mr Springsteen, I would suggest 'Raped in the USA' as your next album . . . You're now harmful to the women and children who have bought your albums.
Jack Thompson (1990)

Squeeze

A band for teachers who can't yet afford their first compact disc.   *'Melody Maker'*

Rod Stewart

He was so mean, it hurt him to go to the bathroom.   *Britt Ekland*

He has an attractive voice and a highly unattractive bottom. In his concert performances he now spends more time wagging the latter than exercising the former, thereby conforming to the established pattern by which popular entertainers fall prey to the delusion that the public loves them for themselves, and not for their work.
Clive James (1981)

'Out of Order' – Whatever the state-of-the-art backing, you can't disguise the fact that it's Rod, hollering away and talking through his cock.   *'Sounds'*

The Style Council

'Confessions of a Pop Group' – A hollow, humourless sham of a record by a couple of yobs with nob pretensions.   *'Sounds'*

Talking Heads

'Naked' – It's great that the Heads have the freedom to create the sort of record they want, but it's dull to listen to.   *'Record Mirror'*

The Temptations

At worst, soporific; at best, pleasantly soporific.
'New Musical Express'

Toto

'The Seventh One' – No cigar for guessing what the eighth one will be like.   *'Melody Maker'*

T'Pau

Their sound inhabits a hitherto no-go area somewhere in between Heart and Lena Zavaroni.   *'Sounds'*

Roger Waters of Pink Floyd

Not so much 'Another Brick in the Wall', but another prick with a haul!   *Anon*

'The Wall: Berlin' – It was going to be a very symbolic, a poignant celebration of the fact that the Berlin Wall was brought down. But it wasn't at all what it was supposed to be. The audience hadn't a clue what was going on . . . Masturbation, that's what it was.
Sinead O'Connor (1990)

[O'Connor had taken part in the massive concert – which cost four million pounds to stage, raising half that sum for disaster relief]

Jody Watley

Pure laughing gravy.   *'Sounds'*

**Paul Weller of
The Jam & The Style Council**
Weller's entire career has been a history of ill-advised haircuts and lamentable musical
gestures. *'Melody Maker'*

Wendy & Lisa
More candyfloss than highbrow. *'Q'*

Wham!
They look like a Gleem Ad.
Christopher Connelly – 'Rolling Stone'

'Music from the Edge of Heaven' – The real
disappointment is that *Music from the Edge of
Heaven* leaves unanswered the burning question
of modern pop. What the hell did Andrew
Ridgeley do in Wham!, anyway, aside from
filling up half the photos?
David Fricke – 'Rolling Stone' (1985)

Whitesnake
'Whitesnake' – There's more lyrical content in a
Pepsi Cola commercial.
J. D. Considine – 'Rolling Stone' (1987)

'Slip of the Tongue' – Slip of the scalpel would
have been more like it . . . Like a musical
lobotomy, it will leave you feeling nothing.
Kim Neely (1990)

Whodini
Don't expect to see Whodini make the Hip-Hop
First XI; they're most likely to be found in the
pavilion making the sandwiches. *'Sounds'*

Bruce Willis
'Return of Bruno' – Bruce Willis doesn't play
harmonica any worse than, say, David
Partridge played bass . . . Quite simply, Willis
can't sing. He may be a big riot on
'Moonlighting', but he has zero presence as a
vocalist. A host of back-up singers and an
arrangement busier than his accountants barely
manage to prop up these songs.
Jimmy Guterman – 'Rolling Stone' (1987)

Shanice Wilson
'Discovery' – Remember Janet Jackson's
'Control' LP for 1986? Shanice Wilson's
producer does. *'Record Mirror' (1988)*

Wilson Phillips
'Wilson Phillips' – Music so oily slick that the
CD nearly slips out of its jewelbox.
'Entertainment Weekly' (1990)

'Hold On' [the video] – Perched on a rocky cliff,
the popsters looked like a cross between
Bananarama and Mount Rushmore. The video
was all seagulls, sunsets and pounding surfs – a
travel ad for paradise with a soundtrack
straight from pop hell. *'Rolling Stone' (1990)*

Stevie Wonder
Who's going to tell him that he's got a macrame
plant holder on his head? *Joan Rivers*

Yes
Five bowls of muesli looking for a spoon.
'New Musical Express'

HEAVY METAL

The idiot-bastard spawn of rock.
Tim Holmes (1987)

The music business doesn't revolve around
heavy metal bullshit. *Michelle Shocked (1988)*

PUNK ROCK

All that punk singers can bring to the
presentations of their songs is the gesture of
sexual obscenity or of impotent rage. There is a
lot of caged simian gibber. British youth needs
a good kick in the pants and a bit of solid
education. *Anthony Burgess – 'Psychology Today'*

Punk is so constipated it should be called
'Hemorrhoid Rock'. *Linda Rondstadt (1977)*

Punks in their silly leather jackets are a cliché.
I have never liked the term and have never
discussed it. I just get on with it and got out of
it when it became a competition. *Johnny Rotten*

I don't really think there's anything
constructive about marching on the Houses of
Parliament or breaking down the walls of
Babylon. Bands like the Jam and the Clash
seem to encourage these sorts of tribal
movements, this gang mentality, and I don't
like it. *John Taylor of Duran Duran (1979)*

MEDIA

Media is a word that has come to mean bad journalism.   *Graham Green*

Looking at yourself through the media is like looking at one of those rippled mirrors in an amusement park.
Ed Muskie – 'Newsweek' (1980)

The word media is plural for mediocre.
Rene Saguisag (1987)

The media. It sounds like a convention of spiritualists.
Tom Stoppard – 'Jumpers' (1972)

THE PRESS

The press is the hired agent of the monied system, and set up for no other purpose than to tell lies where their interests are involved. One can trust nobody and nothing.
Henry Adams (1918)

Generally speaking, the Press lives on disaster.
Clement Attlee

The printing press is either the greatest blessing or the greatest curse of modern times, one sometimes forgets which.
J. M. Barrie – 'Sentimental Tommy'

The most important service rendered by the press and the magazines is that of educating people to approach printed matter with distrust.   *Samuel Butler*

Bit dangerous, y'nt it? Trustin' the Press? Their right 'ands never knows wot their left 'ands is writing'.   *John Galsworthy*

The freedom of the press works in such a way that there is not much freedom from it.
Princess Grace of Monaco

The press is like the peculiar uncle you keep in the attic – just one of those unfortunate things.
G. Gordon Liddy

Freedom of the press is guaranteed to those who own one.   *A. J. Liebling*

On the whole I would not say that our Press is obscene. I would say that it trembles on the brink of it.   *Lord Longford (1963)*

In Czechoslovakia there is freedom of the Press and in England there is no freedom from the Press.   *Martina Navratilova*

Freedom of the press in Britain is freedom to print such of the proprietor's prejudices as the advertisers don't object to.   *Hannen Swaffer*

In the old days men had the rack. Now they have the Press.   *Oscar Wilde (1891)*

NEWSPAPERS

The mission of the modern newspaper is to comfort the afflicted and afflict the comfortable.   *Anon*

Tabloids are fast-reading for the slow thinking.   *Anon*

He had been kicked in the head by a mule when young, and believed everything he read in the Sunday papers.   *George Ade*

Newspaper strikes are a relief.   *Princess Anne*

Have you ever noticed that life, real honest to goodness life, with murders and catastrophes and fabulous inheritances, happens almost exclusively in newspapers?
Jean Anouih – 'The Rehearsal' (1950)

I read the newspaper avidly. It is my one form of continuous fiction.   *Aneurin Bevan*

All the dope this country swallows is not narcotic.   *'Cleveland Times'*

If newspapers are useful in overthrowing tyrants, it is only to establish a tyranny of their own.   *James Fennimore Cooper*

A newspaper is the lowest thing there is!
Richard Daley

Newspapers are so filthy and bestial that no honest man would admit one into his house for a water-closet doormat.   *Charles Dickens*

The more national newspapers there are, the more difficult it is to tell them apart.
Paul Foot – 'New Statesman' (1985)

Headlines twice the size of the events.
John Galsworthy

That ephemeral sheet of paper, the newspaper is the natural enemy of the book, as the whore is of the decent woman.
Edmond & Jules de Goncourt – 'Journal' (1858)

The most truthful part of a newspaper is the advertisements.   *Thomas Jefferson*

Newspapermen learn to call a murderer 'an alleged murderer' and the King of England 'the alleged King of England' to avoid libel suits.
Stephen Leacock

People everywhere confuse what they read in newspapers with news.
A. J. Liebling – 'New Yorker' (1956)

You should believe all you read in the newspapers, as this makes them more interesting.   *Rose Macauley*

The art of newspaper paragraphing is to stroke a platitude until it purrs like an epigram.
Don Marquis

News is by definition a construct of what happened yesterday. Yesterday's newspaper is used to wrap fish and yesterday's broadcast does not exist at all.
Martin Mayer – 'Esquire' (1972)

A newspaper is a device for making the ignorant more ignorant and the crazy crazier.
H. L. Mencken

Whenever I see a newspaper I think of the poor trees. As trees they provide beauty, shade and shelter, but as paper all they provide is rubbish.
Yehudi Menuhin (1970)

Any man with ambition, integrity – and \$10 millon – can start a daily newspaper.
Henry Morgan (1950)

One of the unsung freedoms that go with a free press is the freedom not to read it.
Ferdinand Mount – 'Daily Telegraph' (1986)

I hope we never see the day when a thing is as bad as some of our newspapers make it.
Will Rogers (1934)

Newspapers are unable, seemingly, to discriminate between a bicycle accident and the collapse of a civilisation.
G. B. Shaw– 'Too True to be Good'

Newspapers are the most villainous – licentious – abominable – infernal – Not that I ever read them – no – I make it a rule never to look into a newspaper.   *Richard B. Sheridan*

Anybody who claims to read an entire newspaper is either the world's fastest reader or the world's biggest liar.   *Arthur Sulzberger*

If words were invented to conceal thought, newspapers are a great improvement on a bad invention.   *Henry D. Thoreau*

It is better to dip into 'The Last Days of Pompeii' at breakfast than to peruse the morning paper.   *James Thurber*

Possible? Is anything possible?? Read the newspapers.   *Duke of Wellington*

NEWSPAPERS (BY NAME)

American Papers
The American reading his Sunday paper in a state of lazy collapse is perhaps the most perfect symbol of the triumph of quantity over quality.   *Irving Babbitt*

Trying to be a first-rate reporter on the average American newspaper is like trying to play Bach's 'St Matthew Passion' on a ukele. The instrument is too crude for the work, for the audience and for the performer.   *Ben Bagdikian*

I love the weight of American Sunday newspapers. Pulling them up off the floor is good for the figure.   *Noël Coward*

The average American newspaper, especially of the so-called better sort, has the intelligence of a Baptist evangelist, the courage of a rat, the fairness of a Prohibitionist boob-bumper, the information of a high-school janitor, the taste of a designer of celluloid valentines, and the honour of a police-station lawyer.
H. L. Mencken

Reviewing Upton Sinclair's 'The Brass Check' –
To the best of my knowledge and belief, the average American newspaper, even of the so-called better sort, is not quite as bad as Upton Sinclair says it is, but ten times worse – ten times as ignorant, ten times as unfair and tyrannical, ten times as complaisant and disingenuous, deceitful, pharisaical, pecksniffian, fraudulent, slippery, unscrupulous, perfidious, lewd and dishonest.
H. L. Mencken (1919)

'Chicago Tribune'
The people of Germany are just as responsible for Hitler as the people of Chicago are for *'The Chicago Tribune'*.   *Alexander Woollcott*

'Daily Mail'
Produced by office boys for office boys.
Lord Salisbury

'Harvard Law Review'
The Review's labyrinthine editing process does to the written word what the Cuisinart does to broccoli.   *David Margolick*

'New York Daily News'
An obese, malevolent fishwife, screaming journalistic obscenities at more than two million persons a day, exhorting them to go out and kill a Commie for Christ – or even just for fun.   *James Aronson*

'New York Post'
No New Yorker should take Rupert Murdoch's *'New York Post'* seriously any longer. It makes *'Hustler'* magazine looks like the *'Harvard Law Review'*.   *Abraham Beame*

'New York Times'
We can take *'The New York Times'* – any day. For the editors of the *'National Review'*, it's like swatting flies.
William F. Buckley Jr – Editor of 'The National Review' (1956)

If a newspaper prints a sex crime, it's smut, but when *'The New York Times'* prints it, it's a sociological study.   *Adolph S. Ochs*

'The New York Times' is the official leak of the State Department.   *Mort Sahl*

'New York Tribune'
In the end, the *'Tribune'* lost touch with the world it was supposed to reach; it mattered passionately, but almost exclusively to those who worked for it.   *Paul Gray (1986)*

'Pravda'
'Pravda''s coverage of the first Glassboro conference between Kosygin and LBJ was confined to 37 words, about as much space as a major metropolitan newspaper devotes to the day's weather. The same front page of 'Pravda' announced proudly in an editorial that the millionth Volga car had come off the assembly line at the Gorky auto plant, a news item comparable to something the Ford Motor Company put out along about, say 1911.
William F Buckley Jr – 'On the Right' (1967)

'Wall Street Journal'
If I read 'upcoming' in the *'Wall Street Journal'* again, I shall be downcoming and somebody will be outgoing.   *Bernard Kilgore*

'Washington Post'
If Washington were a circus, as some like to think it is, *'The Washington Post'* would be the ringmaster.   *Phil Gailey (1984)*

MAGAZINES

'Punch'
'Punch' is very much like the Church of England. It is doctrinally inexplicable, but it goes on.   *Malcolm Muggeridge*

The official journal of dentists' waiting rooms.
'The Times' (1981)

'Reader's Digest'
A lot of its readers are of an age where they
forgot to cancel.   *Jerry Della Femina*

'Time'
Backward ran sentences until reeled the mind.
                            Wolcott Gibbs (1985)

'Vogue'
Rona Barrett – Would you ever sell your body to
             survive?
Cher   – No, man! I'd edit' *Vogue'* first.

Women's Magazines
Page one is a diet, page two is a chocolate cake.
It's a no-win situation.   *Kim Williams*

EDITORS

All newspaper editorial writers ever do is come
down from the hills after the battle is over and
bayonet the wounded.   *Anon*

The average editor cannot escape feeling that
telling a writer to do something is almost the
same thing as performing it himself.
                            Heywood C Broun

A big-city newsroom can be a snake-pit. The
politics put Mayor Daley's machine to shame,
the competition proves beyond doubt Darwin's
theory of survival of the fittest and the
hierarchy of editors is more complicated than
the Vatican's.   *Fern Schumer Chapman –
                      'Wall Street Journal' (1985)*

A newspaper editor is a person who knows
precisely what he wants but isn't quite sure.
                            Walter Davenport

I suppose some editors are failed writers – but
so are most writers.   *T. S. Eliot*

Every newspaper editor pays tribute to the
Devil.   *Jean de la Fonataine (1686)*

An editor should have a pimp for a brother, so
he'd have someone to look up to.   *Gene Fowler*

One should fight like the devil the temptation
to think well of editors. They are all, without

exception – at least some of the time –
incompetent or crazy. By the nature of their
profession they read too much, with the result
they grow jaded and cannot recognise talent
though it dances in front of their eyes.
                            John Gardner

Editors used to be known by their authors; now
some of them are known by their restaurants.
                            Robert Giroux

Editors may think of themselves as dignified
head-waiters in a well-run restaurant but more
often operate a snack bar, and expect you to be
grateful that at least they got the food to the
table.   *Thomas Griffith (1974)*

An editor is a person employed on a newspaper,
whose business is to separate the wheat from
the chaff, and to see that the chaff is printed.
                            Elbert Hubbard

Most editors can't recognise bad writing when
they read it. Nor do they try very hard to learn
to recognise it.   *Alfred Knopf*

A newspaper without an editorial page is a
sterile thing – not a newspaper – it means that
the editor either has no opinions or is too timid
to voice them.
            Alan C. McIntosh – 'Rock County Herald'

Editors are no longer father-confessors. Most of
them are acquisition editors who are more
concerned with bringing home the bacon than
in trying to rewrite the bacon.
                            Scott Meredith

Editors are extremely fallible people, all of
them. Don't put too much trust in them.
                            Maxwell Perkins

Editing is the same as quarrelling with writers
– same thing exactly.
                      Harold Ross – 'Time' (1950)

You ask for the distinction between the terms
'Editor' and 'Publisher': an editor selects
manuscripts; a publisher selects editors.
                            M. Lincoln Schuster

An editor has no friends.   *Jack Tanner*

MEDIA

EDITORS (BY NAME)

James Gordon Bennett Jr – *(1841–1918)*
A low-mouthed, blatant, witless, brutal
scoundrel.   *Horace Greeley*

William Lloyd Garrison – *(1805–79)*
Garrison is a tart Luther who neighs like a
horse.   *R. W. Emerson*

Horace Greeley – *(1811–72)*
A nincompoop without genius.
                              James G. Bennett Sr

Irving Howe – *(b 1920)*
Irving Howe, editor of the socialists' 'Dissent',
takes his pleasure mostly from mugging the
United States.
    William F. Buckley Jr – 'On the Right' (1968)

John Middleton Murry – *Editor of 'Adelphi'*
(1889–1957)
Your articles in the 'Adelphi' always annoy me.
Why care so much about your own fishiness or
flabbiness? Why make it so important? Can't
you focus yourself outside yourself? Not for
ever focused on yourself, ad nauseam.
                          D. H. Lawrence (1924)

A. M. Rosenthal –
Editor of 'The New York Times' (b 1922)
He was not a passive person. He involved
himself in everything. There was a Yiddish
word for it: 'kochleffl' – the ladle. That was
Rosenthal – the kochleffl stirring up the pot.
                          Harrison Salisbury

Harold Ross – *Editor of 'New Yorker'*
(1892–1951)
He looks like a dishonest Abe Lincoln.
                              Wolcott Gibbs

His ignorance was an Empire State Building of
ignorance. You had to admire it for its size.
                              Dorothy Parker

Sir Richard Steele – *Founder Editor of 'Tatler'*
(1672–1729)
He maintained a perpetual struggle between
reason and appetite.
        Theophilus Cibber – 'Lives of the Poets'

He was a rake among scholars, and a scholar

among rakes.   *Lord Macaulay*

Steele might become a reasonable good writer if
he would pay a little more attention to
grammar, learn something about the propriety
and disposition of words and, incidentally, get
some information on the subject he intends to
handle.   *Jonathan Swift*

James Wechsler – *Editor of 'The New York*
Post'.
James Wechsler . . . so relentlessly liberal he
ought to be an Exhibit at the World's Fair.
                        William F. Buckley Jr –
                  'National Review Bulletin' (1964)

JOURNALISTS

Doctors bury mistakes. Lawyers hang them.
But journalists put theirs on the front page.
                                      Anon

A journalist is a person who works harder than
any other lazy person in the world.   *Anon*

Journalists are a sort of assassin who sit with
loaded blunderbusses at the corner of streets
and fire them off for hire or sport at any
passer-by they select.   *John Q. Adams (1820)*

Journalists are an effete corps of impudent
snobs who characterise themselves as
intellectuals.   *Spiro Agnew (1969)*

In the US today we have more than our share
of nattering nabobs of negativism. They've
formed their own 4–H club – the hopeless,
hysterical, hypochondriacs of history.
                          Spiro Agnew (1970)

To a newspaperman a human is an item with
the skin wrapped around it.   *Fred Allen*

When a journalist enters the room, your
privacy ends and his begins.   *Warren Beatty*

Journalists say a thing that they knew isn't
true, in the hope that if they keep on saying it
long enough it will be true.
              Arnold Bennett – 'The Title' (1918)

Journalism is the only job that requires no
degrees, no diplomas, and no specialised

knowledge of any kind.   *Patrick Campbell*

Chicago reporters were fast-moving
opportunists encased in cynicism and proud of
it.   *John Carr (1986)*

Journalism largely consists of saying 'Lord
Jones is dead,' to people who never knew Lord
Jones was alive.   *G. K. Chesterton*

A writer who takes up journalism abandons the
slow tempo of literature for a faster one and the
change will do him harm. By degrees the
flippancy of journalism will become a habit and
the pleasure of being paid on the nail and more
especially of being praised on the nail, grow
indispensable.   *Cyril Connolly*

Journalism consists in buying white paper at
two cents a pound and selling it for ten cents a
pound.   *Cyril Connolly*

Journalism is organised gossip.
                                Edward Egglestone

Journalists aren't nearly as interesting as they
think they are.   *Dwight D. Eisenhower*

Our writers are as full of clichés as old barns
are full of bats. There is obviously no rule
about this, except that anything that you
suspect of being a cliché undoubtedly is one
and had better be removed.   *Wolcott Gibbs*

The image of the reporter as a nicotine-stained
Quixote, slugging back Scotch while skewering
city hall with an expose ripped out of a
typewriter on the crack of deadline, persists
despite munificent evidence to the contrary.
                                Paul Gray (1986)

Journalism constructs momentarily arrested
equilibriums and gives disorder an implied
order. That is already two steps from reality.
                                Thomas Griffiths (1974)

I'll tell you what I think of newspaper men: the
hand of God reaching down into the mire
couldn't elevate one of them to the depths of
degradation – not by a million miles.
                                Ben Hecht (1937)

Good taste is, of course, an utterly dispensable

part of any journalist's equipment.
                Michael Hogg – 'Daily Telegraph' (1978)

An investigating journalist is one who can think
up plausible scandals.   *Lambert Jeffries*

The fact that a man is a newspaper reporter is
evidence of some flaw of character.
                                Lyndon B. Johnson

I always said that when we don't have to go
through you bastards, we can really get our
story over to the American people.
                                John F. Kennedy (1962)

At a sports press conference – When I say 'start'
let's have five seconds of silence. [*Pause*] That's
pretty good. That gives something for the news
media to quote with absolute accuracy.
                                Bobby Knight (1982)

The most guileful amongst the reporters are
those who appear friendly and smile and seem
to be supportive. They are the ones who will
seek to gut you on every occasion.
                Ed Koch – 'New York Times' (1984)

Journalists write because they have nothing to
say, and have something to say because they
write.   *Karl Kraus*

Journalism is still an under-developed
profession and, accordingly newspapermen are
quite often regarded as were surgeons and
musicians a century ago, as having the rank,
roughly speaking, of barbers and riding
masters.   *Walter Lippman*

Newspapermen ask dumb questions. They look
up at the sun and ask you if it is shining.
                                Charles 'Sonny' Liston

The day you write to please everyone you no
longer are in journalism. You are in show
business.   *Frank Miller Jr*

A journalist is the paper slave of the day.
                Friedrich Nietzshe – 'The Birth of Tragedy'

People in the media say they must look at the
president with a microscope. Now I don't mind
a microscope, but boy, when they use a

proctoscope, that's going too far.
Richard Nixon (1984)

Journalism – a profession whose business it is to explain to others what it personally doesn't understand. *Lord Northcliffe*

Never trust a reporter who has a nice smile.
William Rauch (1984)

The trouble with daily journalism is that you get so involved with 'Who hit John?' that you never really know why John had his chin out in the first place.
Chalmers Roberts – 'Newsweek' (1958)

When you hear something described by a journalist as disturbing, you know you cannot take it seriously. *Kenneth Robinson*

In America journalism is apt to be regarded as an extension of history, in Britain as an extension of conversation. *Anthony Sampson – 'Anatomy of Britain' (1962)*

Journalists – Nameless men and women whose scandalous low payment is a guarantee of their ignorance and their servility to the financial department. *G. B. Shaw – 'Commonsense About the War' (1914)*

The broads who work in the press are the hookers of the press. I might offer them a buck and a half. I'm not sure. *Frank Sinatra (1974)*

All day long, Hollywood reporters lie in the sun, and when the sun goes down, they lie some more. *Frank Sinatra (1985)*

A foreign correspondent is someone who flies around from hotel to hotel and thinks that the most interesting thing about any story is the fact that he has arrived to cover it.
Tom Stoppard – 'Night and Day' (1978)

Most journalists are restless voyeurs who see the warts on the world, the imperfections in people and places; gloom is their game, the spectacle their passion, normality their nemesis. *Gay Talese (1969)*

It is part of the social mission of every great newspaper to provide a refuge and a home for the largest possible number of salaried eccentrics. *Lord Thompson of Fleet*

The only qualities essential for real success in journalism are rat-like cunning, a plausible manner, and a little literary ability.
Nicholas Tomalin (1969)

Mother [Bess Truman] considered a press conference on a par with a visit to a cage of cobras. *Margaret Truman*

Journalism is the ability to meet the challenge of filling space. *Rebecca West*

Journalism justifies its own existence by the great Darwinian principle of the survival of the vulgarest. *Oscar Wilde (1891)*

The difference between journalism and literature, is that journalism is unreadable and literature is not read. *Oscar Wilde*

You cannot hope to bribe or twist
(Thank God) the British journalist,
But seeing what the man will do
Unbribed, there's no occasion to.
Humbert Wolfe – 'Over the Fire'

Most rock journalism is people who can't write interviewing people who can't talk for people who can't read. *Frank Zappa*

JOURNALISTS (BY NAME)

Anon
On a sycophantic columnist – I see her as one great stampede of lips directed at the nearest derrière. *Noël Coward*

Dear Sir, Your profession has, as usual, destroyed your brain. *G. B. Shaw*

Anon political journalist – She missed the last Lobby briefing, I hear. At the vet's with hard pad, no doubt. *Harold Wilson*

Jack Anderson – *(b 1922)*
Anderson's muckraking is one of the debatable ends constantly used to justify questionable works. *Thomas Griffith (1979)*

Jack Anderson is the lowest form of human

being to walk the earth. He's a muckraker who lies, steals, and . . . he'll go lower than dog shit for a story. *J. Edgar Hoover*

Ambrose Bierce - *(1842–1914)*
Never obliged to match his wits with first-rate minds, he rode his hobbies freely and indulged his whims, dogmatising at his ease with a too facile cynicism that overexpressed his somewhat acrid spirit. *Van Wyck Brooks*

He was an all-inclusive cynic.
C. Hartley Grattan

He repeated himself endlessly, for his harp had a single string. *Stanley Kurnitz & Howard Haycraft – 'American Authors'*

Bierce would bury his best friend with a sigh of relief, and express satisfaction that he was done with him. *Jack London*

There was no more discretion in Bierce, than you will find in a runaway locomotive.
H. L. Mencken

Horatio Bottomley - *(1869–1933)*
England's Greatest Living Humbug.
Reuben Bigland

He had two brains, that man. One linked up with his tongue and the other thought while he talked. *Sir Harry Preston*

Heywood C. Broun - *(1888–1939)*
A one-man slum. *Anon*

A gin-drinking, poker-playing, wicked old reprobate.
Herbert B. Swope – 'As He Seemed to Us'

His speech is an innocent emptying of his mind as a woman empties her purse, himself genuinely curious about its contents.
Alexander Woollcott

No one is so impotent that, meeting Broun face to face, he cannot frighten him into any lie. Any mouse can make this elephant squeal.
Alexander Woollcott

Anthony Burgess - *(b 1917)*
After an 'Observer' interview – He put words into

my mouth which I had to look up in the dictionary. *Graham Greene (1982)*

Cyril Connolly - *(1903–74)*
The key to his behaviour was self-indulgence, which he made almost a rule of life.
Stephen Spender (1983)

Charles Anderson Dana - *(1819–97)*
Poor, despised, disgraced, Old Ananias!
Joseph Pulitzer

A poltroon in an hour of danger. *Joseph Pulitzer*

Murray Kempton - *(b 1918)*
Some go to Kempton for thought, which is like heading south when in search of the North Pole.
William F. Buckley Jr – 'On the Right' (1966)

Dorothy Kilgallen - *(1913–65)*
Dorothy Kilgallen is the only woman I wouldn't mind my wife catching me with. I don't know why she took such umbrage at my comments on birth control, she's such a living argument for it. *Johnny Carson*

Walter Lippman - *(1889–1974)*
Lippman was a true muckraker, a muckraker on the global scale, a man who knew that when statesmen prepare to commit genocide they come to the green baize table in striped pants and morning coats.
Harrison E. Salisbury (1974)

Joseph Pulitzer - *(1847–1911)*
Poor misguided, selfish vulgarian.
James G. Bennett

He was the damnedest best man in the world to have in a newspaper office for one hour in the morning. For the remainder of the day he was a damned nuisance. *John A. Cockerill*

This Dick Turpin of journalism.
Charles A. Dana

Undoubtedly semi-neurasthenic, a disease-demonised soul, who could scarcely control himself in anything, a man who was fighting an almost insane battle with life itself, trying to be omnipotent and what not else, and never to die.
Theodore Dreiser

The only consideration which guides this fellow in the control of his precious paper is to keep out of the reach of criminal prosecution.
Leander Richardson

Ida Tarbell – *(1857–1944)*
Miss Tarbarrel. *John D. Rockefeller*

Muckraking crusader for the middle classes.
Mary E. Tomkins

Dorothy Thompson – *(1894–1961)*
She is the only woman who had her menopause in public and got paid for it.
Alice Roosevelt Longworth

'The Times'
The low and grovelling correspondents of *'The Times'*. *Sir James Simpson (1954)*

Alden Whitman *(b 1913)*
He dropped pejoratives like subliminal seasoning.
Jim Bishop

PUBLISHERS

I am a publisher – a hybrid creature; one part stargazer, one part gambler, one part businessman, one part midwife and three parts optimist. *Cass Canfield*

As repressed sadists are supposed to become policemen or butchers so those with irrational fear of life become publishers.
Cyril Connolly (1938)

Great editors do not discover nor produce great authors; great authors create and produce great publishers. *John Farrar (1957)*

The Englishman loves to roll his tongue around the word, 'extraordinary'. It so pleases him that he is reluctant to finish the sound which goes on into harmonics and overtones. The American publisher is likewise inclined.
R. I. Fitzhenry

Publishers are all cohorts of the devil; there must be a special hell for them somewhere.
Johan Goethe

Publishers are demons, there's no doubt about it. *William James*

Publishers look down on authors simply as a butcher looks upon Southdown mutton, with merely an eye to the number of pounds to be got out of them. *Douglas Jerrold*

If a man makes money by publishing a newspaper, by poisoning the wells of information, by feeding the people a daily spiritual death, he is the greatest criminal I can conceive. *Ferdinand Lassalle (1863)*

A publisher is somebody looking for someone who has something new. *Lorne Pierce*

I object to publishers: the one service they have done me is to teach me to do without them. They combine commercial rascality with artistic touchiness and pettiness, without being either good business or fine judges of literature. All that is necessary in the production of a book is an author and a bookseller, without any intermediate parasite. *G. B. Shaw (1895)*

The trouble with the publishing business is that too many people who have half a mind to write a book do so. *William Trigg*

As for editorial content, that's the stuff you separate the ads with. *Lord Thompson of Fleet*

I could show you all society poisoned by this class of person – a class unknown to the ancients – who, not being able to find any honest occupation, be it manual labour or service, and unluckily knowing how to read and write, become the brokers of literature, live on our works, steal our manuscripts, falsify them, and sell them. *Voltaire*

Publishers kill good trees to put out bad newspapers. *James G. Watt (1982)*

PUBLISHERS (BY NAME)

Anon
On the rejection of his manuscript for 'Sons and Lovers' – Curse the blasted, jelly-boned swines, the slimy, the belly-wriggling invertebrates, the miserable sodding rotters, the flaming sods, the snivelling, dribbling, dithering, palsied, pulseless lot that make up England.
D. H. Lawrence (1912)

Lord Beaverbrook [Max Aitken] –
(1879–1964)
On Beaverbrook and Lord Rothermere – What the
proprietorship of these newspapers is aiming at
is power without responsibility – the
prerogative of the harlot through the ages.
Stanley Baldwin

Beaverbrook is so pleased to be in the
Government that he is like the town tart who
has finally married the Mayor!   *Beverley Baxter*

If Max gets to Heaven he won't last long. He
will be chucked out for trying to pull off a
merger between Heaven and Hell, after having
secured a controlling interest in key subsidiary
companies in both places, of course. *H. G. Wells*

Hugh Hefner *–publisher of 'Playboy' (b 1926)*
If Hugh Hefner truly thinks that being spread-
eagled is so fantastic, how come we haven't
seen his little wahoo with a staple in the
middle?   *'Designing Women'*

He's the kindest, nicest, most selfish man I
have ever met.   *Arnie Morton*

He was a sex junkie with an insatiable habit.
Gay Talese (1980)

William Randolph Hearst – *(1863–1951)*
He wrote so much about the Yellow Peril that
his journalism took its distinctive coloration
from the subject.   *Richard Armour*

Truth for him was a moving target: he never
aimed for the bull and rarely pierced the outer
ring.   *Hugh Cudlipp – 'The Prerogative of
the Harlot' (1980)*

I would rather let my daughters see Mae West's
films regularly than read Randolph Hearst's
newspapers regularly.   *Don Herold*

Edward Livingstone – *(1898–1967)*
He really thought there was nothing he could
not do, so he often did it.   *Archibald MacLeish*

Henry Luce – *(1898–1967)*
Mr Luce's unique contribution to American
journalism is that he placed into the hands of
the people yesterday's newspaper and today's

garbage homogenised into one neat package.
Herbert Block

What Mr Luce needs is a medium through
which to reach the public.
*William F. Buckley Jr –
'National Review' (1966)*

Mr Luce is like a man who owns a shoe store
and buys all the shoes to fit himself. Then he
expects other people to buy them.   *Earl Long*

Robert McCormick – *'Chicago Tribune'*
(1849–1919)
The great, overgrown lummox of a Colonel
Robert McCormick, mediocre in ability, less
than average in brains and a damn physical
coward in spite of his size, sitting on the tower
of the Tribune Building with his guards
protecting him while he squirts sewage at men
whom he happens to dislike.
Harold L. Ickes (1938)

Lord Northcliffe – *(1865–1922)*
The late Lord Northcliffe would not print
anything in criticism of himself. He would
always print the words of praise. Even from the
publicity point of view, he was wrong.
Lord Beaverbrook (1952)

The democracy knows you as the poisoner of
the streams of human intercourse, the
fermenter of war, the preacher of hate, the
unscrupulous enemy of human society.
A. G. Gardner (1914)

He aspired to power instead of influence, and as
a result forfeited both.   *A. J. P. Taylor*

GUTTER PRESS

The English smear campaign is still the best in
the world.   *John Davies – 'Punch'*

The men with the muck-rake are often
indispensable to the well-being of society, but
only if they know when to stop raking the
muck.   *Theodore Roosevelt*

To hell with them. When history is written they
will be the sons of bitches – not I.
Harry S.Truman

TELEVISION

Eyestrain radio. *Anon*

A box that has changed children from an irresistible force into an immovable object. *Anon*

TV is a numbers game. 15-year-old movies on a 21 inch set paid for by 24 easy instalments. *Anon*

Before TV nobody knew what a headache looked like. *Anon*

The electronic device that intersperses gory slaughter with the brushing of teeth. *Anon*

Summer stock in an iron lung. *Anon*

TV is the place where show-biz illiterates can express their ill-informed opinions. *Anon*

Imitation is the sincerest form of television. *Fred Allen*

Television is a device that permits people who haven't got anything to do to watch people who can't do anything. it is radio fluoroscoped; the triumph of machinery over people; a medium because anything good on it is rare. *Fred Allen*

Television is a triumph of equipment over people, and the minds that control it are so small that you could put them in the navel of a flea and still have room beside them for a network vice-president's heart. *Fred Allen*

In California, they don't throw their garbage away – they make it into TV shows. *Woody Allen*

Television has a real problem. They have no page two. *Art Buchwald (1959)*

Every time you think TV has hit its lowest ebb, a new program comes along to make you wonder where you thought the ebb was. *Art Buchwald (1968)*

Television is just one more facet of that considerable segment of our society that never had any standard but the soft buck. *Raymond Chandler*

Television is not the truth. Television is a god-damned amusement park. Television is a circus, a carnival, a travelling troupe of acrobats, story-tellers, dancers, singers, jugglers, sideshow freaks, lion tamers and football players. We're in the boredom-killing business. *Paddy Chayefsky – 'Network' (1976)*

Television is the kind of thing you pay attention to if you wish, and if you don't you go to clean out your drawers. *Cher*

Television is a penny Punch and Judy show. *Sir Winston Churchill*

Television is an avalanche of vulgarity. *Lord Clarke (1954)*

The vast wasteland of television is not interested in producing a better mousetrap but in producing a worse manure. *Laurence C. Coughlin*

Good heavens, television is something you appear on, you don't watch it. *Noël Coward*

Books and plays are diversions about which most of us exercise some decision, even if our selection is based on totally misleading publicity. The movies are in a twilit zone. Television is even lower down the scale of human choice. We nearly always see it by default. *Quentin Crisp (1981)*

Television is a medium of entertainment which permits millions of people to listen to the same joke at the same time, and yet remain lonesome. *T. S. Eliot – 'New York Post' (1963)*

The world is going mad at an accelerating rate and television is the Typhoid Mary of this madness. *Edward Ellis – 'New York Times' (1981)*

In America television can make so much money doing its worst, it cannot afford to do it best. *Fred Friendly (1967)*

Television was supposed to be a national park, it has now become a money machine. It's a

commodity now, just like pork bellies.
Fred Friendly

TV is an invention that permits you to be entertained in your living room by people you wouldn't have in your home. *David Frost (1971)*

I have found the most divine sleeping pill – television. *Eve Gabor*

A medium that has raised writing to a new low.
Samuel Goldwyn

American television must raise its ceiling by some method other than lowering the floor.
Jack Gould – 'New York Times' (1966)

There is something supremely reassuring about television; the worst is always yet to come.
Jack Gould – ibid

Children watch too much TV not only because indolent parents allow them to, but because the standard of most programmes is pitched at their level.
Richard Ingrams – 'The Observer' (1977)

All you have to do on TV is be yourself, provided, that is, that you have a self to be.
Clive James – 'The Observer' (1981)

Most of the blandness which experts presume to detect in TV is just the thinness of overtaxed inspiration. *Clive James – 'The Observer' (1981)*

TV has something in common with the world of horse-racing: it is crowded with untrustworthy characters and bristles with opportunities to cheat. *Paul Johnson*

We are drowning our youngsters in violence, cynicism and sadism piped into the living room and even the nursery. The grandchildren of the kids who used to weep because the Little Matchgirl froze to death now feel cheated if she isn't slugged, raped and thrown into a Bessemer converter. *Jenkin Lloyd Jones*

What this generation was bred to at television's knees was not wisdom but cynicism.
Pauline Kael – 'I Lost It at the Movies'

TV is a medium, because it is neither rare nor well-done. *Ernie Kovacs*

There's a standard formula for success in the entertainment medium, and that is: Beat it to death if it succeeds. *Ernie Kovacs*

In an automobile civilisation, which was one of constant motion and activity, there was almost no time to think; in a television one, there is small desire. *Louis Kronenberger (1954)*

For tens of millions of people TV has become habit-forming, brain-softening, taste-degrading.
Louis Kronenberger – 'The Cart and the Horse' (1964)

I find television very educating. Every time someone turns on the set I go into the other room and read a book. *Groucho Marx*

Television is of great education value. It teaches you while still young how to (a) kill, (b) rob, (c) embezzle, (d) shoot, (e) poison.
George Mikes

Sit down in front of your television set when your station goes on the air and keep your eyes glued to the set until the station signs off. I can assure you that you will observe a vast wasteland. *Newton N. Minow*

Of all the inventions of our time it is likely to prove the most destructive. Whereas nuclear power can only reduce us and our world to cinder, the camera grinds us down to spiritual dust so fine that a puff of wind scatters it, leaving nothing behind.
Malcolm Muggeridge – 'New Statesman' (1968)

The more we elaborate our means of communication, the less we communicate.
J. B. Priestley – 'Thoughts in the Wilderness'

TV offers a banal vision of heaven.
Frederic Raphael – 'The Language of Television' (1980)

Television has lifted the manufacture of banality out of the sphere of handicraft and placed it in that of a major industry.
Nathalie Sarraute

Television is the bland leading the bland.
Murray Schumach – 'The Face on the Cutting Room Floor' (1964)

Television? No good will come out of this new device. The word is half Greek and half Latin.
C. P. Scott – 'Manchester Guardian'

Television may have deteriorated in many ways over the years, but it has triumphed in eliminating the unexpected. *Tom Shales*

If it isn't sex, it's violence. Or it's sex and violence, also known in television as bread and butter. *Tom Shales (1981)*

Television is the best gauge we have of our decay. *John Stevenson – 'Listener' (1978)*

If you read a lot of books, you're considered well-read. But if you watch a lot of TV, you're not considered well-viewed. *Lily Tomlin*

Acting on television is like being asked by the captain to entertain the passengers while the ship goes down. *Peter Ustinov (1957)*

There are days when any electrical appliance in the house, including the vacuum cleaner, seems to offer more entertainment possibilities than the TV set. *Harriet Van Horne (1957)*

Television is now so desperately hungry for material that they're scraping the top of the barrel. *Gore Vidal (1955)*

Television's power for good and evil is roughly equivalent to that of the hula hoop.
Keith Waterhouse – 'Punch' (1966)

Television is a twenty-one inch person. I'm delighted with it, because it used to be that films were the lowest form of art. Now we've got something to look down on. *Billy Wilder*

Soap Operas

The Soaps are like Big Macs . . . a lot of people who won't admit it eat them up. *John Stevenson*

If the Barons of Bad Taste known as network executives believe in chastity as an anti-AIDS measure, it doesn't show on the soaps, day or night.
Margaret Nolan – 'Boston Globe' (1987)

Talk-shows

No TV performance takes such careful preparation as an off-the-cuff talk-show.
Richard Nixon

I view the glittering guests as pests
When what it's all about
Is that they're there
To hawk their wares
Or else to hype and tout. *E. B. de Vito*

Telethons

The telethon invokes in me more terror than mirth. The spectacle of all that self-congratulatory yap masquerading as conscience, of all those chairman of the board passing off public relations as altruism is truly sickening. *Harry Stein*

TV PERSONALITIES

Anon

We call them Twinkies. You've seen them on television acting the news, modelling and fracturing the news while you wonder whether they've read the news – or if they've blow-dried their brains, too.
Linda Ellerbee – 'And So It Goes' (1986)

Johnny Carson – *Talkshow host (b 1925)*
'Johnny Carson: Tonight!' – What we have is a chatterbox-equipped nightlight.
Terry Galanoy (1972)

It has always been my personal conviction that Carson is the most overrated amateur since Evelyn and her magic violin. *Rex Reed*

He's an anaesthetist – Prince Valium. *Mort Sahl*

Connie Chung – *NBC Newscaster/Interviewer (b 1946)*
Is Connie Chung a real journalist or just a reenactment of one? *'Rolling Stone' (1990)*

Walter Cronkite – *CBS Newscaster (b 1916)*
You can learn more by watching 'Let's Make a Deal' than you can by watching Walter Cronkite for a month. *Monty Hall*

Sam Donaldson – *ABC Newscaster (b 1934)*
He is television's sultan of splutter.
Hugh Sidey (1985)

We call him, 'Ol' Shoot from the Lip'.
Larry Speakes

David Frost - *Talk-show host (b 1939)*
David Frost drools OK. *Graffiti*

I always felt Frost was totally absorbed with himself and had a synthetic personality with a fixed smile carefully adapted to the slick phoniness of ad agency types, show business types and broadcast-executive types.
Howard Cosell

The bubonic plagiarist. *Jonathan Miller*

He rose without a trace. *Kitty Muggeridge*

Robin Leach - *Host of 'Lifestyles of the Rich and Famous' (b 1941)*
On his criticisms of a rival show 'On Top All Over the World' - Now that's a case of the pot calling the kettle metal. *Jeff Jarvis - 'People' (1985)*

Malcolm Muggeridge - *(1903-90)*
The wincing, winsome face discharging, as though from some suppurating wound of the spirit, an unstaunchable ooze of sneers.
J. W. Lambert

Muggeridge, a garden gnome expelled from Eden, has come to rest as a gargoyle brooding over a derelict cathedral. *Kenneth Tynan (1968)*

William S. Paley - *President of CBS TV (1901-90)*
He looks like a man who has just swallowed an entire human being. *Truman Capote*

Dan Rather - *Newscaster: '60 Minutes' (b 1931)*
Reporting for '60 Minutes' from Afghanistan -
Rather wore peasant togs that made him look like an extra out of Doctor Zhivago. Vanessa Redgrave wearing the same outfit would have been welcomed at any chic party in Europe. Somehow one got the feeling that this was not so much Dan Rather as Stuart Whitman playing Dan Rather. Or Dan Rather playing Stuart Whitman playing Dan Rather.
Tom Shales - 'Washington Post' (1980)

Geraldo Rivera - *TV investigative reporter (b 1943)*
If Geraldo Rivera is the first journalist in space,

NASA can test weightlessness on weightlessness. *Anon*

Andy Rooney - *Humorist: '60 Minutes' (b 1920)*
We've all had the experience of listening to him talk until an idea comes along. I don't know how Andy can make 60 seconds on '60 Minutes' seem like 60 hours. *Walter Cronkite (1968)*

The resident kvetch of '60 Minutes' - an unabashed fogy.
Sue Halpern - 'New York Times' (1984)

He's a twit. He wastes good airwaves and electrons. He's just plain unbearable.
Jeff Jarvis - 'Entertainment Weekly' (1990)

Dinah Shore - *(b 1917)*
I never watch the Dinah Shore show - I'm a diabetic. *Oscar Levant*

Watching Dinah Shore for just one week is like being imprisoned inside a giant butterscotch sundae. *Harry Waters - 'Newsweek'*

Ed Sullivan - *Variety Host (1901-74)*
Ed Sullivan will be around as long as someone else has talent. *Fred Allen*

Barbara Walters - *Newscaster/Interviewer (b 1931)*
Who would want to bother to try to get along without Barbara Walters? Barbara Walters - manicurist, pedicurist, guru of kitsch, yenta, maven, gadfly, blabbermouth and Mother Confessor to the world.
Tom Shales - 'Washington Post' (1980)

RADIO

A radio announcer is a man who talks until you have a headache, and then tries to sell you an aspirin. *Anon*

Radio is where the law of the jingle operates.
Anon

Radio City is the 'Tower of Babble'. *Anon*

Radio is a bag of mediocrity where little men with carbon minds wallow in sluice of their own making. *Fred Allen (1945)*

On ship they call them barnacles; in radio they attach themselves to desks and are called vice-presidents.
Fred Allen

Radio is the triumph of illiteracy.
John Dos Passos

The transistor radio is the modern leper's bell.
Ian Fleming

Radio – death in the afternoon and into the night.
Arthur Miller

Radio – all the flowing manure of the world's melody.
Francis Ponge – 'Le Grand Recueil'

C.B. – It may stand for Citizens' Band, but soetimes when you listen to it for a long time it stands for 'Constant Bore'.
Ron Rich

Wireless – an instrument with no strings attached.
'Sunday Times'

DISC JOCKEYS

A disc jockey is one who earns a living by putting on airs.
Anon

Disc-jockeys are wriggling ponces of the spoken word.
D. Bridson

Do they merit vitriol, even a drop of it? Yes, because they corrupt the young, persuading them that the mature world, which produced Beethoven and Schweitzer, sets an even higher value on the transient anodynes of youth than does youth itself. They are the Hollow Men. They are electronic lice.
Anthony Burgess – 'Punch' (1967)

This particular rapid, unintelligible patter, Isn't generally heard, and if it is it doesn't matter.
W. S. Gilbert

Ears are assaulted by the manic gibberish of disc-jockeys whose cerebral power wouldn't equip them to engage a chimpanzee in a game of Snap.
Mike Harding

Radio news is bearable. This is due to the fact that while the news is being broadcast the D.J. is not allowed to talk.
Fran Lebowitz

A disc jockey is a person who refers to Australia as being on the flipside of the world.
Robert Orben

PROFESSIONAL

Professionals built the Titanic – amateurs the Ark.   *Anon*

COMMERCE

In matters of commerce, the fault of the Dutch
Is offering too little and asking too much.
George Canning

The rear wheels of commerce are worth a
dollar each.   *'Cheyenne Wyoming State Tribune'*

I niver knew a pollytician to go wrong ontil he's
been contaminated by contact with a
businessman.   *Finlay Peter Dunne*

Businessmen must not break their word twice.
Thomas Fuller

Business is like oil. It won't mix with anything
but business.   *J. Graham*

My father told me that all businessmen were
sons-of-bitches, but I never believed him until
now.   *John F. Kennedy (1962)*

Business is a combination of war and sport.
André Maurois

A businessman is the only one who always
seeks to make it appear, when he attains the
object of his labours, i.e., the making of a great
deal of money, that it was not the object of his
labours.   *H. L. Mencken – 'Smart Set' (1921)*

I resent large corporations. They flatten
personalities.   *Bob Newhart*

The trouble with senior management to an
outsider is that there are too many one-ulcer
men holding down two-ulcer jobs. *Prince Philip*

Commerce is the school of cheating.
*Luc de Clapiers Vauvenargues
– 'Reflexions' (1946)*

Industry is the root of all ugliness.   *Oscar Wilde*

CAPITALISM

The two richest men in the world make motor
cars and sell the gas for them, but the people
maintain the emergency hospitals.
'Charleston Gazette'

CAPITALISTS

John J. Astor – *capitalist (1763–1848)*
An arrant individualist, selfish, narrow-minded,
quite blandly antisocial, he went after whatever
he sought and took it by fair means or foul –
and whoever didn't like it was welcome to a
battle.   *Kenneth W. Porter*

Andrew Carnegie – *philanthropist (1835–1919)*
He had no ears for any charity unless labelled
with his name. He would have given millions to
Greece had she labelled the Parthenon
'Carnegopolis'.
Poultney Bigelow – 'Seventy Summers'

Jason 'Jay' Gould – *financier (1836–92)*
One of the most sinister figures that have ever
flitted bat-like across the vision of the
American people.   *Anon*

Howard Hughes – *industrialist (1905–76)*
The spook of American Capitalism, suspicious
and withdrawn, elusive to the point of being
almost invisible, he is loath to give anything up,
loath to admit error. There is one aspect of his
character on which his former associates are
agreed: he abhors making a decision.
'Fortune Magazine'

Howard Hughes, America's bashful billionaire,
epitomises the dilemma of twentieth century
America: inventive, brilliant, fantastic,
overwhelming in technical precocity and
accomplishment – suspicious, complex,
contradictory, and sometimes downright
antediluvian in social outlook.   *Albert B. Gerber*

A man whose life, more than that of any other
man, resembles the most improbable Grade B
spectacular in glorious Vistavision.   *John Keats*

PROFESSIONAL

John D. Rockefeller – *industrialist (1839–1937)*
We saw a picture in the paper the other day of
a little girl to whom John D. Rockefeller gave
two dimes. It may have been only a
coincidence, but on the same day the price of
gasoline went up one cent.   *'Charleston Gazette'*

John D. Rockefeller can be fully described as a
man made in the image of the ideal money-
maker . . . An ideal money-maker is a machine
the details of which are diagrammed on the
asbestos blueprints which paper the walls of
hell.   *Thomas Lawson*

St John of the Rocks.   *'Life' (1911)*

Donald Trump – *(b 1946)*
'Surviving at the Top' – The book's title alone
. . . is so perversely marvellous that there ought
to be a contest to invent others that could equal
it . . . Marie Antoinette's 'Keeping My Head',
Achilles' 'Recovering from a Tendon Injury',
Gen. Custer's 'Outfoxing the Enemy', and
Jean-Claude Duvallier's 'President for Life'.
       John Rothschild – 'Los Angeles Times' (1990)

ACCOUNTANCY

An accountant is a man hired to explain that
you didn't make the money you did.   *Anon*

Did you ever hear of a kid playing accountant –
even if he wanted to be one?
                          Jackie Mason (1969)

Our experts describe you as an appallingly dull
fellow, unimaginative, timid, spineless, easily
dominated, no sense of humour, tedious
company and irrepressibly drab and awful. And
whereas in most professions these would be
considered drawbacks, in accountancy they are
a positive boon.
           'Monty Python's Flying Circus' (1971)

ADVERTISING

Advertising is something which makes one
think he's longed all his life for a thing he's
never heard of before.   *Anon*

A radio commercial is the pause that depresses.
                                    Anon

Time spent in the advertising business seems to
create a permanent deformity like the Chinese
habit of foot-binding.   *Dean Acheson*

Hype works on the theory that Americans will
put their money where the noise is.
                            Russell Baker (1979)

Advertising has done more to cause the social
unrest of the twentieth century than any other
single factor.   *Clive Barnes Jr (1969)*

They call these pauses station breaks,
But I ask, for my information,
Why six commercials is what it takes,
For station identification?   *S. S. Biddle*

Advertising is what you do when you can't go
see somebody.   *Fairfax Cone*

Advertising is selling and selling is serious
business. There is no place in it for knights on
armoured horses chasing dirt, tornadoes in
kitchen sinks washing dishes, clothes so clean
that they may be safely viewed only through
smoked glasses, blacked eyes based on cigarette
brand loyalty, etc. . . . My favourite recent
headline in a magazine advertisement was,
'How would you like an acid bath', a question
asked by a steel fabricator. The only possible
answer I could think of was, 'How would you
like a punch on the nose?'
            Fairfax Cone – 'Wall Street Journal'

The longest word in the English language is the
one that follows the phrase: 'And now a word
from our Sponsor'.   *Hal Eaton*

Advertising is a racket. Its constructive
contribution to humanity is exactly zero.
                            F. Scott Fitzgerald

TV commercials are the yak in a box.
                             Shelby Friedman

What is needed is a constant intelligence
service to outline all the latest tricks in the
game, so that people do not get too excited by
offers which end up like that 'bathing suit 50%
off' which turned out to be topless, and the
'simple and elegant coathanger' which turned
out to be a nail.   *David Frost*

The advertising quack who wearies
With tales of countless cures,
  His teeth, I've enacted,
  Shall all be extracted
By terrified amateurs.   *W. S. Gilbert*

I remember well the time when a cabbage could sell itself by being a cabbage. Nowadays it's no good being a cabbage – unless you have an agent and pay him a commission. Nothing is free anymore to sell itself or give itself away.
                    Jean Giradoux (1935)

The art of publicity is a black art.
                    Learned Hand

If I were asked to name the deadliest subversive force within capitalism – the single greatest source of its waning morality – I would without hesitation name advertising.
                    Robert L. Heilbroner (1981)

Of course, no rose is complete without thorns, no television show is complete without the following commercial.   *Alfred Hitchcock*

Seeing a murder on TV can help work off one's antagonisms. And if you don't have any antagonisms, the commercials will give you some.
      Alfred Hitchcock – 'National Observer' (1966)

Aristotle once said that a play should have a beginning, a middle and an end. But what did he know? Today, a play must have a first half, a second half, and a station break.
                    Alfred Hitchcock

Advertisements are now so numerous that they are very negligently perused, and it therefore becomes necessary to gain attention by magnificence of promises, and by eloquences sometimes sublime and sometimes pathetic.
                    Samuel Johnson (1758)

Promise, large promise, is the soul of an advertisement.   *Samuel Johnson*

On CBS Radio the news of Ed Murrow's death, reportedly from lung cancer, was followed by a cigarette commercial.   *Alexander Kendrick*

Advertisers of rich cake mixes, desserts, and other calorie-packed indulgences, actually fight to place their colourful, mouth-watering ads, loaded with subliminal triggers, in close proximity to articles on dieting and weight reduction.   *Wilson Key*

An advertiser is the overrewarded court jester and court pander at the democratic court.
          Joseph Wood Krutch – 'Human Nature and the Human Condition'

Advertising may be described as the science of arresting the human intelligence long enough to get money from it.   *Stephen Leacock*

Advertising, in its spirit and purpose, is germinal fascism. *J. Matthews and R. Shallcross*

I think that I shall never see
A billboard lovely as a tree.
Perhaps unless the billboards fall,
I'll never see a tree at all.
          Ogden Nash – 'Song of the Open Road' (1933)

Advertising is the rattling of a stick inside a swill bucket.   *George Orwell (1941)*

Advertising is the art of making whole lies out of half truths.   *Edgar A. Shoaff*

As a whole, advertising is committed to the ways of business, and as the ways of business are seldom straight and narrow, advertising perforce must follow a dubious path.
                    J. Thorne Smith

When the critics of advertising advocate that advertising per se be sharply limited because it is confusing or because it creates demand that some consumers cannot reasonably afford, or because it gives an unfair advantage to the company that is wise enough to do more advertising, they hit at the basic concepts of freedom and practices of marketing that have contributed to the country's high standard of living.   *Stanford Smith*

I am deeply concerned that we are turning out a nation of young cynics – who might be said to know the slogan of every product, and to believe in the merits of none. *Edward H. Weiss*

In advertising terms, an intellectual is anybody who reads a morning newspaper.
Anna-Maria Winchester

Advertising is legalised lying. *H. G. Wells*

ADVERTISING AGENCIES

An advertising agency is eighty-five per cent confusion and fifteen per cent commission.
Fred Allen (1954)

The only thing you can tell an advertising man is that he is fortunate that he isn't in some other business. *Fred Allen (1954)*

Everyone in advertising is ex-something. Ex-actors, ex-artists, ex-writers, and quite a few ex-people too. *Charlotte Bingham*

Public relations specialists make flower arrangements of the facts, placing them so that the wilted and less attractive petals are hidden by sturdy blooms. *Alan Harrington (1959)*

The number of agency people required to shoot a commercial on location is in direct proportion to the mean temperature of the location.
Shelby Page

BANKING AND FINANCE

The difference between a dead skunk and a dead banker on the road is that there are skid marks by the skunk. *Anon*

Banks have done more injury to the religion, morality, tranquillity, prosperity, and even wealth of the nation than they can have done or ever will do good. *John Adams (1799)*

Adventure is the life of commerce, but caution, I had almost said timidity, is the life of banking.
Walter Bagehot (1873)

What you are doing is giving your money to somebody else to hold on to, and I think that it is worth keeping in mind that the businessmen who run banks are so worried about holding on to things that they put little chains on all their pens. *Henry Beard (1986)*

Why do they call them tellers? They never tell you anything. They just ask questions. And why to they call it interest? It's boring. And another thing – how come the Trust Department has all their pens chained to the table? *'Cheers' – NBC TV*

I have always found that a gambler's word is better than a banker's. *Al Farr (1971)*

Banking may well be a career from which no man really recovers. *J. K. Galbraith*

Banking establishments are more dangerous than standing armies. *Thomas Jefferson*

A bank is a thing that will always lend you money if you can prove you don't need it.
Joe E. Lewis

No sane person ever enjoyed visiting a bank.
Martin Mayer

A financier is a pawnbroker with imagination.
A. W. Pinero (1893)

A banker is a fellow who lends you his umbrella when the sun is shining and wants it back the minute it begins to rain. *Mark Twain*

I'd rather be a pimp with a purple hat than be associated with banks. *Pete Zamarello*

ECONOMICS

Economists are people who work with numbers but who don't have the personality to be accountants. *Anon*

Economic theory is a systematic application and critical evaluation of the basic analytic concepts of economic theory, with an emphasis on money and why it's good.
Woody Allen (1970)

Economists' advice is something like patent medicine – people know it is largely manufactured by quacks and that a good percentage of the time it won't work, but they continue to buy the brand whose flavour they like. *Barbara Bergmann (1974)*

A body of occasionally useful truisms.
Kenneth E. Boulding

Economics is what we might call, by way of eminence, the Dismal Science.
Thomas Carlyle

In all recorded history there has not been one economist who had to worry about where the next meal would come from. *Peter Drucker*

An economist is a person who lectures on capital and labour. And the baffling thing is that most of them qualified for this career by having no capital and having done no labour.
Robert Fuoss

Mathematics has given economics rigour, but alas, also mortis. *Robert Heilbroner*

If ignorance paid dividends most Americans could make a fortune out of what they didn't know about economics. *Luther Hodges (1962)*

If an economist becomes certain of the solution of any problem, he can be equally certain that his solution is wrong. *H. A. Innis (1936)*

Ethics is not a branch of economics.
Verachmiel Kugel

The economist can give us the facts. That is his job. He is a good cartographer, but a bad pilot.
Vincent Massey (1924)

The one profession where you can gain great eminence without ever being right.
George Meany (1975)

An economist is a man who tells you what to do with your money after you have done something else with it. *'New York American'*

An economist is a person who talks about something he doesn't understand and makes you feel you are ignorant. *Herbert Prochnow*

An economist's guess is liable to be as good as anybody else's. *Will Rogers*

Economists are the failed priests of our generation. *Louis Rykeyser (1983)*

Economists spend their time rearranging the deck chairs on the Titanic. *Ernest Schumacher*

Most of the modern economic as taught is a form of brain damage. *Ernest Schumacher*

If all economists were laid end to end, they would not reach a conclusion. *G. B. Shaw* [*Arthur H. Motley had a different view* – If all the nation's economists were laid end to end, they would still point in all directions. *(1954)*]

There is no such thing as the science of economics, nor ever will be. It is just cant.
Richard Tawney (1914)

The instability of the economy is equalled only by the instability of the economists.
John H. Williams (1956)

ECONOMISTS

John Kenneth Galbraith – *(b 1908)*
Professor Galbraith is horrified by the number of Americans who have bought cars with tail fins on them, and I am horrified by the number of Americans who take seriously the proposals of Mr Galbraith. *William F. Buckley Jr* – *'Up from Liberalism' (1968)*

John Maynard Keynes – *(1883-1946)*
It is possible to admire Keynes even though one may consider his social vision to be wrong and every one of his propositions to be misleading.
Joseph A. Schumpeter (1936)

His sense of values, and indeed all his feelings, offer the spectacle of a complete paradox. He is a hedonist and a follower of [G. E.] Moore; he is lascivious without lust; he is an Apostle without tears. *Lytton Strachey*

Lady Passfield [Martha Beatrice Webb]
(1858-1943)
There's no more mysticism in Beatrice than in a steam engine. *H. G. Wells*

INSURANCE

Insurance is no substitute for a good alarm system and a twelve-gauge shotgun.
'Cagney and Lacey'

The Act of God designation on all insurance policies means, roughly, that you cannot be insured for the accidents that are most likely to happen to you. *Alan Coren*

I detest life-insurance agents; they always argue that I shall some day die, which is not so. *Stephen Leacock (1910)*

For almost 70 years the life insurance industry has been a smug sacred cow feeding the public a steady line of sacred bull. *Ralph Nader (1974)*

MARKET RESEARCH

Market research is what you call it when you already know the answer you want, but still hunt up the question that will produce it. *Robert Fuoss*

STOCKBROKING

I do not regard a bill-broker as one of the human race. *Honoré de Balzac*

The stock market has caused nine of the last five recessions. *Paul Samuelson (1960)*

With an evening coat and a white tie, anybody, even a stockbroker, can gain a reputation for being civilised. *Oscar Wilde (1891)*

A stockbroker is a man who can take a bankroll and run it into a shoestring. *Alexander Woollcott (1935)*

STOCK EXCHANGES

Stock Exchange, London
If to the Stock Exchange you speed,
To try with bulls and bears your luck,
'Tis odds you soon from gold are freed
And waddle forth a limping duck. *William A. Ireland (1807)*

Wall Street, New York
A Falstaffian joke that frequently degenerates into a madhouse. *Benjamin Graham*

There are only two emotions in Wall Street – fear and greed. *William LeFevre (1978)*

Many Wall Street firms have what they call a capital structure, but which more closely resembles a scaffold. *Donald Regan (1970)*

You've got more crooks in Wall Street than in any other industry I've ever seen. *Louis Wolfson (1969)*

LAWYERS

Ignorance of the law must not prevent the losing lawyer from collecting his fee. *Legal maxim*

A lawyer is a man who prevents someone else from getting your money. *Anon*

A lawyer must first get on, then get honour, and then get honest. *Anon*

A lawyer is merely a college graduate who couldn't get into medical school. *Anon*

A good lawyer is an evil neighbour. *Anon*

Witches fly upon broomsticks – a lawyer may come upon justice. *Anon*

Lawyers and painters can soon change white to black. *Danish proverb*

A lawyer and a cart-wheel must be greased. *German proverb*

A lawyer without cunning, a peasant without manure, a merchant without gold, remain poor. *German proverb*

Of three things the devil makes a salad – lawyers' tongues, notaries' fingers, and the third shall be nameless. *Italian proverb*

Two farmers each claimed to own a certain cow. While one pulled on its head and the other pulled on its tail, the cow was milked by a lawyer. *Jewish proverb*

It is better to be a mouse in a cat's mouth than a man in a lawyer's hands. *Spanish proverb*

The houses of lawyers are roofed with the skins of litigants. *Welsh proverb*

Lawyers are so much used to feign interest in the persons to whom they speak that their features at last assume a grimace which they can put on and off with their official pallium.
Honoré de Balzac

Lawyer – one skilled in the circumvention of the law.
Ambrose Bierce

Liar – a lawyer with a roving commission.
Ambrose Bierce

A lawyer who has not studied economics and sociology is very apt to become a public enemy.
Louis Brandeis

A lawyer is a learned gentleman who rescues your estate from your enemies and keeps it for himself.
Lord Brougham

Lawyers are the only people in whom ignorance of the law is not punished.
Lord Brougham

The courtrooms of America all too often have Piper Cub advocates trying to handle the controls of Boeing 747 litigation.
Warren E. Burger (1973)

The laws I love; the lawyers I suspect.
Charles Churchill

The only civil delinquents whose judges must of necessity be chosen from themselves.
Charles Caleb Cotton

God works wonders now and then. Behold! A lawyer, an honest man.
Benjamin Franklin

There's no better way of exercising the imagination than the study of law. No poet ever interpreted nature as freely as a lawyer interprets truth.
Jean Giradoux (1935)

One trouble with civilisation is that it pays so much more to the lawyer who finds loopholes in laws than to the lawyer who tries to enforce laws.
'Greenville Piedmont'

If you see a Gucci loafer in L.A. today, you're looking at the foot of a lawyer.
Alan Gross

Whatever their other contributions to our society, lawyers could be an important source of protein.
'Guindon'

When there is rift in the lute, the business of the lawyer is to widen the rift and gather the loot.
Arthur G. Hays

Lawyers spend a great deal of their time shovelling smoke.
Oliver Wendell Holmes Jr

A man may as well open an oyster without a knife, as a lawyer's mouth without a fee.
Barton Holyday

Lawyers are people who earn a living by the sweat of their browbeating.
James Huneker

On the increasing problems of litigation in the National Football League – My definition of utter waste is a coach-load of lawyers going over a cliff, with three empty seats.
Lamar Hunt

It is the trade of lawyers to question everything, yield nothing and talk by the hour.
Holbrook Jackson

If the present Congress errs in too much talking, how can it be otherwise in a body to which the people send 150 lawyers?
Thomas Jefferson – 'Autobiography'

Self-defence is the clearest of laws; and for this reason – the lawyers didn't make it.
Douglas Jerrold

A lawyer's smile is dirt cheap at six and eightpence.
Douglas Jerrold

I think we may class the lawyer in the natural history of monsters.
John Keats

Most lawyers are like whores. They serve the client who puts the highest fee on the table.
Florynce Kennedy

Lawyers, I suppose, were children once.
Charles Lamb

It is unfair to believe everything we hear about lawyers – some of it may be true.
Gerald Lieberman

I find in Washington that when you ask what time it is you get different answers from Democrats and Republicans; 435 answers from the House of Representatives; a 500-page report from some consultants on how to tell the time; no answer from your lawyer and a bill for $1000.   *Tim McNamar*

Lawyers are men who hire out their words and anger.   *Martial*

Lawyer – one who protects us against robbers by taking away the temptation.   *H. L. Mencken*

Lawyers are a sort of people whose profession it is to disguise matters.   *Thomas More - 'Utopia'*

I don't want a lawyer to tell me what I cannot do; I hire him to tell me how to do what I want to do.   *J. Pierpont Morgan*

I don't know of any other industry, except the movie business, that has so many stars. Every lawyer thinks he is special.
     Peter Morrison - 'New York Times' (1984)

If you outsmart your own lawyer, you've got the wrong lawyer.   *John Nolan*

A lawyer with a briefcase can steal more than a hundred men with guns.   *Mario Puzo*

Lawyers are the operators of the toll bridge which anyone in search of justice must pass.
                                         Jane B. Quinn

I don't think you can make a lawyer honest by act of legislature. You've got to work on his conscience. And his lack of conscience is what makes him a lawyer.   *Will Rogers (1927)*

The first thing we do, let's kill all lawyers.
                              William Shakespeare

One listens to one's lawyers prattle on as long as one can stand it and then signs where indicated.   *Alexander Woollcott*

A man without money needs no more fear a crowd of lawyers than a crowd of pickpockets.
                             William Wycherley

An incompetent attorney can delay a trial for years or months. A competent attorney can delay one even longer.
     Evelle J. Younger - 'Los Angeles Times' (1971)

EDUCATION

One of the first things schoolchildren in Texas learn is how to compose a simple declarative sentence without the word 'shit' in it.   *Anon*

Nothing in education is so astonishing as the amount of ignorance it accumulates in the form of inner facts.   *Henry Adams*

I didn't need no diploma to do what I do.
Louis Armstrong

Education – that which discloses to the wise and disguises from the foolish their lack of understanding.   *Ambrose Bierce*

Education is learning what you didn't even know you didn't know.   *Daniel J. Boorstin*

Learning is the cobweb of the brain,
Profane, erroneous, and vain.
Samuel Butler – 'Hudibras'

The average PhD thesis is nothing but a transference of bones from one graveyard to another.   *J. Frank Dobie*

A lot of fellows nowadays have a B.A., M.A., or Ph.D. Unfortunately, they don't have a J.O.B.
Fats Domino (1966)

Education is the state-controlled manufactory of echoes.
Norman Douglas – 'How About Europe?'

It doesn't make much difference what you study, as long as you don't like it.
Finlay Peter Dunne

Education should teach us to play the wise fool rather than turn us into the solemn ass.
Kenneth Eble

Education is the process of casting false pearls before real swine.   *Irwin Edman*

Education is the ability to listen to almost anything without losing your temper or your self-confidence.   *Robert Frost*

We must reject that most dismal and fatuous notion that education is a preparation for life.
Northrop Frye

Today's children seem to be born with two strikes against them: teachers and school bus drivers.   *Robert Fuoss*

A lecture is an occasion when you numb one end to benefit the other.   *John Gould*

The advantage of a classical education is that it enables you to despise the wealth which it prevents you from achieving.   *Russell Green*

A diploma is a remembrance of things passed.
Honey Greer

Education is the inculcation of the incomprehensible into the indifferent by the incompetent.   *J. M. Keynes*

Stand firm in your refusal to remain conscious during algebra. In real life, I assure you, there is no such thing as algebra.
Fran Lebowitz (1981)

School days, I believe, are the unhappiest in the whole span of human existence. They are full of dull, unintelligible tasks, new and unpleasant ordinances, brutal violations of common sense and common decency.
H. L. Mencken – 'Baltimore Eveing Sun' (1928)

In large states public education will always be mediocre, for the same reason that in large kitchens the cooking is bad.   *Friedrich Nietzsche*

When a woman inclines to learning there is usually something wrong with her sex apparatus.   *Friedrich Nietzsche*

A little learning is a dangerous thing.
Alexander Pope
[*Bob Edwards added* – But a lot of ignorance is just as bad.]

If there is anything education does not lack

today, it is critics. *Nathan M. Pusey*

To educate a man in mind and not in morale is to educate a menace to society.
Theodore Roosevelt

Education is one of the chief obstacles to intelligence and freedom of thought.
Bertrand Russell

The educated man is a greater nuisance than the uneducated one. *G. B. Shaw*

Words are but wind; and learning is nothing but words; ergo, learning is nothing but wind.
Jonathan Swift (1704)

Education has produced a vast population able to read but unable to distinguish what is worth reading. *G. M. Trevelyan (1944)*

Education is what you must acquire without any interference from your schooling.
Mark Twain

Education appears to be the thing that enables a man to get along without using his intelligence. *A. E. Wiggan*

Education is an admirable thing, but it is well to remember from time to time that nothing that is worth knowing can be taught.
Oscar Wilde (1890)

Sex in the hands of public educators is not a pretty thing. *'The Wonder Years' – US TV show*

EDUCATORS

A professor is a man whose job is to tell students how to solve the problems of life which he himself has tried to avoid by becoming a professor. *Anon*

Parents never appreciate a teacher unless it rains all weekend. *Anon*

A college dean is a man who doesn't know enough to be a professor, but who is too smart to be a president. *Anon*

A lecturer is one with his hand in your pocket,

his tongue in your ear, and his faith in your patience. *Ambrose Bierce*

Most educators would continue to lecture on navigation while the ship is going down.
James H. Boren

Arrogance, pedantry, and dogmatism are the occupational diseases of those who spend their lives directing the intellects of the young.
Henry Canby

A scholar is a man with this inconvenience, that, when you ask him his opinion of any matter, he must go home and look up his manuscripts to know. *R. W. Emerson*

A college professor is someone who talks in other people's sleep. *Bergen Evans*

A lecturer is a literary strumpet, subject for a greater than whore's fee to prostitute himself.
Olive Wendell Holmes

Teaching is the last refuge of feeble minds with classical education. *Aldous Huxley*

I dreamed last night I was teaching again – that's the only bad dream that ever afflicts my sturdy conscience. *D. H. Lawrence*

Whenever the cause of the people is entrusted to professors it is lost. *Nikolai Lenin*

Teachers are overworked and underpaid. True, it is an exacting and exhausting business, this damming up the flood of human potentialities.
George B. Leonard

Our American professors like their literature clear and cold and pure and dead.
Sinclair Lewis (1930)

He may be dead; or, he may be teaching English. *Cormac McCarthy*

The average schoolmaster is and always must be essentially an ass, for how can one imagine an intelligent man engaging in so puerile an avocation? *H. L. Mencken (1922)*

Scholars are unmannered species.
George Meredith

No man ever got a word of sense out of a schoolmaster. You may, at a pinch, take their word about equilateral hexagons but life, life's a closed book to them.
John Mortimer – 'A Voyage Round My Father'

The average small boy believes all teachers should be paid so much salary they could retire – immediately. *'New York World'*

A scholar is a scientific average man.
Friedrich Nietzsche

You don't have to think too hard when you talk to a teacher. *J. D. Salinger*

Lectures can make an audience feel dumb on one end and numb on the other, but they also can reveal the lecturer as both completely dumb and numb.
Arville Schaleben – 'The Milwaukee Journal'

For every person wishing to teach there are thirty not wanting to be taught.
W. C. Sellar and R. J. Yeatman

It is when the gods hate a man with uncommon abhorrence that they drive him into the profession of schoolmaster. *Seneca (64AD)*

He who can does. He who cannot, teaches.
G. B. Shaw

Teaching has ruined more American novelists than drink. *Gore Vidal – 'Oui' (1975)*

Everybody who is incapable of learning has taken to teaching – that is exactly what our enthusiasm for education has come to.
Oscar Wilde – 'The Decay of Lying' (1889)

He is either dead or teaching school.
Zenobius (100 BC)

SEATS OF LEARNING

College bred is a four-year loaf made out of the old man's dough. *Anon*

College is a fountain of knowledge where students gather to drink. *Anon*

More often than not the only thing a man gets out of college is himself. *Anon*

Administering a college today is like playing chess on the open deck of the sinking Titanic.
Edward Bloustein (1971)

A university is what a college becomes when the faculty loses interest in students.
John Ciardi

Public schools are becoming a nuisance, a pest, and an abomination; and it is fit that the eyes and noses of mankind should, if possible, be open to perceive it. *William Cowper*

Public schools are the nurseries of all vice and immorality. *Henry Fielding*

The best you can say for most day care nurseries is that they fill a crying need.
Robert Fuoss

A college is a place where pebbles are polished and diamonds dimmed. *Robert G. Ingersoll*

University politics are vicious precisely because the stakes are so small. *Henry Kissinger*

Show me a college dean whose professors are out on strike and I'll show you someone who's no longer in possession of his faculties.
Bert Murray

Most colleges trample whole fields of wheat trying to put salt on a sparrow's tail.
Austin O'Malley

The schools ain't what they used to be and never was. *Will Rogers*

A child only educated at school is an uneducated one. *George Santayana*

School is where you go between when your parents can't take you and industry can't take you. *John Updike*

It is a pity so many men get a college training without getting an education. *'Washington Post'*

SCHOOLS AND UNIVERSITIES

Christ's College, Cambridge
A stony-hearted stepmother.   *John Milton*

Eton, Slough
Entry in 'Who's Who' – Educated: In the
holidays from Eton.   *Osbert Sitwell*

Harvard, Massachusetts, USA
You can tell a Harvard man, but you can't tell
him much.   *Anon*

A Harvard professor is an educator who thinks
the American eagle has two left wings.
                John M. Ashbrook

Studying literature at Harvard is like learning
about women at the Mayo Clinic.
                Ray Blount Jr

On the 1970s oil crisis – The real villain of the oil
crisis is the Harvard Business School. Almost

every Arab sheik now in charge of his country's
oil policy was trained at Harvard.
                Art Buchwald (1973)

*On its reputation as 'the greatest storehouse of
knowledge in the nation'* – In all likelihood it is
because the freshmen bring in so much of it
and the seniors take away so little.
                Dr Charles W. Eliot

If Moses had gone to Harvard Law School and
spent three years working on the hill, he would
have written the Ten Commandments with
three exceptions and a savings clause.
                Charles Morgan Jr

Magdalen College, Oxford
I spent fourteen months at Magdalen: they
proved the most idle and unprofitable fourteen
months of my life.   *Edward Gibbon*

Oxford
It is Oxford that has made me unsufferable.
                Max Beerbohm

RELIGION

Many bring their clothes to church rather than themselves.   *Anon*

Don't stay away from church because there are so many hypocrites. There's always room for one more.   *A. R. Adams*

Not only is there no God, but try getting a plumber at weekends.   *Woody Allen*

Religion is a Daughter of Faith and Hope, explaining to Ignorance the nature of the Unknowable.   *Ambrose Bierce*

To pray is to ask that the laws of the universe be annulled on behalf of a single practitioner confusedly unworthy.   *Ambrose Bierce*

All popular theology is a bright bubble, blown into life by the fervour of devout passion, and pictured all round with the most pleasing forms and colours of devout fancy. Very pretty as long as it floats loosely in the air, but pricked with the slightest touch of severe reason or shrewd common sense, it bursts into nothing.
                                    John S. Blackie

Theology, as we encounter it, is philosophy seasoned with popular passion and decorated by popular imagination.   *John S. Blackie*

Religion is excellent stuff for keeping common people quiet.   *Napoleon Bonaparte*

For me the single word 'God' suggests everything that is slippery, shady, squalid, foul, and grotesque.   *André Breton*

Every day people are straying away from the church and going back to God.   *Lenny Bruce*

It is usually when men are at their most religious that they behave with the least sense and the greatest cruelty.   *Ilka Chase*

Religion is by no means a proper subject of conversation in mixed company.
                                    Lord Chesterfield

Isn't God a shit!   *Randolph Churchill*

Men will wrangle for religion, write for it, fight for it, die for it, anything but live for it.
                                    Charles Caleb Cotton

I don't believe in God because I don't believe in Mother Goose.   *Clarence Darrow*

And of all the plagues with which mankind are cursed,
Ecclesiastic tyranny's the worst.   *Daniel Defoe*

The idea of a Supreme Being who creates a world in which one creature is designed to eat another in order to subsist, and then pass a law saying, 'Thou shalt not kill', is so monstrously, immeasurably, bottomlessly absurd that I am at a loss to understand how mankind has entertained or given it house room all this long.
                                    Peter De Vries

So far as religion of the day is concerned, it is a damned fake . . . Religion is bunk.
                                    Thomas A. Edison

Science without religion is lame, religion without science is blind.   *Albert Einstein*

Faith is a stiffening process, a sort of mental starch, which ought to be applied as sparingly as possible.
          E. M. Forster – 'Two Cheers for Democracy'

If men are so wicked with religion, what would they be without it?   *Benjamin Franklin*

Theologians are all alike – their aim is always to wield despotic authority over men's consciences.   *Frederick the Great (1736)*

When a man is freed of religion, he has a better chance to live a normal and wholesome life.
                                    Sigmund Freud

Religion is an illusion and it derives its strength from the fact that it falls in with our intellectual desires.   *Sigmund Freud*

All religions are ancient monuments to superstitions, ignorance, ferocity; and modern religions are only ancient follies rejuvenated.
Baron d'Hollbach (1772)

Theology is an attempt to explain a subject by men who do not understand it; the intent is not to tell the truth but to satisfy the questioner.
Elbert Hubbard – 'The Philistine'

A mystic is a person who is puzzled before the obvious, but who understands the non-existent.
Elbert Hubbard

Perhaps the most lasting pleasure in life is the pleasure of not going to church.   *William Inge*

No man with any sense of humour ever founded a religion.   *Robert G. Ingersoll (1884)*

A monumental chapter in the history of human egotism.   *William James (1902)*

'Twas only fear first in the world made gods.
Ben Johnson – 'Sejanus'

I do not believe in God. I believe in cashmere.
Fran Lebowitz

I do believe our army chaplains, taken as a class, are the worst men we have in our service.
Abraham Lincoln

How many evils have flowed from religion!
Lucretius (60 BC)

Theology is taught by demons, it teaches about demons, and it leads to demons.
St Albertus Magnus

I count religion but a childish toy.
Christopher Marlowe – 'The Jew of Malta'

Religion is the sign of the oppressed creature, the feeling of a heartless world and the spirit of conditions which are unspiritual. It is the opium of the people.   *Karl Marx (1884)*

What mean and cruel things people do for the love of God!   *W. Somerset Maugham*

I've always been a man of God. God's green and He folds.   *Robert McGammon*

Religion is a conceited effort to deny the most obvious realities.   *H. L. Mencken*

The Creator is a comedian whose audience is afraid to laugh.   *H. L. Mencken*

Faith is an illogical belief in the occurrence of the improbable.   *H. L. Mencken – 'Prejudices'*

We must respect the other fellow's religion, but only in the sense and to the extent that we respect his theory that his wife is beautiful and his children smart.   *H. L. Mencken (1956)*

I detest converts almost as much as I do missionaries.   *H. L. Mencken*

It is impossible to believe that the same God who permitted His own son to die a bachelor regards celibacy as an actual sin.   *H. L. Mencken*

A comedian is not an actor. His work bears the same relation to acting as that of a hangman, a midwife or a divorce lawyer bears to poetry, or that of a bishop to religion.
H. L. Mencken (1929)

Religion is the venereal disease of mankind.
Henri de Montherlant

After coming in contact with a religious man I always feel that I must wash my hands.
Friedrich Nietzsche – 'The Antichrist' (1888)

God is a thought that makes crooked all that is straight.   *Friedrich Nietzsche*

Whoever has theological blood in his veins is shifty and dishonourable in all things.
Friedrich Nietzsche (1888)

Religion is induced insanity.
Madalyn Murray O'Hair

Difference of religion breeds more quarrels than difference in politics.   *Wendell Phillips*

Jesus was a crackpot.   *Bhagwan Shree Rajneesh*

I think all the great religions of the world – Buddhism, Hinduism, Christianity, Islam and Communism – both untrue and harmful. It is evident as a matter of logic that, since they disagree, not more than one of them can be true. With very few exceptions, the religion which a man accepts is that of the community in which he lives, which makes it obvious that the influence of the environment is what has led him to accept the religion in question.

Bertrand Russell – 'Why I Am Not a Christian'

Everyone prefers belief to the exercise of judgment. *Seneca*

There are three sexes – men, women and clergymen. *Sydney Smith*

The world is proof that God is a committee. *Bob Stokes*

Man is the only animal that has the true religion – several of them. *Mark Twain*

Religion is the source of all imaginable follies and disturbances; it is the parent of fanaticism and civil discord; it is the enemy of mankind. *Voltaire*

Maybe there isn't a devil; perhaps it's just God when he's drunk. *Tom Waits*

Religion is the fashionable substitute for belief. *Oscar Wilde*

Most religious teachers spend their time trying to prove the unproven by the unprovable. *Oscar Wilde*

SCIENCE

Science is the orderly arrangement of what, at the moment, seems to be the facts. *Anon*

Science is really going away at a rapid pace. Now it's only a hundred years behind comic strips. *Joey Adams*

Research is the process of going up alleys to see if they are blind. *Marston Bates*

The trouble with scientists is that they can't leave well enough alone. *Art Buchwald (1971)*

Science is an exchange of ignorance for that which is another kind of ignorance. *Lord Byron*

Science in the modern world has many uses; its chief use, however, is to provide long words to cover the errors of the rich. *G. K. Chesterton*

Science, which was to be the midwife of progress, became the angel of death, killing with a precision and a rapidity that reduced the wars of the Middle Ages to the level of college athletics. *Will Durrant*

The whole of science is nothing more than a refinement of everyday thinking.
Albert Einstein

Now that we have demonstrated that man can walk on the moon, it's time we proved he can walk down Main Street after dark. *Robert Fuoss*

Science is the topography of ignorance.
Oliver Wendell Holmes Sr

Science says the first word on everything, and the last word on nothing. *Victor Hugo*

It is inexcusable for scientists to torture animals; let them make their experiments on journalists and politicians. *Henrik Ibsen*

Scientists are Peeping Toms at the keyhole of eternity. *Arthur Koestler*

Modern science is generally practised by those who lack the flair for conversation.
Fran Lebowitz – 'Metropolitan Life' (1978)

In studying the science of yesteryear one comes upon such interesting notions as gravity, electricity, and the roundness of the earth – while an examination of more recent phenomena shows a strong trend towards spray cheese, stretch denim, and the Moog synthesiser. *Fran Lebowitz – ibid*

Scientists – a crowd that when it comes to style and dash makes the general public look like the Bloomsbury set. *Fran Lebowitz – ibid*

Science! Pooh! Whatever good has science done the world? Damned bosh! *George Moore (1932)*

I almost think it is the ultimate destiny of science to exterminate the human race.
Thomas L. Peacock (1860)

Science is nothing but developed perception, interpreted intent, common sense rounded out and minutely articulated.
George Santayana – 'The Life of Reason' (1906)

What is called science today consists of a haphazard heap of information, united by nothing, often utterly unnecessary, and not only failing to present one unquestionable truth, but as often as not containing the grossest errors, today put forward as truths, and tomorrow overthrown. *Leo Tolstoy (1902)*

Science is a bar of gold made by charlatan scientists. You want to simplify it, to make it accessible to all: you find that you have coined a lot of false coins. When the people realise the real value of these coins, they won't thank you.
Leo Tolstoy

Science robs men of wisdom and usually converts them into phantom beings loaded up with facts. *Miguel de Unamuno – 'Essays' (1925)*

Science is a cemetery of dead ideas.
Miguel de Unamuno

SCIENTISTS

Viscount William Brouncker –
President of the Royal Society (1629–84)
I perceive he is a rotten-hearted, false man as
any else I know, even as Sir W. Pen himself,
and, therefore, I must beware of him
accordingly, and I hope I shall.
Samuel Pepys – 'Diary' (1666)

Charles Darwin – *naturalist (1809–82)*
A good sort of man is this Darwin and well
meaning, but with very little intellect.
Thomas Carlyle – 'The Times' (1877)

'On the Origin of Species' – I have no patience
whatever with these gorilla damnifications of
humanity. *Thomas Carlyle*

While Darwinian man, though well-behaved,
At best is only a monkey shaved.
W. S. Gilbert – 'Princess Ida'

If the whole of the English language could be
considered into one word, it would not suffice
to express the utter contempt those invite who
are so deluded as to be disciples of such an
imposture as Darwinism.
Francis O. Morris (1877)

'On the Origin of Species' – I laughed till my sides
were sore. *Adam Sedgwick (1859)*

'On the Origin of Species' – A rotten fabric of
guess and speculation.
Samuel Wilberforce – Bishop of Oxford (1859)

Albert Einstein – *physicist (1879–1955)*
There is a famous family named Stein –
There's Gert, and there's Ep, and there's Ein;
  Gert's poems are bunk,
  Ep's statues are junk,
And nobody understands Ein. *Anon*

A stitch in time would have confused Einstein.
Anon

I have never met a man yet who understands in
the least what Einstein is driving at . . . a cloak
which hides the ghastly apparition of atheism.
Cardinal W. O'Connell (1929)

Any man whose errors take ten years to correct,

is quite a man. *J. Robert Oppenheimer*

The genius of Einstein leads to Hiroshima.
Pablo Picasso

Sigmund Freud – *founder of psychoanalysis
(1856–1939)*
Freud put the 'anal' into psychoanalysis.
Graffiti

'Moses and Monotheism' – This book is poorly
written, full of repetitions, replete with
borrowings from unbelievers, and spoiled by
the author's atheistic bias and his flimsy
psychoanalytic fancies. *'Catholic World' (1939)*

He formulated his ideas in extravagant and
exclusive forms, which have since got quietly
modified – I doubt whether psychoanalysts
would now maintain that dreams of overcoats,
staircases, ships, rooms, tables, children,
landscapes, machinery, airships and hats
commonly represent the genitals.
Rosemary Dinnage (1980)

Nobody can read Freud without realising he
was the scientific equivalent of another
nuisance, George Bernard Shaw.
Robert M. Hutchins

He was ill-informed in the field of contemporary
psychology and seems to have derived only
from hearsay any knowledge he had of it.
*Ernest Jones – 'Life and
Works of Sigmund Freud'*

I just want to make one brief statement about
psychoanalysis: 'F*** Dr Freud!' *Oscar Levant*

Did Freud ever write the word 'happiness'?
André Malraux

I think he's crude, I think he's medieval, and I
don't want an elderly gentleman from Vienna
with an umbrella inflicting his dreams upon
me. *Vladimir Nabokov*

Surely he never wrote his 'sexy' books? What a
terrible man. I am sure he has never been
unfaithful to his wife. It's quite abnormal and
scandalous. *Anna de Noailles*

The greatest villain that ever lived, a man

worse than Hitler or Stalin. I am speaking of
Sigmund Freud.   *Telly Savalas (1975)*

Sigmund Freud was a half-baked Viennese
quack. Our literature, and the films of Woody
Allen would be better today if Freud had never
written a word.   *Ian Shoales*

Galileo Galilei - *astronomer (1564–1692)*
The revolution of thought initiated by Galileo's
observations of January 7, 1610, proved to be
the most catastrophic in the history of the race.
Sir James Jeans – 'The Universe About Us'

Thor Heyerdahl - *explorer (b 1914)*
'Kon-Tiki' – Who in hell wants to read about a
bunch of crazy Scandinavians floating around
the ocean on a raft?   *Anon (1947)*

'Kon-Tiki' – This is a long, solemn, tedious
Pacific voyage best suited, I think, to some kind
of drastic abridgement in a journal like the
National Geographic.   *William Styron (1947)*

Thomas Huxley - *biologist (1825-95)*
One who is continually taking two irons out of
the fire and putting three in; and necessarily,
along with the external congestion entailed,
there is apt to come internal congestion.
Herbert Spencer

Sir Isaac Newton - *mathematician
(1642–1727)*
Newton was a great man, but you must excuse
me if I think that it would take many Newtons
to make one Milton.
Samuel T. Coleridge – 'Table Talk'
[*In a later letter Coleridge expounded his
Newtonian theory* – I believe the souls of five
hundred Sir Isaac Newtons would go to the
making up of a Shakespeare or a Milton.]

Sir Walter Raleigh - *explorer (1552–1618)*
I will prove you the notoriousest traitor that
ever came to the bar . . . Nay, I will prove all;
thou art a monster; thou hast an English face
but a Spanish heart.   *Edward Coke (1603)*

BRANCHES OF SCIENCE

ASTROLOGY

Anybody who believes in astrology must have
been born under the wrong sign.   *Anon*

Astrology is framed by the devil.
Martin Luther – 'Table-Talk'

MATHEMATICS

There are three kinds of lies – lies, damned lies,
and statistics.   *Benjamin Disraeli*

I don't believe in mathematics.   *Albert Einstein*

I have hardly ever known a mathematician who
was able to reason.
Plato – 'The Republic' (370 BC)

The only science where one never knows what
one is talking about, nor whether what is said is
true.   *Bertrand Russell (1918)*

MEDICINE

Drill, fill and bill.   *Old dental saying*

A physician is a man who pours drugs of which
he knows little into a body of which he knows
less.   *Anon*

A virus is a Latin word translated by doctors to
mean 'Your guess is as good as mine.'   *Anon*

An ignorant doctor is no better than a
murderer.   *Chinese proverb*

A young physician should have three
graveyards.   *German proverb*

No physician is really good before he has killed
one or two patients.   *Hindu proverb*

If you have a friend who is a physician send
him to the house of your enemy.
Portuguese proverb

Heaven defend me from a busy doctor.
Welsh proverb

We may lay down a maxim, that when a nation
abounds in physicians it grows thin of people.
Joseph Addison (1711)

An apothecary is a physician's accomplice,
undertaker's benefactor, and grave worm's
provider.   *Ambrose Bierce*

Medicine as a collection of uncertain prescriptions, the results of which, taken collectively, are more fatal than useful to mankind. *Napoleon Bonaparte*

The whole imposing edifice of modern medicine, for all its breathtaking successes, is, like the celebrated Tower of Pisa, slightly off balance. It is frightening how dependent on drugs we are all becoming and how easy it is for doctors to prescribe them as the universal panacea for our ills. *Prince Charles (1985)*

Doctors are the same as lawyers; the only difference is that lawyers merely rob you, whereas doctors rob you and kill you too. *Anton Chekhov – 'Ivanov' (1887)*

The best doctor is the one you run for and can't find. *Dennis Diderot*

I wonder why you can always read a doctor's bill and you can never read his prescription. *Finlay Peter Dunne*

Some doctors make the same mistakes for twenty years and call it clinical experience. *Dr Noah Fabricant*

God heals, the doctor takes the fee. *Benjamin Franklin*

Doctors think a lot of patients are cured who have simply quit in disgust. *Don Herold*

I often say a great doctor kills more people than a great general. *G. W. Leibnitz*

To live by medicine is to live horribly. *Linnaeus*

Nearly all men die of their medicines and not of their illnesses. *Molière*

The trouble with doctors, I find, is that they seldom admit that anything stumps them. *George J. Nathan*

Perhaps the relatives of the massacred Armenians may find comfort in the report that an American dentist has been in attendance on the Sultan of Turkey. *George J. Nathan – 'New York Morning Telegraph'*

I hate doctors! They'll do anything – anything to keep you coming to them. They'll sell their souls! What's worse, they'll sell yours, and you never know it till one day, you find yourself in hell! *Eugene O'Neill – 'Long Day's Journey Into Night'*

Cured yesterday of my disease, I died last night of my physician. *Matthew Prior*

A doctor is someone who kills you today to prevent you from dying tomorrow. *'Punch'*

A male gynaecologist is like an auto mechanic who has never owned a car. *Carrie Snow*

The art of medicine consists of amusing the patient while nature cures the disease. *Voltaire*

DOCTORS

Benjamin Rush – *physician (1745–1813)*
He is a man born to be useful to society. And so is a mosquito, a horse-leech, a ferret, a polecat, a weasel: for these are all bleeders, and understand their business full as well as Doctor Rush does it. *William Cobbett – 'Peter Porcupine Works'*

METAPHYSICS

A metaphysician is a man who goes into a dark cellar at midnight without a light looking for a black cat that isn't there. *Anon*

The finding of bad reasons for what we believe on instinct. *Francis Bradley*

The attempt of the mind to rise above the mind. *Thomas Carlyle*

The art of being sure of something that is not so. *Joseph Wood Krutch*

A metaphysician is one who, when you remark that twice two makes four, demands to know what you mean by twice, what by two, what by makes, and what by four. *H. L. Mencken*

Metaphysics is almost always an attempt to prove the incredible by an appeal to the unintelligible. *H. L. Mencken*

METEOROLOGY

The science of being up in the air and all at sea.
Anon

PARANORMAL

We still say ESP is spinach and stands for Essentially Silly People. *Cleveland Amory*

PHILOSOPHY

I wanted to be a philosopher, but cheerfulness kept breaking in. *Anon*

A philosopher is a man who can get the fun out of defunct. *Anon*

Philosophy is unintelligible answers to insoluble solutions. *Henry Adams*

A philosopher is a man up in a balloon, with his family and friends holding the ropes which confine him to earth and trying to pull him down. *Louisa May Alcott*

The philosophy of one century is the common sense of the next. *Henry Ward Beecher*

Philosophy is a route of many roads leading from nowhere to nothing. *Ambrose Bierce*

Philosophy is common sense in a dress suit. *Oliver S. Braston*

All philosophies, if you ride them home, are nonsense, but some are greater nonsense than others. *Samuel Butler (1912)*

There is nothing so ridiculous but some philosopher has said it. *Cicero*
[*René Descartes agreed* – There is nothing so strange and so unbelievable that it has not been said by one philosopher or another.]

Philosophy is the purple bullfinch in the lilac tree. *T. S. Eliot*

I hate the philosopher who is not wise to himself. *Euripides*

Most philosophical treatises show the human cerebrum loaded far beyond its Plimsoll Mark.
H. L. Mencken – 'Prejudices' (1924)

Wonder is the foundation of all philosophy, inquiring the process, ignorance the end.
Michel Montaigne – 'Essays'

A terrible explosive in the presence of which everything is in danger. *Friedrich Nietzsche*

Bad philosophers may have a certain influence, good philosophers, never. *Bertrand Russell*

Philosophers are as jealous as women; each wants a monopoly of praise.
George Santayana (1925)

Philosophy is nothing but discretion.
John Selden

For there was never yet philosopher
That could endure toothache patiently.
William Shakespeare – 'Much Ado About Nothing'

The various opinions of philosophers have scattered through the world as many plagues of the mind as Pandora's Box did those of the body; only with this difference, that they have not left hope at the bottom.
Jonathan Swift (1707)

The reason philosophers are not to the public taste is that they do not talk enough of the things we know. *Luc Vauvenargues*

PHILOSOPHERS

Aristotle – *(384–322 BC)*
He did not consult experience, as he should have done, in the framing of his decisions and axioms; but, having first determined the question according to his will, he then resorted to experience, and bending her into conformity with his precepts, led her about like a captive in a procession. *Francis Bacon*

Criticism, as it was first introduced by Aristotle, was meant as a standard of judging well. *Samuel Johnson*

James L. Austin – *(1911–60)*
You are like a greyhound who doesn't want to run himself, and bites the other greyhounds, so

they cannot run either.   *A. J. Ayer*

Francis Bacon – *(1561-1626)*
An atheist pretending to talk against Atheism!
                                        William Blake

He could as easily have created the planets as
he could have written Hamlet.   *Thomas Carlyle*

John Dewey – *(1859-1952)*
In the bedlam, melodrama and light opera in
which we live, Dewey is still the master of the
commonplace.   *C. E. Ayres*

Not only is his own style dull, but his dullness
infects everybody who has anything to write
about his theories of education.
                                    Max Eastman

Thomas Hobbes – *(1588-1679)*
Here lies Thomas Hobbes, the Bug-bear of the
    Nation,
Whose Death hath frightened Atheism out of
    Fashion.   *Anon*

In fine, after a thousand shams and fobs,
Ninety years eating and immortal jobs,
Here matter lies, and that's the end of Hobbes.
                                    Anon epitaph

Ah! poor Hobbes, he possessed fine talents; in
forming his theories, however, he fancied the
first link of his chain was fastened to a rock of
adamant, but it proved to be a rock of ice.
                        Samuel Taylor Coleridge

His strong mind and body appear to have
resisted all impressions but those which were
derived from the downright blows of matter: all
his ideas seemed to lie like substances in his
brain: what was not solid, tangible, distinct,
palpable object was to him nothing.
        William Hazlitt – 'On the Writings of Hobbes'

Eric Hoffer – *(1902-83)*
Hoffer, our resident Peasant Philosopher, is an
example of articulate ignorance.   *John Seelye*

David Hume – *(1711-76)*
Hume is always idiomatic, but his idioms are
constantly wrong.   *Walter Bagehot*

His face was broad and flat, his mouth wide,

and without any other expression than that of
imbecility. His eyes were vacant and spiritless,
and the corpulence of his whole person was far
better to communicate the idea of a turtle-
eating Alderman, than of a refined philosopher.
                                    James Caulfield

The philosophy of Hume was nothing more
than the analysis of the word 'cause' into
uniform sequence.   *Benjamin Jowett*

Friedrich Jacobi – *(1743-1819)*
The virtues of his work are quenched and
smothered by the multitude and monstrosity of
its vices. They say that he was born of human
parentage; but if so he must have been suckled
by Caucasian tigers.   *A. E. Housman*

William James – *(1842-1910)*
James confronted all dogma with skepticism
and made skepticism itself a dogma.
                            Henry Steele Commanger

John Locke – *(1632-1704)*
Against Locke's philosophy I think it an
unanswerable objection that, although he
carried his throat about with him in this world
for seventy-years, no man ever condescended to
cut it.   *Thomas de Quincey – 'Murder Considered
                            as One of the Fine Arts'*

Sir James Mackintosh – *(1765-1832)*
Though thou'rt like Judas, an apostate black,
In the resemblance thou dost one thing lack;
When he had gotten his ill-purchas'd pelf,
He went away, and wisely hang'd himself:
This thou may do at last, yet much I doubt
If thou hast any bowels to gush out!
                                    Charles Lamb

Karl Marx – *(1818-83)*
'Capital' – The first volume of 'Capital' is badly
written, ill put together, lacking in order, logic,
and homogeneity of material.   *Jacques Barzun*

The world would not be in such a snarl,
Had Marx been Groucho instead of Karl.
                                    Irving Berlin

M is for Marx
And clashing of the classes
And movement of masses
And massing of asses.   *Cyril Connolly*

John Mill – *(1773-1836)*
'Essay on Government' – Our objection to the essay of Mr Mill is fundamental. We believe it is utterly impossible to deduce the science of government from the principles of human nature.
Thomas Macaulay – 'Edinburgh Review' (1829)

John Stuart Mill – *(1806-73)*
As for Mill as a thinker – a man who knew nothing of Plato and Darwin gives me very little. His reputation is curious to me. I gain nothing, I have gained nothing from him – an arid, dry man with moods of sentiment – a type that is poor, and, I fancy, common.
Oscar Wilde (1889)

Friedrich Nietzsche – *(1844-1900)*
An agile but unintelligent and abnormal German, possessed of the mania of grandeur.
Leo Tolstoy (1902)

Thomas Paine – *(1737-1809)*
For such a mongrel between pig and puppy, begotten by a wild boar on a bitch wolf, never before in any age of the world was suffered by the poltrooney of mankind, to run through such a career of mischief. Call it then the Age of Paine.
John Adams (1805)

That dirty little atheist.
Theodore Roosevelt

Jean Jacques Rousseau – *(1712-78)*
He is surely the blackest and most atrocious villain in the world; and I am heartily ashamed of anything I ever wrote in his favour.
David Hume (1766)

He clothed passion in the garb of philosophy, and preached the sweeping away of injustice by the perpetuation of further injustices.
Thomas Huxley – 'On the Natural Inequality of Man'

Plato – *(427-347 BC)*
Plato is dear to me but dearer still is truth.
Aristotle

Take from him his sophisms, futilities and incomprehensibilities and what remains? His foggy mind.
Thomas Jefferson (1814)

Plato is a bore.
Friedrich Nietzsche

You have heard me quote from Plato
A thousand times no doubt;
Well, I have discovered that he did not know
What he was talking about.
Ella W. Wilcox

With all his brilliance and subtle insight, Plato, the architect of the eternal ideas, builds what is after all a magnificent palace of half-truths.
A. D. Winspear

Josiah Royce – *(1855-1916)*
His thinking was marred by profusion and sheer power, rather than by refinement, pointedness, or focal illumination. He carried big guns but they were too big to hit the centre of a small target.
Ralph Perry

There was a suggestion about him of the benevolent ogre or the old child, in whom a preternatural sharpness of insight lurked beneath a grotesque mask.
George Santayana

Bertrand Russell – *(1873-1970)*
The Ass in the Lion's Skin and the Wolf in Sheep's Clothing represent familiar human types, but we have no image for the traitor who pretends to be a Mugwump.
Anonymous War Office memo (1916)

He is a sophist; practises sophism; that by cunning contrivances, tricks and devices and by mere quibbling, he puts forth fallacious arguments and arguments that are not supported by sound reasoning; and he draws inferences which are not justly deduced from a sound premise; that all his alleged doctrines which he calls philosophy are just cheap, tawdry, worn out, patched up fetishes and propositions, devised for the purpose of misleading the people. *Joseph Goldstein (1940)*

The next time anyone asks you, 'What is Bertrand Russell's philosophy?', the correct answer is 'What year?' *Sidney Hook*

Poor Bertie Russell! He is all Disembodied mind. *D. H. Lawrence*

You are really the super-war-spirit. What you want is to jab and strike, like the soldier with the bayonet, only you are sublimated into words. And you are saying like a soldier who might jab man after man with his bayonet, saying, 'This is for peace.'

D. H. Lawrence (1915)

The enemy of all mankind, you are, full of the lust of enmity. It is not hatred of falsehood which inspires you. It is the hatred of people, of flesh and blood. It is perverted, mental bloodlust. Why don't you own it?

D. H. Lawrence (1915)

He only feels life through his brain, or through sex, and there is a gulf between these two separate departments. *Lady Ottoline Morrell*

George Santayana - *(1863-1962)*
He stood on the flat road to heaven and buttered slides to hell for all the rest.

Oliver W. Holmes (1913)

The perfection of rottenness. *William James*

Jean-Paul Sartre - *(1905-80)*
I much prefer Sartre's plays to his philosophy. Existentialism works much better in the theatre than in theory. *A. J. Ayer*

Socrates - *Athenian philosopher (470-399 BC)*
I hate this Socrates, this babbling beggar, who has meditated more than anybody else, but has never asked where he was going to get his dinner. *Eupolis*

The character of Socrates does not rise upon me. The more I read him, the less I wonder that they poisoned him. *Thomas B. Macaulay*

Socrates belonged to the lowest of the low; he was the mob. You can still see for yourself how ugly he was. *Friedrich Nietzsche - 'Twilight of the Idols' (1889)*

Herbert Spencer - *(1820-1903)*
The most unending ass in Christendom.

Thomas Carlyle

He was very thin skinned under criticism, and shrank from argument; it excited him overmuch, and was really bad for his health.

Sir Francis Galton

Oh! you know Spencer's idea of a tragedy is a deduction killed by a fact. *T. H. Huxley*

PSYCHIATRY

Anyone who has to see a psychiatrist needs to have his head examined. *Sam Goldwyn*

PSYCHIATRISTS

Thomas Szasz - *(b 1920)*
'*Schizophrenia*' - Szasz blasts society with all the explosive force of a popgun.

Richard Jacoby - 'The Nation' (1976)

PSYCHOLOGY

The science that tells you what you already know in words you don't understand. *Anon*

Of course behaviourism works. So does torture.

W. H. Auden

Psychology is as unnecessary as directions for using poison. *Karl Kraus*

PSYCHOLOGISTS

Dr Ruth Westheimer - *sex psychologist (b 1929)*
She has become the Julia Child of sex.

Gloria Steinem (1987)

SOCIOLOGY

The guilty science. *Hortense Calisher (1977)*

The science with the greatest number of methods and the least results. *J. H. Poincaré*

Sociologists are those academic accountants who think that truth can be shaken from an abacus. *Peter S. Prescott (1972)*

The study of people who do not need to be studied by people who do. *E. S. Turner*

These terrible sociologists, who are the astrologers and alchemists of our twentieth century. *Miguel de Unamuno (1925)*

SOCIOLOGISTS

Thorstein Veblen – *(1857–1929)*
Tunnel under his great moraines and
stalagmites of words, dig down into his vast
kitchen midden of discordant and raucous
polysyllables, blow up the hard, thick shell of
his almost theological manner and what you
will find in his discourse is chiefly a mass of
platitudes – the self-evident made horrifying,
the obvious in terms of the staggering.

H. L. Mencken (1919)

TECHNOLOGY

One cannot walk ʳhrough a mass-production
factory and not feel that one is in Hell.

W. H. Auden (1953)

Modern technology
Owes ecology
An apology.

Alan M. Eddison – 'Worse Verse' (1969)

Technological progress is like an axe in the
hands of a pathological criminal.

Albert Einstein

The marvels of modern technology include the
development of a soda can which, when
discarded, will last forever – and a $7,000 car
which, when properly cared for, will rust out in
two or three years.
Paul Harwitz – 'Wall Street Journal'

Technological society has succeeded in
multiplying the opportunities for pleasure, but
it has great difficulty in generating joy.

Pope Paul VI (1975)

Nothing you can't spell will ever work.

Will Rogers (1924)

Technology is a queer thing. It brings you great
gifts with one hand, and it stabs you in the back
with the other. *C. P. Snow*

POLITICS

One would risk being disgusted if one saw politics, justice, and one's dinner in the making.
Anon

Politics, as a practice, whatever its professions, had always been the systematic organisation of hatred.
Henry Adams – 'The Education of Henry Adams' (1906)

Practical politics consists in ignoring facts.
Henry Adams

Politics is the gentle art of getting votes from the poor and campaign funds from the rich, by promising to protect each other from the other.
Oscar Ameringer

I find politics the single most uninspiring, unemotional, insensitive activity on this planet.
Adam Ant

Politics, it seems to me, for years, or all too long,
Has been concerned with right or left instead of right or wrong.
Richard Armour

Bureaucracy is a giant mechanism operated by pigmies.
Honoré de Balzac

The worst thing in the world, next to anarchy, is government.
Henry Ward Beecher

Politics is the art of looking for trouble, finding it whether it exists or not, diagnosing it incorrectly, and applying the wrong remedy.
Sir Ernest Benn

Politics is a blood sport.
Aneurin Bevan

Politics is the conduct of public affairs for private advantage.
Ambrose Bierce

Politics is the art of the next best.
Otto von Bismarck

I always wanted to get into politics but I was never light enough to make the team.
Art Buchwald

Government is a contrivance of human wisdom to provide for human wants.
Edmund Burke

If you take yourself seriously in politics, you've had it.
Lord Carrington

The only good government is a bad one in a hell of a fright.
Joyce Cary – 'The Horse's Mouth' (1944)

It is the fate of the great in political life to be criticised, condemned and hated. It is the mediocre who are popular.
Carrie C. Catt

Politics are almost as exciting as war, and quite as dangerous. In war you can only be killed once, but in politics many times.
Sir Winston Churchill

Every political pull, in due time, is found to exert itself on the leg of the public.
'Columbia Record'

Political gas is not of the illuminating variety.
ibid

If our democracy is to flourish, it must have criticism; if our government is to function, it must have dissent.
Henry Commanger

A political convention is a chess tournament disguised as a circus.
Alistair Cooke

In politics there is no honour. *Benjamin Disraeli*

Politics makes strange bedfellows.
Charles Dudly
[*Wayne Haisey added* – Politics makes strange bedfellows rich.

While Kin Hubbard thought – Politics makes strange postmasters

Though Harwitz had the final word – The reason politicians make strange bedfellows is because they all use the same bunk!]

Politics is a deleterious profession, like some poisonous handicrafts. *Ralph Waldo Emerson*

Bureaucracy is just an officious circle.
Robert Fitch

If you take a close look at the government's economic predictions you have to wonder if the Weather Bureau hasn't taken over the forecasts.
Robert Fuoss

Politics is not the art of the possible. It consists in choosing between the disastrous and the unpalatable.
J. K. Galbraith – 'Ambassador's Journal' (1969)

Nothing is so admirable in politics as a short memory.
J. K. Galbraith – ibid

The political platform is just a preach of promise.
Arnold Glasgow

The cardinal rule of politics – never get caught in bed with a live man or a dead woman.
J. R. Ewing – 'Dallas'

What is politics but persuading the public to vote for this and support that and endure these for the promise of those.
Gilbert Highet

Politics is the science of how who gets what, when and why.
Sidney Hillman

Politics is nothing more than a means of rising in the world.
Samuel Johnson

Politics is a dog's life without a dog's decencies.
Rudyard Kipling

A political election is a circus wrestling match.
Nikita Kruschev

Elections are held to delude the populace into believing that they are participating in government.
Gerald Lieberman

Being in politics is like being a football coach. You have to be smart enough to understand the game and stupid enough to think it's important.
Eugene MacArthy

Politics is the art of looking for trouble, finding it everywhere, diagnosing it incorrectly and applying the wrong remedy.
Groucho Marx

Politics is a field where action is one long

second best and where the choice constantly lies between two blunders.
John Morley

Government is the only institution that can take a valuable commodity like paper, and make it worthless by applying ink.
Ludwig van Moses

Politics is the diversion of trivial men who, when they succeed at it, become important in the eyes of more trivial men.
George Jean Nathan

Politics is the skilled use of blunt objects.
Lestor Pearson

Politics, as the word is commonly understood, are nothing but corruptions.
Plato

A political party is the madness of many, for the gain of a few.
Alexander Pope

Government is the only known vessel that leaks from the top.
James Reston

All politics are based on the indifference of the majority.
James Reston

If you ever injected truth into politics you would have no politics.
Will Rogers

The more you read about politics, the more you got to admit that each party is worse than the other.
Will Rogers

I don't make jokes; I just watch the government and report the facts.
Will Rogers

Politics has got so expensive that it takes a lot of money even to get beat with.
Will Rogers

There is no more independence in politics than there is in jail.
Will Rogers

Government is the political representative of natural equilibrium, of custom, of inertia; it is by no means a representative of reason.
George Santayana

The art of government is the organisation of idolatry.
G. B. Shaw

Elections are a moral horror, as bad as a

battleground except for the blood; a mud bath for every soul concerned on it.   *G. B. Shaw*

When political ammunition runs low, inevitably the rusty artillery of abuse is always wheeled into action.   *Adlai Stevenson (1952)*

Politics is perhaps the only profession for which no preparation is thought necessary.
      Robert Louis Stevenson

Government is an association of men who do violence to the rest of us.   *Leo Tolstoy*

Politics is the art of preventing people from busying themselves with what is their own business.   *Paul Valery*

POLITICIANS

The first requirement of a statesman is that he be dull. This is not aways easy to achieve.
      Dean Acheson (1970)

A horrible voice, bad breath and a vulgar manner – the characteristics of a popular politician.   *Aristophanes*

Dangerous lunatics to be avoided when possible, and carefully humoured: people, above all, to whom we must never tell the truth.
      W. H. Auden

No diet will remove all the fat from your body because the brain is entirely fat. Without a brain you might look good, but all you could do is run for public office.   *Covert Bailey*

Just say the word 'politician' and I think of chicanery.   *Lucille Ball*

The politician is an acrobat. He keeps his balance by saying the opposite of what he does.
      Maurice Barres

Every politician is emphatically a promising politician.   *G. K. Chesterton*

The politicians owe their most valuable discovery to Phineas T. Barnum.
      'Columbia Record'

A politician is an arse upon which everyone has sat except a man.   *e. e. cummings*

A statesman is a man who plays both ends against the muddle.   *Raymond Cvikota*

Politics is developing more comedians than radio ever did.   *Jimmy Durante*

A mugwump is one of those boys who always has his mug on one side of the political fence and his wump on the other.
      Albert J. Engel (1936)

Self-criticism is a luxury all politicians should indulge in, but it is best done in private.
      Malcolm Fraser (1977)

When a politician changes his position it's sometimes hard to tell whether he has seen the light or felt the heat.   *Robert Fuoss*

I have come to the conclusion that politics are too serious a matter to be left to the politicians.
      Charles de Gaulle

Since a politician never believes what he says, he is surprised when others believe him.
      Charles de Gaulle

In politics as on the sickbed people toss from one side to the other thinking they will be more comfortable.   *Johann Goethe*

Politics means the art of compromise. Most politicians are all-too-well schooled in this art. They compromise to get nominated; they compromise to get elected; and they compromise time and time again, after they are elected, to stay in office.
      Dick Gregory – 'Why I Want to Be President'

The most distinctive characteristic of the successful politician is selective cowardice.
      Richard Harris – 'New Yorker' (1968)

You cannot adopt politics as a profession and remain honest.   *Louis Howe*

A statesman is a politician who is held upright by equal pressure from all directions.
      Erica A. Johnston

Mothers all want their sons to grow up to be President but they don't want them to become politicians in the process.   *John F. Kennedy*

Men play at being God, but lacking God's experience they wind up as politicians.
Harry W. King

Politicians are the same all over. They promise to build a bridge even when there's no river.
Nikita Kruschev (1960)

The more I see of the representatives of the people, the more I admire my dogs.
Alphonse de Lamartine

The candidate never wore diapers as a baby way back when;
It seems that no one could ever pin him down, even then.   *George O. Ludcke*

Politicians as a class radiate a powerful odour. Their business is almost as firmly grounded on false pretences as that of the quack doctor or the shyster lawyer.   *H. L. Mencken*

A good politician under democracy is quite as unthinkable as an honest burglar.
H. L. Mencken (1924)

A politician is an animal that can sit on the fence and keep both ears to the ground.
H. L. Mencken

I have spent much of my life fighting the Germans and fighting the politicians. It is much easier to fight the Germans.
Field Marshal Montgomery (1967)

The reason there are so few female politicians is that it is too much trouble to put makeup on two faces.   *Maureen Murphy*

Bad officials are elected by good citizens who do not vote.   *George Nathan*

It is no wonder politicians get hard-boiled. They're always in hot water.
'New Orleans Times'

A politician divides mankind into two classes: tools and enemies.   *Friedrich Nietzsche*

The statesman shears the sheep, the politician skins them.   *Austin O'Malley*

To be a chemist you must study chemistry; to be a lawyer or a physician you must study law or medicine; but to be a politician you need only study your own interests.   *Max O'Rell*

Public office is the last refuge of the incompetent.   *Boies Penrose*

Those who are too smart to engage in politics are punished by being governed by those who are dumber.   *Plato*

Politicians who complain about the media are like ships' captains who complain about the sea.
Enoch Powell

A statesman is a successful politician who is dead.   *Thomas Reed*
[Bob Edwards added to this – Now I know what a statesman is, he's a dead politician. We need more statesmen.]

The most successful politician is he who says what everybody else is thinking most often and in the loudest voice.   *Theodore Roosevelt*

A politician should have three hats. One for throwing in the ring, one for talking through, and one for pulling rabbits out of if elected.
Carl Sandburg

A bad politician is one that would circumvent God.   *William Shakespeare – 'Hamlet'*

A politician knows nothing. He thinks he knows everything – that clearly points to a political career.   *G. B. Shaw*

That insidious and crafty animal, vulgarly called a statesman or politician, whose councils are directed by momentary fluctuations or affairs.   *Adam Smith*

A politician is a statesman who approaches every question with an open mouth.
Adlai Stevenson

Every government is run by liars and nothing they say should be believed.   *I.F. Stone*

One of the principal qualifications for a political job is that the applicant know nothing much about what he is expected to do.
Terry Townsend

My choice early in life was either to be a piano-player in a whorehouse or a politician. And to tell the truth, there's hardly any difference.
Harry S. Truman

In statesmanship get the formalities right, never mind about the moralities. *Mark Twain*

Two members of the acting profession who are not needed by that profession, Mr Ronald Reagan and Mr George Murphy, entered politics, and they've done extremely well. Since there has been no reciprocal tendency in the other direction, it suggests to me that an actor's job is still more difficult than their new one.
Peter Ustinov

I am not a politician, and my other habits are good. *Artemus Ward*

The best time to listen to a politician is when he's on a stump on a street corner in the rain late at night when he's exhausted. Then he doesn't lie.
Theodore White – 'New York Times' (1969)

A liberal is a person who believes that water can be made to run uphill. A conservative is someone who believes everybody should pay for his water. I'm somewhere in between: I believe water should be free, but that water flows downhill. *Theodore White*

Politicians make good company for a while just as children do – their self-enjoyment is contagious. But they soon exhaust their favourite subjects – themselves. *Gary Wills*

On the rhinoceros – Here is an animal with a hide two feet thick, and no apparent interest in politics. What a waste.
James C. Wright – 'New York Times' (1986)

A statesman is an easy man,
  He tells his lies by rote;
A journalist makes up his lies
And takes you by the throat;
So stay at home and drink your beer

And let the neighbours vote.
William B. Yeats – 'The Old Stone Cross'

PARTY POLITICS

BOLSHEVISM

Bolshevism is merely Czarism in overalls.
George J. Nathan

COMMUNISM

A Communist is one who has nothing and wishes to share it with the world. *Anon*

The illegitimate child of Karl Marx and Catherine the Great. *Clement Attlee*

One big phone company. *Lenny Bruce*

All that communism needs to make it successful is somebody to feed and clothe it.
'Columbia Record'

A communist is a socialist without a sense of humour. *George Cutton*

The Communist is a Socialist in a violent hurry. *W. Gough*

Communism is the enemy of free men.
Robert H. Hinckley

Communism might be likened to a race in which all competitors come in first with no prizes. *Lord Inchcape*

Communism, like any other revealed religion, is largely made up of prophecies. *H. L. Mencken*

'Down with the betrayers of the workers!' says the hand-bill issued by the Communist party. A good example of self-condemnation.
'New York Star'

A communist is a person who publicly airs his dirty Lenin. *Jack Pomeroy*

A 'Red' is one who hasn't read enough.
'Richmond News Leader'

Communism is one-third practice and two-thirds explanation.
Will Rogers – 'Autobiography'

Communism, like prohibition, is a good idea but it won't work. *Will Rogers – ibid*

Communism is the corruption of a dream of justice. *Adlai Stevenson*

CONSERVATIVISM

A Conservative is a fellow who is standing athwart history yelling 'Stop!'.
William F. Buckley Jr

Conservatism offers no redress for the present, and makes no preparation for the future.
Benjamin Disraeli

Conservatism is the unhappy cross-breed, the mules of politics that engenders nothing.
Benjamin Disraeli

A conservative is a man who is too cowardly to fight and too fat to run. *Elbert Hubbard*

Some fellows get credit for being conservative when they are only stupid. *Kin Hubbard*

A Conservative is a man who will not look at the moon, out of respect for that ancient institution, the old one. *Douglas Jerrold*

Conservatism is the adherence to the old and tried, against the new and untried.
Abraham Lincoln (1860)

Conservatives are not necessarily stupid, but most stupid people are conservatives.
John Stuart Mill

A conservative is a liberal who got mugged the night before. *Frank Rizzo (1972)*

A conservative is a man with two perfectly good legs who, however, has never learned to walk forward. *Franklin D. Roosevelt*

Conservatism is the worship of dead revolutions. *Clinton Rossiter*

A conservative is someone who believes in reform. But not now. *Mort Sahl*

A conservative is a man who does not think

anything should be done for the first time.
Frank Vanderlip

Conservatism is the maintenance of conventions already in force.
Thorstein Veblen

A conservative is a man who thinks and sits, mostly sits. *Woodrow Wilson*

DEMOCRACY

Democracy is a government in the hands of man of low birth, no property and unskilled labour. *Aristotle*

Democracy means government by discussion but it is only effective if you can stop people talking. *Clement Attlee*

An aristocracy of blackguards. *Lord Byron*

Democracy means government by the uneducated, while aristocracy means government by the badly educated.
G. K. Chesterton

A festival of mediocrity. *E. M. Cioran*

Democracy consists of choosing your dictators, after they've told you what it is you want to hear. *Alan Coren (1975)*

The government of bullies, tempered by editors. *R. W. Emerson*

Two cheers for democracy; one because it admits variety and two because it permits criticism. Two cheers are quite enough; there is no occasion to give three. *E. M. Forster (1951)*

Our real disease – which is Democracy.
Alexander Hamilton

A democracy is no more than an aristocracy.
Thomas Hobbes

Democracy is a form of government by popular ignorance. *Elbert Hubbard*

One fifth of the people are against everything all the time. *Robert Kennedy*

The art of running the circus from the monkey cage. *H. L. Mencken*

Democracy is the theory that the common people know what they want, and deserve to get it good and hard. *H. L. Mencken*

The worship of jackals by jackasses. *H. L. Mencken*

Government under democracy is thus government by orgy, almost orgasm. *H. L. Mencken*

Democracy is hypocrisy without limitation. *Iskander Mirza – 'Time' (1958)*

Democracy is a kingless regime infested by many kings who are sometimes more exclusive, tyrannical, and destructive than one, if he is a tyrant. *Benito Mussolini*

Democracy is finding proximate solutions to insoluble problems. *Reinhold Niebuhr*

A process by which the people are free to choose the man who will get the blame. *Laurence J. Peter*

An institituion in which the whole is equal to the scum of the parts. *Keith Preston*

Democracy is a form of government you have to keep for four years no matter what it does. *Will Rogers*

Democracy substitutes selection by the incompetent many for the appointment by the corrupt few. *G. B. Shaw*

Democracy is a device which ensures we shall be governed no better than we deserve. *G. B. Shaw*

Democracy is the worst of all forms of government. *Robert Welch*

The recurrent suspicion that more than half of the people are right more than half of the time. *E. B. White*

The bludgeoning of the people, by the people, for the people. *Oscar Wilde*

FASCISM

Fascism is Capitalism in decay. *Nikolai Lenin*

Fascism is above all the unconscious awakening of our profound racial instinct. *Alfredo Rocco*

Fascism is Capitalism plus Murder. *Upton Sinclair*

LIBERALISM

A liberal is conservative who's been mugged by reality. *Anon*

A man with both feet firmly planted in the air. *American Proverb*

A man who tells others how to spend their money. *Imamu A. Baraka*

A conservative is enamoured of existing evils, as distinguished from a liberal – who wishes to replace them with others. *Ambrose Bierce*

If God had been a Liberal, we wouldn't have had the ten commandments – we'd have the ten suggestions. *Malcolm Bradbury*

A man who leaves the room when the fight begins. *Heywood C. Broun*

A person who understands everything but the people who don't understand him. *Lenny Bruce*

What the liberal really wants is to bring about change which will not in any way endanger his position. *Stokely Carmichael*

Though I believe in liberalism, I find it difficult to believe in liberals. *G. K. Chesterton*

A man who will give away everything he doesn't own. *Frank Dane*

The Liberals are the flying saucers of politics. No one can make head nor tail of them and they never are twice seen in the same place. *John G. Diefenbacker (1962)*

One who is too broadminded to take his own side in a quarrel. *Robert Frost*

The middle of the road is where the white line is - and that's the worst place to drive.
Robert Frost

A man who is willing to spend someone else's money.
Carter Glass

A power worshipper without the power.
George Orwell

A liberal is a person whose interests aren't at stake at the moment.
Willis Player

I can remember way back when a liberal was one who was generous with his own money.
Will Rogers

Liberalism is the first refuge of political indifference and the last refuge of Leftists.
Harry Roskolenko

SOCIALISM

The inherent virtue of Socialism is the equal sharing of miseries.
Winston Churchill

Socialism is Bolshevism with a shave.
Detroit Journal

Socialism is a boring way to speed up the mess.
Buckminster Fuller

I criticise, doctrinaire State Socialism because it is, in fact, little better than a dusty survival of a plan to meet the problems of fifty years ago, based on a misunderstanding of what someone said a hundred years ago.
J. M Keynes

The function of socialism is to raise suffering to a higher level.
Norman Mailer

As with the Christian religion, the worst advertisement for Socialism is its adherents.
George Orwell (1937)

Socialism is workable only in heaven where it isn't needed, and in hell where they've got it.
Cecil Palmer

All socialism involves slavery.   *Herbert Spencer*

No more and no less than a criticism of the idea

of property in the light of public good.
H. G. Wells

Any man who is not something of a socialist before he is forty has no heart. Any man who is still a socialist after he is forty has no head.
Wendell L. Willkie

TRADE UNIONS

Unions run by workers are like alcoholic homes run by alcoholics, a sure recipe for tyranny.
Roy Kerridge (1984)

Unionism seldom, if ever, uses such power as it has to insure better work; almost aways it devotes a large part of that power to safeguarding bad work.   *H. L. Mencken (1922)*

Unions are getting such a bad name, it's no wonder they're called Brother Hoods.
Robert Orben

MEMBERS OF PARLIAMENT

Anon
He had one arm round your waist and one eye on the clock.
Margot Asquith

Member of the House of Lords - His mouth is for export and his head has no entrance.
Douglas Feaver

The Right Honourable gentleman is indebted to his memory for his jests and to his imagination for his facts.   *Richard B. Sheridan*

Henry Addington - *Prime Minister (1757-1844)*
The indefinable air of a village apothecary inspecting the tongue of the State.
Lord Rosebery

Herbert Asquith - *Prime Minister (1852-1928)*
For twenty years he has held a season ticket on the line of least resistance, and gone wherever the train of events has carried him, lucidly justifying his position at whatever point he has happened to find himself.   *L. S. Amery (1916)*

His modesty amounts to deformity.
Margot Asquith

Black and wicked and with only a nodding
acquaintance with the truth.   *Lady Cunard*

Asquith's mind is a perfect instrument, and he
takes points after the manner of a trained
lawyer. But he lacks some element of character;
perhaps hardiness, I should say he was a soft
man; and his chin recedes when an attack is
possible or imminent.
                    Lord Esher – 'Diary' (1907)

A forensic gladiator who never made a heart
beat quicker by his words, and who never by
any possibility, brought a lump into his hearers'
throats.
          W. T. Stead – 'Review of Reviews' (1906)

In Asquith's case the inveterate lack of ideals
and imagination seems really unredeemed;
when one has peeled off the brown-paper
wrapping of phrases and compromises – just
nothing at all.   *Lytton Strachey*

Nancy Astor – *(1879–1964)*
Viscount Astor owned Britain's two most
influential newspapers, The Times and the
'Observer', but his American wife, Nancy, had
a much wider circulation than both papers put
together.   *Emery Klein*

Debating against her is like playing squash with
a dish of scrambled eggs.
                    Harold Nicolson (1943)

Nannie was a devout Christian Scientist, but
not a good one. She kept confusing herself with
God. She didn't know when to step aside and
give God a chance.   *Mrs Gordon Smith*

Clement Attlee – *Prime Minister (1883–1967)*
On his autobiography – 'As It Happened' – A good
title – things happened to him. He never did
anything.   *Aneurin Bevan*

He seems determined to make a trumpet sound
like a tin whistle. He brings to the fierce
struggle of politics the tepid enthusiasm of a
lazy summer afternoon at a cricket match.
                    Aneurin Bevan

He is a sheep in sheep's clothing.
                    Sir Winston Churchill (1945)

A modest little man with much to be modest
about.   *Sir Winston Churchill*

Charisma? He did not recognise the word,
except as a clue in his beloved 'Times'
crossword.   *James Margach –*
                    'The Abuse of Power' (1981)

As a public speaker, he is compared to Winston
Churchill, like a village fiddler after Paganini.
                    Harold Nicholson (1947)

He reminds me of nothing so much as a dead
fish before it has had time to stiffen.
                    George Orwell (1942)

Stanley Baldwin – *Prime Minister (1867–
1947)*
I think Baldwin has gone mad. He simply takes
one jump in the dark; looks around and then
takes another.   *Lord Birkenhead*

Decided only to be undecided, resolved to be
irresolute, adamant for drift, solid for fluidity,
all-powerful to be impotent.
                    Sir Winston Churchill (1936)

Baldwin occasionally stumbles over the truth,
but he always hastily picks himself up and
hurries on as if nothing had happened.
                    Sir Winston Churchill

An inexperienced nonentity of the utmost
insignifance.   *Lord Curzon*

One could not even dignify him with the name
of stuffed shirt. He was simply a hole in the air.
                    George Orwell (1941)

Baldwin always hits the nail on the head, but it
doesn't go in any further.   *G. M. Young*

Lord Beaverbrook – *(1879–1964)*
If you talk to him no good will come of it.
Beware of flattery.   *Clement Attlee (1945)*

He is so pleased to be in the Government that
he is like the town tart who has finally married
the Mayor.   *Beverley Baxter*

Tony Benn – *(b 1925)*
The Bertie Wooster of Marxism.   *Anon*

The Minister of Technology flung himself into the Sixties technology with the enthusiasm (not to say the language) of a newly enrolled Boy Scout demonstrating knot-tying to his indulgent parents.   *Bernard Levin* – *'The Pendulum Years' (1970)*

I have always said of Tony that he immatures with age . . . He was a very good Postmaster-General.   *Harold Wilson (1981)*

Jeremy Bentham – *(1748–1832)*
The arch-philistine Jeremy Bentham was the insipid, pedantic, leather-tongued oracle of the bourgeois intelligence of the Nineteenth Century.   *Karl Marx* – *'Das Kapital'*

Aneurin [Nye] Bevan – *(1897–1960)*
If thy Nye offend thee, pluck it out.
           Clement Attlee (1955)

He will be as great a curse to this country in peace as he was a nuisance in time of war.
           Sir Winston Churchill (1945)

Replying to a speech by Bevan – I should think it hardly possible to state the opposite of the truth with more precision.   *Sir Winston Churchill*

He enjoys prophesying the imminent fall of the capitalist system and is prepared to play a part, any part, in its burial – except that of a mute.
           Harold Macmillan

Ernest Bevin – *(1881–1951)*
Bevin thought he was Palmerston wearing Keir Hardie's cloth cap, whereas he was really the Foreign Office's Charlie McCarthy.
           Konni Zilliacus

Lord Birkenhead – *(1872–1930)*
He is very clever, but sometimes his brains go to his head.
           Margot Asquith – *'Autobiography' (1936)*

The trouble with Lord Birkenhead is that he is so un-Christlike.   *Margot Asquith*

This dark Hermes.
           Henry Channon – *'Diary' (1934)*

A man with the vision of an eagle but with a blind spot in his eye.   *Andrew Bonar Law*

Brendan Bracken – *(1901–58)*
You're phoney. Everything about you is phoney. Even your hair – which looks false – is real.   *Anon US Diplomat (1944)*

Lord Brougham – *(1778–1868)*
If he were a horse, no one would buy him; with that eye, no one could answer for his temper.
           Walter Bagehot

As author, lawyer, and politician, he is triformis, like Hecate; and in every one of his three forms he is bifrons, like Janus; the true Mr Facing-both-ways of Vanity Fair.
           Thomas L. Peacock

He might have been any one of the ten first-rate kinds of men, but he tried to be all ten, and has failed.   *'The Times'*

He was so marvellously ill-favoured as to possess some of the attractiveness of a gargoyle. He had neither dignity, nor what a Roman would call gravity.   *Esmé Wingfield-Stratford*

Edmund Burke – *(1729–97)*
The final event to himself has been, that as he rose like a rocket, he fell like the stick.
           Thomas Paine

John Burns – *(1858–1943)*
Mr John Burns is the only gaol-bird in the Ministry.
           W. T. Stead – *'Review of Reviews' (1906)*

James Callaghan – *Prime Minister (b 1912)*
Living proof that the short-term schemer and the frustrated bully can be made manifest in one man.   *Hugo Young* – *'Sunday Times' (1980)*

George Canning – *Prime Minister (1770–1827)*
Canning in office is like a fly in amber. Nobody cares about the fly; the only question is, 'How the devil did it get there?'   *Sydney Smith*

John Carteret – *(1690–1763)*
A careless, lolling, laughing love of self: a sort of Epicurean ease, roused to action by starts and bounds – such was his real character.
           Lord Mahon – *'History of England'*

Viscount Castlereagh – *(1739–1821)*
Thou intellectual eunuch Castlereagh.
Lord Byron – 'Don Juan'

Posterity will ne'er survey
A nobler grave than this:
Here lie the bones of Castlereagh;
Stop, traveller, and piss.
Lord Byron – 'Epitaph'

Why is a pump like Viscount Castlereagh? –
Because it is a slender thing of wood,
That up and down its awkward arm doth sway,
And coolly spout and spout and spout away,
In one weak, washy, everlasting flood.
Thomas Moore

Lord Hugh Cecil – *(1869–1956)*
I saw him riding in the Row, clinging to his
horse like a string of onions. *Margot Asquith*

**The Chamberlains
[Austin, Joseph and Neville]**
The Chamberlain family govern the country as
if they were following hounds – where
according to hunting conventions it is mean-
spirited to look before you leap.
Lord Salisbury (1904)

Austen Chamberlain – *(1863–1937)*
Sir Austen Chamberlain said, when he was
Foreign Secretary, that he loved France like a
mistress. Poor Sir Austen doesn't know
anything about mistresses.
Lord Beaverbrook (1931)

The mind and manners of a clothes-brush.
Harold Nicolson – 'Diary' (1936)

Joseph Chamberlain – *(1836–1914)*
The master of the feast has the manners of a
cad and the tongue of a bargee.
H. H. Asquith (1900)

Mr Chamberlain who looked and spoke like a
cheese-monger. *Benjamin Disraeli (1880)*

He was not born, bred or educated in the ways
which alone secure the necessary tact and
behaviour of a real gentleman.
Sir Edward Hamilton – 'Diary' (1899)

Dangerous as an enemy, untrustworthy as a

friend, but fatal as a colleague.
Sir Hercules Robinson

Neville Chamberlain – *Prime Minister
(1869–1940)*
He has the lucidity which is the by-product of a
fundamentally sterile mind. *Aneurin Bevan*

The worst thing I can say about democracy is
that it has tolerated the right hon. gentleman
for four and a half years. *Aneurin Bevan (1929)*

Listening to a speech by Chamberlain is like
paying a visit to Woolworths; everything in its
place and nothing above sixpence.
Aneurin Bevan – 'Tribune' (1937)

He is no better than a Mayor of Birmingham,
and in a lean year at that. Furthermore he is
too old. He thinks he understands the modern
world. What should an old hunk like him know
of the modern world? *Lord Hugh Cecil*

He looked at foreign affairs through the wrong
end of a municipal drainpipe.
Sir Winston Churchill

Lord Chesterfield [Philip Stanhope] –
(1694–1773)
On his letters to his son – They inculcate the
morals of a whore, and the manners of a
dancing master. *Samuel Johnson*

This man I thought had been a Lord among
wits; but I find, he is only a wit among Lords.
Samuel Johnson

A half-lazy man. *Sir Lewis Namier*

If justice and truth take place, if he is rewarded
according to his desert, his name will stink to
all generations. *John Wesley*

Sir Winston Churchill – *Prime Minister
(1874–1965)*
Fifty per cent genius, fifty per cent bloody fool.
Clement Attlee

Comparing him to a cake – One layer was
certainly 17th century. The 18th century in
him is obvious. There was the 19th century,
and a large slice, of course, of the 20th century:
and another, curious, layer, which may possibly

have been the 21st.   *Clement Attlee*

I thought he was a young man of promise, but it appears he was a young man of promises.
Arthur Balfour (1899)

'*World Crisis*' – Winston has written four volumes about himself and called it 'World Crisis'.   *Arthur Balfour (1899)*

Churchill? He's a busted flush.
Lord Beaverbrook (1932)

He has the habit of breaking the rungs of any ladder he puts his foot on.
Lord Beaverbrook (1932)

Churchill on top of the wave has in him the stuff of which tyrants are made.
Lord Beaverbrook

The mediocrity of his thinking is concealed by the majesty of his language.   *Aneurin Bevan*

A man suffering from petrified adolescence.
Aneurin Bevan

He never spares himself in conversation. He gives himself so generously that hardly anybody else is permitted to give anything in his presence.   *Aneurin Bevan*

He mistakes verbal felicities for mental inspiration.   *Aneurin Bevan*

His ear is so sensitively attuned to the bugle note of history that he is often deaf to the more raucous clamour of contemporary life.
Aneurin Bevan

He refers to a defeat as a disaster as though it came from God, but to a victory as though it came from himself.   *Aneurin Bevan*

Replying to Churchill's speech – I welcome the opportunity of pricking the bloated bladder of lies with the poniard of truth.   *Aneurin Bevan*

Winston has devoted the best years of his life to preparing his impromptu speeches. *F. E. Smith*

WANTED! Dead or alive! Winston Churchill. 25 years old. 5 feet 8 inches tall. Indifferent build. Walks with a bend forward. Pale complexion. Red-brownish hair. Small toothbrush moustache. Talks through his nose and cannot pronounce the letter 'S' properly.
Jan Smuts

On his book 'Life of Marlborough' – As history it is beneath contempt, the special pleading of a defence lawyer. As literature it is worthless. It is written in a sham Augustan prose which could only have been achieved by a man who thought always in terms of public speech, and the antitheses clang like hammers in an arsenal.
Evelyn Waugh

He is not a man for whom I ever had esteem. Always in the wrong, always surrounded by crooks, a most unsuccessful father – simply a 'Radio Personality' who outlived his prime.
Evelyn Waugh (1965)

Winston is always expecting rabbits to come out of empty hats.   *Lord Wavell*

Sir Alfred 'Duff' Cooper – *(1890–1954)*
On his death aboard ship on a cruise – Mr Duff Cooper has died where he always was – at sea.
Anon Irish journalist

Sir Stafford Cripps – *(1899–1952)*
He has a brilliant mind, until he makes it up.
Margot Asquith – 'Autobiography' (1936)

There, but for the grace of God, goes God.
Sir Winston Churchill

He has built a high stone wall around his mind, as though it was an intellectual nudist colony.
'Tribune'

John Croker – *(1780–1857)*
He was, in short, a man who possessed, in very remarkable degree, a restless instinct for adroit baseness.   *Benjamin Disraeli*

That impudent leering Croker . . . I detest him more than cold boiled veal.
Thomas Macaulay (1831)

Oliver Cromwell – *Lord Protector (1599–1658)*
He lived a hypocrite and died a traitor.
John Foster

Cromwell. To the eternal condemnation of Oliver. Seditionist, traitor, regicide, racialist, protofascist and blasphemous bigot. God save England from his like. *'The Times'*

The English Monster, The Center of Mischief, a shame to the British Chronicle, a pattern for Tyranny, Murther and Hypocrisie, whose bloody Caligula, Domatian, having at last attained the height of his Ambition, for Five years space, he wallowed in the blood of many Gallant and Heroick Persons.

Gerard Winstanley

Richard Crossman - *(1907-74)*
He is a man of many opinions, most of them of short duration.

Bessie Braddock - 'The Braddocks'

A charming companion and a virtuous conversationalist and not a selfish one. He was a wonderful hand at conducting a general conversation and could bring out the best in shy and the alien. But he had his handicaps. The chief of these was his failure to tell the truth. He also had no sense of humour.

Dame Rebecca West (1977)

Earl of Danby [Thomas Osborne] -
(1631-1712)
His short neck, his legs uneven, the vulgar said, as those of a badger, his forehead low as that of a baboon, his purple cheeks, and his monstrous length of chin. *Thomas Macaulay*

Earl of Derby [Edward Stanley] -
(1865-1948)
D. is a very weak-minded fellow, I am afraid, and, like the feather pillow, bears the marks of the last person who sat on him! I hear he is called in London 'genial Judas'!

Douglas Haig - 'Diary' (1914)

Bernadette Devlin - *(b 1947)*
Bernadette Devlin is Fidel Castro in a miniskirt. *Stratton Mills (1969)*

Benjamin Disraeli - *Prime Minister (1804-81)*
The Great Panjandrum.
Alfred Munby - 'Diary' (1874)

He is a self-made man and worships his creator.
John Bright

His life is a living lie. He is the most degraded of his species and kind; and England is degraded in tolerating or having upon the face of her society a miscreant of his abominable, foul, and atrocious nature. If there be harsher terms in the British language I should use them, because it is the harshest of all terms that would be descriptive of a wretch of his species.
Daniel O'Connell

Anthony Eden - *Prime Minister (1897-1977)*
He had antennae in all directions, but no brains. *Gladwin Jebb*

He is forever poised between a cliché and an indiscretion. *Harold Macmillan*

He was not only a bore; he bored for England.
Malcolm Muggeridge - 'Tread Softly for You May Tread on My Jokes' (1966)

He is an overripe banana – yellow outside, squishy in. *Reginald Paget (1956)*

Eden did not face the dictators, he pulled faces at them. *A. J. P. Taylor*

Sir Walter Eliot
He is a man walking backwards with his face to the future. *Aneurin Bevan*

Michael Foot - *(b 1913)*
A leg end in his own lifetime. *Graffiti*

A good man fallen among politicians.
'Daily Mirror' (1983)

Hugh Gaitskell - *(1906-63)*
I know that the right kind of political leader of the Labour Party is a desiccated calculating machine. *Aneurin Bevan (1954)*

Gaitskell has a Wykehamistical voice and manner and a 13th-century face.
Henry Channon - 'Diary' (1951)

William Gladstone - *Prime Minister (1809-98)*
On his budget speeches – He talked shop like a tenth muse. *Anon*

Gladstone appears to me one of the contemptiblest men I ever looked on. A poor ritualist; almost spectral king of phantasm of a man – nothing in him but forms and ceremonies and outside wrappages; incapable of seeing veritably any fact whatever, but seeing, crediting, and laying to heart the mere clothes of the fact and fancying that all the rest does not exist. Let him fight his own battle, in the name of Beelzebub the god of Ekron, who seems to be his God. Poor phantasm.

Thomas Carlyle

An old man in a hurry.

Randolph Churchill (1886)

He was generally thought to be very pusillanimous in dealing with foreign affairs. That is not at all the impression I derived. He was wholly ignorant. *Lord Cromer (1913)*

A sophistical rhetorician, inebriated with the exuberance of his own verbosity, and gifted with an egotistical imagination that can at all times command an interminable and inconsistent series of arguments to malign an opponent and glorify himself.

Benjamin Disraeli (1878)

Posterity will do justice to that unprincipled maniac Gladstone – extraordinary mixture of envy, vindictiveness, hypocrisy, and superstition; and with one commanding characteristic – whether preaching, praying, speechifying or scribbling – never a gentleman!

Benjamin Disraeli (1878)

He has not a single redeeming defect.

Benjamin Disraeli

A misfortune is if Gladstone fell into the Thames; a calamity would be if someone pulled him out. *Benjamin Disraeli*

Honest in the most odious sense of the word.

Benjamin Disraeli

If you weren't such a great man you'd be a terrible bore. *Mrs Gladstone*

I don't object to the Old Man's always having the ace of trumps up his sleeve, but merely to his belief that God Almighty put it there.

Henry du Pre Labouchere

George Grenville – *Prime Minister (1712–70)*
A fatiguing orator and indefatigable drudge; more likely to disgust than offend. As all his passions were expressed by one livid smile, he never blushed at the variations in his behaviour; scarce any man ever wore in his face such outward and visible marks of the hollow, cruel and rotten heart within.

Horace Walpole – 'Memoirs'

Viscount Grey of Fallodon – *(1862–1933)*
He was absolutely worthless. He was pure funk. He was a mean man. *David Lloyd George (1933)*

Alexander Hamilton – *(1757–1804)*
A bastard brat of a Scottish peddlar.

John Adams

Edward Heath – *Prime Minister (b 1916)*
In any civilised country Heath would have been left hanging upside-down on a petrol pump years ago.

Auberon Waugh – 'Private Eye' (1974)

'Travels' – A reminder that Morning Cloud's skipper is no stranger to platitude and longitude.

Christopher Wordsworth – 'The Observer'

Sir Samuel Hoare-Belisha – *(1880–1959)*
To Prince George, Duke of Kent – And does my George know this whore, Belisha?

Princess Marina of Greece

Alec Douglas-Home – *(b 1903)*
I have seen better-looking faces on pirate flags.

Anon

The only real and distinctive achievement of the fourteenth Earl was to have been born the heir of the thirteenth. *'Sunday Express' (1960)*

Florence Horsbrugh – *(1889–1969)*
As Minister for Education – A face which has sunk a thousand scholarships.

Aneurin Bevan (1953)

Geoffrey Howe – *(b 1926)*
Being attacked in the House by him is like being savaged by a dead sheep.

Denis Healey (1978)

Henry Hunt – *(1773–1835)*
The incarnation of an empty, blustering,

restless, ignorant, and selfish demagogue.
Harriet Martineau

Andrew Bonar Law *-Prime Minister*
(1858-1923)
Has not the brains of a Glasgow baillie.
Herbert Asquith (1916)

It is fitting that we should have buried the
Unknown Prime Minister by the side of the
Unknown Soldier. *Herbert Asquith (1923)*

Bonar would never make up his mind on
anything. Once a question had been decided,
Bonar would stick to it and fight for it to a
finish, but he would never help in the taking of
a decision. *David Lloyd-George*

Earl of Liverpool [Robert Jenkinson] –
Prime Minister (1770-1828)
The Arch-Mediocrity.
Benjamin Disraeli – 'Coningsby'

David Lloyd George – *Prime Minister*
(1863-1945)
He could not see a belt without hitting below it.
Margot Asquith – 'Autobiography' (1936)

He spent his whole life in plastering together
the true and the false and therefrom extracting
the plausible. *Stanley Baldwin*

He didn't care in which direction the car was
travelling, so long as he remained in the
driver's seat.
Lord Beaverbrook – 'New Statesman' (1983)

The Happy Wanderer of Squandermania.
Sir Winston Churchill

Trying to argue with Lloyd George is like
trying to go for a walk with a grasshopper.
Eamonn de Valera

Lloyd George is rooted in nothing; he is void
and without content. *John M. Keynes – 'Essays'*

This goat-footed bard, this half-human visitor
to our age from the bag-ridden magic and
enchanted woods of Celtic antiquity.
John M. Keynes – ibid.

Ramsay MacDonald – *Prime Minister*
(1866-1937)
The Boneless Wonder sitting on the Treasury
bench. *Sir Winston Churchill (1931)*

We know that he has, more than any other
man, the gift of compressing the largest amount
of words into the smallest amount of thought.
Sir Winston Churchill (1933)

He has sufficient conscience to bother him, but
not sufficient to keep him straight.
David Lloyd George

Harold Macmillan – *Prime Minister*
(1894-1986)
The Prime Minister has an absolute genius for
putting flamboyant labels on empty luggage.
Aneurin Bevan

It was almost impossible to believe that he was
anything but a down-at-heel actor resting
between engagements at the decrepit theatres of
minor provincial towns. *Bernard Levin –*
'The Pendulum Years' (1976)

The Right Honourable Gentleman has
inherited the streak of charlatanry in Disraeli
without his vision and the self-righteousness of
Gladstone without his dedication to principle.
Harold Wilson

Colin Moynihan – *Minister for Sport (b 1955)*
The Miniature for Sport. *'Spitting Image'*

Frederick North – *Prime Minister (1732-92)*
Lord North was a coarse and heavy man, with a
wide mouth, thick lips, and puffy cheeks, which
seemed typical of his policy. *J. H. Rose*

Henry Palmerston – *Prime Minister*
(1784-1865)
If the Devil has a son
It is surely Palmerston. *Anon*

Your Lordship is like a favourite footman on
easy terms with his mistress. Your dexterity
seems a happy compound of the smartness of
an attorney's clerk and the intrigue of a Greek
lower empire. *Benjamin Disraeli*

Sir Robert Peel - *Prime Minister (1788–1850)*
The Right Honourable Gentleman is
reminiscent of a poker. The only difference is
that a poker gives off occasional signs of
warmth.   *Benjamin Disraeli*

His life has been one great appropriation
clause. A burglar of others' intellect – there is
no statesman who has committed political
larceny on so grand a scale.   *Benjamin Disraeli*

His smile is like the silver plate on a coffin.
Daniel O'Connell – Quoting
J. P. Curran – 'Hansard' (1835)

I have no small talk and Peel has no manners.
Duke of Wellington

Spencer Perceval - *Prime Minister*
(1762–1812)
It is a great misfortune to Mr Perceval to write
in a style that would disgrace a washerwoman.
King George IV (1812)

Mr Perceval is a very little man.
Lord Sidmouth (1809)

William Pitt the Younger - *Prime Minister*
(1759–1806)
He was not merely a chip off the old block, but
the old block itself.   *Edmund Burke*

The great snorting bawler.
William Cobbett – 'Rural Rides'

Pitt deem'd himself an Eagle – what a flat!
What was he? A poor wheeling, fluttering Bat –
An Imp of Darkness – busy catching flies!
Here, there, up, down, off, on – shriek, shriek –
snap, snap –
His gaping mouth a very lucky trap,
Quick seizing for his hungry maw – Supplies.
John Wolcot – 'Odes to the Ins and Outs'

John Profumo *(b 1915)*
On the 'Profumo Scandal' –
'What have you done?' cried Christine,
'You've wrecked the whole party machine!
'To lie in the nude
'May be rude,
'But to lie in the House is obscene.' *Anon (1963)*

Sir John Reith - *(1889–1971)*
Dante without the poetry;
Irving without the mystery;
Mephistopheles without the fun.
Alan Dent (1939)

Marquis of Rockingham - *Prime Minister*
(1730–82)
He could neither speak nor write with ease, and
was handicapped by inexperience, boils, and a
passion for Newmarket.   *O. A. Sherard*

Lord Roseberry - *Prime Minister (1847–1929)*
He is a one-eyed man in blinkers.
David Lloyd George

A dark horse in a loose box.   *John Morley*

A man who never missed an occasion to let slip
an opportunity.   *G. B. Shaw*

Gladstone's successor is a poor creature . . .
when he tries to roar like a lion, he only brays
like an ass.   *Sir Garnett Wolseley*

Lord John Russell - *Prime Minister (1792–1878)*
The foreign policy of the Noble Earl . . . may
be summed up in two truly expressive words,
'meddle' and 'muddle'.   *Lord Derby (1864)*

If a traveller were informed that such a man
was the Leader of the House of Commons, he
might begin to comprehend how the Egyptians
worshipped an insect.   *Benjamin Disraeli*

He was impulsive, very selfish, vain, and often
reckless and impulsive.
Queen Victoria – 'Diary' (1878)

Lord Salisbury - *(1563–1612)*
Here lieth Robin Crookback; unjustly reckoned
A Richard the Third, he was Judas the Second.
Anon epitaph

Lord Salisbury - *Prime Minister (1830–1903)*
His face is livid, gaunt his white body, his
breath green with gall, his tongue drips poison.
John Quincey Adams

That strange, powerful, inscrutable and
brilliant obstructive deadweight at the top.
Lord George Curzon

I am always very glad when Lord Salisbury makes a great speech. It is sure to contain at least one blazing indiscretion which it is a delight to remember.   *A. E. Parker (1887)*

Herbert Samuel – *(1870–1963)*
When they circumcised Herbert Samuel, they threw away the wrong bit.
David Lloyd George (1930)

Lord Shaftesbury – *(1621–83)*
A little, limping peer – though crazy yet in action nimble and as busy as a body-louse.
Anon – 'Letter to Bishop of Meath' (1680)

The King and Duke of York used to call him 'Little Sincerity', while with others at court, he went under the title of 'Lord Shiftesbury'.
Augustus Jessop

Sir John Simon – *(1873–1954)*
The Right Honourable and Learned Gentleman has twice crossed the floor of this House, each time leaving behind a trail of slime.
David Lloyd George – 'Speech: House of Commons' (1931)

The Right Honourable Gentleman has sat so long on the fence that the iron has entered his soul.   *David Lloyd George – 'Speech: House of Commons' (1931)*

Norman St John Stevas – *(b 1929)*
A Catholic layman who has never been averse to giving advice to the Pope, or indeed anybody else who he thought might be in need of it.
Bernard Levin

Norman Tebbitt – *(b 1931)*
A semi-house-trained polecat.
Michael Foot – 'Speech: House of Commons'

Margaret Thatcher – *Prime Minister (b 1925)*
Margaret Thatcher is David Owen in drag.
Anon

She is trying to wear the trousers of Winston Churchill.   *Leonid Brezhnev (1979)*

She cannot see an institution without hitting it with her handbag.
Julian Critchley – 'The Times' (1982)

She is a cross between Isadora Duncan and Lawrence of Arabia.   *'Daily Telegraph' (1986)*

The improbable PM; she seems totally humourless, with the nervous system usually attributed to fishes. Surely she has never read a book or looked at a picture? *Ann Fleming (1985)*

Attila the Hen.
Clement Freud – 'BBC Radio 4' (1979)

She approaches the problem of our country with all the one-dimensional subtlety of a comic strip.   *Denis Healey (1979)*

For the past few months she has been charging about like a bargain basement Boadicea.
Denis Healey (1982)

La Pasionara of middle-age privilege.
Denis Healey (1986)

The nanny seemed to be extinct until 1975, when, like the coelacanth, she suddenly and unexpectedly reappeared in the shape of Margaret Thatcher.
Simon Hoggart – 'Vanity Fair' (1983)

She is the Enid Blyton of economics. Nothing must be allowed to spoil her simple plots.
Richard Holme (1980)

She sounded like the book of Revelations read out over a railway station public address system by a headmistress of a certain age wearing calico knickers. *Clive James – 'Observer' (1979)*

On attending a conference in Venice – She only went to Venice because someone told her should could walk down the middle of the street.   *Neil Kinnock (1987)*

She's one of the most splendid headmistresses there has ever been.   *Arthur Marshall (1982)*

She is democratic enough to talk down to anyone.   *Austin Mitchell*

I'm thoroughly in favour of Mrs Thatcher's visit to the Falklands. I find a bit of hesitation, though, about her coming back.
John Mortimer – 'Any Questions?' (BBC Radio)

She's a handbag economist who believes that
you pay as you go.   *'New Yorker' (1986)*

If I were married to her, I'd be sure to have
dinner ready when she got home. *George Schulz*

Plunder Woman.   *Harry Unwin (1980)*

I cannot bring myself to vote for a woman who
has been voice-trained to speak to me as though
my dog has just died.   *Keith Waterhouse*

Sir Robert Walpole – Prime Minister
(1676–1745)
Achieving of nothing – still promising
     wonders –
By dint of experience improving in blunders,
Oppressing true merit, exalting the base,
And selling his country to purchase his place.
A jobber of stocks by retailing false news –
A prater at court in the style of the stews:
Of virtue and worth by profession a giber,
Of injuries and senates the bully and briber.
Though I name not the wretch, yet you know
     whom I mean –
'Tis the cur-dog of Britain, and spaniel of
     Spain.   *Jonathan Swift*

Shirley Williams – *(b 1930)*
She achieved that kitchen-sink-revolutionary
look that one cannot get unless one has been to
a good school.   *Dame Rebecca West (1976)*

Harold Wilson – *Prime Minister (b 1916)*
All facts and no bloody ideas.   *Aneurin Bevan*

Talk about a credibility gap, Harold Wilson is
undoubtedly the world's most unbelievable
politician. Indeed, one could have made a
handsome living over the past three years
betting on the opposite of everything Harold
Wilson has averred, whether on Rhodesia, the
common market, economic controls, or – most
recently – the value of the pound.
          William F. Buckley Jr – 'On the Right' (1967)

Referring to his austere childhood – If Harold
Wilson ever went to school without any boots it
was merely because he was too big for them.
          Ivor Bulwer-Thomas (1949)

The Rt Hon Gentleman always keeps his ear so
close to the ground that I suppose he is bound
to get it full of dirt.   *Sir Jocelyn Simon*

MILITARY

It is the blood of the soldier that makes the general great. *Anon*

Make love not war. *Pacifist slogan*

War is the science of destruction. *John Abbott*

Ah! the generals! they are numerous but not good for much! *Aristophanes*

From the happy expresson on their faces, you might have supposed they welcomed the War. I had met people who loved stamps, and men who loved stones and snakes – but I could not imagine any man loving war. *Margot Asquith*

I have never understood this liking for war. It panders to instincts already catered for within the scope of any respectable domestic establishment.
Alan Bennett – 'Forty Years On' (1968)

Soldiers can win battles and generals get the medals. *Napoleon Bonaparte*

There are no bad regiments, only bad colonels.
Napoleon Bonaparte

I am convinced that the best service a retired general can perform is to turn in his tongue along with his suit and to mothball his opinions. *General Omar N. Bradley (1959)*

War is a brain-spattering, windpipe-slitting art.
Lord Byron – 'Don Juan'

The feat of vultures, and the waste of life.
Lord Byron – 'Lara'

There are no warlike peoples – just warlike leaders. *Ralph Bunche*

To jaw-jaw is better than war-war.
Sir Winston Churchill (1954)

The services in wartime are only fit for desperadoes, but in peace are fit only for fools.
Benjamin Disraeli – 'Vivian Grey'

A chest full of medals is nothing more than a résumé in 3-D and Technicolor.
Owen Edwards (1985)

There is nothing that war has ever achieved that we could not have better achieved without it. *Havelock Ellis*

It takes 15 000 casualties to train a major-general. *Ferdinand Foch*

There never was a good war or a bad peace.
Benjamin Franklin

A soldier is a man whose business it is to kill those who never offended him, and who are the innocent martyrs of other men's iniquities. Whatever may become of the abstract question of the justifiableness of war, it seems impossible that the soldier should not be a depraved and unnatural thing. *William Godwin*

The trouble with military rule is that every colonel or general is soon full of ambition. The navy takes over today and the army tomorrow.
Yakubu Gowon (1970)

War knocks the 'l' out of glory.
'Greenville Piedmont'

What the world needs is more mistletoe and less missile talk. *Anna Herbert*

War is death's feast. *George Herbert*

Older men declare war. But it is the youth that must fight and die. *Herbert Hoover (1944)*

Militarism is a fever for conquest, with peace as a shield, using music and brass buttons to dazzle and divert the populace. *Elbert Hubbard*

What is absurd and monstrous about war is that men who have no personal quarrel should be trained to murder one another in cold blood.
Aldous Huxley

Better to live in peace than to begin war and lie

dead. *Chief Joseph*

The first advice I am going to give my successor is to watch the generals and to avoid feeling that just because they were military men their opinions on military matters were worth a damn. *John F. Kennedy*

An excellent figurehead for battleships would be a formal design of a weeping taxpayer. *'Kingston Whig'*

Military glory is the attractive rainbow that rises in showers of blood. *Abraham Lincoln*

Military intelligence is a contradiction in terms. *Groucho Marx*

Military justice is to justice what military music is to music. *Groucho Marx*

Military men are the scourges of the world. *Guy de Maupassant*

War will never cease until babies begin to come into the world with larger cerebrums and smaller adrenals. *H. L. Mencken*

What would our government think of a citizen who spent ninety-three per cent of his income on ammunition? *George J. Nathan*

When there are no war profits, there will be fewer prophets of war. *'Nelson News'*

Very little is known about the War of 1812 because the Americans lost it. *Eric Nicol*

No one hates war more than who has seen a lot of it. *Richard Nixon (1959)*

If war is hell, earth is no place for it. *'Norfolk Virginian-Post'*

History is littered with wars which everybody knew would never happen. *Enoch Powell*

The world must finally understand that we cannot settle disputes by eliminating human beings. *Jeanette Rankin*

You can no more win a war than you can win an earthquake. *Jeanette Rankin*

You can't say civilisation don't advance – for every war they kill you a new way. *Will Rogers*

War is not an adventure. It is a disease. *Antoine de Saint-Exupery*

Sometime they'll give a war and nobody will come. *Carl Sandburg – 'The People, Yes' (1936)*

Oh, war! war! the dream of patriots and heroes! A fraud. A hollow sham, like love. *G. B. Shaw (1894)*

A soldier is an anachronism of which we must get rid. *G. B. Shaw*

I never expected a soldier to think. *G. B. Shaw*

Soldiering is the coward's art of attacking mercilessly when you are strong, and keeping out of harm's way when you are weak. *G. B. Shaw – 'Arms and the Man'*

When the military man approaches, the world locks up its spoons and packs it off womankind. *G. B. Shaw – 'Man and Superman' (1903)*

I bomb, therefore I am. *Philip Slater*

War is much too serious to be left to military men. *Charles M. Talleyrand*

The chief attraction of military service has consisted and will consist in this compulsory and irreproachable idleness. *Leo Tolstoy – 'War and Peace'*

War is the unfolding of miscalculations. *Barbara Tuchman*

A general who is stupid and courageous is a calamity. *Tu Mu*

War is a wasteful, boring, and muddled affair. *A. P. Wavell*

There is nothing on earth as stupid as a gallant officer. *Duke of Wellington*

We want to get rid of the militarist not simply because he hurts and kills, but because he is an intolerable thick-voiced blockhead who stands hectoring and blustering in our way to achievement. *H. G. Wells (1920)*

Before a war military science seems like a real science, like astronomy. But after a war it seems more like astrology. *Rebecca West*

MILITARY LEADERS

Anon
US General – He is an imitation rough diamond.
Margot Asquith

General Gebhardt von Blücher – *(1742-1819)*
That drunken hussar. *Napoleon Bonaparte*

Colonel Jim Bowie – *(1796-1838)*
On the fall of the Alamo – Colonel William Travis died like a hero, gun in hand, stretched across the carriage of a cannon, but the boastful Bowie died like a woman, almost concealed beneath a mattress.
Edward C. Sears – 'The Lowdown on Jim Bowie'

General Benjamin Butler – *(1818-93)*
After outraging the sensibilities of civilised humanity he returns, reeking crime, to his own people, and they receive him with joy – the beastliest, bloodiest poltroon and pickpocket the world has ever seen. *Anon*

A man whom all the waters of Massachusetts Bay cannot wash back into decency.
'New York World' (1863)

Karl von Clausewitz – *(1780-1831)*
The Mahdi of mass and mutual massacre.
Sir B. Liddell Hart

General Robert Clive [of India] – *(1725-74)*
A savage old Nabob, with an immense fortune, a tawny complexion, a bad liver, and a worse heart. *Thomas Macaulay – 'Essays'*

General George Custer – *(1836-76)*
He has gone down in history as the man who blew the Little Big Horn. *Anon*

Lord Fisher of Kilverstone –
Admiral of the Fleet (1841-1920)
He was a mixture of Machiavelli and a child.
Esther Meynell – 'A Woman Talking'

Ferdinand Foch – *Allied Commander-in-Chief (1851-1929)*
Only a frantic pair of moustaches.
T. E. Lawrence (1932)

General Ulysses S. Grant – *(1822-85)*
He is a scientific Goth, resembling Alaric, destroying the country as he goes and delivering the people over to starvation. Nor does he bury his dead, but leaves them to rot on the battlefield. *John Tyler (1964)*

Alexander Haig – *US Secretary of State (b 1924)*
One thing I don't want around me is an intellectual military. I don't have to worry about you on that score. *Henry Kissinger*

Earl [Douglas] Haig – *Commander-in-Chief (1861-1928)*
What a rascal Haig was. One of the biggest rascals of our time. His is a disgraceful story.
Lord Beaverbrook

Haig had a first-rate General Staff, mind.
Lord Haldane

Haig was devoid of the gift of intelligible and coherent expression.
David Lloyd George – 'War Memoirs'

Major-General Henry Wager Halleck – *(1815-72)*
Originates nothing, anticipates nothing, takes no responsibility, plans nothing, suggests nothing, is good for nothing.
Gideon Welles – 'Diary' (1862)

Saddam Hussein – *Iraqi Commander-in-Chief (b 1937)*
Saddam Insane is the SCUD of the Earth!
Colin M. Jarman (1991)

As far as Saddam Hussein being a great military strategist, he is neither a strategist, nor is he schooled in operational arts. He's not a tactician. He's not a general. He's not a soldier. Other than that, he's a great military man.
General H. Norman Schwarzkopf (1991)

Admiral John Jellicoe – *(1859-1935)*
A sailor with a flawed cutlass. *Correlli Barnett*

Jellicoe was the only man on either side who could lose the war in an afternoon.
Sir Winston Churchill – 'The World Crisis'

John Jervis [Lord St Vincent] – *(1735-1823)*
Where I would take a penknife Lord St Vincent takes a hatchet. *Lord Nelson*

Marshal Jean-Jacques Joffre – *(1825-1931)*
The only time he ever put up a fight in his life was when we asked him for his resignation.
Georges Clemenceau

Captain Barney Kelly
After he allowed the 'USS Enterprise' to run aground in San Francisco Bay – He grounds the warship he walks on. *John Bracken (1983)*

General Douglas MacArthur – *(1880-1964)*
I studied dramatics under him for 12 years.
Dwight D. Eisenhower

MacArthur is the type of man who thinks that when he gets to heaven, God will step down from the great white throne and bow him into His vacated seat. *Harold Ickes – 'Diary' (1933)*

He was a great thundering paradox of a man.
William Manchester

I fired him because he wouldn't respect the authority of the President. I didn't fire him because he was a dumb son-of-a-bitch, although he was, but that's not against the law for generals. If it was, half to three-quarters of them would be in jail. *Harry S. Truman*

General George B. McClellan – *(1826-85)*
He is an admirable Engineer, but he seems to have a special talent for the stationary engine.
Abraham Lincoln

My dear McClellan,
   If you don't want to use the army, I should like to borrow it for a while.
   Yours respectfully, *Abraham Lincoln*

Field-Marshal B. L. Montgomery –
(1887-1976)
In defeat he was unbeatable; in victory, unbearable. *Edward Marsh*

General George S. Patton Jr – *(1885-1945)*
Patton was an acolyte to Mars.
Col. J. Farley (1964)

Earl of Peterborough – *(1658-1735)*
His career was a series of unconnected actions. His motives were mere impulses. He sailed with all canvas spread, but without a rudder; he admitted of no rule of duty, and his sole, but unacknowledged end, was gratification of his inordinate self-esteem. *E. B. Warburton*

General Zebulon Pike – *(1779-1813)*
Pike's name remains perpetuated in a great natural monument more than 14 000 feet in height, an honour totally unjustified and totally undeserved. *John Terrell – 'Zebulon Pike'*

Major-General John Pope – *(1823-92)*
Pope was utterly outgeneralled; he never knew where his enemy was; he fought to no purpose.
Theodore A. Dodge – 'Civil War'

General Winfield Scott – *(1786-1866)*
Old Fuss and Feathers. *Anon*

General Philip H. Sheridan – *(1831-88)*
The general is a stumpy, quadrangular little man, with a forehead of no promise and hair so short that it looks like a coat of black paint.
George Strong

General William Sherman – *(1820-91)*
It would seem as if in him, all the attributes of man were merged into the enormities of the demon, as if Heaven intended in him to manifest depths of depravity yet untouched by a fallen race. *'Macon Telegraph' (1864)*

Sir Arthur Wellesley – Duke of Wellington
(1769-1852)
That long-nosed Bugger that beat the French.
Anon private (1811)

Waterloo was a battle of the first rank won by a captain of the second. *Victor Hugo*

OTHER

ARMY

An army captain wears a uniform with two chips on the shoulder. *Anon*

A paratrooper is a man who descends from trees he did not climb.   *Anon*

Join the Army, see the world, meet interesting people – and kill them.
                    Pacifist reply to army recruitment poster

DRAFT

The draft is white people sending black people to fight yellow people to protect the country they stole from red people.
                    Gerome Gragni and James Rado (1967)

MARINE CORPS

They have a propaganda machine that is almost equal to Stalin's.   *Harry S. Truman (1956)*

NAVY

Traditions of the Royal Navy? I'll give you traditions of the Navy – rum, sodomy and the lash.   *Sir Winston Churchill (1939)*

The Navy's a very gentlemanly business. You fire at the horizon to sink a ship and then you pull people out of the water and say, 'Frightfully sorry, old chap.'   *William Golding*

There were gentlemen and there were seamen in the Navy of Charles II. But the seamen were not gentlemen and the gentlemen were not seamen.   *Thomas Macaulay (1848)*

NUCLEAR WEAPONS

Ban the bomb.   *Pacifist slogan*

Better Red than dead.   *Pacifist slogan*

Make Love, not Bombs.   *Pacifist slogan*

It's like having a cobra in the nursery with your

grandchildren. You get rid of the cobra or you won't have any grandchildren.
                    Theodore M. Hesburgh – '60 Minutes'
                    – CBS TV (1982)

Preparing for suicide is not a very intelligent means of defence.   *Bruce Kent (1986)*

The survivors of a nuclear attack would envy the dead.   *Nikita Khrushchev*

If the Third World War is fought with nuclear weapons, the Fourth will be fought with bows and arrows.   *Lord Mountbatten*

THE PENTAGON

A log going down the river with 25 000 ants on it, each thinking he's steering.
                    Anon Assistant Secretary of State

During the Vietnam War – Bombing can end the war: bomb the Pentagon now!   *Pacifist slogan*

That immense monument to man's subservience to the desk.   *Oliver Frank (1952)*

A place where costs are always rounded to the nearest tenth of a billion dollars.
                    C. Merton Tyrrell (1970)

WAR OFFICE

The British soldier can stand up to anything except the British War Office.
                    G. B. Shaw – 'The Devil's Disciple'

WORLD WAR I

This was a war of no tactics, no strategy, no mind. Just slaughter.   *Paul Fussell (1975)*

A war of plugging shellholes with live soldiers.
                    Sanche de Gramont (1975)

ROYALTY

Aristocracy is that form of government in which education and discipline are qualifications for suffrage and officeholding.
Aristotle

Aristocracy is a government in which the attention of the nation is concentrated on one person doing interesting actions.
Walter Bagehot

A queen is a woman by whom the realm is ruled when there is a king, and through whom it is ruled when there is not. *Ambrose Bierce*

Democracy means government by the uneducated, while aristocracy means government by the badly educated.
G. K. Chesterton

For the first time I was aware of that layer of blubber which encases an English peer, the sediment of permanent adulation.
Cyril Connolly – 'Enemies of Promise' (1938)

Everyone likes flattery; and when you come to Royalty you should lay it on with a trowel.
Benjamin Disraeli

An aristocrat is a democrat ripe and gone to seed. *Ralph W. Emerson*

A king is an ordinary kind of man who has to live in a very extraordinary kind of way that sometimes seems to have little sense of it.
King George V

The aristocracy is composed of asses – asses who talk about horses. *Heinrich Heine*

In all ages, hypocrites, called priests, have put crowns upon the heads of thieves, called kings.
Robert G. Ingersoll

Offending is the aristocratic pleasure.
Françoise Montesquieu

When royalty leaves the room it is like getting a seed out of your tooth. *Mrs P. Phipps*

The right divine of kings is to govern wrong.
Alexander Pope

Kings are not born; they are made by artificial hallucination.
George B. Shaw – 'Man and Superman'

An aristocrat is a demokrat with hiz pockets filled. *Henry W. Shaw*

We adore titles and heredities in our hearts, and ridicule them with our mouths. This is our democratic privilege. *Mark Twain*

The kingly office is entitled to no respect. It was originally procured by highwayman's methods; it remains a perpetuated crime, can never be anything but the symbol of a crime. It is no more entitled to respect than is the flag of a pirate. *Mark Twain – 'Notebook' (1935)*

There is always more brass than brains in an aristocracy.
Oscar Wilde – 'A Woman of No Importance' (1893)

BRITISH ROYALTY

Prince Albert – *husband of Queen Victoria (1819–61)*
Albert was merely a young foreigner, who suffered from having no vices, and whose only claim to fame was that he had happened to marry the Queen of England. *Lytton Strachey*

Queen Anne – *(1665–1714)*
Queen Anne was one of the smallest people ever set in a great place. *Walter Bagehot*

Anne when in good humour was meekly stupid, and when in bad humour was sulkily stupid.
Thomas Macaulay

The Princess Royal [Anne] – *(b 1950)*
Such an active lass. So outdoorsy. She loves nature in spite of what it did to her.
Bette Midler

Anne of Cleeves – *fourth wife of Henry VIII (1515-57)*
They have brought me the Flanders Mare.
Henry VIII

King Charles I – *(1600-49)*
On seeing Van Dyck's portrait in three positions –
Never have I beheld features more unfortunate.
Gianlorenzo Bernini

Caroline of Brunswick – *wife of George IV (1768-1821)*
On seeing her for the first time – Harris, I am not well; pray get me a glass of brandy.
King George IV

Catherine of Braganza – *consort to Charles II (1638-1705)*
A little woman, no breeder.
Anthony à Wood – 'Life and Times' (1664)

King Charles II – *(1630-85)*
He would fain be Despot, even at the cost of being another's Underling . . . I look on him as one of the moral Monsters of History.
Samuel Taylor Coleridge

Charles I lived and died a hypocrite. Charles II was a hypocrite of another sort, and should have died upon the same scaffold.
Franciscus Junius

Here lies a great and mighty king,
Whose promise none relies on;
He never said a foolish thing,
Nor ever did a wise one.
John Wilmot, Earl of Rochester

Merry monarch, scandalous and poor.
John Wilmot, Earl of Rochester

Charlotte – *consort of George III (1744-1818)*
Yes, I do think that the bloom of her ugliness is going off.
Colonel Disbrowe

King Edward VII – *(1841-1910)*
His intellect is of no more use than a pistol packed in the bottom of a trunk if one were attacked in the robber-infested Apennines.
Prince Albert (1858)

Bertie seemed to display a deepseated

repugnance to every form of mental exertion.
Lytton Strachey (1921)

Queen Elizabeth I – *(1533-1603)*
Oh dearest Queen
I've never seen
A face more like a soup-tureen.
Anon

As just and merciful as Nero and as good a Christian as Mahomet.
John Wesley – 'Journal' (1768)

Queen Elizabeth II – *(b 1926)*
She is a woman who acts her age, which is 50. She has, in fact, acted that age since she was little more than 20.
Fern Marja Eckman – 'New York Post' (1976)

The personality conveyed by the utterances which are put into her mouth is that of a priggish school-girl, captain of the hockey team, a prefect and a recent candidate for confirmation.
John Grigg – 'National Review' (1955)

A very pleasant middle to upper-class type of lady, with a talkative retired Navy husband.
Malcolm Muggeridge – 'Saturday Evening Post'

She is frumpish and banal.
Malcolm Muggeridge (1957)

Ethelred the Unready – *(968-1016)*
The career of his life is said to have been cruel in the beginning, wretched in the middle, and disgraceful in the end. *William of Malmesbury*

Sarah Ferguson – *Duchess of York*
On her weight problem – The Duchess of Pork.
Anon

Maria Anne Fitzherbert – *'wife' of George IV (1756-1837)*
What is the difference between Mrs Fitzherbert and a demi-mondaine?
Mrs Fitzherbert would break the Seventh Commandment for a sovereign, but not for half-a-crown. *Anon*

The Georges I-IV
George the First was always reckoned
Vile, but viler George the Second;
And what mortal ever heard

Any good of George the Third?
When from earth the Fourth descended,
God be praised, the Georges ended.
Walter S. Landor

King George I – *(1660–1727)*
George I was lazy and inactive even in his
pleasures, which therefore were lowly sensual.
Importunity alone could make him act, and
then only to get rid of it.   *Lord Chesterfield*

George I kept his wife in prison because he
believed she was no better than he was.
Will Cuppy

A dull, stupid and profligate King, full of drink
and low conversation, without dignity of
appearance or manner, without sympathy of
any kind with the English people and English
ways, and without the slightest knowledge of
the English language.   *Justin McCarthy*

King George II – *(1683–1760)*
The best, perhaps, that can be said of him is
that on the whole, all things considered, he
might have been worse.   *Justin McCarthy*

King George III – *(1738–1820)*
Throughout the greater part of his life George
III was a kind of consecrated obstruction.
Walter Bagehot

George the Third
Ought never to have occurred.
One can only wonder
At so grotesque a blunder.   *E. C. Bentley*

There is a certain continuity in his prejudices,
but hardly any in his policy.
F. S. Oliver – 'The Endless Adventure'

His maxims, in mid-career, were those of a
conscientious bull in a china shop.
Richard Pares

King George IV – *(1762–1830)*
Alvanney – who's your fat friend?
Beau Brummel (1813)

As a son, as a husband, as a father, and
especially as an adviser of young men, I deem it
my duty to say that, on a review of his whole
life, I can find no one good thing to speak of, in

either the conduct or character of this king.
William Cobbett

A more contemptible, cowardly, selfish,
unfeeling dog does not exist than this king . . .
with vices and weaknesses of the lowest and
most contemptible order.   *Charles Greville*

As Prince Regent – A corpulent Adonis of fifty.
Leigh Hunt – 'London Examiner' (1813)

King George V – *(1865–1936)*
Born into the ranks of the working class, the
new King's most likely fate would have been
that of a street-corner loafer.
James Keir Hardie (1910)

King Henry VII – *(1457–1509)*
What the man lacked apparently was any
personal charm. They called his son Bluff King
Hal and granddaughter Good Queen Bess, but
none ever gave Henry VII a nickname. He
never seems to have caught the popular
imagination. What contemporaries chiefly
remarked in him was his wisdom, by which
they meant his sound common sense. Men
feared him, admired him, depended on him, but
they did not love him.
Conyers Red – 'The Tudors'

King Henry VIII – *(1491–1547)*
The plain truth is, that he was a most
intolerable ruffian, a disgrace to human nature,
and a blot of blood and grease upon the History
of England.   *Charles Dickens*

A pig, an ass, a dunghill, the spawn of an adder,
a basilisk, a lying buffoon, a mad fool with a
frothy mouth, a blubbery ass.   *Martin Luther*

Henry VIII perhaps approached as nearly to the
ideal standard of perfect wickedness as the
infirmities of human nature will allow.
Sir James Mackintosh

King James I – *(1566–1625)*
The loathsome Lackwit, James I.
Samuel T. Coleridge – 'Notebook'

King James II – *(1633–1701)*
The most incompetent man I have ever seen in
my life. A child of seven years would not make

such silly mistakes as he does.
Duchess of Orleans (1692)

Under the morose face there seemed to be a
heart of stone.
Alexander Smellie – 'Men of the Covenant'

King John – *(1167–1216)*
He was the very worst of all our kings; a man
whom no oaths could bind, no pressure of
conscience, no consideration of policy, restrain
from evil; a faithless son, a treacherous brother,
an ungrateful master; to his people a hated
tyrant . . . John seems as incapable of receiving
a good impression as of carrying into effect a
wise resolution.   *Bishop William Stubbs*

He had the mental abilities of a great king, but
the inclinations of a petty tyrant.
W. C. Warren – 'King John'

Princess Margaret – *(b 1930)*
The Billy Carter of the British monarchy.
Robert Lacey

Queen Mary I – *(1516–58)*
Her appearance was formidable, her manner –
well, it was like talking to St Paul's Cathedral.
Henry Channon

Cursed Jezebel of England.   *John Knox*

Mary, Queen of Scots – *(1542–87)*
The most notorious whore in all the world.
Peter Wentworth

Prince Philip, Duke of Edinburgh – *(b 1921)*
Whatever happens to him in his present
capacity as royal poor relation can't do him
much good in the long run. My advice to him
would be: give up being a royal personage, stick
to the sea, learn a trade and find an anchorage
with an average wife.   *'Daily Worker' (1946)*

I'm prepared to take advice on leisure from
Prince Philip. He's a world expert on leisure.
He's been practising for most of his adult life.
Neil Kinnock (1981)

King Richard II – *(1367–1400)*
A weak, vain, frivolous, and inconstant prince;
without weight to balance the scales of
government; without discernement to chuse a

good ministry; without virtue to oppose the
measures and advice of evil counsellors, even
when they happened to clash with his own
principles and opinion. He was a dupe to
flattery, a slave to ostentation . . . He was idle,
profuse, and profligate, and, though brave by
starts, naturally pusillanimous and irresolute.
Tobias Smollett

King Stephen – *(1097–1154)*
He was a man of great renown in the practice
of arms, but for the rest almost an incompetent,
except that he was rather inclined to evil.
Walter Map

Queen Victoria – *(1819–1901)*
She had the temper of the Tudors but none of
the charm of the Stuarts. She was German – a
German hausfrau – down to her fingertips.
Worst of all, when her dogs were ill, or cold,
she sent them away.   *Ouida*

A mixture of national landlady and actress.
V. S. Pritchett

Nowadays, a parlour-maid as ignorant as
Queen Victoria was when she came to the
throne would be classed as mentally defective.
G. B. Shaw

Wallis Simpson – *Duchess of Windsor
(1896–1986)*
On refusing to co-operate on her memoirs – You
can't make the Duchess into Rebecca of
Sunnybrook Farm.   *Cleveland Amory*

King William I [the Conqueror] –
(1027–87)
William, indeed, seems to have been astute
without wisdom, resolute without foresight,
powerful without ultimate purpose, a man of
very limited aims and very limited vision,
narrow, ignorant and superstitious.
R. G. Richardson

King William II – *(1056–1100)*
There exists no proof as
To who shot William Rufus,
But shooting him would seem
To have been quite a sound scheme.
E. C. Bentley

King William III – *(1650–1702)*
He's ugly and crooked

His nose it is hooked
The Devil to him is beauty
Nor father nor mother
Nor sister nor brother
Can ever bring him to his duty.   *Anon (1688)*

In Hyde Park he rides like a hog in armour,
In Whitehall he creeps like a country farmer;
Old England may boast of a godly reformer,
A dainty fine king indeed.   *Anon*

King William IV – *(1765–1837)*
Etiquette is a thing he cannot comprehend.
    Charles Greville – 'Diary' (1830)

FOREIGN ROYALTY

Napoleon Bonaparte – *Emperor of France (1769–1821)*
One could forgive the fiend for becoming a torrent, but to become an earthquake was really too much.   *Prince Charles-Joseph*

Of his face was written:
Thou shalt have no other God but me.
    Heinrich Heine

God was bored by him.   *Victor Hugo*

A cold-blooded, calculating, unprincipled usurper, without a virtue; no statesman, knowing nothing of commerce, political economy, or civil government, and supplying ignorance by bold presumption.
    Thomas Jefferson (1814)

'Memoirs' – A querulous sick man on a sub-tropical island dictating a drab and meaningless record to while away times. The memoirs of Napoleon suggest that there is something to be said for not thinking you are God.
    A. J. P. Taylor

Bonaparte's whole life, civil, political, and military, was fraud. There was not a transaction, great or small, in which lying and fraud were not introduced.   *Duke of Wellington*

Julius Caesar – *(100–44 BC)*
Caesar was a failure. Otherwise he would not have been assassinated.   *Napoleon Bonaparte*

Tsar Ferdinand of Bulgaria – *(1861–1948)*
He's a low cunning clown. He ought to be in jail, and if I ever catch him in Germany, I shall put him there.   *Kaiser Wilhelm II*

Frederick the Great – *King of Prussia (1712–86)*
The King of Prussia is a mischievous rascal, a base friend, a bad ally, and bad relation and a bad neighbour; in fact, the most dangerous and evil-disposed Prince in Europe.
    Napoleon Bonaparte

A mixture of Puck and Machiavelli.
    J. F. Fuller (1939)

King Louis XIV of France – *(1638–1715)*
Strip your Louis Quatorze of his king-gear, and there is left nothing by a poor forked radish with a head fantastically carved.
    Thomas Carlyle (1841)

King Louis XVI of France – *(1754–93)*
His features showed no nobility of expression. His laugh was heavy and lethargic, his face lifeless, his appearance slovenly. He was short-sighted, overgrown, shy and awkward. He had the countryman's graceless walk, his voice at times rose to an undignified squeak and he hated dancing.
    John Fisher – 'Six Summers in Paris'

King Louis XVIII of France – *(1755–1824)*
The courtiers who surrounded him have forgotten nothing and learnt nothing.
    Charles-François Dumouriez

Monaco Royal Family
Look, it's our 'Dallas', our serial, and they are our Kennedys, and we didn't invent any of it. The scenario is beyond belief.
    Roger Therond – 'Paris-Match' (1984)

Napoleon III – *(1808–73)*
He is a great unrecognised incapacity.
    Carl Otto von Bismarck

His mind is like an extinct sulphur-pit giving out the smell of rotten eggs.   *Thomas Carlyle*

He never speaks – and always lies.   *Lord Cowley*

Ideas run in and out of his head like rabbits in a warren.   *Lord Palmerston*

Prince Philip II of Spain - *(1527–98)*
I cannot find it in me to fear a man who took ten
years a-learning his alphabet.

Queen Elizabeth I

Queen of Tonga
On being asked who the short man sitting next to the

amply proportioned Queen was – Probably her
lunch!   *Noël Coward*

Kaiser Wilhelm II – *(1804–73)*
He never wrote a letter or a message wherein he
did not speak of God as if the Creator was
waiting to see him in the lobby.   *Elbert Hubbard*

SPORT

Hang gliding, blast baseball, and sod cycling.
Anon

The greatest dread of all, the dread of games.
John Betjeman

Sport is an armoured apparatus for coercion, an instrument of bourgeois hegemony in a Gramscian sense, dominated by a phallocratic and fascitoid idea of virility. It is mechanisation of the body conceived as a robot, ruled by the principle of productivity.
Jean-Marie Brohm (1975)

Organised sport is an occasion of pure waste – waste of time, energy, ingenuity, skill, and often money.   *Roger Caillois – 'Men Play Games'*

Sports and games are entirely non-creative; no game yet played had any lasting effect on human well-being.   *H. Campbell*

Athletes live a life quite contrary to the precepts of hygiene, and I regard their mode of living as a regime far more favourable to illness than to health.   *Galen*

Like every other instrument man has invented, sport can be used for good and evil purposes. Used badly, it can encourage personal vanity and group vanity, greedy desire for victory and even hatred for rivals, an intolerant esprit de corps and contempt for people who are beyond an arbitrary selected pale.   *Aldous Huxley*

I hate all sports as rabidly as a person who likes sports hates common sense.   *H. L. Mencken*

Athletic sports, save in the case of young boys, are designed for idiots. *George J. Nathan (1931)*

He that spends his time in sports is like him whose garment is all made of fringes, and his meat nothing but sauces; they are healthless, chargeable and useless.   *Jeremy Taylor*

AMERICAN FOOTBALL

Rugby is a beastly game played by gentlemen. Soccer is a gentleman's game played by beasts. Football is a beastly game played by beasts.
Harry Blaha (1972)

Football? Hell, what is it? It's a sick game – a whole lot of guys trying to beat the crap out of one another. If I could play golf just as well, I'd do it.   *Jim McMahon*

On refusing Cornell University leave to play a game in Michigan – I will not permit 30 men to travel 400 miles to agitate a bag of wind.
Andrew White

ATHLETICS

Carl Lewis
On his pony-tail look – He looks like the love child of Grace Jones and Paul Revere.
Tony Kornheiser – 'Washington Post' (1990)

Ben Johnson
After his positive drug test in the Seoul Olympics – From hero to zero in 9.79 seconds.
Graffiti in the Olympic village (1988)

The human cheetah.   *Colin M. Jarman (1988)*

BASEBALL

A game which consists of tapping a ball with a piece of wood, then running like a lunatic.
H. J. Dutiel

You remember baseball. A sort of razzamatazz rounders, played by rowdy rough-necks, wielding oversized clubs and oversized tennis balls.   *Robert Steen*

I don't think I can be expected to take seriously a game which takes less than three days to reach its conclusion.   *Tom Stoppard (1984)*

The underprivileged people of the Americas play some strange game with a bat which looks like an overgrown rolling pin.   *Fred Trueman*

Baseball is the favourite American sport because it's so slow. Any idiot can follow it. And just about any idiot can play it.
                              Gene Vidal

BOXING

Professional boxing is no longer worthy of civilised society. It's run by self-serving crooks, who are called promoters. Professional boxing is utterly immoral. It's not capable of reformation. I now favour the abolition of professional boxing. You'll never clean it up. Mud can never be clean.   *Howard Cosell (1982)*

All boxers are prostitutes and all promoters are pimps.   *Larry Holmes*

BOXERS

Muhammad Ali
He stings like a bee, but lives like a W.A.S.P.
                        Eamonn Andrews (1972)

He's not only a lousy fighter, he's a bad actor. Louis or Marciano could have whipped him by telephone.   *Dan Digilio (1965)*

Aged 39 – He floats like an anchor, stings like a moth.   *Ray Gandolf (1982)*

For Ali to compose a few words of real poetry would be equal to an intellectual throwing a punch.   *Norman Mailer*

Joe Bugner
Jesus Christ, 60 per cent of all the Aussies I know think Joe Bugner is something you find up the Queensland Premier's nose.
                'New Australasian Express' (1987)

Joe Frazier
Before their first meeting – He's so ugly they ought to donate his face to the World Wildlife Fund.   *Muhammad Ali (1971)*

Brian London
Brian London possesses the most unbeautiful face – it looks as if it, at one time, fell apart and was re-assembled by a drunken mechanic.
                          Michael Parkinson

Ray 'Boom-Boom' Mancini
If bullshit was poetry, Boom-Boom's last name would be Shakespeare.   *Dennis Rappaport*

BOXING PROMOTERS

Bob Arum
Bob Arum is one of the worst people in the western hemisphere. I don't know the eastern hemisphere very well, but I suspect he'd be one of the worst people there too, if he went.
                            Cus D'Amato

Don King
The man's so insecure he goes around wearing his hair like a f****** idiot, so people will recognise him.   *Rich Giachetti*

Don King dresses like a pimp and speechifies like a store-front preacher.   *John Schulian*

CARDS AND DICE

Cards and dice are the Devil's books and bones.
                                   Anon

Cards are the Devil's prayer book.
                            German proverb

Whenever dice are thrown or cards shuffled the Dark Ages get another turn on this planet.
                          Jack Richardson

BRIDGE

Bridge, because of its tendency to encourage prolonged smoking and its deadly immobility, is probably the most dangerous game played in England now.   *Anon doctor*

Bridge I regard as only one degree better than absolutely vacuous conversation, which is certainly the most fatiguing thing in the world.
                          Arthur C. Benson

I say, let's banish bridge. Let's find some pleasant way of being miserable together.
                             Don Herold

If you play bridge badly you make your partner suffer; but if you play bridge very badly you make everybody suffer.   *Joe Laurie Jr*

I hate people who play bridge as though they were at a funeral and knew their feet were getting wet. *W. Somerset Maugham (1921)*

CHESS

Bobby Fischer
Finally, the USA produces its greatest chess genius, and he turns out to be another stubborn boy. *'Chess Life'*

Bobby Fischer is a chess phenomenon, it is true, but is also a social illiterate, a political simpleton, a cultural ignoramus, and an emotional baby.
Mary Kenny – 'Evening Standard'

CRICKET

Oh God, if there be cricket in heaven, let there also be rain. *Alec Douglas Home*

Cricket is not a twentieth century game and nearly all modern-minded people dislike it.
George Orwell (1944)

Personally, I look up cricket as organised loafing. *William Temple*

I do not play cricket, because it requires me to assume such indecent positions. *Oscar Wilde*

PLAYERS

Ian Botham
This fellow is the most over-rated player I have ever seen. He looks too heavy, and the way he's been bowling out here, he wouldn't burst a paper bag. *Harold Larwood*

He couldn't bowl a hoop downhill.
Fred Trueman (1985)

A guerrilla fighter impatient of discipline.
Graeme Wright

Geoff Boycott
Telegram after he had taken an age to score fifty at Perth – You have done for Australian cricket what the Boston Strangler did for door-to-door salesmen. *Jack Birney (1978)*

Geoff Boycott has the uncanny knack of being

where fast bowlers aren't. *Tony Greig*

The tragedy of Geoff Boycott is that his batting was always going to entitle him to a place in cricket's Hall of Fame. *Don Mosey*

Sir Don Bradman
Twenty years of cricket do not seem to have taught Bradman the real British Empire meaning of the word. *Anon*

Had Bradman been built with more backbone, it is possible the 'Bodyline' story might have been different. *Warwick Armstrong*

W. G. Grace
Unless I'm crackers or something, I've scored a bloody sight more runs than that bearded old bugger. *Geoff Boycott*

He has one of the dirtiest necks I have kept wicket behind. *Viscount Cobham*

W. G. Grace was by no conceivable standards a good man. He was a cheat on and off the cricket field. *C. P. Snow*

Tony Greig
There's only one head bigger than Tony Greig's – and that's Birkenhead. *Fred Trueman*

Michael Holding
A perfect running specimen, but I don't go to a Test to see running; if I wished to see that I would go to Crystal Palace to see Coe and Ovett. *Jack Fingleton (1981)*

F. R. Spofforth
Spofforth was the Australian of Australians, a stark man that let in with him the coldest blast of antagonism that ever blew over a June field.
Sir Neville Cardus

Fred S. Trueman
Henry Irving never made greater impact with a stage entrance than Freddie Trueman in a pub.
John Hampshire (1983)

CROQUET

That ineffably insipid diversion they call croquet. *Mark Twain*

DARTS

I was watching sumo wrestling on the TV for
two hours before I realised it was darts.
Hattie Hayridge (1989)

PLAYERS

Eric Bristow
If Eric Bristow was at Cape Canaveral, he'd
take off before the rocket. *Sid Waddell*

EXERCISE AND HEALTH

I believe every human has a finite number of
heart-beats. I don't intend to waste any of mine
running around doing exercises. *Neil Armstrong*

Bodily exercise profiteth little.
The Bible: Timothy 4 v.8

The only reason I would take up jogging is so
that I could hear heavy breathing again.
Erma Brombeck

Health is what my friends are always drinking
to before they fall down. *Phyllis Diller*

Exercise is bunk. If you are healthy, you don't
need it; if you are ill, you shouldn't take it.
Henry Ford

Whenever I feel like exercise, I lie down until
the feeling passes. *Robert Hutchins*

The only exercise I get is when I take the studs
out of one shirt and put them in another.
Ring Lardner

The only thing running and exercise can do for
you is make you healthy. *Mickey Lolich*

The popular belief in athletics is grounded
upon the theory that violent exercise makes for
bodily health and that bodily health is
necessary for mental vigour. Both halves of this
theory are highly dubious. Athletes, as a class,
are not above the normal in health, but below
it. *H. L. Mencken (1951)*

I bought all those Jane Fonda videos. I love to
sit and eat cookies and watch 'em.
Dolly Parton

I prefer the bar to the gym any day. I like to
drink and I like to brawl. *Sean Penn*

I'm Jewish. I don't work out. If God had
wanted us to bend over he'd put diamonds on
the floor. *Joan Rivers*

What a troublesome affliction to have to
preserve one's health by too strict a regime.
François, Duc de La Rochefoucauld

The need for exercise is a modern superstition,
invented by people who ate too much and had
nothing to think about. Athletics don't make
anybody either long-lived or useful.
George Santayana

Exercise? I get it on the golf course. When I see
my friends collapse, I run for the paramedics.
Red Skelton

The beneficial effects of the regular quarter of
an hour's exercise before breakfast is more than
offset by the mental wear and tear in getting
out of bed fifteen minutes earlier than one
otherwise would. *Simeon Strunsky*

I consider exercise vulgar. It makes people
smell. *A. Y. Thornton*

I have never taken any exercise, except for
sleeping and resting, and I never intend to take
any. Exercise is loathsome. *Mark Twain*

As a nation we are dedicated to keeping
physically fit – and parking as close to the
stadium as possible. *Bill Vaughan*

Jogging is for people who aren't intelligent
enough to watch Breakfast TV.
Victoria Wood (1989)

FOOTBALL

I loathed the game, and since I could see no
pleasure or usefulness in it, it was very difficult
for me to show courage at it. Football, it
seemed to me, is not really played for the
pleasure of kicking a ball about, but is a species
of fighting. The lovers of football are large,
boisterous, nobby boys who are good at
knocking down and trampling on slightly
smaller boys. *George Orwell*

PLAYERS

Trevor Brooking

Trevor Brooking floats like a butterfly and stings like one too.   *Brian Clough (1981)*

Kenny Dalglish

Kenny Dalglish has about as much personality as a tennis racket.   *Mike Channon*

Glen Hoddle

You can scare Hoddle out of a match and you couldn't depend on him to bring you a cup of tea if you were dying.   *Tommy Smith*

Kevin Keegan

To call Keegan a superstar is stretching a point. He's been very, very lucky, an average player who came into the game when it was short of personalities. He's not fit to lace my boots as a player.   *George Best*

He is the Julie Andrews of football.
                              Duncan McKenzie

Keegan is not fit to lace George Best's drinks.
                              John Roberts

Remi Moses

On his transfer – Half a million for Remi Moses? You could get the original Moses and the tablets for that price.   *Tommy Docherty*

Ray Wilkins

He can't run, he can't tackle and he can't head the ball. The only time he goes forward is to toss the coin.   *Tommy Docherty*

MANAGERS

Ally McLeod

Ally McLeod believes that tactics are a new kind of peppermint.
                    Anon Scottish international (1978)

Don Revie

Don Revie's appointment as England manager was a classic example of poacher turned game-keeper.   *Alan Hardaker*

Bobby Robson

His natural expression is that of a man who fears he might have left the gas on.
                              David Lacey – 'The Guardian'

PLONKER!   *'Sun' – headline (1988)*

TEAMS

Everton F.C.

If Everton were playing down at the bottom of my garden, I'd draw the curtains.   *Bill Shankly*

When I've got nothing better to do, I look 'down' the league table to see how Everton are getting along.   *Bill Shankly*

This city has two great teams – Liverpool and Liverpool reserves.   *Bill Shankly*

Fulham F.C.

Poor Fulham, with no real method up front, resembled a fire engine hurrying to the wrong fire.   *Geoffrey Green*

Nottingham Forest

They could put ten dustbins out there and do the job they do.   *Terry McDermott (1980)*

GOLF

A golf player is someone who can drive 70 miles an hour in heavy traffic with perfect ease, but blows up on a two-foot putt if somebody coughs.   *Anon*

On subscribing a shilling to W. G. Grace's testimonial – It's not in support of cricket, but as an earnest protest against golf.
                              Sir Max Beerbohm

Golf is cow-pasture pool.   *O. K. Bovard*

I don't like to watch golf on TV because I can't stand people who whisper.
                              David Brenner (1977)

I regard golf as an expensive way of playing marbles.   *G. K. Chesterton*

Golf is an ineffectual attempt to direct an uncontrollable sphere into an inaccessible hole with instruments ill-adapted to the purpose.
                              Sir Winston Churchill

Golf is hockey at the halt.
Arthur Marshall (1985)

I'd rather watch a cabbage grow, than a man worrying his guts over a two-foot putt.
Michael Parkinson
[*Parkinson was a former president of the Anti-Golf League.*]

Excessive golf dwarfs the intellect.
Sir Walter Simpson

Golf is a good walk spoiled.
Mark Twain

Golf is a day spent in a round of strenuous idleness.
William Wordsworth

HOCKEY

The most odious of all games for a woman.
'Badminton Magazine' (1900)

HORSE RACING

I do not say that all those who go racing are rogues and vagabonds, but I do say that all rogues and vagabonds seem to go racing.
Sir Abe Bailey

Everyone knows that horse racing is carried on mainly for the delight and profit of fools, ruffians and thieves.
George Gissing (1903)

A bookie is just a pickpocket who lets you use your own hands.
Henry Morgan

Flat racing? No thanks. They're like battery hens – if they don't lay so many eggs they've had their chips.
Jenny Pitman

The swindling, dangerous and absurd practice of steeple-chasing, things merely got up by publicans and horse-dealers to pillage the unwary and enrich themselves.
'The Times' (1838)

Horse-racing I hate.
Anthony Trollope

Instead of a month's jail someone should be sentenced to read 'The Sporting Life' on non-racing days.
Lord Wigg (1959)

HUNTING

Hunting, a detested sport, that owes its pleasure to another's pain.
William Cowper

Wild animals never kill for sport. Man is the only one to whom the torture and death of his fellow creatures is amusing in itself.
James A. Froude

Deer hunting would be fine sport, if only the deer had guns.
William Gilbert

Biography, like big-game hunting, is one of the recognised forms of sport, and it is as unfair as only sport can be.
Philip Guedalla

When a man wantonly destroys one of the works of man, we call him a vandal. When he wantonly destroys one of the works of God, we call him a sportsman.
Joseph Wood Krutch

How anyone can profess to find animal life interesting and yet take delight in reducing the wonder of any animal to a bloody mass or fur or feathers is beyond my comprehension.
Joseph Wood Krutch (1957)

You call pheasant shooting a sport, do you? Why? What is it? Up gets a guinea – off goes a penny-farthing – and, if you're lucky, down comes two-and-six. Bah!
'Punch' (1889)

When a man wants to murder a tiger he calls it sport; when a tiger wants to murder him he calls it ferocity.
G. B. Shaw

No sportsman wants to kill a fox or the pheasant as I want to kill him when I see him doing it.
G. B. Shaw

For as long as one hears the anguished wailing of a hare as the blood gushes from its ears, and its eyes come out on stalks under the pressure of a hound's teeth, then our countryside can never be the green and pleasant place of our birthright.
Peter Wilson – 'Daily Mirror'

I hate all blood pursuits involving animals whose panting death provides a thrill for the pursuers. But at least those who hunt the fox and the noble stag do put their own limbs at some risk. I loathe bull-fighting – but the great

SPORT

matador is not a coward. Hare-coursing puts no
one, save the hare, at any worse risk than over-
indulgence in eating and drinking can bring.
Peter Wilson – 'Daily Mirror'

ICE HOCKEY

I went to a fight the other night and an Ice
Hockey game broke out.
Rodney Dangerfield (1978)

Hockey is where a fan pays his money and
almost a fifth of the time sees nothing decided.
Robert Fachet – 'New York
Herald/Tribune' (1978)

To his Olympic team – Every day you guys look
worse and worse. And today you played like
tomorrow.   *John Mariucci*

MOTOR RACING

René Arnoux
A real whacko from Grenoble, lacked the one
essential quality of the modern racing driver –
intelligence.   *Keith Botsford*

Niki Lauda
He is a single minded chap. If he found you
lying on the ground, he would sooner walk over
you than round you.   *James Hunt*

ROWING

Henley Regatta is full of haughty happiness,
hats, haves and very few have-nots.
Frank Keating – 'The Guardian' (1983)

The Oxford/Cambridge Boat Race would be
much more attractive if the rules were changed
to allow the boats to ram each other.
Miles Kington

SKIING

Skiing? Why break my leg at 40 degrees below
zero when I can fall downstairs at home?
Corey Ford

SKIERS

Eddie 'The Eagle' Edwards
What about Eddie the bloody stupid eagle?

Don't tell me he's a sportsman . . . thick as two
short planks.   *Eric Bristow (1989)*

He has done for British winter sports what
Screaming Lord Sutch has done for the British
electoral system.   *Colin M. Jarman (1988)*

SNOOKER

Steve Davis
You have as much class as my backside.
Cliff Thorburn (1981)

Alex 'Hurricane' Higgins
A lot of people are using two-piece cues,
nowadays. Alex Higgins hasn't got one, because
they don't come with instructions.
Steve Davis

It is all very attractive, the talent, the tears, the
tantrums, the highs and lows, and all that so-
called human stuff, but underneath there is a
selfishness and ruthlessness that makes me look
like a choirboy.   *Steve Davis*

SQUASH

Squash – that's not exercise, it's flagellation.
Sir Noël Coward

SWIMMING

What on earth has this synchronised swimming
got to do with anything, let alone sport?
Frank Keating – 'Guardian' (1984)

Britain's swim girls are just not tough enough.
At the World Championships they were no
more than a glee club for the men.
Jack Queen (1975)

TENNIS

André Agassi
On his avoiding Wimbledon, 'for a rest' – That's
like a football player who skips the Super Bowl
because he has got to get ready for training
camp.   *Martina Navratilova (1990)*

Looks like he missed the last train to
Woodstock. With neon-coloured spandex worn

under denim-look shorts, he's tennis's flower-child gone to seed.

Mr Blackwell – 'Tennis' (1990)

Tracy Austin

Tracy was never the cute little kid that she looks.   *Martina Navratilova (1980)*

Bjorn Borg

Like a Volvo, Bjorn Borg is rugged, has good after-sales service, and is very dull.

Clive James – 'The Observer'

Jimmy Connors

Jimmy Connors is loud, aggressive and, with the face and hairstyle of a medieval varlet, he personifies a generation which tips its hat to no man.   *Ian Wooldridge – 'Daily Mail'*

John McEnroe

Hair like badly turned broccoli.

Clive James – 'The Observer'

Tennis players are a load of w***ers. I'd love to put McEnroe in the centre for Fulham [Rugby League club] and let some of the big players sort him out.   *Colin Welland (1980)*

Ilie Nastase

On being asked to address him as 'Mr Nastase' –
Look, Nastase, we used to have a famous cricket match in this country called Gentlemen versus Players. The Gentlemen were put down on the scorecard as 'Mister' because they were gentlemen. By no stretch of the imagination can anybody call you a gentleman.

Trader Horn – Wimbledon umpire

Nastase is a Hamlet who wants to play a clown. He is no good at it.

Clive James – 'The Observer' (1975)

Nastase rarely grins and bears it. More commonly he grins, groans, shrugs, slumps, spins around, shakes his head, puffs out his cheeks, rolls on the ground and bears it. Even more commonly, he does all that and doesn't bear it.   *Clive James – 'The Observer'*

Martina Navratilova

In her leather-appliquéd skirts and '70s wire-rim eye-glasses, she's the 'Tootsie' of tennis.

Mr Blackwell – 'Tennis' (1990)

Charlie Pasarell

Charlie Pasarell moves so slowly between points that at times he seems to be flirting with reverse gear.   *Rex Bellamy – 'The Times'*

Bobby Riggs

He can't hear, can't see, walks like a duck and is an idiot.   *Rosemary Casals*

Gabriella Sabatini

She is very beautiful, but she walks like Robert Mitchum.   *Teddy Tinling*

Aranxta Sanchez-Vicario

She looks like a refugee from a Bruce Springsteen concert hitting all the wrong fashion shots.   *Mr Blackwell – 'Tennis' (1990)*

WEIGHTLIFTING

Canadian Olympic weightlifting team

After four of their seven lifters had been banned for 'drug-abuse' – Canadian weightlifters: three clean and four jerks.   *Graffiti*

WRESTLING

Professional wrestling is just rehearsed acrobatics. It's not the sort of thing you would let your children go to see.

George Hackenschmidt

Professional wrestling's most mysterious hold is on its audience.   *Luke Neely (1953)*

YACHTING

Watching an America's Cup is like watching the grass grow.   *Ring Lardner*

FOOD

You are what you eat. *Anon*
[*Paul Theroux thought otherwise* – You are not what you eat; but where you eat is who you are.]

Eating food with a knife and fork is like making love through an interpreter. *Anon*

Nutrition makes me puke. *Jimmy Piersall*

Jack Sprat could eat no fat. His wife could eat no lean. A real pair of neurotics. *Jack Sharkey*

Cooking is a minor art. I can't imagine an hilarious soufflé, or a deeply moving stew.
Kenneth Tynan (1975)

REGIONAL FOODS

If you are what you eat, a visit to North Carolina could make you a very interesting person. *Anon*

English Cooking – You just put things in hot water and take them out again after a while.
Anon French Chef

Chinese food – you do not sew with a fork and I see no reason why you should eat with knitting needles. *Henry Beard (1981)*

The food in Yugoslavia is fine if you like pork tartare. *Ed Begley Jr*

American food is a plenitude of peanut butter and a dearth of hot mustard. *Patrick Dean*

If you are going to America, bring food.
Fran Lebowitz

Japanese food is very pretty and undoubtedly a suitable cuisine in Japan, which is largely populated by people of below average size. Hostesses hell-bent on serving such food to occidentals would be well advised to supplement it with something more substantial and to keep in mind that almost everybody likes French fries. *Fran Lebowitz (1978)*

An Englishman teaching an American about food is like the blind leading the one-eyed.
A. J. Liebling

To eat well in England, you should have a breakfast three times a day.
W. Somerset Maugham

Never eat Chinese food in Oklahoma.
Bryan Miller

The trouble with eating Italian food is that five or six days later you're hungry again.
George Miller

Americans can eat garbage, provided you sprinkle it liberally with ketchup, mustard, chili sauce, tabasco sauce, cayenne pepper, or any other condiment which destroys the original flavour of the dish. *Henry Miller –'Remember to Remember' (1947)*

German cooking, above all! – How much it has upon its conscience! Soup before the meal, meats cooked to death, fat and mealy vegetables.
Friedrich Nietszche – 'Ecce Homo' (1888)

You can't barbecue in New York, you'd have to keep vacuuming the meat. *'Rhoda' – CBS TV*

If the English can survive their food, they can survive anything. *G. B. Shaw*

The United States have thirty-two religions and only one dish. *Charles-Maurice de Talleyrand*
[*Unfortunately M. Talleyrand did not specify what the dish was.*]

Even today, well-brought up English girls are taught by their mothers to boil all vegetables for at least a month and a half, just in case one of the dinner guests turns up without his teeth.
Calvin Trillin (1983)

CHEFS AND COOKS

A chef who would dilute his bernaise with a

FOOD

cream sauce to save a few pennies ought to
have his toque ripped off and tossed into the
fire.   *Anon*

Murder is commoner among cooks than among
members of any other profession.
                            W. H. Auden (1973)

God sends meat, but the Devil sends cooks.
                            Thomas Deloney

Old Italian chefs never die – they're just put
out to pasta.   *Shelby Friedman*

The British cook is a foolish woman who
should be turned for her iniquities into a pillar
of salt which she never knows how to use.
                            Oscar Wilde

SPECIFIC

BREAD

A sandwich is an unsuccessful attempt to make
both ends meat.   *Anon*

Bagels are made with love and a little cement.
                                         Anon

Bagel – an unsweetened doughnut with rigor
mortis.   *Beatrice & Ira Freeman –*
                    'New York Times' (1960)

The staff of life, once healthy fare,
Is cotton gauze now, mostly air,
Such plastic foam, pneumatic bread
Should stay on grocers' shelves instead,
Unless you need a loaf for fluffing
A pillow that has lost its stuffing.
                            Ethel Jacobson

Anyhow, the hole in the doughnut is at least
digestible.
        H. L. Mencken – 'Chrestomathy' (1949)

I understand the big food companies are
developing a tearless onion. I think they can do
it – after all, they've already given us tasteless
bread.   *Robert Orben*

The first time I tried organic wheat bread, I
thought I was chewing on roofing material.
                            Robin Williams

BREAKFAST
Continental breakfasts are very sparse, usually
just a pot of tea or coffee and a teensy roll that
looks like a suitcase handle. My advice is to go
right to lunch without pausing.   *Henry Beard*

Do you know what breakfast cereal is made of?
It's made of all those little curly wooden
shavings you find in pencil sharpeners!
                Roald Dahl – 'Charlie and the
                            Chocolate Factory'

It takes some skill to spoil a breakfast – even
the English can't do it.   *J. K. Galbraith (1969)*

Danish pastry – The word 'Danish' has been
synonymous with fun, fun, fun. Who else would
have the sense of humour to stuff prunes and
toecheese into lumps of wet dough and serve it
to you for breakfast?
        Tony Hendra – 'National Lampoon' (1976)

Oats is a grain which in England is generally
given to horses, but in Scotland supports the
people.   *Samuel Johnson*

Breakfast cereals that come in the same colours
as polyester leisure suits make oversleeping a
virtue.   *Fran Lebowitz (1978)*

Some breakfast food manufacturer hit upon the
simple notion of emptying out the leavings of
carthorse nosebags, adding a few other things
like unconsumed portions of chicken layer's
mash, and the sweepings of racing stables,
packing the mixture in little bags and selling
them in health food shops.   *Frank Muir*

Remember the days when you let your child
have some chocolate if he finished his cereal?
Now, chocolate is one of the cereals.
                            Robert Orben

DINNER PARTIES

If the soup had been as hot as the claret, if the
claret had been as old as the bird, and if the
bird's breasts had been as full as the waitress's,
it would have been a very good dinner.   *Anon*

On dinner at Emile Zola's – House-warming at
Zola's . . . very tasty dinner including some

241

grouse whose scented flesh compared to an old courtesan's flesh marinaded in a bidet.
Edward de Goncourt

The English never smash a face. They merely refrain from asking it to dinner.
Margaret Halsey

Summer has an unfortunate effect upon hostesses who have been unduly influenced by the photography of Irving Penn and take the season as a cue to serve dinners of astonishingly meagre proportions. These they call light, a quality, which, while most assuredly welcome in comedies, cotton shirts and hearts, is not an appropriate touch at dinner. *Fran Lebowitz*

A dinner invitation, once accepted, is a scared obligation. If you die before the dinner takes place, your executor must attend.
Ward McAllister (1890)

Dinner at the Huntercombes' possessed only two dramatic features – the wine was a farce and the food a tragedy. *Anthony Powell –*
'The Acceptance World' (1955)

The social dinner is of medieval inefficiency.
Jean-Jacques Schreiber – 'New York Times' (1968)

DAIRY PRODUCE

Custard is a detestable substance produced by a malevolent conspiracy of hen, cow and the cook. *Ambrose Bierce*

My illness is due to my doctor's insistence that I drink milk, a whiteish fluid they force down helpless babies. *W. C. Fields*

As for butter versus margarine, I trust cows more than chemists. *Joan Gussow (1986)*

Cream is the very head and flower of milk; but it is somewhat of a gross nourishment, and by reason of the unctuosity of it, quickly cloyeth the stomach, relaxeth and weakeneth the retentive faculty thereof, and is easily converted into phlegm, and vaporous fumes.
Tobia Venner – 'Via Recta' (1620)

DIETS & HEALTH FOODS

Diets are for those who are thick and tired of it all. *Anon*

A dieter is one who wishes others wouldn't laugh at his expanse. *Al Bernstein*

Those magazine dieting stories always have the testimonial of a woman who wore a dress that could slipcover New Jersey in one photo and thirty days later looked like a well-dressed thermometer. *Erma Brombeck*

I've been on a constant diet for the last two decades. I've lost a total of 789 pounds. By all accounts, I should be hanging from a charm bracelet. *Erma Brombeck*

Liquid diets – the powder is mixed with water and tastes exactly like powder mixed with water. *Art Buchwald –*
'New York Herald/Tribune' (1960)

I feel about airplanes the way I feel about diets. It seems to me they are wonderful things for other people to go on. *Jean Kerr (1960)*

I went on a diet, swore off drinking and heavy eating, and in fourteen days I lost two weeks.
Joe E. Lewis

What some call health, if purchased by anxiety about diet, isn't much better than tedious disease. *George Prentice (1860)*

Health food may be good for the conscience but Oreos taste a hell of a lot better. *Robert Redford*

Remember the good old days when a liquid protein diet was chicken soup? *Gil Stern*

Dieticians are the worst enemy of the great cuisine. It is impossible to have low calories in excellent food. *Louis Vaudable*

My wife is on a diet. Coconuts and bananas. She hasn't lost any weight, but she can sure climb a tree. *Henny Youngman*

DRINK

ALCOHOL

Here's to champagne, the drink divine
  That makes us forget our troubles.
It is made of a dollar's worth of wine
And three dollar's worth of bubbles.   *Anon*

Alcohol is a liquid that can put the wreck into
recreation.   *Anon*

A martini is an olive with an alcohol rub.   *Anon*

When the wine is in, the wit is out.   *Proverb*

The Norwegians live to eat and the Danes eat
to live, while the Swedes eat to drink.
                            Scandinavian saying

The point about white Burgundies is that I hate
them myself. They so closely resemble a blend
of cold chalk soup and alum cordial with an
additive or two to bring it to the colour of
children's pee.
        Kingsley Amis – 'The Green Man' (1969)

Champagne for my sham friends; real pain for
my real friends.   *Francis Bacon*

Drinking makes such fools of people, and
people are such fools to begin with that it's
compounding a felony.   *Robert Benchley*

Brandy is a cordial composed one part thunder-
and-lightning, one part remorse, two parts
bloody murder, one part death-hell-and-the-
grave and four parts clarified Satan.
                              Ambrose Bierce

Beer is not a good cocktail party drink,
especially in a home where you don't know
where the bathroom is.   *Billy Carter (1977)*

'Cold Duck' – a carbonated wine foisted upon
Americans (who else would drink it) by winery
ad agencies as a way of getting rid of inferior
champagne by mixing it with inferior
burgundy.
                            John Ciardi (1983)

A cocktail is to a glass of wine what rape is to
love.   *Paul Claudel*

Corn Liquor – It smells like gangrene starting in
a mildweed silo, it tastes like the wrath to
come, and when you absorb a deep swig of it
you have all the sensations of having swallowed
a lighted kerosene lamp. A sudden, violent jolt
of it has been known to stop the victim's watch,
snap his suspenders and crack his glass eye
right across.
                          Irvin S. Cobb (1931)

Apart from cheese and tulips, the main product
of Holland is advocaat, a drink made from
lawyers.
        Alan Coren – 'The Sanity Inspector' (1974)

I hate champagne more than anything in the
world next to Seven-Up.
        Elaine Dundy – 'The Dud Avocado' (1958)

The only way they could improve upon Coca
Cola . . . is to put rum or bourbon in it.
                          Lewis Grizzard (1985)

Show me a nation whose national beverage is
beer, and I'll show you an advanced toilet
technology.   *Paul Hawkins (1977)*

I like liquor – its taste and effects – and that is
just the reason why I never drink it.
                    Thomas 'Stonewall' Jackson

One of the disadvantages of wine is that it
makes a man mistake words for thoughts.
                              Samuel Johnson

Brandy and water spoils two good things.
                                Charles Lamb

The Spanish wine, my God, it is foul, catpiss is
champagne compared, this is the sulphurous
urination of some aged horse.
                            D.H. Lawrence (1929)

Cocktails have all the disagreeability without
the utility of a disinfectant.
        Shane Leslie – 'The Observer' (1939)

Only Irish coffee provides in a single glass all
four essential food groups – alcohol, caffeine,
sugar, and fat.   *Alex Levine*

A man takes a drink, the drink takes another,
and the drink takes the man.   *Sinclair Lewis*

A good general rule is to state that the bouquet is better than the taste, and vice versa.
Stephen Potter (1952)

It's a naive domestic Burgundy without any breeding, but I think you'll be amused by its presumption. *James Thurber (1943)*

The Germans are exceedingly fond of Rhine wines. One tells them from vinegar by the label.
Mark Twain (1880)

How to mix a Mint Julep – Pluck the mint gently from its bed, just as the dew of the evening is about to form upon it. Select the choicer sprigs only, but do not rinse them. Prepare the simple syrup and measure out a half-tumbler of whiskey. Pour the whiskey into a well-frosted cup and throw away the other ingredients and drink the whiskey. *Henry Waterson*

BEVERAGES

Coffee – Trifle away their time, scald their chops, and spend money, all for a little base, black, nasty, little nauseous puddle of water.
Anon

Tea, although an oriental,
Is a gentleman at least;
Cocoa is a cad and coward,
Cocoa is a vulgar beast.
G. K. Chesterton (1927)

I view tea-drinking as a destroyer of health, an enfeebler of the frame, an endangerer of effeminacy and laziness, a debaucher of youth and a maker of misery for old-age.
William Cobbett (1835)

English coffee – just toasted milk.
Christopher Fry (1962)

Ladies' Afternoon Tea – Giggle – gabble – gobble – git. *Oliver Wendell Holmes*

Cocoa? Cocoa? Damn miserable puny stuff, fit for kittens and unwashed boys. Did William Shakespeare drink cocoa?
Shirley Jackson (1954)

Tea – its proper use is to amuse the idle, relax the studious and dilute the full meals of those who cannot use exercise and will not use abstinence. *Samuel Johnson*

English cuisine is generally so threadbare that for years there has been a gentleman's agreement in the civilised world to allow the Brits pre-eminence in the matter of tea – which, after all, comes down to little more than the ability to boil water.
Wilfred Sheed – 'GQ' (1984)

Teas: Where small talk dies in agony.
Percy B. Shelley

Tea possesses an acrid astringent quality, peculiar to most leaves and exterior bark, and corrodes and paralyses the nerves.
Jesse Torrey (1819)

EGGS

There is no such thing as a pretty omelette.
French Proverb

Be content to remember that those who can make omelettes properly can do nothing else.
Hilaire Belloc

I'm frightened of eggs, worse than frightened, they revolt me. That white round thing without any holes. Have you ever seen anything more revolting than an egg yolk breaking and spilling its yellow liquid? Blood is jolly, red. But egg yolk is yellow, revolting. I've never tasted it.
Alfred Hitchcock (1963)

FAST-FOOD

It would be healthier if parents told their children, 'Go out and play in traffic'.
Dr Tazewell Banks (1985)

We were taken to a fast-food café where our order was fed into a computer. Our hamburger, made from the flesh of chemically impregnated cattle, had been broiled over counterfeit charcoal, placed between slices of artificially flavoured cardboard and served to us by recycled juvenile delinquents.
Jean-Michel Chapereau (1975)

The Rise of fast-food restaurants,
Though convenient in many respects,
Is sure to increase the sightings of,
Unidentified Frying Objects.
Edward F. Dempsey

Eating at fast-food restaurants, still drives me
    to distraction,
  But I wouldn't call it snobbery, just a kind of
  gut reaction.
                                    Edward F. Dempsey

All those fast-food indigestion huts.
                                    Bryan Miller (1983)

Macdonalds is a reductive kitchen for a
classless culture that hasn't time to dally on its
way to the next rainbow's end.
                        Tom Robbins – 'Esquire' (1983)

FROZEN FOOD

In these days of frozen dinners, cake mixes and
instant coffee, poison ivy is the only thing left
that starts from scratch.   *W. J. Croneberger*

  The frozen pie you're moved to buy
By the colour photo that dazzles the eye
On the gaudy package for which you fall,
Believe me, won't look like that at all!
But still, what's important is, how does it taste?
  You want to know? Like library paste.
                                    Ethel Jacobson

On some occasions, the most effective way to
improve the flavour of a TV dinner is to turn
off the TV.   *Robert Orben*

FRUIT

A prune is a plum that has seen better days. *Anon*

A raisin is a worried looking grape.   *Anon*

GOURMET COOKING
I don't like gourmet cooking or 'this' cooking or
'that' cooking. I like good cooking.
                                    James Beard (1985)

A gourmet is just a glutton with brains.
            Phillip W. Haberman Jr – 'Vogue' (1961)

It's ironic that in this age when anybody who's
cut his second molars considers himself a
gourmet, the quality of our staple food is so
dreary.   *Harriet van Horne (1972)*

HERBS & SAUCES
There is no such thing as a little garlic.   *Anon*

Edmund McIlhenny's Tabasco Sauce – he
chopped up peppers, mixed them with vinegar
and Avery Island salt, put the mixture in
wooden barrels to age and funnelled the
resulting sauce into a secondhand cologne
bottle.   *James Conway*

MEAT

Three million frogs' legs are served in Paris –
daily. Nobody knows what became of the rest of
the frogs.   *Fred Allen*

A chop is a piece of leather skilfully attached to
a bone and administered to the patients at
restaurants.   *Ambrose Bierce*

  Did I not know my wife's ragout
  Is Boeuf-au-something, Cordon Bleu –
    I'd swear that I am eating stew.
                                    F. R. Canning

What a shocking fraud the turkey is. In life
preposterous, insulting – what a foolish noise
they make to scare you away! In death
unpalatable. The turkey has practically no taste
except a dry fibrous flavour reminiscent of a
mixture of warmed-up plaster of paris and
horse hair. The texture is like sawdust and the
whole vast feathered swindle has the piquancy
of a boiled mattress.
                        'Cassandra' [William Connor] –
                                'Daily Mirror' (1953)

Pâté – nothing more than a French meat loaf
that's had a couple of cocktails.   *Carol Cutler*

  One often yearns
For the land of Burns –
The only snag is
  The haggis!   *Lils Emslie (1983)*

I did not say that this meat was tough. I just
said I didn't see the horse that usually stands
outside.   *W. C. Fields (1941)*

Avoid fried meats, which angry the blood.
                                Leroy 'Satchel' Paige

I am a great eater of beef and I believe that does
harm to my wit.
                William Shakespeare – 'Twelfth Night'

FOOD

It is only by softening and disguising dead flesh
by culinary preparation that it is rendered
susceptible of mastication or digestion; and that
the sight of its bloody juices and raw horror
does not excite intolerable loathing and disgust.
Percy B. Shelley (1913)

They served haggis at the last dinner I
attended. I didn't know whether to kick it or eat
it. Having eaten it, I wished I'd have kicked it.
Stuart Turner

A few years ago it was considered chic to serve
Beef Wellington; fortunately, like Napoleon, it
met its Waterloo. *Rene Veaux*

I've often wondered what goes into a hot dog.
Now I know and I wish I didn't.
William Zissner (1970)

NOUVELLE CUISINE

It's so beautifully arranged on the plate – you
know someone's fingers have been all over it.
Julia Child

Food is to eat, not to frame and hang on the
wall. *William Denton*

I don't go for the nouvelle approach – serving a
rabbit rump with coffee extract sauce and a
slice of kiwi fruit. *Jeff Smith*

NUTS

Don't eat too many almonds; they add weight
to the breasts. *Colette*

OVER-EATING

A glutton is a man who eats his dessert before
the echo of his soup has stopped. *Anon*

Obesity is a fat accompli. *Len Elliott*

A glutton is an abominable stow man, while a
reducing diet is the taming of the chew.
Shelby Friedman

Obesity is really widespread. *Joseph Kern III*

Gluttony is not a secret vice. *Orson Welles*

SEAFOOD

I will not eat oysters. I want my food dead – not
sick, not wounded – dead. *Woody Allen (1966)*

Clams – I simply cannot imagine why anyone
would eat something slimy served in an
ashtray. *Henry Beard (1981)*

Oysters – a slimy, gobby shellfish which
civilisation gives men the hardihood to eat
without removing the entrails! The shells are
sometimes given to the poor. *Ambrose Bierce*

I have eaten octopus – or squid, I can never
quite tell the difference – but never with
wholehearted enjoyment on account of not
caring for the taste of hot india rubber.
Noël Coward

She ate so many clams that her stomach rose
and fell with the tide.
Louis Kronenberger – 'The Cutting Edge'

In Mexico we have a word for sushi – bait.
José Simon

In the selection of seafood you won't go wrong
if you stick to things the other fish won't eat.
Charles M. Smith (1972)

School food – The piece of cod which passeth
understanding.
Geoffrey Willans & Ronald Searle (1958)

Oh, no doubt the cod is a splendid swimmer –
admirable for swimming purposes but not for
eating. *Oscar Wilde*

SOUP

The food is so bad that pigmies come here to
dip their arrows in the soup. *Anon*

There is nothing wrong with cold soup . . . But,
that gazpacho and all manner of liquids
employing watercress have no right to vanquish
the hors d'oeuvres. You should give up soup for
a year. Above all, no soup must be inflicted on
guests (if you really can't do without, be like
the French dogs and have a bowl for breakfast).
Solid hors d'oeuvres only!
Digby Anderson – 'Spectator'

Soup is corpse water. *Adolf Hitler*

I don't take soup. You can't build a meal on a lake. *Lady Mendl [Elsie de Wolfe]*

After being served Matzo Ball soup, three days in a row – Isn't there any other part of the matzo you can eat? *Marilyn Monroe*

SWEETS & DESSERTS

Desserts remain for a moment or two in your mouth and for the rest of your life on your hips.
Peg Bracken – 'The I Hate to Cook Book'
[*More popularly* – A moment on your lips
A lifetime on your hips]

Choco Taco – a kind of crunchy novelty snack that children and dentists dream about.
'Time' (1985)

Sugar – pure, white and deadly. *Dr John Yudkin*

VEGETABLES

Vegetables are substances used by children to balance their plate while carrying it to and from the dining table. *Anon*

The french fried potato has become an inescapable horror in almost every public eating place in the country. 'French fries' say the menus, but they are not French fries any longer. They are a furry-textured substance with the taste of plastic wood.
Russell Baker – 'New York Times' (1968)

'Tis not her coldness father,
That chills my labouring breast;
It's that confounded cucumber
I've eaten and can't digest. *R. H. Barham*

Now scientists say youth can be prolonged by eating cabbage. As between sauerkraut and monkey glands, give us old age. *'Beloit News'*

A cabbage is a familiar kitchen-garden vegetable about as large and wise as a man's head. *Ambrose Bierce*

Rhubarb is the vegetable essence of stomach ache. *Ambrose Bierce*

The local groceries are all out of broccoli,
Loccoli.
Ray Blount Jr – 'Atlantic Monthly'

The sprout was developed by Belgian agronomists, this being the largest cabbage a housewife could possibly carry through the teeming streets. *Alan Coren (1974)*

I write at high speed because boredom is bad for my health. It upsets my stomach more than anything else. I also avoid green vegetables. They're greatly overrated. *Noël Coward*

How to eat spinach like a child – Divide into little piles. Rearrange again into new piles. Repeat. After five or six manoeuvres, sit back and say you are full. *Delia Ephron*

Nobody really likes capers, no matter what you do with them. Some people pretend to like capers, but the truth is that any dish that tastes good with capers in it, tastes even better with capers not in it. *Nora Ephron*

I hate with a bitter hatred the names of lentils and haricots – those pretentious cheats of appetite, those tabulated humbugs, those certificated aridities calling themselves human food. *George Gissing (1903)*

A cucumber should be well sliced and dressed with pepper and vinegar, and then thrown out, as good for nothing. *Samuel Johnson*

Vegetables are interesting but lack a sense of purpose when unaccompanied by a good cut of meat. *Fran Lebowitz (1978)*

Large, naked, raw carrots are acceptable as food only to those who live in hutches eagerly awaiting Easter. *Fran Lebowitz*

I have no religious or moral objection to vegetables but they are, as it were, the also-rans of the plate. One takes an egg, or a piece of meat, or fish, with pleasure but then one has, as a kind of penance, to dilute one's pleasure with a damp lump of boskage. *Frank Muir –
'You Can't Have Your Kayak and Heat It' (1973)*

Any dish that has either a taste or an appearance that can be improved by parsley is

ipso facto a dish unfit for human consumption.
Ogden Nash (1938)
[*Ogden Nash continued to treat parsley harshly*]
Parsley
Is gharsley.
'Further Reflections on Parsley' (1942)

I have no truck with lettuce, cabbage and similar chlorophyll. Any dietician will tell you that a running foot of apple strudel contains four times the vitamins of a bushel of beans. Every time I crush a stalk of celery, there is a whirring crash, a shriek of tortured capillaries, and my metabolism goes to the graveyard.
S. J. Perelman – 'Acres and Pains' (1947)

Asparagus makes my urine smell.   *Babe Ruth*

VEGETARIANISM

A meal without flesh is like eating grass.
Indian Proverb

Most vigitaryans I iver see looked enough like their food to be classed as cannybals.
Finlay Peter Dunne (1900)

Vegetarianism is harmless enough, though is apt to fill a man with wind and self-righteousness.   *Sir Robert Hutchinson*

Vegetarians have wicked, shifty eyes and laugh in a cold, calculating manner. They pinch little children, steal stamps, drink water, favour beards.   *J. B. Morton – 'Daily Express'*

Refusing an invite to a vegetarian dinner – The thought of two thousand people crunching celery at the same time horrified me.
G. B. Shaw

Vegetarianism isn't simply a distaste for animal products. It's a way of life: faddish, cranky and

holier-than-thou.
Harriet van Horne – 'New York Post' (1978)

RESTAURANTS

Never eat in a place called 'Moms'.
Nelson Algren

I ate on the motorway. At the Grill 'n' Griddle. I had Ham 'n' Eggs. And now I've got 'ndigestion.   *Alan Bennet – 'Getting On' (1971)*

If Broadway shows charge preview prices while the cast is in dress rehearsal, why should restaurants charge full price when their dining room and kitchen staffs are still practising?
Marion Burros – 'New York Times' (1986)

The murals in restaurants are on a par with the food in museums.   *Peter de Vries (1977)*

The disparity between a restaurant's price and food quality rises in direct proportion to the size of the pepper mill . . . The quality of food is in inverse proportion to a dining room's altitude, especially atop bank and hotel buildings (airplanes are an extreme example).
Bryan Miller (1983)

Whenever I go to a restaurant I don't know, I always ask to meet the chef before I eat. For I know that if he is thin, I won't eat well. And if he's thin and sad, there's nothing for it but to run.   *Fernand Point*

Once upon a time we occasionally got half-fare on the railroads. Now we get it in the restaurants all the time.   *'Syracuse Herald'*

I never eat in a restaurant that's over a hundred feet off the ground and won't stand still.
Calvin Trillin (1979)

NATIONS

NATIONALITIES

What are the six most dangerous things in the world?
A drunken Irishman with a broken whiskey bottle,
An Italian with an education,
A Mexican with a driver's licence,
A Jew with authority,
A Greek with tennis shoes, and
A Frenchman with a chipped tooth. *Anon*

What are the five shortest books in the world?
Jewish Business Ethics,
Italian War Heroes,
The Complete History of German Humour,
Great British Lovers, and
Who's Who in Puerto Rico. *Anon*

Frustrate a Frenchman, he will drink himself to death; an Irishman, will die of angry hypertension; a Dane, he will shoot himself; an American, he will get drunk, shoot you, then establish a million dollar aid program for your relatives. Then he will die of an ulcer.
Stanley Rudin (1963)

If one only could teach the English how to speak and the Irish how to listen – society would be quite civilised. *Oscar Wilde*

SPECIFIC

ARGENTINA

An Argentine is an Italian who speaks Spanish, thinks he's French, but would like to be English. *Anon*

AUSTRALIA

The Australian temper is at bottom grim, it is as though the hot sun has dried up his nature.
Sir Neville Cardus (1934)

Australians can, and do, quite readily and often in my experience, throw off all their 180 years of civilised nationhood; they gaily revive every

prejudice they ever knew, whether to do with accent, class consciousness or even the original convict complex, and sally forth into battle with a dedication which would not disgrace the most committed of the world's political agitators. *Ted Dexter (1972)*

Violently loud alcoholic roughnecks whose idea of fun is to throw up in your car.
P. J. O'Rourke – 'National Lampoon' (1976)

AUSTRIA

No Italian can hate the Austrians more than I do; unless it be the English, the Austrians seem to me the most obnoxious race under the sun.
Lord Byron (1820)

The Viennese, speaking generally, dislike and misunderstand anything serious and sensible; they care only for trash – burlesques, harlequinades, magical tricks, farces and antics.
Leopold Mozart (1768)

BELGIUM

A Belgian is a hell living on earth.
Charles Baudelaire (1864)

CANADA

A Canadian is a person who knows how to make love in a canoe. *Pierre Berton*

Canadians are concerned about the rape of our country by the Americans. And I say that it is not true – how can you rape a prostitute?
Dave Broadfoot

You have to know a man awfully well in Canada to know his surname. *John Buchan*

Canadians have been accustomed to define themselves by saying what they are not.
William Kilbourn

A Canadian is someone who knows he is going somewhere, but isn't sure where. *W. L. Morton*

Canadians are the white, Protestant, heterosexual ghetto of the north.

Mordecai Richler

Canadians are generally indistinguishable from Americans, and the surest way of telling the two apart is to make the observation to a Canadian.

Richard Staines

A Torontonian is a man who leaves culture to his wife.

B. K. Sandwell

CHINA

Chinese is a language of 15 000 words and none of them in English.

Anon

CYPRUS

Realising that they will never be a world power, the Cypriots have decided to settle for being a world nuisance.

George Mikes

DENMARK

Beer is the Danish national drink and the Danish national weakness is another beer.

Clementine Paddleford (1964)

ENGLAND

English inventions tend to mechanise other nations. England seems bent on seeing the whole world as dull as itself, and dull in the same way.

Honore de Balzac

The most dangerous thing in the world is to make a friend of an Englishman, because he'll come sleep in your closet rather than spend ten shillings on a hotel.

Truman Capote

The English never draw a line without blurring it.

Sir Winston Churchill

The English think incompetence is the same thing as sincerity.

Quentin Crisp

An Englishman is a man who lives on an island in the North Sea governed by Scotsmen.

Philip Guedella – 'Supers and Superman'

From every Englishman emanates a kind of gas,

The deadly choke-damp·of boredom.

Heinrich Heine

I am firmly convinced that a blaspheming Frenchman is a spectacle more pleasing to the Lord than a praying Englishman.

Heinrich Heine

In dealing with Englishmen you can be sure of one thing only, that the logical solution will not be adopted.

William Inge

The English are so bloody nosey.

Elton John

Curse the blasted jelly-boned swines, the slimy belly-wriggling invertebrates, the miserable sodding rotters, the flaming sods, the snivelling, dribbling, dithering, palsied pulseless lot that make up England today. They've got white of egg in their veins, and their spunk is that watery it's a marvel they can breed. Why, why, why, was I born an Englishman!

D. H. Lawrence (1912)

England is a country infested with people who love to tell us what to do, but who very rarely seem to know what's going on.

Colin MacInnes

Three things to beware of – The hoof of a horse, the horn of a bull, and the smile of an Englishman.

Seumas MacManus

The English are always ready to admire anything so long as they can queue up.

George Mikes – 'How to be an Alien'

The English are a busy people; they do not have time to become elegant and refined.

Charles Montesquieu

Not only is England an island, but so is every Englishman.

Novalis

An Englishman is a creature who thinks he is being virtuous when he is only being uncomfortable.

G. B. Shaw

The whole strength of England lies in the fact that the enormous majority of the English people are snobs.

G. B. Shaw

The English are a nation of shopkeepers.

Adam Smith – 'The Wealth of Nations'

The Englishman's truly distinctive disease is his cherished habit of waiting until the 13th hour.   *Arnold Toynbee*

The English think soap is civilisation.
                    Heinrich von Treitschke

Nothing is more evident than that Nature hates Mind. Thinking is the most unhealthy thing in the world, and people die of it just as they die of any other disease. Fortunately, in England at any rate, thought is not catching.   *Oscar Wilde*

The English have an extraordinary ability for flying into a great calm.   *Alexander Woollcott*

In order to appreciate England one has to have a certain contempt for logic.   *Lin Yutang*

Shake a bridle over a Yorkshireman's grave and he will rise and steal a horse.
                    Lancashire saying

FRANCE

The French are a low lot. Give them two more legs and a tail, and there you are.
                    Helen Choate Bell

The simple thing is to consider the French as an erratic and brilliant people, who have all the gifts except that of running their country.
    James Cameron – 'News Chronicle' (1954)

Frenchmen are like grains of gunpowder – each by itself smutty and contemptible, but mass them together and they are terrible indeed.
    Samuel T. Coleridge – 'Table Talk' (1831)

A Frenchman is a German with good food.
                    Fran Lebowitz

If you're going to Paris you would do well to remember this: no matter how politely or distinctly you ask a Parisian a question he will persist in answering you in French.
                    Fran Lebowitz

When Frenchmen are talking, never lift the needle off the gramophone: it only goes back to the beginning.   *Oliver Lyttleton*

The French are sawed-off cissies who eat snails and slugs and cheese that smells like people's feet. Utter cowards who force their own children to drink wine, they gibber like baboons even when you try to speak to them in their own wimpy language.
    P. J. O'Rourke – 'National Lampoon' (1976)

The ignorance of French society gives one a rough sense of the infinite.   *Joseph E. Renan*

French is the true and native language of insincerity.   *Alfred Sutro*

GERMANY

A German always has the courage of his Jewish neighbour's convictions.   *Anon*

The German mind has a talent for making no mistakes but the very greatest.   *Clifton Fadiman*

Everything German is odious to me.
Everything German affects me like an emetic.
The German language rends my ears.
                    Heinrich Heine

Germans abroad are no better than exported beer.   *Heinrich Heine*

One German makes a philosopher, two a public meeting, three a war.   *Robert MacDonald –
                    'Summit Conference' (1982)*

German is a language which was developed solely to afford the speaker the opportunity to spit at strangers under the guise of polite conversation.   *'National Lampoon' (1973)*

Everything ponderous, viscous, and solemnly clumsy, all long-winded and boring types of style are developed in profuse variety among Germans.   *Friedrich Nietzsche*

The Germans are like women, you can scarcely ever fathom their depths – they haven't any.
                    Friedrich Nietzsche (1888)

German is the most extravagantly ugly language – it sounds like someone using a sick bag on a 747.   *Willy Rushton (1984)*

Whenever the literary German dives into a sentence, that is the last you are going to see of him till he emerges on the other side of his Atlantic with his verb in his mouth.

> *Mark Twain – 'A Connecticut Yankee in King Arthur's Court' (1889)*

GREAT BRITAIN

After the rebuilding of the House of Commons – The British have the distinction above all other nations of being able to put new wine into old bottles without bursting them.

> *Clement Attlee (1950)*

British Xenophobia takes the form of Insularism, and the Limeys all moved to an island some time ago to 'keep themselves to themselves', which as far as I am concerned is a good thing. *National Lampoon (1973)*

GREECE

After shaking hands with a Greek, count your fingers. *Albanian proverb*

The Greeks – dirty and impoverished descendants of a bunch of la-de-da fruit salads who invented democracy and then forgot how to use it while walking around dressed up like girls.

> *P. J. O'Rourke – 'National Lampoon' (1976)*

HUNGARY

If you have a Hungarian for a friend you don't need any enemies. *Hungarian proverb*

IRELAND

Every Irishman has a potato in his head. *Anon*

A nation of brilliant failures – the Irish.
> *Max Beerbohm*

The quiet Irishman is about as harmless as a powder magazine built over a math factory.
> *James Dunne*

The Irish people do not gladly suffer common sense. *Oliver St John Gogarty (1935)*

The Irish are a fair people; they never speak well of one another. *Samuel Johnson*

An Irishman is a guy who:
Believes everything he can't see, and nothing he can.
Has such great respect for the truth, he only uses it in emergencies.
Can lick any man in the house he is sole occupant of.
Believes salvation can be achieved by means of a weekly envelope.

> *Jim Murray – 'Los Angeles Times' (1976)*

An Irish queer is a fellow who prefers women to drink. *Sean O'Faolain*

An Irishman is a human enthymeme – all extremes and no middle. *Austin O'Malley*

An Englishman thinks while seated; a Frenchman, standing; an American, pacing; an Irishman, afterwards. *Austin O'Malley*

A fighting race who never won a battle; a pious race excelling in blasphemy; who sing of love and practise fratricide; have a harp for an emblem and no musicians, whose tongue is silver and whose heart is black.

> *Tom Penhaligon – 'The Impossible Irish'*

The Irish are an English-piquing people.
> *'Washington Post'*

ISRAEL

The Jewish man with parents alive is a fifteen-year-old boy and will remain a fifteen-year-old boy till they die.

> *Philip Roth – 'Portnoy's Complaint' (1969)*

There is only one race greater than the Jews – and that is the Derby. *Victor Sassoon*

ITALY

Except for white ruffles, pasta and opera, the Italians cannot be credited with anything.
> *Pierre Berge*

Italy is a paradise for horses, a hell for women.
> *Robert Burton (1621)*

The median Italian is a cowardly baritone who consumes 73.8 kilometres of carbohydrates a month and drives about in a car slightly smaller

than he is, looking for a divorce.
Alan Coren – 'The Sanity Inspector' (1974)

Their talk is always one octave above their
actions. *'Newsweek' (1971)*

The Italians – you can't find one who is honest.
Richard Nixon

By 1948 the Italians had begun to pull
themselves together, demonstrating once more
their astonishing ability to cope with disaster
which is so perfectly balanced by their absolute
inability to deal with success.
Gore Vidal (1977)

JAPAN

The Japanese are a people with a genius for
doing anything they set out to do as a matter of
national decision.
George Ball – 'Newsweek' (1975)

Are extremely good imitators – and so polite
they even copy the mistakes.
Earl Scruggs (1968)

The Japanese have perfected good manners and
made them indistinguishable from rudeness.
Paul Theroux

MIDDLE EAST

An Arab is a man who will pull down a whole
temple to have a stone to sit on. *Proverb*

An Arab is just a Jew on horseback. *Anon*

PERU

The only way to handle a Peruvian is to agree
with his pessimism. *Paul Theroux – 'The Old
Patagonian Express' (1979)*

POLAND

There are few virtues that the Poles do not
possess – and there are few mistakes they have
ever avoided. *Sir Winston Churchill*

SCOTLAND

There are few more impressive sights in the

world than a Scotsman on the make. *J. M. Barrie*

Their fumbled attempt at speaking the English
language has been a source of amusement for
five centuries, and their idiot music has been
dreaded by those not blessed with deafness for
at least as long.
P. J. O'Rourke – 'National Lampoon' (1976)

It requires a surgical operation to get a joke
well into Scotch understanding. *Sydney Smith*

It is never difficult to distinguish between a
Scotsman with a grievance and a ray of
sunshine. *P. G. Wodehouse (1935)*

SOUTH AFRICA

Fancy, a whole nation of lower-middle-class
Philistines! *Olive Schreiner*

SPAIN

Three Spaniards, four opinions.
Spanish proverb

A Feeble, imbecile, and superstitious race.
Napoleon Bonaparte

SWEDEN

The Swedes have their medical expenses taken
care of, all of their welfare costs paid for, their
rent subsidised, and so much done for them,
that if they lose their car keys they promptly
commit suicide. *Godfrey Cambridge*

Tedious, clean-living boy-scout types, strangers
to graffiti and littering but who possess of an
odd suicidal mania. Speculation is that they're
slowing boring themselves to death.This is
certainly the case if their cars and movies are
any indication.
P. J. O'Rourke – 'National Lampoon' (1976)

SWITZERLAND

The Swiss are not a people so much as a neat,
clean, quiet solvent business. *William Faulkner*

The Swiss are a neat and industrious people,
none of whom is under seventy-five years of
age. They make cheeses, milk chocolate, and

watches, all of which, when you come right down to it, are fairly unnecesaary.
Dorothy Parker - 'New Yorker' (1931)

A whole country of phobic handwashers living in a giant Barclays Bank.
Jonathan Raban (1979)

In Italy for thirty years under the Borgias, they had warfare, terror, murder, bloodshed. They produced Michelangelo, Leonardo da Vinci, and the Renaissance. In Switzerland, they had brotherly love, five hundred years of democracy and peace, and what did they produce? The cuckoo clock. *Orson Welles - 'Third Man' (1949)*

USA

If you can speak three languages – you're trilingual. If you can speak two languages – you're bilingual. If you can only speak one language – you're an American. *Anon*

If God had meant for Texans to ski, he would have made bullshit white. *Anon*

The palavery kind of Southerner; all that slushy gush on the surface, and no sensibilities whatever: a race without consonants and without delicacy. *Willa Cather (1926)*

The Americans are a funny lot; they drink whisky to keep them warm; then they put ice in it to make it cool; they put some sugar in it to make it sweet, and then they put a slice of lemon in it to make it sour. Then they say 'here's to you' and drink it themselves.
B. N. Chakravarty (1966)

The Yankee is a dab at electricity and crime,
He tells you how he hustles and it takes him quite a time.
I like his hospitality that's cordial and frank,
I do not mind his money, but I do not like his swank. *G. K. Chesterton -*
'A Song of Self-esteem' (1933)

Americans think of themselves as a huge rescue squad on twenty-four hour call to any spot on the globe where dispute and conflict may erupt.
Eldridge Cleaver

The American language is in a state of flux based on the survival of the unfittest.
Cyril Connolly - 'Sunday Times' (1966)

A Yankee is one who, if he once gets his teeth set on a thing, all creation can't make him let go. *R. W. Emerson*

Americans are like a rich father who wishes he knew how to give his sons the hardships that made him rich. *Robert Frost*

No one can be as calculatedly rude as the British, which amazes Americans, who do not understand studied insult and can only offer abuse as a substitute. *Paul Gallico*

I am willing to love all mankind, except an American. *Samuel Johnson*

Californians are the biggest collection of losers who ever met on one piece of real estate.
David Karp - 'New York Times' (1968)

Americans are the great Satan – the wounded snake. *Ayatollah Khomeini (1986)*

Americans are people who laugh at African witch doctors and spend 100 million dollars on fake reducing systems. *L. L. Levinson*

Nobody ever went broke underestimating the taste of the American public. *H. L. Mencken*

The American people, taking one with another, constitute the most timorous, snivelling, poltroonish, ignominious mob of serfs and goosesteppers ever gathered under one flag in Christendom since the end of the Middle Ages.
H. L. Mencken - 'Prejudices' (1922)

America's dissidents are not committed to mental hospitals and sent into exile; they thrive and prosper and buy a house in Nantucket and take flyers in the commodities market.
Ted Morgan -
'On Becoming an American' (1978)

America is where the wildest human on the planet came to do anything they damn well pleased. *P. J. O'Rourke - 'Rolling Stone' (1982)*

Look at the typical American family scene:

Man walkin' around fartin'. Woman walkin'
around scratchin'. Kids goin' around hollerin'.
Hey man, f*** that!   *Elvis Presley*

The people of America are just not born with
culture.   *Phil Spector*

The trouble with the American public is that it
thinks something is better than nothing.
                                       Alfred Stieglitz

For every American Art has no marvel, and
Beauty has no meaning, and the Past has no
message.   *Oscar Wilde*

Pessimism is as American as apple pie – frozen
apple pie with a slice of processed cheese.
                                       George F. Will (1982)

The thing that impresses me most about
America is the way parents obey their children.
                                       The Duke of Windsor

In the USA 'First' and 'Second' class can't be
painted on railroad cars, for all passengers,
being Americans, are equal and it would be 'un-
American.' But paint 'Pullman' on a car and
everyone is satisfied.   *Owen Wister*

A Bostonian is an American, broadly speaking.
                                       G. E. Woodberry

USSR

The essential clue to Russian literature, as
indeed to the mysterious Russian character, is
that all Russians are shits.   *Evelyn Waugh*

WALES

A Welshman is a man who prays on his knees
on Sundays and preys on his neighbours all the
rest of the week.   *Anon*

PLACES

Aberystwyth, Wales
The perfect town for the unambitious man.
                                       Wynford Vaughan-Thomas –
                                       'Trust to Talk' (1980)

The Alamo, Texas
On what he might do with his $30 000 [1967 US

Open] prize-money – I may buy the Alamo and
give it back to Mexico.   *Lee Trevino*
After seeing the Alamo – I'm not going to buy this
place, it doesn't have any inside plumbing.

All-Hallows, England
All-Hallows-on-Sea looked as though it was
built for fun, and something happened to
frighten the revellers away. *Norman Shrapnell –*
                                       'A View of the Thames' (1977)

The Alps, Europe
Such uncouth rocks and such uncomely
inhabitants! I hope I shall never see them again.
                                       Horace Walpole (1739)

Amsterdam, Holland
A paltry, rubbishy Venice.
                                       William Hazlitt – 'Notes' (1826)

Ancona, Italy
Filthy hole, like rotten cabbage.
                                       James Joyce (1906)

Atlantic Ocean
Disappointing.   *Oscar Wilde*

Baden-Baden, Germany
One is left with a strong impression that
Baden-Baden was built on undelivered faeces.
                                       Alex Comfort – 'The Anxiety Makers' (1967)

Baltimore, USA
Baltimore is such a lousy town, Francis Scott
Key went out in a boat to write 'The Star
Spangled Banner'.   *Billy Martin*

Barry, Wales
A one-eyed Godforsaken town, made out of
odds and ends stuck down anywhere, all new
houses, docks, coal tips, and railway sidings,
and nowhere to go. It's best to stay aboard in
Barry.   *H. M. Tomlinson – 'The Seas and*
                                       the Jungle' (1912)

Bath, England
One of the most disagreeable places in the
world.   *Sydney Smith (1820)*

Bedford, England
A cemetery with traffic lights.
                                       Anon American G.I. (1946)

Beverly Hills, USA

If you stay in Beverly Hills too long you become a Mercedes.   *Robert Redford*

Bexhill, England

Filthy hole, dull, and I gather, purseproud.
James Agate – 'Ego 2' (1934)

Birmingham, England

One has not great hopes from Birmingham. I always say there is something direful in the sound.   *Jane Austen – 'Emma' (1816)*

Boston, USA

I have just returned from Boston. It is the only thing to do if you find yourself up there.
Fred Allen

A festering mud puddle.   *Ellis Arnall*

Boston is a city with champagne tastes and beer pocketbooks.   *Alan Friedberg*

A moral and intellectual nursery always busy applying first principles to trifles.
George Santayana

Tomorrow night I appear for the first time before a Boston audience – 4,000 critics.
Mark Twain

If I lived there, I'd move.   *Sarah Vaughan*

Clear out eight hundred thousand people and preserve it as a museum piece.
Frank Lloyd Wright

Cairo, Egypt

There is not perhaps upon earth a more dirty metropolis.
John Carne – 'Letters from the East' (1830)

This dismal Cairo, an ugly sepulchre, a grave uncheered by any gleam of promise.
Charles Dickens

Calcutta, India

One of the most wicked Places in the Universe.
Robert Clive (1765)

Calcutta is a definition of obscenity.
Geoffrey Moorehouse – 'Calcutta' (1971)

California, USA

His great aim was to escape from civilisation, and, as soon as he had money, he went to Southern California.   *Anon*

California is so wonderful – on a clear day when the fog lifts, you can see the smog.   *Anon*

California is the only place where you can have all four seasons in one day.   *Anon*

I wouldn't live in California. All that sun makes you sterile.   *Alan Alda*

A fine place to live in – if you happen to be an orange.   *Fred Allen*

It's a scientific fact that if you stay in California you lose one point of your IQ every year.   *Truman Capote*

The department store state.   *Raymond Chandler*

The West coast of Iowa.   *Joan Didion*

California is a place in which a boom mentality and a sense of Chekovian loss meet in uneasy suspension.   *Joan Didion*

A wet dream in the mind of New York.
Erica Jong

There's nothing wrong with South California that a rise in the ocean level wouldn't cure.
Ross MacDonald

Mistresses are more common in California – in fact, some of them are very common. It's easier for a man to conceal his mistress there because of the smog.   *Groucho Marx*

The California climate makes the sick well and the well sick, the old young and the young old.
H. L. Mencken

In Southern California the vegetables have no flavour and the flowers have no smell.
H. L. Mencken

California is where you can't run any farther without getting wet.   *Neil Morgan (1967)*

California is where the twentieth-century is a

burning and a shining neon light, and where, anyway, cows are rarely seen out-of-doors nowadays.
Malcolm Muggeridge - 'The Observer' (1965)

A place with lots of warm weather and lots of cold people. *Vanessa Redgrave*

Living in California adds ten years to a man's life. And those extra ten years I'd like to spend in New York. *Harry Ruby*

Most people in California came from somewhere else. They moved to California so they could name their kids Rainbow or Mailbox, and purchase tubular Swedish furniture without getting laughed at. *Ian Shoales*

Cambridge, England
An asylum in more senses than one.
A. E. Housman (1911)

Chicago, USA
It's a joint where the bulls and the foxes live well and the lambs wind up head-down from the hook.
Nelson Algren - 'Chicago: City on the Make'

An October sort of city even in spring.
Nelson Algren

Merely a place to change trains. *Jane Byrne*

Chicago is not the most corrupt American city, it's the most theatrically corrupt.
Dick Cavett (1978)

Chicago is a product of modern capitalism, and like other great commercial centres is unfit for human habitation. *Eugene Debs (1908)*

A town with a Queen Anne front and a Queen Mary back.
Paul H. Douglas - 'New York Times' (1977)

A façade of skyscrapers facing a lake and behind the façade every kind of dubiousness.
E. M. Forster

A city of terror and light, untamed. *W. L. George*

Most cities have a smell of their own. Chicago

smells like it's not sure. *Alan King*

Having seen it, I urgently desire never to see it again. It is inhabited by savages. Its air is dirt.
Rudyard Kipling

A pompous Milwaukee. *L. L. Levinson*

Hog Butcher for the World . . . Stormy, husky, brawling. City of the Big Shoulders.
Carl Sandburg - 'Chicago'

Here is the difference between Dante, Milton and me. They wrote about hell and never saw the place. I wrote about Chicago after looking the town over for years and years.
Carl Sandburg

This vicious, stinking zoo, this mean-grinning, mace-smelling boneyard of a city; an elegant rockpile of a monument to everything cruel and stupid in the human spirit. *Hunter S. Thompson*

Cleveland, USA
Suggested motto - You gotta live somewhere.
Jimmy Brogan

We are now arriving in Cleveland. Set back your watches forty-two minutes. *Tim McCarver*

Two Hobokens back-to-back. *Joan Holman*

Cologne, Germany
In Koln, a town of monks and bones,
And pavements, fang'd with murderous stones,
And rags, and hags, and hideous wenches;
I counted two and seventy stenches,
All well defined, and several stinks!
Ye nymphs that reign o'er sewers and sinks,
The river Rhine, is well known,
Doth wash your city of Cologne;
But tell me, nymphs, what power divine
Shall henceforth wash the river Rhine?
Samuel T. Coleridge

Cologne is in size considerable, in aspect uncompromising, and in smell odious.
William Thackeray (1830)

Colorado, USA
This state has more sunshine and more bastards than any place on earth! *Anon*

The Rift Valley makes the Grand Canyon of the Colorado look like a line scratched with a toothpick.   *John Gunther – 'Inside Africa' (1955)*

Coney Island, NY, USA
A place where surf is one third water and two thirds people.   *Anon*

Costa del Sol, Spain
Variously known as the Coca Cola Coast and Costa Mierda, for which a genteel translation would be the Coast of Dung.   *Kenneth Tynan – 'Tynan Right and Left' (1967)*

Delaware, USA
A state that has three counties when the tide is out, and two when it is in.   *J. J. Inglis*

Delhi, India
Delhi is the capital of the losing streak. It is the metropolis of the crossed wire, the missed appointment, the puncture, the wrong number.   *Jan Morris – 'Destinations' (1980)*

The East
The world's getting too small. The Near East is too near and the Far East isn't far enough.   *Lou Erickson – 'Atlanta Journal'*

Eastern Europe
I've played [*tennis*] behind the Iron Curtain, and those squalid East European countries are disastrous. I hate it there. I mean, it's a luxury if you can eat eggs for breakfast.   *'Buster' Mottram*

Edinburgh, Scotland
That most picturesque (at a distance) and nastiest (when near) of all capital cities.   *Thomas Gray*

Florida, USA
God's waiting room.   *Glenn le Grice*

Alaska with Jai-alai games.   *Robert Orben*

Frankfurt, Germany
When God made Frankfurt-am-Main, he shat a lump of concrete.   *Gunter Grass*

Giant's Causeway, Ireland
Worth seeing, but not worth going to see.   *Samuel Johnson*

Glasgow, Scotland
When I hear the word Glasgow, I reach for my revolver.   *Colin M. Jarman (1989)*

Gloucestershire, England
Gloucestershire is now one big car park for Volvos with a few scattered trees.   *Stephen Pile – 'Sunday Times'*

Hamburg, Germany
It's a sad place. In this epithet you have the soul and essence of all the information which I have been able to gather.   *William Wordsworth (1798)*

Houston, Texas
This city has been an act of real estate rather than an act of God or man.   *Ada Louisa Huxtable – 'New York Times' (1976)*

Houston is twenty of the most innovative buildings in this country and 2000 rather ordinary gas stations.   *Denis Williams – 'Newsweek' (1977)*

Hudson's Bay, Canada
I've never seen such a Miserable Place in my life.   *Captain James Knight – 'Journal' (1717)*

Indiana, USA
The home of more first-rate second-class men than any other state in the union.   *Thomas Marshall*

Jaffa, Israel
The streets of Jaffa are narrow and are composed of four equal parts of donkey, camel, native and mud.   *Lilian Leland – 'Travelling Alone' (1890)*

Jerusalem, Israel
In Tel Aviv the weekends last 48 hours. In Jerusalem they last 6 months.   *Zev Chavets (1967)*

Las Vegas, USA
The land of the spree and home of the knave.   *Anon*

It's like a garbage disposal for money.
Robert Orben

A monument to the Mafia's ability to cater to the lowest form of lust in the souls of the American people; to give the suckers what they want. It's the biggest joke that's ever been played on the people of the United States.
Thomas Perry (1982)

Llantrisant, Wales

After the Royal Mint had been relocated there –
The hole with a Mint! *Anon*

London, England

Take a perfect day, add six hours of rain and fog, and you have instant London. *US saying*

London is a splendid place to live for those who can get out of it. *Lord Balfour*

That monstrous tuberosity of civilised life, the capital of England. *Thomas Carlyle*

That great cesspool into which all the loungers of Europe are irresistibly drained.
Arthur Conan Doyle

A place you go to get bronchitis. *Fran Lebowitz*

Dirty little pool of life. *B. M. Malabari*

I hate London when it's not raining.
Groucho Marx

When it's three o'clock in New York, it's still 1938 in London. *Bette Midler (1978)*

Hell is a city much like London –
A populous and smoky city. *Percy B. Shelley*

London, like a bowl of viscid human fluid, boils sullenly over the rim of its encircling hills and slops messily and uglily into the home counties.
H. G. Wells

Los Angeles, USA

A big hard-boiled city with no more personality than a paper cup. *Raymond Chandler*

A city lost and beaten and full of emptiness.
Raymond Chandler

Everything in L.A. is too large, too loud and usually banal in concept. The plastic asshole of the world. *William Faulkner*

Oh to be in L.A. when the polyethyl-vinyl trees are in bloom. *Herb Gold*

A kind of post-urban process rather than a city.
Herb Gold (1978)

A large citylike area surrounding the Beverly Hills Hotel.
Fran Lebowitz – 'Social Studies' (1981)

In 1956 the population of Los Angeles was 2 243 901. By 1970 it had risen to 2 811 801, 1 650 917 of whom are currently up for a series.
Fran Lebowitz

The chief products of LA are novelisations, salad, game-show hosts, points, muscle tone, mini-series and rewrites. They export all of these items with the twin exceptions of muscle tone and points, neither of which seem to travel well. *Fran Lebowitz*

L.A. – that Queen City of Plastic.
Norman Mailer (1969)

Nineteen suburbs in search of a metropolis.
H. L. Mencken

A pasture foreordained for the cow-town evangelism of a former sideshow wriggler.
H. L. Mencken

Los Angeles is fertile soil for every kind of imposter that the face of the earth has been cursed by. The suckers all come sooner or later and the whole twelve months is open season.
H. L. Mencken

It is hereby earnestly proposed that the USA would be much better off if that big, sprawling incoherent, shapeless, slobbering civic idiot in the family of American communities, the City of Los Angeles, could be declared incompetent and placed in charge of a guardian like any individual mental defective. *Westbrook Pegler*

On how he would train for the L. A. Olympics Marathon – I'll start the car in the garage and run in there. *Alberto Salazar (1982)*

The city seems dead as putrefying squid with plastic varicose veins stapled into a plastic body.

Harrison Salisbury (1976)

The serial mass murder capital of the world.

Sheriff Alfred Sett

The city of angels; where every cockroach has a screenplay and even the winos wear roller-skates. It's that kind of town.   *Ian Shoales*

When it's five below in New York, it's 78 in Los Angeles, and when it's 110 in New York, it's 78 in Los Angeles. There are two million interesting people in New York, and only seventy-eight in Los Angeles.

Neil Simon – 'Playboy' (1979)

The difference between Los Angeles and yoghurt, is that yoghurt has real culture.

Tom Taussik (1982)

If you tilt the whole country sideways, Los Angeles is the place where everything loose will fall.   *Daniel Webster*

Los Angeles has of course been called every name in the book, from 'nineteen suburbs in search of a metropolis' to 'a circus without a tent' to 'less a city than a perpetual convention'.   *Frank Lloyd Wright*

Lusaka, Zambia
Lusaka looks like a Wild West set in early, shabby movies.

John Gunther – 'Inside Africa' (1955)

Lyons, France
It's a great nightmare – a bad conscience – a fit of indigestion – the recollection of having done a murder. An awful place!

Charles Dickens (1844)

Madrid, Spain
At best Madrid is a hole but in rainy weather it is a place fit only to drown rats.

Henry Adams (1870)

Maine, USA
Maine is as dead, intellectually, as Abyssinia. Nothing is ever heard from it.   *H. L. Mencken*

Manchester, England
I would like to live in Manchester, England. The transition between Manchester and death would be unnoticeable.   *Mark Twain*

Manhattan, New York, USA
The only real advantage of New York is that all its inhabitants ascend to heaven right after their deaths, having served their full term in hell right on Manhattan Island.

'Barnard Bulletin' (1967)

A narrow island off the coast of New Jersey devoted to the pursuit of lunch.

Raymond Sokolov – 'Wall Street Journal' (1984)

Margate, England
The curse of the Ministry of Health, the despair of the architect, the salvation of the umbrella trade.   *'Manchester Guardian' (1941)*

Messina, Italy
This place is vastly dirty. Dirtyissimo.

Edward Lear (1866)

Miami, USA
Miami Beach is where neon goes to die.

Lenny Bruce

Minneapolis, USA
May your soul be forever tormented by fire and your bones dug up by dogs and dragged through the streets of Minneapolis.

Garrison Keillor (1982)

Mississippi River, USA
By what words shall we describe the Mississippi, great father of waters, who (praise to Heaven) has no children like him! An enormous ditch, sometimes two or three miles wide, running liquid mud.

Charles Dickens (1842)

Montreal, Canada
Montreal is the only place where a good French accent isn't a social asset.   *Brendan Behan*

Moscow, USSR
Moscow is a depressing place. To me its atmosphere is somehow suggestive of servants' bedrooms.

Peter Fleming – 'One's Company' (1934)

Moscow is the only city where, if Marilyn Monroe walked down the street with nothing on but a pair of shoes, people would stare at her feet first.

John Gunther – 'Inside Russia Today' (1962)

New England, USA
The most serious charge which can be brought against New England is not Puritanism, but February.   *Joseph Wood Krutch (1949)*

I wonder if anybody ever reached the age of thirty-five in New England without wanting to kill himself?   *Barrett Wendell (1924)*

Newhaven, England
Newhaven is spot and rash and pimple and blister; with the incessant cars like lice.

Virginia Woolf – 'Diary' (1921)

New Jersey, USA
New Jersey looks like the back of an old radio.

Josh Greenfeld

Suggested motto – What died?   *Steven Pearl*

The cities are indifferent and dingy, the people are seedy and dull, a kind of sloppiness and mediocrity seems to have fallen on the fields themselves, as if Nature had turned slattern and could no longer keep herself dressed.

Edmund Wilson (1924)

New York, USA
An island full of clip joints.   *Anon*

A city of brotherly shove.   *Anon*

The first thing that strikes a stranger in the Big Apple is a taxi-cab.   *Anon*

New York has absolutely everything except a past.   *Louis Auchinloss*

The only city in the world where you can get deliberately run down on the sidewalk by a pedestrian.   *Russell Baker*

This muck heaves and palpitates. It is multidirectional and has a mayor.

Donald Barthelme

I hate the city, the environment . . . they should

drop an A-Bomb on the place.   *Kevin Curren*

Hell is New York city with all the escape hatches sealed.   *James R. Frakes (1972)*

The only New York image that has permanently impressed itself on the national mind is that of Wall Street – a street on which nobody lives. Paris may be France, London may be England, but New York we continue to reassure ourselves, is not America.

*Nathan Glazer & Daniel Moynihan –
'Beyond the Melting Pot'*

If there ever was an aviary overstocked with jays it is that Yaptown-on-the-Hudson called New York.   *O. Henry*

A city where everyone mutinies but no one deserts.

Harry Hershfield – 'New York Post' (1974)

The posthumous revenge of the Merchant of Venice.   *Elbert Hubbard*

New York is appalling, fantastically charmless and elaborately dire.   *Henry James (1904)*

I don't like the life here in New York. There is no greenery. It would make a stone sick.

Nikita Krushchev (1960)

When you leave New York, you are astonished at how clean the rest of the world is.

Fran Lebowitz

Every year when it's Chinese New Year in New York, there are fireworks going off at all hours. New York mothers calm their frightened children by telling them it's just gunfire.

David Letterman

A car is useless in New York, essential everywhere else. The same with good manners.

Mignon McLaughlin (1966)

A third-rate Babylon.   *H. L. Mencken*

It is simply a sort of free port – a place where the raw materials of civilisation are received, sorted out, and sent on further.   *H. L. Mencken*

The nation's thyroid gland.   *Christopher Morley*

The Bronx?
No, thonx!   *Ogden Nash – 'New Yorker' (1931)*

Vulgar of manner, overfed,
Overdressed and underbred;
Heartless, Godless, hell's delight,
Rude by day and lewd by night . . .
Crazed with avarice, lust and rum,
New York, thy name's Delirium.
            Brian Rufus Newton (1906)

A New Yorker is a person with an almost
inordinate interest in mental health, which is
only natural considering how much of that it
takes to live here.   *'New York Times' (1986)*

I've been a New Yorker for ten years, and the
only people who are nice to me are the
Moonies.   *P. J. O'Rourke*

When I went to New York in the airplane, I saw
a picture in the clouds and I got my pencil right
out. I drew something with long tail and horns.
            Nellie Mae Rowe

New York is not Mecca. It just smells like it.
     Neil Simon – 'California Suite' (1976)

The pneumatic noisemaker is becoming the
emblematic Sound of New York, the way the
bells of Big Ben are the Sound of London.
            Horace Sutton

A disco without the music.   *Elaine Strich*

A city of 7,000,000 so decadent that when I
leave it I never dare look back lest I turn into
salt and the conductor throw me over his
shoulder for good luck.   *Frank Sullivan*

Nova Scotia, Canada
Bangladesh on the St Lawrence.   *Anon*

Oakland, USA
The trouble with Oakland is that when you get
there, there isn't any there.   *Gertrude Stein*

The trouble with Oakland is that when you get
there, it's there.   *Herb Caen*

Odessa, USSR
The dingiest, most dog-eared town I saw . . . it

looks as if mould were growing all over it.
     John Gunther – 'Inside Russia' (1962)

Omaha, USA
Omaha is a little like Newark [New Jersey] –
without Newark's glamour.   *Joan Rivers*

Ottawa, Canada
A city where nobody lives, though some of us
may die there.   *Michael Macklen*

A sub-arctic lumber village converted by royal
mandate into a political cock-pit.
            Goldwin Smith

Oxford, England
I had always assumed that cliché was a suburb
of Paris, until I discovered it to be a street in
Oxford.   *Philip Guedella*

Paris, France
Paris is a disease; sometimes it is several
diseases.   *Honoré de Balzac*

Paris is a great city of gaieties and pleasures,
where four-fifths of the inhabitants die of grief.
            Nicholas de Chamfort

A city asleep – and snoring loudly.   *Ned Rorem*

Paris is what it has always been: a pedant-
ridden failure in everything that it pretends to
be.
     G. B. Shaw – 'London Music'

A chaos, a throng where everybody hunts for
pleasure and hardly anybody finds it.   *Voltaire*

It is the ugliest town in the universe.
            Horace Walpole (1765)

Pasadena, USA
A cemetery with lights.   *Anon*

Peking [Beijing], China
What this place needs is a few good paint
salesmen.   *Anon Australian visitor*

Philadelphia, USA
Philadelphia is an old wino sleeping it off in the
doorway littered with busted dreams. Its teams
are doomed to lose and its fans are cruel and
crabbed.   *Jimmy Cannon*

Philadelphia is not a town, it's a jungle. They don't have gyms there; they have zoos. They don't have sparring session; they have wars.
Angelo Dundee

All the filth and corruption of a big city; all the pettiness and insularity of a small town.
Howard Ogden

A metropolis sometimes known as the City of Brotherly Love, but more accurately as the City of Bleak November Afternoons.
S. J. Perelman

The streets are safe in Philadelphia, it's only the people who make them unsafe. *Frank Rizzo*

Pittsburgh, USA
Hell with the lid off. *Charles Dickens*

Abandon it. *Frank Lloyd Wright – 'New York Times' (1955)*

Port Au Prince, Haiti
A sort of slum Venice in which the canals are open drains.
Norman Lewis – 'The Changing Sky' (1959)

Princeton, USA
Princeton is a wonderful little spot. A quaint and ceremonious village of puny demigods on stilts. ` Albert Einstein

Quebec, Canada
Quebec is one of the ten provinces against which Canada is defending itself. *Carl Dubuc*

Reno, USA
The land of the free and the home of the grave.
Anon

Sue City. *Anon*

Rhine River, Europe
Seems to me one of the few really ugly rivers in the world. *Leonard Woolf – 'Downhill All the Way' (1967)*

Rome, Italy
Rome, Italy, is an example of what happens when the buildings in a city last too long.
Andy Warhol –'The Philosophy of . . .' (1975)

Ronciglione, Italy
A little town like a large pig-sty.
Charles Dickens – 'Pictures from Italy' (1946)

San Diego, USA
San Diego didn't look like the kind of town where people get born. *Steve Elman*

San Francisco, USA
The moral penal colony of the world.
Ambrose Bierce

Nothing important has ever come out of San Francisco, Rice-A-Roni aside.
Michael O'Donoghue

The coldest winter I ever spent was a summer in San Francisco. *Mark Twain*

Selma, USA
Just as in the anatomy of man, every nation must have its hind part.
Robert Indiana [Robert Clark] (1966)

South Dakota, USA
A part of hell with the fires burnt out.
General Custer

South Pole
Great God! This is an awful place.
Robert F. Scott – 'Journal' (1912)

St Moritz, Switzerland
St Moritz, the heart of the broken-limb country, where a man must prove himself first on skis and then on a stretcher.
Art Buchwald – 'I Chose Caviar" (1957)

Sun City, USA
The average age of Sun City is deceased.
Bob Uecker

Sydney, Australia
Manchester with a harbour backdrop.
Robert Morley (1968)

Texas, USA
Parts of Texas look like Kansas with goitre.
Anon

Texas is the third most urbanised state (behind New York and California) with all the tangles, stench, random violence, architectural rape,

historical pillage, neon blight, pollution and ecological imbalance the term implies.
Larry King (1975)

The place where there are the most cows and the least milk and the most rivers and least water in them, and where you can look the farthest and see the least. *H. L. Mencken*

If I owned Texas and Hell, I would rent out Texas and live in Hell.
Gen. Philip H. Sheridan (1855)

Toronto, Canada

The whole city is an immense house of ill-fame.
C. S. Clark (1826–1909)

Methodism and money in this city have produced a sort of hell of dullness.
Wyndham Lewis

Valencia, Spain

The wart on the Mediterranean lip. *Anon*

Pittsburgh with the air pollution. *Anon*

Venice, Italy

The only place where you can get seasick by crossing the street. *Anon*

Telegram to his Editor– Streets flooded. Please advise. *Robert Benchley*

A city for beavers.
Ralph Waldo Emerson – 'Journal' (1833)

Venice is excessively ugly in the rain: it looks like King's Cross. *John Gielgud (1953)*

Venice would be a fine city if it were only drained. *Ulysses S. Grant (1879)*

Washington DC, USA

A city where half of the people wait to be discovered and the other half are afraid they will be. *Anon*

Hubbub of the Universe. *Anon*

The more I observed Washington, the more frequently I visited it, and the more people I interviewed there, the more I understood how prophetic L'Enfant was when he laid it out as a city that goes around in circles.
John Mason Brown

No place for a civilised man to spend the summer. *James Buchanan*

A place where men praise courage and act on elaborate personal cost-benefit calculations.
J. K. Galbraith

My God! What is there in this place that a man should ever want to get into it? *James Garfield*

Washington is not a place to live in. The rents are high, the food is bad, the dust is disgusting and the morals are deplorable.
Horace Greeley – 'New York Tribune' (1865)

A town of famous men and the women they married when they were young.
Mrs Oliver Wendell Holmes

An endless series of mock palaces clearly built for clerks. *Ada Louisa Huxtable*

A city of southern efficiency and northern charm. *John F. Kennedy*

A city of cocker spaniels . . . a city of people who are more interested in being petted and admired, loved, than rendering the exercise of power. *Elliot L. Richardson –*
'New York Times' (1982)

The only place where sound travels faster than light. *C. V. R. Thompson –*
'Reader's Digest' (1949)

SEXES

MEN

Women have their faults. Men have only two:
Everything they say. Everything they do.
Anon

If they can put one man on the moon, why
can't they put them all there? *Anon*

Man is the missing link between the ape and
the human being. *Anon*

Adam came first, but men always do. *Anon*

A gentleman is any man who wouldn't hit a
woman with his hat on. *Fred Allen*

I married beneath me. All women do.
Nancy Astor

The fastest way to a man's heart is through his
chest. *Roseanne Barr*

Behind almost every woman you ever heard
stands a man who let her down. *Naomi Bliven*

A puny, slow, awkward, unarmed animal.
Jacob Bronowski

God Created Adam – Then Corrected HER
Mistake. *Brooklyn Women's Bar Association*

I refuse to consign the whole male sex to the
nursery. I insist on believing that some men are
my equals. *Brigid Brophy*

Men are the cause of women hating one
another. *Jean de La Bruyère*

The man is a domestic animal which, if treated
with firmness and kindness, can be trained to
do most things.
Jilly Cooper – 'Cosmopolitan' (1972)

Men's men; be they gentle or simple, they're
much of a muchness. *George Eliot*

A man in love is incomplete until he has

married. Then he's finished. *Zsa Zsa Gabor*

A kind of inverted thermometer, the bulb
uppermost, and the column of self-evaluation is
all the time going up and down.
Oliver Wendell Holmes

Men are the funniest things since silly putty.
Florence King

The average girl would rather have beauty than
brains because she knows the average man can
see much better than he can think.
'Ladies' Home Journal'

The male sex still constitutes in many ways the
most obstinate vested interest one can find.
Lord Longford

A man is a creature with two legs and eight
arms. *Jayne Mansfield*

Men are nicotine-soaked, beer-besmirched,
whisky-greased, red-eyed devils. *Carry Nation*

Husbands are a small band of men, armed only
with wallets, besieged by a horde of wives and
children. *'National Lampoon' (1979)*

I require three things of a man. He must be
handsome, ruthless, and stupid. *Dorothy Parker*

God made man, and then said I can do better
than that and made woman.
Adele Rogers St John

A husband is what is left after the nerve is
extracted. *Helen Rowland*

Inconsistency is the only thing in which men
are consistent. *Horatio Smith*

A woman needs a man like a fish needs a
bicycle. *Gloria Steinem*

Why was man created on the last day? So that
he can be told, when pride possesses him: God
created the gnat before thee. *'Talmud'*

Man – a creature made at the end of the week's work when God was tired.   *Mark Twain*

The first time you buy a house you think how pretty it is and sign the cheque. The second time you look to see if the basement has termites. It's the same with men.   *Lupe Velez*

Whatever women do they must do twice as well as men to be thought half as good. Luckily, this is not difficult.   *Charlotte Whitton*

Men become old, but they never become good.
                    Oscar Wilde

Why are women so much more interesting to men than men are to women?   *Virginia Woolf*

WOMEN

Give a woman an inch and she thinks she's a ruler.   *Anon*

A man without a woman is like a neck without a pain.   *Anon*

Some men try to climb mountains, others try to date them.   *Anon*

The tongue of woman is their sword and they take care not to let it rust.   *Chinese proverb*

A beautiful woman who is pleasing to men is good only for frightening fish when she falls into the water.   *Zen proverb*

Women have a passion for mathematics. They divide their age in half, double the price of their clothes and always add at least five years to the age of their best friend.   *Marcel Achard*

In twenty centuries scarcely twenty great women are to be counted.   *Honoré de Balzac*

Women ruin music.   *Sir Thomas Beecham*

Most women are not so young as they are painted.   *Max Beerbohm*

Woman is the organ of the devil.   *St Bernard*

Why haven't women got labels on their foreheads saying, 'Danger; Government Health Warning: women can seriously damage your brains, genitals, current account, confidence, razor blades and good standing among your friends'?   *Jeffrey Bernard – 'Spectator' (1984)*

In various stages of her life, a woman resembles the continents of the world. From: 13 to 18, she's like Africa – virgin territory; from 18 to 30, she's like Asia – hot and exotic; from 30 to 45, she's like America – fully explored and free with her resources; from 45 to 55, she's like Europe – exhausted, but not without places of interest; after 55, she's like Australia – everybody knows it's down there, but nobody much cares.   *Al Boliska*

Women are most adorable when they're afraid; that's why they frighten so easily.   *Ludwig Borne*

I wish that Adam had died with all ribs inside his body.   *Dion Boucicault*

A woman is but an animal, and an animal not of the highest stock.   *Edmund Burke*

Woman is a necessary evil, a natural temptation, a desirable calamity, a deadly fascination, and a painted ill.
                    St John Chrysostom

A woman never sees what we do for her, she only sees what we don't do.   *Georges Courteline*

What men desire is a virgin who is a whore.
                    Edward Dahlberg – 'Reasons
                    of the Heart' (1965)

The Bible says that woman is the last thing which God made. He must have made it Saturday night. It shows fatigue.
                    Alexandre Dumas

Women are like elephants to me; they're nice to look at but I wouldn't want to own one.
                    W. C. Fields

Give a woman a job and she grows balls.
                    Jack Gerber

I would not want a woman flying on my wing. I want them back where they belong. I have always said I have nothing against a woman doing anything a man can do as long as she gets home in time to cook dinner.   *Barry Goldwater*

An influential woman is one who makes a dent in the pillow next to the leader of the Western world.   *Lois Gould – 'New York Times'*

Hell is paved with women's tongues.   *Albe Guyon*

Woman is at once apple and serpent.
Heinrich Heine

In point of morals, the average woman is, even for business, too crooked.
Stephen Leacock – 'The Woman Question'

Women do not find it hard to behave like men, but they often find it extremely difficult to behave like gentlemen.   *Compton MacKenzie*

You don't know a woman until you've met her in court.   *Norman Mailer*

On one issue at least, men and women agree – they both distrust women.   *H. L. Mencken*

American women: How they mortify the flesh in order to make it appetising! Their beauty is a vast industry, their enduring allure a discipline which nuns or athletes might find excessive.
Malcolm Muggeridge – 'The Most of . . .'

When two women suddenly become friendly, it is a sign that some third woman has lost two friends.   *George J. Nathan*

Nothing is more wearying than a supremely dull woman unless it is an extremely witty one.
George J. Nathan – 'Smart Set'

Now that women astronauts are moving into the space program, we wonder if spacecraft will be redesigned with rear seats so that the ladies may exercise their rare talents for backseat driving.   *'No Comment'*

Woman was made from man's ribs, which, as any butcher will tell you, isn't the best cut.
Robert Orben

Women are one and all a set of vultures.
Petronius

I consider that women who are authors, lawyers and politicians are monsters.
Pierre Auguste Renoir

It's little questions from women about tappets that finally push men over the edge. *Philip Roth*

Women in general have no love of art; they have no proper knowledge of any; and they have no genius.   *Jean Jacques Rousseau*

Men have more problems than women. In the first place, they have to put up with women.
Françoise Sagan

A woman reading 'Playboy' feels a little like a Jew reading a Nazi manual.   *Gloria Steinem*

To endow a woman with reason, thought, wit, is to put a knife into the hands of a child.
Hippolite Taine

A woman's place is in the wrong.   *James Thurber*

Woman is generally so bad that the difference between a good and a bad woman scarcely exists.   *Leo Tolstoy*

God created man, and finding him not sufficiently alone, gave him a companion to make him feel his solitude more.
Paul Valery – 'Tel Quel' (1943)

A woman will flirt with anyone in the world as long as other people are looking on.
Oscar Wilde – 'The Picture of Dorian Gray' (1891)

Women are made to be loved, not understood.
Oscar Wilde

Women have a wonderful instinct about things. They can discover everything except the obvious.
Oscar Wilde – 'An Ideal Husband' (1895)

SEX

The conventional position makes me claustrophobic. And the others either give me a stiff neck or lockjaw.   *Tallulah Bankhead*

I could be content that we might procreate like trees, without conjunction, or that there were

any way to perpetuate the world without this trivial and vulgar way of coition: it is the foolishest act a wise man commits in all his life.
Thomas Browne (1642)

Sexual intercourse is a grossly overrated pastime; the position is undignified, the pleasure momentary and the consequences utterly damnable.
Lord Chesterfield

Whatever else can be said about sex, it cannot be called a dignified performance.
Helen Lawrenson

I think it's disgusting. Sex has always been with us, but never so flamboyantly as it is today. I was known as the 'kissless star'. My leading men used to say, 'What's the matter with me, do I have bad breath?' I said, 'No, but I'm against kissing on the screen.' In a way, a kiss is a promise, and I didn't want to create the wrong impression.
Mary Pickford

All this fuss about sleeping together. For physical pleasure I'd sooner go to my dentist any day.
Evelyn Waugh

SEX SYMBOLS

Being a sex symbol is a heavy load to carry, especially when one is tired, hurt and bewildered.
Clara Bow

A sex symbol becomes a thing. I hate being a thing.
Marilyn Monroe

They labelled me the 'Ooomph Girl'. To me, 'Ooomph' is the sound that a fat man makes when he bends over to tie his shoelaces in a phone booth.
Ann Sheridan

RETORTS

ART

James Whistler
What has Oscar in common with Art? Except that he dines at our tables and picks from our platters the plums for the pudding he peddles in the provinces. Oscar – the amiable, irresponsible, esurient Oscar – with no more sense of a picture than the fit of a coat, has the courage of the opinions of others.

Oscar Wilde
As for borrowing Mr Whistler's ideas about art, the only thoroughly original ideas I have ever heard him express have had reference to his own superiority as a painter over painters greater than himself.

Whistler
A poor thing, Oscar! – but for once, I suppose, your own!

Oscar Wilde
On Whistler's hurried pencil sketch of himself – It's a pretty poor work of art.

James Whistler
Yes. And you're a pretty poor work of nature.

Sir Edwin Landseer
How is it you never finish your work? I never understand artists who leave their paintings unfinished.

James Whistler
And I can never understand why you ever begin yours.

Jacob Epstein
Do you remember the days before we knew each other?

Mark Gertler
Yes.

Jacob Epstein
Well then, let's go back to them.

FASHION

Anon
Isn't your dress a little too young for you, dear?

Dorothy Parker
Do you think so, dear? I think yours suits you

perfectly. It always has.

Mrs Horace Greeley
Commenting on her acquaintance's kid-gloves – Skin of a beast!

Miss Fuller
Why, what do you wear?

Mrs Greeley
Silk!

Miss Fuller
Entrails of a worm!

Anon
Do you call that thing on your head a hat?

Ludwig Holberg
Do you call that thing under your hat a head?

LITERATURE

Thomas Boswell
Drinking drives away care. Would you not allow a man to drink for that reason?

Samuel Johnson
Yes, sir, if he sat next to you.

Elinor Glyn
Would you please publish the enclosed manuscript or return it without delay, as I have other irons in the fire.

Anon publisher
On returning the manuscript – Put this with your other irons.

Anon writer
Last week you rejected my story. I know that you did not read it for, as a test, I pasted together pages 15, 16 and 17 and the manuscript came back with the pages still pasted. You are a fraud and you turn down stories without even reading them.

George Horace Latimer
Madam, at breakfast when I open an egg, I don't have to eat the whole egg to discover it is bad.

Anon actress
I enjoyed your book [*Past Imperfect*]. Who wrote it for you?

Ilka Chase
Darling, I'm so glad you liked it. Who read it to you?

Clare Booth Luce
On coming to a door – Age before beauty.
Dorothy Parker
Sweeping through first – Pearls before swine.

George Lewes
I'm not like that, I commence to write at once, directly the pen is in my hand! In fact, I boil at a low temperature.
Thomas Huxley
Indeed. That is very interesting, for, as you know, to boil at a low temperature implies a vacuum in the upper region.

William Faulkner
Hemingway has never been known to use a word that might send a reader to the dictionary.
Ernest Hemingway
Poor Faulkner. Does he really think big emotions come from big words? He thinks I don't know the ten-dollar words. I know them all right. But there are older and simpler and better words, and those are the ones I use.

Sir Lewis Morris
The press are neglecting my poems. It is a conspiracy of silence. What ought I do, Oscar?
Oscar Wilde
Join it!

William Wordsworth
I believe I could write like Shakespeare, if I had a mind to try.
Charles Lamb
Yes, nothing would be wanting, but the mind.

Samuel T. Coleridge
Did you ever hear me preach?
Charles Lamb
I never heard you do anything else.

Alfred Austin
On the lack of money in poetry – I manage to keep the wolf from the door.
Lord Young
How – by reading your poems to him?

Admetus
How do you like this extraordinary epitaph that

I've written for myself?
Demonax
It's so beautiful, I wish it were in place already!

THEATRE

Oscar Wilde
Do you mind if I smoke?
Sarah Bernhardt
I don't care if you burn.

Lady Diana Manners
Are you the Noël Coward who wrote a play called 'Private Lives'?
Noël Coward
Yes, I am he.
Lady Diana
Very funny.
Noël Coward
Tell me, could you be the Lady Diana Manners who played the Virgin in 'The Miracle'?
Lady Diana
Yes I am she.
Noël Coward
Very funny.

Noël Coward
You look almost like a man.
Edna Ferber
Dressed in a trouser suit – So do you!

Lord Northcliffe
The trouble with you, Shaw, is that you look as if there was a famine in the land.
G. B. Shaw
The trouble with you, Northcliffe, is that you look as if you were the cause of it.

G. B. Shaw
Telegram exchange with Cornelia Otis Skinner, who opened in his 'Candida' on Broadway (1935) – Excellent! Greatest!
Cornelia Otis Skinner
A million thanks, but undeserving such praise.
Shaw
I meant the play.
Skinner
So did I.

G. B. Shaw
Invitation to the opening night of 'Pygmalion' – Am reserving two tickets for you for my première. Come and bring a friend – if you have one.

Winston Churchill
Impossible to be present for the first performance. Will attend the second – if there is one.

Anon society hostess
Invitation – Lady X will be at home Thursday between four and six.
G. B. Shaw
Mr Bernard Shaw likewise.

G. B. Shaw
Isn't it true, my dear, that male judgement is superior to female judgement?
Mrs Shaw
Of course, dear. After all, you married me and I you.

Ruth Gordon
Explaining her latest role – There's no scenery at all. In the first scene, I'm on the left side of the stage and the audience has to imagine I'm eating dinner in a restaurant. Then in scene two, I run over to the right side of the stage, and the audience imagines I'm in the drawing-room.
George S. Kaufman
And the second night, you have to imagine there's an audience out front.

Tallulah Bankhead
How lucky you are to be married to Alfred Lunt, darling! His directing, his acting, his theatre sense. Where would you be without him?
Lynne Fontaine
Probably playing your roles.

Anon actor
What's the matter, Kelcey? Aren't you asleep yet?
Kelcey Allen – *critic*
You are not on stage yet.

Anon actor
Last night I was a sensation at the Roxy. I had the audience glued to their seats.
George Jessel
How clever of you to think of it.

Alexander Woollcott
I don't think you'd make a good Lady Macbeth, Peggy. Do you?

Peggy Wood
No, but you would.

DANCE

Isadora Duncan
Imagine a child with my body and your brain.
G. B. Shaw
Yes, but suppose it had my body and your brain!

MUSIC

Franz Liszt
That was a march I have written on the death of Meyerbeer. How do you like it?
Giacomo Rossini
I liked it. But might it have been better had it been you who died and Meyerbeer written the music?

Anon composer
After his recital – What did you keep doffing your hat for?
Giacomo Rossini
I always take my hat off when I meet an old acquaintance. And every few bars in your music I recognised one I had met here and there.

George Gershwin
If you had it all over again, would you fall in love with yourself again?
Oscar Levant
Play us a medley of your hit!

Anon singer
You know, my dear, I insured my voice for fifty thousand dollars.
Miriam Hopkins
That's wonderful. And what did you do with the money?

Frank Sinatra
After the female singer had refused to perform in New Jersey if the U.S. national anthem was played – Someone should kick her in the ass!
Sinead O'Connor
If you believe all that you read, I wouldn't be the first woman he's threatened to do that to.

CINEMA

Katharine Hepburn
Meeting her co-star for the first time – I'm afraid

I'm a little tall for you, Mr Tracy.
Spencer Tracy
Never mind, Miss Hepburn. I'll soon cut you down to size.

Katharine Hepburn
On finishing a film – Thank goodness, I don't have to act with you any more.
John Barrymore
I didn't know you ever had, darling.

MEDIA

Female journalist
Mr Marx, we met at Mrs Glynthwaite's. I'm sure you remember me.
Groucho Marx
I never forget a face, but in your case I'll make an exception.

William Paley – *chairman of CBS TV*
Fran, terrific book, terrific book!
Fran Lebowitz – *author of 'Metropolitan Life'*
Pretty good network, Bill, pretty good network!

LEGAL

Convicted criminal
As God is my judge – I am innocent.
Judge Norman Birkett
He isn't; I am, and you're not!

RELIGION

Country squire
If I had a son who was an idiot, I'd make him a parson.
Reverend Sydney Smith
Quite so, though I see your father was of a different mind.

Anon clergyman
I would like to thank you for all the enjoyment you have brought the world.
Groucho Marx
And I would like to thank you for all the enjoyment you have taken out of the world.

POLITICS

Lord Sandwich
Really, Mr Wilkes, I don't know whether you'll die on the gallows or of the pox.

John Wilkes
That depends, my lord, on whether I embrace your principles or your mistress.

Heckler
Vote for you? I'd as soon vote for the devil!
John Wilkes
And if your friend is not standing?

William Pitt the Younger
If I cannot speak standing, I will speak sitting, and if I cannot speak sitting, I will speak lying.
Lord North
Which he will do in whatever position he speaks.

Chauncey Depew
All you need to get a speech out of Mr Choate is to open his mouth, drop in a dinner and up comes a speech.
Joseph Choate
Dr Depew says that if you open my mouth and drop in a dinner, up will come a speech. But I warn you that if you open your mouths and drop in one of Dr Depew's speeches, up will come your dinner.

Chauncey Depew
Referring to his portly acquaintance's well-developed stomach – I hope if it is a girl, Mr Taft will name it for his charming wife.
William Taft
If it is a girl, I shall, of course, name it for my lovely helpmate of many years. And if it is a boy, I shall claim the father's prerogative and name it Junior. But if, as I suspect, it is only a bag of wind, I shall name it Chauncey Depew.

Lord Charles Beresford
I suggest that Winston Churchill is suffering from beri-beri, the cardinal symptom of which is a swollen head.
Sir Winston Churchill
My Right Honourable friend is wrong. The disease of which he speaks has for its chief symptom swollen feet.
Lord Beresford
That's even better. What I mean to imply is that you are too big for your boots.

Bessie Braddock
Winston, you're drunk!

Sir Winston Churchill
Bessie, you're ugly. And tomorrow morning I shall be sober.

Sir Winston Churchill
I venture to say that my Right Honourable friend, so redolent of other knowledge, knows nothing of farming. I'll even make a bet that she doesn't know how many toes a pig has!
Lady Astor
Oh, yes I do! Take off your little shoosies and have a look!

Lady Astor
What is the difference between you and me?
Sir Winston Churchill
I can't conceive, madam!

Lady Astor
Winston, if I were married to you, I'd put poison in your coffee.
Sir Winston Churchill
Nancy, if you were my wife – I'd drink it.

Henry Clay
I would rather be right than be President.
Congressman Reed
He doesn't have to worry. He'll never be either.

Alexander Smith
You, sir, speak for the present generation, but I speak for posterity.
Henry Clay
Yes, and you seem resolved to speak until the arrival of your audience.

Heckler
Go ahead, Al, tell 'em all you know.
Alexander Smith
I'll tell them all we both know. It won't take any longer.

Barry Goldwater
I won't say that the papers misquote me, but I sometimes wonder where Christianity would be today if some of these reporters had been Matthew, Mark, Luke and John.
Walter Lippman
The senator might remember that the Evangelists had a more inspiring subject.

Czar of Russia
I see Turkey as the sick man of Europe.

Prince Metternich
Is your Majesty speaking of it so as its doctor, or as its heir?

Richard Sheridan's son
If I were in Parliament, I would write on my forehead – 'To Let'.
Richard Sheridan
Add 'Unfurnished'.

Heckler
I wouldn't vote for you if you were the Archangel Gabriel.
Robert Menzies
If I were the Archangel Gabriel, madam, you would scarcely be in my constituency.

James Callaghan
May I congratulate you on being the only man in your team.
Margaret Thatcher
That's one more than you've got in yours.

SPORTS

Jeremy Tree
I've got to speak to my old school, Lester, and tell them all I know about horse-racing. What should I tell them?
Lester Piggott
Tell 'em you have got the flu!

Joe Bugner
After being accused of not trying in a fight against Muhammad Ali – Get me Jesus Christ, I'll fight Him tomorrow!
Hugh McIlvanney
Joe, you're only saying that because you know He's got bad hands.

SEXES

Male heckler
Are you a lesbian?
Florence Kennedy
Are you my alternative?

Jean Harlow
Why, you're MargoT Asquith, aren't you?
Margot Asquith
No, my dear. The 't' in Margot is silent, as in Harlow.

SELF-CRITICISM

Franklin P. Adams
I am easily influenced. Compared with me a weather vane is Gibraltar.

Louisa May Alcott
When I don't look like the tragic muse, I look like a smoky relic of the great Boston Fire.

Sherwood Anderson
For all my egotism I know I am but a minor figure.

Margot Asquith
I have no face - only two profiles clapped together.

I am the kind of woman I would run away from.

W. H. Auden
My face looks like a wedding cake left out in the rain.

Jane Austen
I think I may boast myself to be, with all possible vanity, the most unlearned and uninformed female who ever dared to be an authoress.

Tallulah Bankhead
I'm as pure as the driven slush.

They used to photograph Shirley Temple through gauze. They should photograph me through linoleum.

Rona Barrett
I'm really a pussycat - with an iron tail.

James M. Barrie
Some of my plays peter out, and some pan out.

Marlon Brando
I have eyes like those of a dead pig.

James M. Cain
I am 54 years old, weigh 220 pounds, and look like the chief dispatcher of a long-distance hauling concern.

Mrs Patrick Campbell
I look like a burst paper bag . . . I must borrow a chair with a high back so that I can hide my chins behind it.

Billy Carter
I'm not the Carter who'll never tell a lie.

Raymond Chandler
Having just read the admirable profile of Hemingway in the New Yorker I realise that I am much too clean to be a genius, much too sober to be a champ, and far, far too clumsy with a shotgun to live the good life.

G. K. Chesterton
Just the other day in the Underground I enjoyed the pleasure of offering up my seat to three ladies.

Agatha Christie
A sausage machine, a perfect sausage.

George M. Cohan
I can write better plays than any living dancer and dance better than any living playwright.

Cyril Connolly
I have always disliked myself at any given moment; the total of such moments is my life.

Calvin Coolidge
I think the American people wants a solemn ass for President. And I think I'll go along with them.

Princess Diana
I'm as thick as a plank.

Phyllis Diller
If my jeans could talk they'd plead for mercy.

It's a good thing beauty is only skin deep, or I'd be rotten to the core.

Errol Flynn
My problem lies in reconciling my gross habits with my net income.

Jane Fonda
I hope there's no one else like me.

Nell Gwynn
When mistaken for a Catholic duchess – I am the Protestant whore.

Heinrich Heine
At times my own poems nauseate me.

Ernest Hemingway
As a war correspondent – I'm Ernie Hemorrhoid, the poor man's Pyle.

Kiri Te Kanawa
I'm anorexic for an opera singer – but I'm a fat anorexic.

Ring Lardner
Robert Taft looked at me as if I was a side dish he hadn't ordered.

Charles Laughton
I have a face like the behind of an elephant.

Oscar Levant
Under this flabby exterior is an enormous lack of character.

Groucho Marx
I eat like a vulture. Unfortunately, the resemblance doesn't end there.

Golda Meir
I may not have been a great prime minister, but I would have been a great farmer.

Grace Metalious
On 'Peyton Place' – I'm a lousy writer; a helluva lot of people have got lousy taste.

David Niven
I have a face that is a cross between two pounds of halibut and an explosion in an old clothes cupboard.

Dorothy Parker
My verses are damn no good.

S. J. Perelman
Under a forehead roughly comparable to that of Javanese and Piltdown man are visible a pair of tiny pig eyes, lit up alternately by greed and concupiscence.

Tyrone Power
I've done an awful lot of stuff that's a monument to public patience.

Joan Rivers
I was so flat, I used to put x's on my chest and write, 'You are here.'

Damon Runyon
I am like a day-coach boy in a parlour car seat.

Billy Sample
I'm like Daffy Duck in the cartoons. I'm black, I've got big feet and I'm always bitching.

George Bernard Shaw
I am like a dentist, there is so much that is wounding about my work.

'Red' Smith
He might have been a great athlete, except that he is small, puny, slow, inept, uncoordinated, myopic and yellow.

Robert Louis Stevenson
I am a rogue at egotism myself; and, to be plain, I have rarely liked a man who was not.

Evelyn Waugh
You have no idea how much nastier I would be if I was not a Catholic. Without supernatural aid I would hardly be a human being.

Mae West
I used to be Snow White, but I drifted.

Alexander Woollcott
I am a pretty trivial, rootless person, a fellow of motley and diffused affections, permanently adrift.

INDEX

INDIVIDUALS QUOTED OR MENTIONED IN QUOTATION
(including publications)

James RESTON 204
Don REVIE 236
Kenneth REXROTH 74
Burt REYNOLDS 115
Sir Joshua REYNOLDS 27, 33, 81
RHODA (CBS TV) 240
Jean RHYS 68
Frank RICH 16, 98, 105, 109, 121
Ron RICH 178
Cliff RICHARD 162
King RICHARD II 229
Eliot L. RICHARDSON 264
Jack RICHARDSON 233
Leander RICHARDSON 172
Natasha RICHARDSON 141
R. G. RICHARDSON 229
Ralph RICHARDSON 141
Samuel RICHARDSON 54
Mordecai RICHLER 250
Don RICKLES 147
Andrew RIDGELY 163
Diana RIGG 141
Bobby RIGGS 239
James W. RILEY 84
Martin RINGWAY 115
Geraldo RIVERA 177
Joan RIVERS 131, 158, 160, 161,
  163, 235, 262, 275
Frank RIZZO 208, 263
Harold ROBBINS 58
Tom ROBBINS 245
Chalmers ROBERTS 170
Dale ROBERTS 147
John ROBERTS 236
Cliff ROBERTSON 113
Lord Patrick ROBERTSON 68, 84
David ROBINSON 121
Edward ROBINSON 154
Henry ROBINSON 137
Henry C. ROBINSQN 132
Kenneth ROBINSON 170
Lennox ROBINSON 93
Sir Hercules ROBINSON 213
Bobby ROBSON 236
Alfredo ROCCO 209
Francois, Duc de la
  ROCHEFOUCAULD 62, 235
John D. ROCKEFELLER 172, 180
Marquis of ROCKINGHAM 218
ROEBUCK 33
Nicholas ROEG 123
Kenny ROGERS 161
Samuel ROGERS 39, 84
Will ROGERS 45, 113, 121, 147,
  165, 183, 186, 189, 202, 204, 208,
  209, 210, 222
Adele ROGERS ST JOHN 265
ROLLING STONES 158, 160, 161,
  176
Linda RONSTADT 161, 163
Andy ROONEY 177
Mickey ROONEY 141
Eleanor ROOSEVELT 105
Franklin D. ROOSEVELT 208
Theodore ROOSEVELT 173, 188,
  200, 206
Ned ROREM 262
Salvator ROSA 33

J. H. ROSE 217
Robert ROSE 32
Lord ROSEBERY 210, 218
A. M. ROSENTHAL 168
ROSKOLENKO 210
Dante ROSSETTI 33, 85
Diana ROSS 161
Harold ROSS 50, 167, 168
Robert ROSS 63
Giaocchino ROSSINI 151, 154, 155,
  271
Clinton ROSSITER 206
Leo ROSTON 39
David Lee ROTH 161
Philip ROTH 39, 68, 252, 267
Lord ROTHERMERE 173
John ROTHSCHILD 180
Johnny ROTTEN 161, 163
Richard ROUD 121
Pierre ROULLE 96
Henri ROUSSEAU 33
Jean B. ROUSSEAU 85
Jean-Jacques ROUSSEAU 39, 200,
  267
Nellie Mae ROWE 262
Helen ROWLAND 265
Josiah ROYCE 200
Harry RUBY 257
Julius RUDEL 109
Stanley RUDIN 249
Bernard RUDOFSKY 20
Todd RUNDGREN 161
Dagobert RUNES 9, 27, 74
Damon RUNYON 51, 275
Mrs RUPPERT 141
Willy RUSHTON 251
John RUSKIN 11, 16, 20, 23, 25, 26,
  27, 30, 31, 34, 36, 64, 70, 151
Bertrand RUSSELL 17, 59, 62, 90,
  105, 188, 193, 196, 198, 200, 201
John RUSSELL 27
Lord John RUSSELL 218
Babe RUTH 248
Dame Margaret RUTHERFORD
  141
Louis RYKEYSER 183

S

Gabriella SABATINI 239
Victoria SACKVILLE-WEST 12
SADE 161
Françoise SAGAN 267
Rene SAGUISAG 164
Mort SAHL 121, 166, 176, 208
Charles SAINTE-BEUVE 11
Antoine de SAINT-EXUPERY 222
Camille SAINT-SAENS 153, 154
SAKI (H. H. Munro) 80, 97
Alberto SALAZAR 259
J. D. SALINGER 189
Harrison SALISBURY 168, 260
Harrison E. SALISBURY 171
Lord SALISBURY 166, 213, 218,
  219
Claudius SALMASIUS 83
Billy SAMPLE 275
Anthony SAMPSON 170
Herbert SAMUEL 219

Paul SAMUELSON 184
SAN FRANCISCO CHRONICLE 47,
  95
SAN FRANCISCO EXAMINER 51,
  62
SAN JUAN COUNTY RECORD 47
Aranxta SANCHEZ-VICARIO 239
George SAND 68
Carl SANDBURG 68, 85, 206, 222,
  257
Ed SANDERS 74
George SANDERS 142
George SANDS 113
B. K. SANDWELL 250
Lord SANDWICH 272
George SANTAYANA 9, 40, 80, 148,
  189, 194, 198, 200, 201, 204, 235,
  256
John Singer SARGENT 27, 31, 33
Peggy SARGENT 35
Nathalie SARRAUTE 175
May SARTON 68
Siegfried SASSOON 155
Victor SASSOON 252
Vidal SASSOON 159
Erik SATIE 16, 150, 152
Jean-Paul SATRE 201
SATURDAY EVENING POST 122
SATURDAY REVIEW 56, 58, 72,
  122
Richard SAVAGE 85
Telly SAVALAS 196
SAXON 162
Dorothy L. SAYERS 68
Prunella SCALES 142
Arville SCHALEBEN 189
Dore SCHARNY 9
Johann SCHEIBE 151
Steven H. SCHEURER, 122
Richard SCHICKEL 134, 141
Robert SCHICKEL 122
Friedrich von SCHILLER 85
Karl F. SCHINKEL 21
Louis SCHNEIDER 152
Arthur SCHNITZLER 122
Arnold SCHONBERG 154
Mark SCHORER 63
Jean-Jaques SCHREIBER 242
Olive SCHREINER 253
Franz SCHUBERT 154
John SCHULIAN 233
Milton SCHULMAN 131, 140
Montgomery SCHULYER 30
Charles SCHULZ 74
George SCHULZ 220
Ernest SCHUMACHER 183
Murray SCHUMACK 175
Robert SCHUMANN 151, 154
Joseph A. SCHUMPETER 183
Lincoln M SCHUSTER 167
Arnold SCHWARZENEGGER 142
General H. Norman
  SCHWARZKOPF 223
Paul SCOFIELD 142
SCORPIO 20
C. P. SCOTT 176
Clement SCOTT 105
George C. SCOTT 142

GENERAL REFERENCE